CW00346521

The Trouble With Money

London 9/7/98

The Trouble With Money

and other essays

IAN HAMILTON

BLOOMSBURY

This collection first published 1998

Copyright © Ian Hamilton 1998

The moral right of the author has been asserted

Bloomsbury Publishing Plc,
38 Soho Square,
London W1V 5DF

A CIP catalogue record for this book
is available from the British Library

ISBN 0 7475 3965 0

Typeset in Great Britain by
Palimpsest Book Production Limited,
Polmont, Stirlingshire
Printed in Great Britain by
Clays Ltd, St Ives plc

Contents

Author's Note

The 'new' pieces collected here were written between 1994 and 1997 and to these I have added a selection from *Walking Possession*, which was published in hardback by Bloomsbury in 1994. My thanks to the editors and publishers of *Granta*, *London Review of Books*, *The New Yorker*, *The New York Times*, *Punch*, *Sunday Telegraph*, *The Times Literary Supplement*, *The Times*, and *Vogue* (USA).

1

Down Grub Street Way

The Trouble with Money

Did you know that a hundred-gram jar of Nescafé filled with 1p coins buys two packets of Benson and Hedges? Did you know that a two-litre flagon of Paul Masson burgundy filled with 2p coins buys three regular-size bottles of Safeway's claret? Did you know that a Steradent tube filled with 10p coins buys just over one-and-a-half bottles of Night Nurse?

Perhaps you didn't. Why should you? Why should I? And yet I dote on such statistics; rarely do they fail to cheer me up. I can be twenty grand down at the bank, the tax on my heels and a heap of nasties on the mat, but for some reason the spectacle of my three-quarters-full-and-rising coffee jar gives me a sense of high accomplishment, a feeling that I've licked, have nearly licked, will lick the system. As long as those bronze chiplets continue to pile up, I tell myself, I'm not out of the game. I am a saver.

There are, of course, other ways of saving. For these, though, you need to be 'in funds'. For example, you can hide a fiver in a coat you never wear, or tuck a tenner in a sock that's had its day. The idea is that you'll forget about these minor-league deposits. After all, what's fifteen pounds when you are packing a new wad? And then, when things turn rough again and you just happen to be trying on old coats and socks – you know, the way one does when things turn rough – there they will be: salvation, a new start! The loopholes in this stratagem are self-evident, and it's not one that I recommend for workaday survival. But it does have some poetic substance. It makes money seem like magic. As with the coffee jars, although more chancily, it tells you that you're still in with a chance.

Childish stuff, you may well think, and you'd probably be right. But for some of us, it has become the stuff of life – the stuff, that is, of literary life. Knowing how many days pass between a final notice and a cut-off, knowing how much time you gain with a carefully-phrased 'WAFDA pdc' (post-dated cheque on which the 'words and figures don't agree'), knowing the phone codes for Northampton, Worthing and Southend ('A friendly-sounding fellow called. Could you please ring him back?'): such information is the small change of a life that's sometimes financed by small change. And you can easily get hooked on your own expertise. A sudden access of riches can induce a sense of desolation. What to do with all this know-how, all this *change*?

Back in the early Sixties, when I first started out, insolvency spelt glamour. It was OK to be broke – more than OK, since money was well known to be the super-foe of books. It was Mammon v. the Muses: take your pick. In those days, if a writer owned up to caring about money, he was instantly branded a dud. 'He's got a *what*? A mortgage? Well, I have to say I always had my doubts. I mean, his line-breaks did seem a bit *arbitrary*.' The avowed aim was to treat money rather as money seemed likely to treat us: with altitudinous contempt.

There was, of course, an easy fraudulence in this, since none of us was poor – well, not *poor* poor – but we weren't ready then to spot it. We intended to set up as 'sons of literature' (in Dr Johnson's noble phrase). Had not literature itself decreed that we should not make friends with Mammon? The modern texts we had learned to decipher for our school exams were all to do with tensions between money and non-money. For A-level English I studied *The Waste Land* and *Howards End* and I still have the actual books I worked from. The margins of each resemble a roster of sports fixtures: 'inner life v. outer', 'money values v. culture values', 'Wilcoxes (money) v. Schlegels (sensibility)', 'Mr Eugenides (merchant) v. hyacinth girl (spiritual illumination)'. With the Forster, I am glad to see, there is the odd underlining or question mark, as if I might now and then have been trying to work out something for myself: 'To trust people is a luxury only the wealthy can indulge' is marked with a combative 'Trust you!' The overall impression, though, is of tame capitulation to the belief that works of art are like messages in bottles from some dire cultural shipwreck – a wreck caused, of course, by money. As students, it was our clear duty to man life-rafts and set sail.

There was, then, a near-priestly kind of romance in the idea that a high-purposed literary career would be profitless, at least in terms of cash. Here was the Thorny Way, the way of deprivation. And for a period, I went along with this, nose in the air. At the same time, though, I knew I could handle only so much deprivation. That painting of the dead Chatterton sprawled on his pallet never made me want to be like him. Nor, come to that, did I want to be like Keats and Shelley. And the then-recent cult of Dylan Thomas left me cold. Thomas's whipped-dog act when he was cadging the price of his next drink seemed horribly demeaning. And look at the way he carried on when he had swallowed his next drink: all that intoning-from-above, that bardic blethering. He too was like a priest. He seemed to think the world owed him a living.

With attitudes like these, I was clearly in something of a fix. On the one hand, it was contemptible to have a mortgage; on the other, a fellow ought to be able to pay for the next round. What did that leave? It left the Cobbled Way, the way of compromise. And my compromise was to start up a small poetry magazine. How better to reconcile the importunities of art and commerce?

In those days – this was 1962 – I was much fired by the early letters of Ezra Pound, the ones that deal with his efforts on behalf of magazines like the *Little Review* and *Poetry (Chicago)*. Pound was a superb backs-to-the-wall businessman, it seemed to me. An enemy of money, or of 'money-values', he recognised yet did not flinch from money's power. He was brilliant at locating and tapping likely sources of largesse. With him, though, there was none of Thomas's spare-a-penny-guv self-humbling. His benefactors were usually left feeling grateful: such was the high vehemence of his belief in the world-altering potential of his cause. And they were even more grateful when Pound from time to time slipped them a Joyce worksheet or a drawing by Gaudier-Brzeska. Pound never made the mistake of despising his money-men. He treated them like converts. I remember being mightily impressed by his retort to his two arty-crafty co-editors on the *Little Review*, when they spoke scornfully of the millionaire John Quinn. It was Quinn's money that guaranteed the magazine's survival. Pound wrote to them:

> Re: Quinn, remember. Tis he who hath bought the pictures: tis he who both getteth me an American publisher and smacketh the same with rods; tis he who sendeth me the Spondos Oligos, which is by interpretation the small tribute or spondoolicks wherewith I do pay my contributors, WHEREFORE is my heart softened toward the said J.Q. and he in mine eyes can commit nothing heinous.

This seemed to me to strike precisely the right note. For Pound, the trouble with money was that it kept bad company. With his help, it would learn to make new friends. At the time, I didn't pay much attention to the economic theories of Pound's later years, nor did I brood deeply on *Hugh Selwyn Mauberley*, in which he calls himself 'wrong from the start . . . born in a half-savage country, out of date.' What mattered to me then – or so I said – was the man's energy and style, his fiercely-held conviction that money could be made to see the light.

Cultural high-mindedness allied with pecuniary cunning: well, why not? I set up shop – first of all with *The Review* and later with *The New Review*. I got myself an office in Soho, a big desk, two telephones, a small staff of willing helpers, a franking machine. Much thought went into our letterhead design. And in the pub downstairs I dreamed up savage business schemes, thought big. 'A mailshot of so-and-so costs such-and-such. Working on a two-and-a-half per cent return we'll effectively be *buying* readers at so-much a head.' The fight was on, the life-raft had set sail. The axe fell in 1979, and by then I had a long list of why-nots: booksellers who wouldn't stock the magazine, publishers who wouldn't advertise, readers who threw away the mailshot without reading it, and so on. Then there was Edward Heath, the three-day week, television, the Beatles. Overarchingly, there was the general state of things, the culture, the shipwreck. By the end of it, I was pretty glad to disembark.

For a year or two afterwards, however, I went around with a long face. For some reason, and in spite of all the evidence, I wanted people to believe that it hadn't been my fault. Significantly, one of my darkest gripes was directed at the Arts Council's Literature Panel. The Arts Council had been *The New Review*'s John Quinn. Like Quinn, it came up with the spondoolicks and for that it deserved, it still deserves, my thanks. Without its backing not even five issues of the magazine would have appeared, let alone the fifty that we eventually came through with. That was the Council, though. The Literature Panel was, as they say, a different kettle of fish. This powerful committee was staffed, alas, by writers.

And I mean alas. The truth is that when you give a bunch of writers any kind of money-muscle, they go slightly mad. I ought to know. And when you put them on committees that give money to other writers, they go madder still. I can hear their voices now: 'Mr Chairman, on a point of order, I feel it my duty to observe . . .' And this would be some foppish, dreamy-faced poetaster fresh from a three-absinthe lunch. But nearly all of them behaved like this. Wild-eyed anarchic novelists would transmute into prim-lipped accountants. Tremulous lyric poets would rear up like tigers of the bottom line. Book-reviewers who, I knew, lived in daily terror of being rumbled by the Revenue were all at once furrow-browed custodians of *public funds*. Happily, I was only once called up to meet the Panel face to face. The event was like a cross between Star Chamber and our Prefects' Court at school. Afterwards I made a vow: from now on, I told the Council, I will deal only with career bureaucrats, with philistines. Show me an enemy of literature, and I will show him my accounts.

In a way, though, I was just as fake as those mad panellists. Like them I was pretending to be good with money, a safe pair of hands. And in November 1980, sitting in front of the Official Receiver, I was still faking. 'Our accumulated deficit was, let's say, thirty thousand pounds. Divide that by the fifty issues we produced and that's – what – about six hundred pounds per issue in arrears. Well, with our new typesetting machine, we might easily have taken in six hundred pounds worth of outwork, given half a chance. So we were not, as you seem to suggest, trading when non-viable. In my view, we were just about to turn the corner when those bastards pulled the plu . . . that is to say, when our creditors foreclosed.'

And so it went. The Receiver smiled me through it, but he knew. He knew what I knew and what Pound knew. The whole thing had been 'wrong from the start', impossible, not on. For all Pound's craftiness, his skill at penetrating the corridors of wealth, for all his commonsensical acknowledgement of money's power, its self-regard, he was at heart a heretic, a money-apostate, a fake. And so was I.

Looking back on my first reading of Pound's letters, I can see now that it was not Pound the crusader who excited me so much as Pound the cultural outlaw. I liked the idea of being up against it, on the run and in the right. Certainly my best memories of those magazine years are of situations where the battle-lines were clearly marked, the hostilities explicit. When asked about *The New Review*, I am always more likely to boast about how I outwitted some bailiff than about this or that poem or short story. And my colleagues on the magazine feel much the same – especially those who are still waiting to be paid.

Granta, 49, Winter, 1994.

Us and Them

A couple of years ago, I was asked by an American magazine to write a piece about the newly opened Channel Tunnel. The idea was that I would catch the morning Eurostar from London's Waterloo, have lunch in Paris and get back to London just in time for dinner. My piece would tell the story of my trip and ponder its significance in terms of Anglo-French relations.

As things turned out, you will not be surprised to learn, the whole endeavour was a non-event: no story, no significance. For the first hour, I sat in my high-speed window seat staring out at the blurred fields of Kent. Then came a whizzing, darkened stretch, as the train passed through the underwater tunnel. Then more fields, the fields of Northern France. Then Paris. Lunch ensued, just round the corner from the Gare du Nord, and – *naturellement* – lunch was not too bad. And after lunch, the train again, and yet more fields. And yes, I did get home for my substandard English dinner. The journey, as advertised, had been extremely quick. And that was that.

But that could not be that, was not allowed to be. Not just like that. I had a piece to write, a fee to bank. In these circumstances, the clear temptation was to get creative: i.e. to invent. Normally, this would have been straightforward. I would simply have dreamed up a few vivacious en route confrontations, bowler hat v. beret; I'd have enlivened the scenery somewhat, and – as my centrepiece – pretended that the submarine phase of the journey had been thrillingly suspenseful. This central sequence I'd have done, perhaps, in sub-poetic dream-speak, as a kind of Waterworld 'what-if?'. All of this, plus an upmarket quip or two about Napoleon and, well, Q.E.D.

That would have been the normal way to go about it. By 'normal' I mean: if I'd been writing for a British magazine. But this piece was destined for America and American editors, I knew from past experience, don't like it when you make things up. They don't like it when you day-dream on the job. All too vividly I could anticipate the late-night calls: 'Did this guy really wear a bowler hat?', 'Where did those Napoleon jokes come from; we can't find them anywhere,' 'That paragraph in which you say that you could "almost see" a gang of lobsters clawing at your window-pane: do they *have* lobsters in the English Channel?'

The next day I made a second trip on Eurostar, and this time I was taking notes. This time a field was more than just a field, a Britcow altogether different from a Gallic *vache* (and not just because most of our Britcows, we have since been told, had BSE). I even talked to a few of my co-passengers, thus stirring up at least two paragraphs of lively inter-cultural exchange: 'French dogs – they've all got rabies, no?', 'No, non, non, *non!*' In Paris, I pocketed a copy of the lunch menu, just in case I needed to prove what I'd eaten. This time, when I got back, it seemed to me that I had earned my English crust. The piece I wrote may not have been so very different from the piece I almost wrote, but it was true. Each word of it was checker-proof, or so I thought.

The American magazine fact-checker occupies a special place in London's Grub Street demonology. When English writers gather at their drinking holes, the talk is usually to do with money: crooked publishers, dumb agents, and the like. But if the writers in question have regular experience of writing for America, you can be pretty sure that Tales of the Fact-Checker will soon enough flow thick and fast. Over the years, I must have heard dozens of these comic horror yarns. They tend to follow the same pattern: verifiers in pursuit of the unverifiable, literal minds at odds with the imagination, humourless pedants out to throttle the free play of fancy.

In England, you are lucky if an editor reads your piece before he prints it. About the worst that can happen to you here is that your most stylish insight gets cut out at the last minute – 'for space reasons'. Consultation hardly ever happens; rarely do you get to see a set of proofs. This being so, English writers find it particularly irksome and demeaning when they get hauled up before the New York Magistrates of Fact: so thorough, so remorseless, and so deeply unimpressed. The English way of coping – as with most of their indignities – is to try to make a joke of it.

Some of the jokes, it must be said, are pretty good. One of my favourites was told to me by a South African friend who'd written a piece for America in which he made passing reference to the 'red roof' of his old Kimberley high school (a school he'd left some forty years before). His magazine's fact-checkers were not happy. 'Was that roof really red?' My friend contrived to keep his cool. 'Why don't you ask my brother? After all, he went there too.' Not good enough, came the reply: a blood relative was hardly an impartial witness.

The checkers then made contact with the school itself, and got to speak to the headmaster, whom they sent outside to check the colour of his roof. 'It seems to be a kind of grey', was his report, 'but forty years ago, who knows?' By which he meant, presumably, who cares? The checkers cared, but in the end even they had to admit defeat – though not before the hapless head had been made to trawl around for several hours in the school archives. All his old roof-photographs, alas, were black and white.

Some types of reportage cannot, of course, be fact-checked: best of all are those which speak of the deep-buried past or the unreachably subjective. To illustrate the point, the novelist Julian Barnes once concocted a spoof version of the ultimately check-proof prose submission. Such a piece, he said, would lure the checkers into seeking to confirm 'that dream about hamsters which your grandfather had on the night Hitler invaded Poland – a dream never written down but conveyed personally to you on the old boy's knee, a dream of which, since your grandfather's death, you are the sole repository.'

Even in such a hopeless case as this, says Barnes, the checkers would still check: all the grandfather's living associates would be lined up 'against a wall' and all known 'dictionaries of the unconscious' would be scoured. Only after long hours of tireless sleuthing would the fact-police agree to close the case, and add the magic words 'on author' (or 'blame *him*') to Barnes's piece. Barnes himself, by then, would no doubt have been marked down as a deeply suspect person.

In the world of the fact-checker, all writers are perceived as suspect persons – or at any rate as persons much more likely to be wrong than right. This attitude can certainly be hard to take. Most wordsmiths like to be thought of as truth-bearers. In my case, though, I'm sad to say, there seems to be a need for stern invigilation. Before I came up against the fact-checkers I had seen myself as pretty rigorous on points of fact: had I not once edited a magazine myself? It didn't take the checkers very long to find me out. Even before we spoke, they knew something that I didn't know. After a couple of intensive late-night calls (and because of the time-difference, these checkers' calls do tend to be late-night), I felt like visiting my doctor, or a shrink. My literary check-up had revealed some ugly symptoms: inability to remember dates correctly, compulsive misquotation, persistent tendency to muddle up the names of characters in novels, and – overarchingly – an infantile refusal to plead guilty when exposed. In other words, a refusal to face facts.

I remember, with a special shame, one late-night call, about some novel I had mentioned in a piece. When challenged by my checker, I was 'absolutely sure' that it was Anthony who had tried to seduce Celia on page sixteen. After a short silence, the checker asked me, most politely, if I'd care to 'take another look at page sixteen'. 'Yes, very well, if you insist' – and there it was: the lecher's name was not Anthony but *Alfred*. And his victim was called Jill.

Well, anyone can make a mistake, and – as anyone could see – I'd made a big one. What shames me now, though, looking back, is my absurd reluctance to own up, to simply say that, sorry, yes, I'd erred. 'And which edition, exactly, are you working from?', I heard myself enquire – and in a voice quivering with haughty indignation. The checker's tone at once began to soften. 'It's the one you're working from, or so you said.' By this time she'd quite properly decided that I needed help, perhaps in something of a hurry. I could hear her thinking: if only this author had been properly fact-checked as a child.

The checker herself, I ought to say, sounded distinctly under-age. But then they always do. To be despised, to be checked out, by one so young! It was a sorry night in Scribbleton, UK. And yet, thanks to that checker, I now triple-check my prose. I hoard all items of 'supportive data' as if they were expense-claims. All in all, as with the Eurostar experience, I have become quite usefully disdainful of my own inventive skills. The price of this new conscientiousness may well have been a certain loss of *joie d'écrire*, but I'm not sure that I had much of that to lose.

'Joyless', it so happens, is a word I've more than once heard used about American fact-checkers: as if a shaky grasp of factual detail were somehow essential to the merry thrill of literary composition. 'So killjoy; so American', it's said. Killjoy America? Thirty years ago, when I first visited New York, this formulation would have made me laugh. America was then the place to go it you wanted to recharge your nervous system. It was a place where you would either cheer up or crack up. It was the home of on-the-edge intensity.

Some British writers of 'a certain age' still think of it/her/him this way. In the late Sixties, the New York literary scene was regarded here as the very Utopia of glamorous disorder. The best American writers, it was widely and admiringly believed, were crazy, drunk or dead by their own hands. Their champ-sized books were fuelled by grandscale private turbulence. The British literati lapped this up. At the same time, they managed to look down on it. The British are expert at transmuting envy into scorn. Americans, they'd say, don't want to be grown-up.

Nowadays, we understand, the scene has changed. America is now the place to go to if you want to smarten up, get verified, checked-out. Nobody drinks, nobody smokes, nobody even *thinks* of going mad. And certainly nobody dares to fall out with his editor or publisher. Indeed publishers, or so I'm told, have now become more glamorously wacky than most of their now resolutely stable authors. Tales of manic rights-directors are now more commonplace than tales of suicidal poets. When I speak with American writers these days, they are forever complaining that X or Y conglomerate-big-cheese never returns their calls. 'I guess he's always out to lunch. If, after ten messages, he calls you back, you know you're riding high.' And the messages had better be cold-sober.

In the bad old days, it would have been the other way around. Writers then were expected to be negligent, preoccupied and difficult to reach. The publisher's function was to serve – or rather, to marvel and to serve. But this was the epoch of Vietnam, the bomb, and –

coming soon – the trials of Richard Nixon. There was an atmosphere of moral and political upheaval, of impending chaos. Writers of course flourish in such ether. In bad times, they are seen as seers, as spirit-of-the-age seismologists. On the page they are attended to, with urgency. Off-duty they are licensed to do as they please: whatever it might take to keep their insights fresh and frightening.

Not so today. Social complacency now rules, or so I'm told, and writers have been stripped of their druidic heft. They are now expected to project themselves as cool, well-organised achievers, just like everybody else. Rumour has it that many of them prefer the new arrangement. They would much rather talk targets with the marketing division than slump over a sodden set of galleys with some latterday Max Perkins. But for those writers to whom the marketing division rarely speaks, something magical does seem to have been lost.

Against this background, the rise of the too-rigorous fact-checker can easily be seen as a symptom of some larger disposition, as – perhaps – the small-print expression of a revitalised American work-ethic. To catch a writer out on points of fact is, in effect, to say: you are accountable – we all are, and don't let's forget it. Accountable to whom, to what? To God, to Random House, to 'public taste', to market forces? Who can tell: all we know for certain is that what we have here is no joke. Americans these days do not go in for jokes: not jokes that are *just* jokes. There is a resolute mistrust of the gratuitous, the mischievous, the risky. Hence, presumably, the whole minefield of political correctness. 'Be careful what you say' is, for most writers, a deeply scary exhortation.

This, anyway, is the perhaps-caricature vision of America now popular in British literary circles. The fact-checker is thus laughingly portrayed as a significant symbolic presence. If you want the cheques, get ready to be checked. And this, we Brits will tend to say, is a downturn towards the Slough of Deadly Earnestness. Not so long ago, English writers would have told their American colleagues to sober up and get more 'balanced'. Now they are likely to deride them for excessive sanity and purposeful resolve. All the old transatlantic prejudices are still happily in place: we have the culture, America has the money; we have the old, they have the new; we have the irony, they have the innocence. But now there is this strange new twist: we're right to be wrong and they're wrong to be right. At any rate, I think this is the twist. Don't ask me to prove it.

New York Times, 1997

I Love Concordances

What was T.S. Eliot's favourite colour? Which season – summer, autumn, winter, spring – would you expect to feature most often in the works of Philip Larkin? And which of these two poets would you reckon was the more self-centred, fond of flowers, susceptible to hyphens, keen on using the word *mother*?

Such are the questions that can spin off from too many hours spent browsing in the realms of the Concordance. It so happens that both Larkin and Eliot have lately had their works 'concorded' – that's to say, worked over with a scanner in order that the world might know how many and which words each of them used, how often, when and where. Don't ask me why. A concordance is, I think, meant to assist us in the checking of quotations, the remembering of half-forgotten lines. In my hands, it becomes a kind of toy.

But then, I love such toys. I love compiling lists. A few years ago, when I was editing an Oxford Companion to twentieth-century poetry, one of the rare pleasures of the job was in trying to work out how many of my poets had done what – apart, that is, from writing verse. How many had been policemen, say, or boxers, or management consultants? How many had played hockey for their country, been murdered, died in battle? How many had served time in jail? Who cares? you will retort, and I'd agree. Back then, though, for a day or two, I *had* to know these things. Again, don't ask me why.

With some of my lists, I tried to kid myself that I was not just playing games. For instance: surely it was worth knowing how many modern poets died young, were alcoholic, or went mad? In these areas, it must be said, the lists I ended up with revealed little that could not have easily been guessed. And yet this hardly seemed to matter. Thanks to me, guesswork had been hardened into fact, statisticised. From now on, I could say, it was a matter of official record that the majority of modern poets had been not only sane and sober but also, survival-wise, extremely shrewd. Most of them, my final list disclosed, had spent their lives in universities and, come pension-time, been good for at least one further decade of 'productive work'.

And this list, I need hardly say, led to another list, a list-within-a-list. Now and then, during the course of my labours, some churlish friend would remind me that only a small handful of my listed poets was, had ever been, could ever be, well, 'any good'. Was it statistically correct to call these people poets, 'just because they said they were'? In retaliation, I took to totting up the century's 'real talents', as decreed by me. And this list, when I finally got through with it, ran to about two dozen names − from a total of something like a thousand. Disconcertingly, about a third of these real talents had, alas, gone mad, been alcoholic, and/or died at a (statistically) young age.

So where did that get us? Not very far − and in my case especially not far, since I had no wish to be persuaded, by arithmetic, that great wits are, or have to be, unstable. There was a clear need for yet another list, a list-within-a-list-within-a-list: one that would demonstrate, to my personal satisfaction, that insane/drunk/ill poets wrote their best work when sane/sober/in good nick. Yes, yes, I know. My statistics had turned into a chaos of begged questions. There was madness in my methodologies, and it was beginning to show through.

All the same, I can't help loving these concordances. The mere look of them − page after page of headwords, numerals, page refs, original pub. dates and all the rest of it − is marvellously soothing. The Eliot concordance, done by a Cambridge team of literary and linguistic statisticians, is a giant volume of some 1,250 pages (twice the length of T.S.E.'s Collected Works) − and this without full listings of *and, the, this, that* and other functional connectives (though it is vouchsafed that Eliot employed *the* − 6,940 usages − nearly twice as frequently as he had use for *and* − 3,926 − and that his *that*s − 2,085 − almost contemptuously outrank his *this*es − 538. Who would have thought?). Larkin, whose output was about a third the size of Eliot's, nonetheless concords at a hefty 660 pages. His Collected Works weigh in at 338.

When books as big as these land on your desk, you can't just sit and smile at them. You feel a duty to get in there and start counting. *Memory* – 37 usages; *desire* – 25; *waste* – 26; *land* – 31; *Jew* – three; and so on. And since there are two poets on parade here, there is also a temptation to compare and contrast. Thus Larkin, you can now be told, used *sex* 11 times to Eliot's none. Eliot, on the other hand, has three *lusts* where Larkin can manage only one. *Mad* is much the same: Larkin here scores three to Eliot's nine. Of course, with *lust* and *mad* you have to bear in mind that Larkin's figures ought really to be multiplied by three, so as to reflect his smaller output. There is no knowing what Larkin's vocabulary might have got up to had he been three times more prolific; as things stand, though, the two poets must – on *lust* and *mad* – be rated neck-and-neck. Not so with *know*, which turns out to be Eliot's all-time number-one word, scoring an impressive 677 to Larkin's 42. *Time* is T.S.'s second-favourite. Here Eliot clocks in with 357 to Larkin's laggard 74.

At a brisk flick-through, it might seem that Eliot's word-hoard was on the whole more prosy and various than Larkin's. To take just the 'A' section of the two concordances, there are Eliot-words like *abnormal, absent-minded, agitate, absorption, allowance* etc which don't appear at all in Larkin's poems. But nor do they appear in Eliot's. These words are all taken from the plays. And the inclusion of his plays does somewhat falsify the Eliot picture. For instance, the Eliot concordance reveals 93 uses of the word *mother* (compared to Larkin's six). But only three of Eliot's 93 appear in poems. The others are spoken by characters in plays: 'Is this your mother?', 'The mother of my child was Mrs Guzzard's sister', or 'I've never had a father and a mother.' Similarly, about 50 per cent of Eliot's 102 *God* mentions come from *Murder in the Cathedral*. *God* appears five times in the *Four Quartets*, and four times in 'Ash Wednesday' – which in each case is somewhat less often than I would have guessed. If, as is sometimes claimed, concordances expose authorial obsessions, we need to tread carefully with Eliot, the bulk of whose lexicon was deployed as dramatic speech.

Certainly, we need to be more nervous than I've been when comparing him with Larkin. In truth, even joke-comparisons don't actually stand up, not least because the two concordances don't follow the same editorial guidelines. The Eliot, for example, is much stricter than the Larkin in its exclusions of the poet's 'small words' – prepositions, conjunctives, articles, dead-common verbs. It leaves out high-scoring Larkin-words like *you* and *I*, *could*, *come* and *did*. Thus, the best I can offer, using words common to both listings, is the information that Larkin's most-frequent usages – compared to Eliot's *know* and *time* – are *like* (175), *their* (112), *up* (92) and *down* (75), which could I suppose be juggled into the beginnings of a sombre Larkin line.

In his Preface to the Eliot book, co-editor Peter Holland says that it is not his task 'to indicate the potential uses of the concordance'. He does suggest, though, that concordances can have 'a peculiar magic in their consequential revelations'. He speaks also of 'the serendipity of scholarship, the critical chance of conjunction' and points with pride to 'the intriguing juxtaposition of *god-given* and *god-shaken*', as revealed by 'our index of Words Containing Hyphen or Apostrophe'. He could happily have pointed elsewhere – to his 'Reverse Index', for example, where we get 'investigate/margate/moorgate/gallowgate/hate/ appreciate/ associate/ immediate/ repudiate/ humiliate/ multifoliate/ expiate/appropriate', which makes Eliot sound like a mountingly ecstasised rap poet. Or, under 'Statistical Ranking List of Word Forms' there is (each word has 11 usages) the rather poignant observation that 'perpetual/powers/prefer/priests/problem'. Mr Holland also directs us to a surreal pile-up under *bark*. 'Computers have no sense of humour,' he remarks, but 'their output is sometimes amusing.' So it is:

BARK
222Pekes Pols 8 they join in to the fray/And
     they/Bark bark bark bark/Bark bark BARK BARK
222Pekes Pols 8 join in to the fray/And they/Bark
     bark bark bark/Bark bark BARK BARK/Until
222Pekes Pols 8 in to the fray/And they/Bark bark
     bark bark/Bark bark BARK BARK/Until you
222Pekes Pols 8 to the fray/And they/Bark bark
     bark bark/Bark bark BARK BARK/Until you can
222Pekes Pols 8 fray/And they/Bark bark bark
     bark/Bark bark BARK BARK/Until you can hear
222Pekes Pols 8/And they/Bark bark bark bark/

    Bark bark BARK BARK/Until you can hear them all
222Pekes Pols 8 they/Bark bark bark bark/Bark
    bark BARK BARK/Until you can hear them all over

And so it continues for a further 20 lines, barking all the way. Glanced at on the page it has a crazed and frantic look – an impression which, close-up, the intense pedantry serves happily to underscore. This *bark* item is pretty funny, I'd agree, but it is from Eliot's *Practical Cats* book and was in the first place pitched for laughs. My own favourite, in terms of serendipitous eeriness, comes under 'knock'. The entry begins: 'Pressing lidless eyes and waiting for a knock upon the door/ When Lil's husband got'. And then proceeds:

I'd like to know about that coffin/KNOCK KNOCK KNOCK/
                                     KNOCK.
know about that coffin/KNOCK KNOCK KNOCK/ KNOCK
                                       KNOCK
that coffin/KNOCK KNOCK KNOCK/KNOCK KNOCK KNOCK

careers on through a further 30 KNOCKS and ends:

ha ha/Hoo/Hoo/Hoo/KNOCK KNOCK KNOCK/ KNOCK KNOCK
/Hoo/Hoo/Hoo/KNOCK KNOCK KNOCK/KNOCK KNOCK
                                       KNOCK
/Hoo/KNOCK KNOCK KNOCK/KNOCK KNOCK KNOCK/
                                       KNOCK
KNOCK KNOCK/KNOCK KNOCK KNOCK/KNOCK/ KNOCK/
                                       KNOCK
KNOCK/KNOCK KNOCK KNOCK/KNOCK/KNOCK/ KNOCK
/KNOCK KNOCK KNOCK/KNOCK/KNOCK/KNOCK/ Coriolan
KNOCK KNOCK/KNOCK/KNOCK/KNOCK/Coriolan Triumphal
                                       March
KNOCK/KNOCK/KNOCK/KNOCK/Coriolan Triumphal March/
                                       Stone.
bull by the horns/And this is one/(Knock: and enter DOWNING)/
                                       Good.

Concordances needn't be all fun-and-games. Indeed, the Larkin editor, R.J.C. Watt, makes a good case for the critical usefulness of his word-lists. He points, for instance, to 'the extraordinary series of words beginning with the prefix *un*—' that can be found in Larkin's work, and certainly the series, ploughed through at one sitting, over seven pages, does have a deeply dampening relentlessness. At the same time, though, Watt is correct to emphasise how often Larkin used the *un* – prefix not simply in order to negate but rather, on occasions, to restrain or sorrowingly mitigate a positive: 'the unraised hand', 'the apple unbitten', 'love unused, in unsaid words', 'unchilded and unwifed'.

Watt's compilation also has the merit (not shared by the Eliot) of dating each of its word-entries – on the page, in an adjoining column, 'making it possible', he says, 'to see at a glance whether Larkin favoured a particular word at a particular stage of his career'. Hence, there are Auden-words during his Auden phase, Yeats-words when he was influenced by Yeats. There is also a discernibly deepening distrust of language that might be thought of as too 'poetic' or too overtly fervent. *Blood* never crops up after 1950. *Bright* stops at 1959. *Heart* makes 26 appearances pre-1958 and is used again but twice (and one of these is in a line about 'a boy puking his heart out in the Gents'). Nine of Larkin's 14 *God*-mentions are in early poems. Post-'Church Going', we get 'No God any more', 'Talking to God (who's gone too)', and the like.

All this is of real interest, and one can easily imagine Watt's concordance serving as the basis of some future, and perhaps valuable analysis of Larkin's changing way with words. For me, though, the toy-appeal of these two mammoth list-books seems likely to remain paramount. So: to go back to the questions I put to you at the beginning. The answers to the first two, since you press me, are *grey* (or *gray*) – 22 usages – and *summer* – 34. As to the others, even I can't be bothered to check them out right now. As T.S. Eliot might have said, I'll let you know some other time.

A *Concordance to the Complete Poems and Plays of T.S. Eliot*, edited by J.L. Dawson, P.D. Holland and D.J McKitterick (Faber).

A *Concordance to the Poetry of Philip Larkin*, edited by R.J.C. Watt (Olms-Weidmann).

London Review of Books, 1996

Poor Cyril

Cyril Connolly is famous now, and was famous in his lifetime, for not having written a masterpiece. A peculiar sort of fame: after all, many thousands of literary persons share the same distinction. Connolly, though, made a career out of insisting that his failure had a special poignancy, a poignancy which we should all attend to.

Others fail at literature because they don't have the necessary talent. With Connolly it was different. It was not an insufficiency of giftedness that kept him from delivering the goods. With him it was something altogether more complex and intriguing: something to do with Eton, mother, Ireland, wartime, sex, the cultural zeitgeist, laziness, food, money, publishers, disloyal or too-loyal friends, and so on. Above all, and influencing most of the above, it was to do with his unfaultable – nay, altitudinous – Good Taste. And this Good Taste, he wished it to be known, was both a blessing and a curse.

Connolly knew a masterpiece when he encountered one. He couldn't help himself: he had the palate. Furthermore he knew he possessed the kind of sensibility that went into the making of a masterpiece. He belonged, by natural kinship, in the company of high-art writers like Flaubert, Proust and James (or, as he contended for a while, Edith Sitwell, Aldous Huxley and Virginia Woolf), and therefore he could scarcely be expected to function at the same level as industrious pen-pushers like, say, Bennett or Galsworthy. He would much rather talk Proust over a posh dinner than sit at home and read a new novel by Jack Priestley. In many respects, and in spite of all the talk about becoming, or not becoming, a great artist, Connolly's true vocation was to score points as a literary socialite. This being so, he had no wish to be praised for effortful near-misses. Far better not to try than to be thought of as a trier.

Of course, he did try – although, to judge from what we now know of his several inglorious false starts, he didn't try too hard. The stance of 'promise-victimised' was picked up early on. At first, it was a self-defensive social ploy but over the years it was coaxed into a thoroughgoing style: a life-style and a work-style. Observing the dinner-table impact of lordly non-producers like Logan Pearsall Smith and Desmond MacCarthy, Connolly in his mid-twenties realised that failure, if worked on, could handsomely pay off. At worst, the notion of gifts wasted or withheld might lend a dark coherence to the most fragmentary output. At best, it might guarantee that any books he did vouchsafe would be greeted as provisional: mere preludes to the one that mattered. And if this book that mattered failed to happen, readers would scarcely blame its 'author'. On the contrary, they might very well find in the book's non-appearance both pathos and significance, a lesson to be learned.

And this, for almost five decades, was how it worked for Cyril Connolly – and still works, so it seems. His literary life is now studied as a kind of parable, or cautionary tale – which is pretty much how he saw it, and wished it to be seen. There have been five respectful books about Connolly since his death in 1974: about the same number as he himself produced, if we include collections of his book reviews. In the shops it is easier to find books about him than books by him. Nobody any longer wants to read *The Rock Pool* or *The Unquiet Grave*, except as period-pieces. Only *Enemies of Promise* (1938) has proved to have real staying power, and this largely because of a few golden phrases. And yet Connolly's reputation is probably as high as it has ever been. Nice one, to be sure.

Philip Larkin once wrote that Connolly was 'at his best when able to assimilate his subject into the scenario of his own temperament'. But for Connolly, such assimilation was compulsive. Almost everything he wrote was touched with woebegone self-consciousness. His humblest book reviews gave out an air of grievance: why am I doing this? If things were otherwise, he seemed to say, if he were richer, thinner, better-looking, luckier, more disciplined, we wouldn't be reading this review, and he would not have had to write it.

When other people wrote scornfully about these same reviews, he got annoyed. He wanted to be admired for his professionalism almost as badly as he wanted to be pitied for his damaged promise. He liked always to be in-between: in between art and its enemies, in between wives, in between books, in between countries, North and South. He liked to draw up self-dissecting lists: 'I can't bear to be unpopular, though I enjoy being hated'; 'I am too much of a snob to be a bohemian'; 'I am always trying to wound others, while remaining infinitely vulnerable.' To be Cyril Connolly meant being 'a lazy, irresolute person, over-vain and over-modest, unsure in my judgments and unable to finish what I have begun'. It also meant being pitilessly self-revealing (or tediously self-obsessed, as some believed). 'In myself,' he used to say, 'I recognise three beings. 1. The romantic, melancholy artist. 2. The eighteenth-century hedonist. 3. The efficient twentieth-century left-wing intellectual.' Small wonder, runs the subtext, that I'm finding it difficult to write a book. As Jeremy Lewis's admirable biography shows, Connolly's life was pimpled with 'if onlys'. His dream, he once testified, was to 'live in one lovely place always pining for another, with the perfect woman imagining one more perfect'.

Sexually, he was forever in a state of indecision. At school, he pined for perfect boys, and with boys his wooing style was spiritual and bookish. These Eton crushes were more painfully intense than anything that afterwards happened to him in this line. Once he discovered women, he became more casual and abrupt in his liaisons, though always likely to set up a mighty howl when things went wrong. Women were like mothers (Connolly's own mother was mostly absent from his childhood, having run off with her husband's boss): he liked them to cuddle him and give him pocket money. There was always a feeling, though, that he blamed them for not having been to Eton. 'A certain austerity of taste,' he once observed, 'has made me always revolt from the curves of the feminine shape.' As with his writing, women could never quite shape up, could never be the masterworks he yearned for. Only now and again was he fortunate enough to find 'a lovely boy-girl . . . like a casual, loving, decadent Eton athlete'. Connolly's conduct with women was alternately bossy and babyish – a winning formula, to judge from his strike-rate. Lewis amiably guides us through Connolly's numerous affairs and marriages without ever being able to tell us what these women saw in him. But then the women themselves seemed not to know, much of the time. He was – well, he was just 'poor Cyril'.

In *Enemies of Promise*, Connolly divided current fiction into the Mandarin and the Vernacular (this was the late 1930s). To which mode did he belong? Needless to say, this was not altogether clear, except that his testy judgements on the Mandarin were pretty mandarin: lots of showy condescension, and not much substance. Most readers were probably left with the idea that Connolly was too gutsily realistic to be like Virginia Woolf, and too elegantly mannered to be like D.H. Lawrence. As always, he was somewhere in between. This was his natural terrain. When there were two things to be had, he wanted both. He wanted to be old-fashioned. He also wanted to be up to date. He preened himself as a high-grade connoisseur of by-gone beauties. At the same time, he liked to be seen as a rule-breaking avant-gardist. He dreamed of being a bookman of vast leisure, with a private income, a well-stocked cellar in the country and a great library of first editions, but he also got a kick out of studying the mechanics of down-at-heel Grub Street survival. He wanted to be left-wing; he wanted to be right-wing. Most of all, and without equivocation, he wanted his equivocations to be talked about. And talked about by people who knew how to talk, and who spent lots of time talking to each other. Waughs, Flemings, Mitfords, Bowras, Nicolsons, Woolfs, Powells, Clarks: the list was wonderfully challenging, ineffably discordant in its inner workings. What, though, if they could all be made to love Cyril as they ought to: love him but never finally quite fathom him?

It is perhaps not surprising that Connolly's peak writing triumphs – the words of his we want to keep – turned out to be in modes like parody and aphorism: humble modes which nonetheless thrive on a rhetoric of self-assurance, modes in which his irresolution could be projected as a form of social dominance. As jester or as sage, he was loftily above the fray and yet mysteriously on the ball. Another winning formula, and Lewis traces its drawing-room effects in ardent detail. The kind of people Connolly most wanted to impress, and did impress, were the kind of people who wrote lots of determinedly well-written letters. Lewis is skilful in his use of these – would indeed be somewhat lost without them. His intelligent and conscientious book ought not to be described as 'gossipy', but almost everybody in it was a gossip. And Cyril, as he himself had hoped and planned, was first-rate gossip fodder.

Connolly's parodies of his literary contemporaries were rightly considered to be brilliant at the time, and they still raise a laugh, but were they intended to be spiteful or admiring? When pressed, Connolly would own that they were probably a bit of both. His aphorisms (heavily indebted to Logan Pearsall Smith's *Trivia* books: he worked as Smith's secretary for a time, and envied his employer's well-heeled otherworldliness) were in general less sparkling than his literary take-offs but quite a few have now become part of the language. One need only check the standard dictionaries of modern quotations to realise that here, if anywhere, lies Connolly's true immortality. The best of his maxims were from the heart: 'Whom the gods wish to destroy they first call promising'; 'There is no more sombre enemy of art than the pram in the hall'; 'Imprisoned in every fat man a thin man is wildly signalling to be let out.' (According to Lewis, incidentally, this fat man/thin man trope was probably lifted from George Orwell.) The worst of them – indeed the average – now seem pompous and banal: 'No one can make us hate ourselves like an admirer'; 'All charming people have something to conceal, usually their total dependence on other people'; 'Literature is the art of writing something that will be read twice: journalism what will be grasped at once.' But even with these lead balloons we are meant to catch a whiff of the authentic Cyril: meant to marvel at his stoic poise, then scratch our heads. Poor Cyril. Poor impressive Cyril.

During the war years, Connolly's in-betweenness found its perfect monthly outlet, in the magazine *Horizon* (1940–50). In *Horizon*'s early issues, Connolly found himself, he said, caught between the 'aesthetic Twenties' and the 'puritan Thirties'. Prewar he had dabbled in both manners, without settling for either – at least not for long. Now he could change his stance from month to month. In May he could be aesthetic: September might find him veering just a shade towards the puritan. Some readers followed his fluctuating moods with fond solicitude. Others found them to be symptoms of an irritating spinelessness. Connolly was sympathetic to both points of

view – although, when feeling particularly spineless, he preferred the
fond approach.

On the subject of the war itself, Connolly was also in-between.
War was anti-art, he'd say, and therefore artists should keep it at a
distance: get on with their proper work while fighters fought. On
the other hand, he was no pacifist and had no wish to be thought
of as a shirker. This war was a just war, he decided, after a few
months of dithering, and *Horizon* was a legitimate contribution to
the war effort. Its offices had, after all, been bombed during the Blitz.
He bridled when people reproached him for even thinking about
Culture at a time like this. He disliked it intensely when 'warriors'
(his name for the soldiery) put on their butcher-than-thou airs. Of
one writer-conscript who attacked *Horizon* for its artiness, he wrote
that 'unless the dashing captain has now left these shores, it is he who
is under the obligation to us for carrying on through the craters, and
amid the looped and windowed raggedness of our offices, to provide
him and his stern followers with something to read in their quarters in
the West Country.' This note of 'you're lucky you have me' cropped
up rather often, and never more irascibly than when Connolly got
on to the subject of his magazine's subscription list: 'If we can go
on producing a magazine in these conditions, the least you can do
is read it.'

Although *Horizon* is now thought of as Connolly's most substantial
achievement, the truth is that during the war years his self-centred
elegiacs were bound to grate on many people's nerves. On the
other hand, nobody took him seriously when he tried to present
himself as a jaw-jutting patriot. He simply did not have the style,
or the sensibility, for times like these: times of moral urgency, of
selflessness. Almost any note he struck was sure to be the wrong one;
and nobody was more relieved than he was when the war came to
an end. At last he could resurrect the old world-weary plangencies,
the old disdains. The marquee of civilisation had collapsed, he wrote,
and there was relish in his sonority. Europe, he declared, was finished.
Even France was no longer the last outpost of Good Taste. She, too,
was on her knees. Towards the end of the Forties, he began smiling
towards America. American food parcels were arriving at the office,
in response to an appeal, and Connolly was first in line. In October

1947, *Horizon* published a double issue on 'The Arts in America' and
exhorted its readers to look to the New World for cultural renewal:

> As Europe becomes more helpless the Americans are forced to
> become far-seeing and responsible, as Rome was forced by the
> long decline of Greece to produce an Augustus, a Vergil. *Our
> impotence liberates their potentialities.* Something important is about
> to happen, as if the wonderful *jeunesse* of America were suddenly
> to retain their idealism and vitality and courage and imagination
> into adult life, and become the wise and good who make use
> of them.

Even this, alas, produced no US funding for the magazine, and by 1949
the food parcels had stopped coming. *Horizon*, Connolly announced,
would close down for a year, then reappear in 'an invigorated form'.
It never did, and to judge from what proved to be its final editorial,
it never really thought it would. 'It is closing time in the gardens of
the West,' the editor intoned, 'and from now on an artist will be
judged only by the resonance of his solitude or the quality of his
despair.' But what about that wonderful American *jeunesse*? What
about 'idealism and vitality and courage and imagination'? We can
be fairly certain that no regular reader of *Horizon*, or of Connolly,
demanded an explanation. After all, as he himself would surely have
retorted, that was two years ago – and anyway, it didn't work.

Cyril Connolly: A Life by Jeremy Lewis (Cape)

London Review of Books, 1997

2

Lives and Letters

Edmund Wilson's Wounds

When I first heard of Edmund Wilson, in the late 1950s, the stories about him were all to do with his prodigious learning. He had read everything, knew all manner of languages, was planning to learn more – including, we were told, Hungarian. He had written with masterful lucidity on a breathtakingly wide range of subjects: history, politics, religion, anthropology, psychology, world-travel – all this in addition to the books about literature for which I knew him. In old age – he was born in 1895 – Wilson's curiosity was boundless and undimmed, his industry unceasing.

And he had suffered too. He had the bow but he also had the wound. According to legend, Wilson's hands were afflicted with strange sores, brought on by too much contact with antique leather bindings. There was talk also of a breathing problem: the great bibliophile – and his biographer confirms it – suffered from 'a nose and throat infection from reading old books and bound periodicals that give out clouds of dust'. In 1961, a student has recalled, 'Wilson seemed to wheeze every time he turned a page in a book.'

Following Wilson's career from the mid-fifties, it was easy enough to build on this cartoon of the relentless polymath. The titles told the tale: *The Scrolls from the Dead Sea* (1955), *Red, Black, Blond and Olive: Studies in Four Civilizations: Zuni, Haiti, Soviet Russia, Israel* (1956), *Apologies to the Iroquois* (1960), *Patriotic Gore: Studies in the Literature of the American Civil War* (1962), *O Canada: An American's Notes on Canadian Culture* (1965). Was Wilson trying to make the rest of us feel shrivelled, locked into our mean little specialities? Was there an element of look-at-me?

John Updike (who can have a similar effect on his admirers) would later on suggest that Wilson's essay-collection, *A Piece of My Mind*, should really have been titled *Kiss My Mind*, and every one knew what he meant. Wilson had learned Hebrew in order to introduce some commonsense into the study of the Dead Sea Scrolls. For *Red, Black, Blond and Olive*, he had mugged up on the Shalako religion and on Haitian voodoo. For the Iroquois book, he had fathomed the mysteries of The Little Water Ceremony. An amateur magician, Wilson apparently 'enchanted' the Iroquois with his own 'mice and coin tricks'. He even used some of their good medicine to cure his gout.

Just in case these researches might have seemed too flamboyantly arcane, Wilson every so often turned his attention to the humdrum. Stale-seeming topics were enlivened by his magisterial disdain. *The Cold War and the Income Tax* was essentially self-serving (Wilson was in deep trouble with the IRS) but it did have a point: why *should* such small earnings from such giant learning be used for the bombing of Vietnam? And there was sense too in his famously pugnacious attack on the Modern Language Association. Wilson objected to the MLA wasting its funds on over-edited editions of bad books, and his pamphlet on the subject – *The Fruits of the MLA* (1968) – is now reckoned to have helped launch the excellent Library of America series: uniform hardbacks of America's best writing, with a minimum of 'apparatus' and a book-design that aims for readability and 'frequent use'.

From 1955 until his death in 1972, there was almost a Wilson book a year: essays, poems, plays as well as the big scholarly outpourings. And in the mid-Sixties Wilson even had time to engage in a long public argument with Vladimir Nabokov over Nabokov's translation of *Eugene Onegin*. According to Wilson, Nabokov was 'not quite at home with Russian'. Famous for his learning, Wilson was also known for his competitive hubris. Nabokov, after all, had claims to be thought of as one of America's great minds, and he was Russian. The ploy was to out-Russian the upstart, even though Wilson's own mastery of Pushkin's tongue was, by all accounts, a good deal less than perfect. Interestingly, Wilson rarely spoke the languages he learned from books. Whenever he did, the idiom was quite likely to be nineteenth-century.

At his death Wilson was honoured as America's foremost man of letters, and there was much marvelling that such a mighty thinker had never occupied a regular university position. In fact, Wilson did teach from time to time but was so bad at it – shy, stumbling, dogmatic – that he gave it up. And it, on the whole, gave him up: all the more so when he took to attacking academics as idlers and pedants. Academics, in their turn, sometimes described him as a charlatan, a magpie. His manner, when he met an expert in whatever field, was brusquely interrogative: it was as if he believed that the expert's expertise would be better off in the hands of someone who knew what to do with it; i.e. Edmund Wilson.

In America, Wilson liked to present himself as a custodian of threatened values, or as a patriot-curmudgeon in the style of H.L. Mencken, one of the heroes of his youth. In spite of his leftist flirtations of the 1930s (he once voted Communist and wrote a book about the Russian Revolution), nobody doubted that for him America came first. Europe was finished, but were Americans yet fit to rule the world? Although Wilson travelled a lot, he was always uncomfortable in European settings, and especially in England, where he was treated – so he felt – as just another pushy Yank. More than once he was subjected to what he called 'the Oxford brush-off: getting rid of importunate and troublesome questions by laughing gently about some aspect of the country or class or person which is totally irrelevant to the question in hand.' Camp figures like Maurice Bowra or snobs like Evelyn Waugh particularly riled him. So too did Cyril Connolly, although Wilson tried to be his friend. Connolly once said to him: 'I wish I had your *grasp*. I am really only a napkin folder,' and Wilson was not sure how to take it.

This, then, was Wilson's persona at his death: the solemn sage, America's champ-intellectual. He was known to have a sharp tongue and a short fuse but these failings merely served to enhance his reputation as one who functioned on an unreachably elevated plane. When admirers asked to meet him, he would say: 'If you like my work so much, why don't you go away and let me get on with it.' He had a card printed which listed all the things that Edmund Wilson did not want to do: Read manuscripts/Make statements for publicity purposes/Deliver lectures/Answer questionnaires/Autograph books for strangers/Contribute manuscripts for sales/Take part in symposiums or 'panels', and so on. The list ran to more than twenty items; the idea was that Wilson, or his secretary, would tick the appropriate rebuff. As Jeffrey Meyers points out, Wilson actually did most of the things he said he never did, but that was not the point. This man is of another world, do not disturb, was the intended message. Americans quite like their intellectuals to be hard to reach, and Wilson's books, for all his great prestige, were usually purchased in small numbers. Only with the scandalous novel, *Memoirs of Hecate County* – banned as pornographic in his home New York State – did he score anything approaching a popular success. Throughout his twenties and thirties he struggled as a highbrow journalist. Years of poverty writing book reviews for *Vanity Fair* and *The New Republic* were followed by a near-affluent stretch with *The New Yorker*, but Wilson was forever short of cash.

Towards the end of his life he was routinely honoured as – in Daniel Aaron's words – 'the moral and intellectual conscience of his generation' – and was showered with prizes and awards, including a Presidential Medal from John Kennedy. The IRS tried to block this honour on the grounds that the tax-evading Wilson was hardly one 'whose talent enlarges the public vision of the dignity with which life can be graced'. Kennedy retorted that the Medal was not 'for good conduct but for literary merit'.

If Kennedy had known more about Wilson's conduct over the years, he might have given him a medal for that too. In his own circle, Wilson's sexual exploits were spoken of with baffled admiration – short, fat and bald, he was not everyone's idea of a good-looker – but not until the posthumous publication of his journals did he emerge as what Jeffrey Meyers calls 'one of the great literary fornicators of all time'. (Wilson was indeed a literary fornicator: he had a taste for neurotic women-poets and was quite ready to praise their work in print so as to further his low aims.)

At the time of Kennedy's Medal, though, not much was known about Wilson's personality or private life. He liked to psychologise in print and his criticism was historical-biographical rather than New Critical (another reason, perhaps, for his low standing in some universities). His novels sometimes seemed to be confessions-in-disguise. *I*

Thought of Daisy, for example, was known to have its roots in Wilson's anguished love affair with Edna St Vincent Millay. It was also believed that Wilson figured unpleasantly in the vengeful fictions of Mary McCarthy, his third wife.

When, in the 1920s, someone suggested that Wilson might attempt '*un confession d'un enfant du siècle*', his response was to recoil: the idea, he said, was repugnant – he wanted 'to become more objective instead of more personal'. And this was early on, shortly after he left Princeton. In those days his ambition was to 'get to know something about all the main departments of human thought', or so he said. He was also ambitious as an artist. In the 1920s, he wrote eight plays and a ballet, and his first four publications were 'creative'.

His first triumph, though, was as a critic. In 1931, his *Axel's Castle* introduced Americans to European modernism (Diana Trilling, in 1927, had never heard of Eliot, Proust or Yeats), and still stands as a landmark text. But *Axel's Castle* was more than just a work of criticism; it was also an exploration of Wilson's own aesthetic inclinations, inclinations he had come to fear, or to mistrust. The book examined the ways in which the modernist writer employed a 'medley of metaphors – to communicate unique personal feelings'. The modernist was seen as a direct descendant of the 1890s, neurotically estranged from ordinary life, holed up in some private citadel of Art. Wilson wrote of what Pater called the 'large dissidence between an inward and somewhat exclusive world of vivid personal apprehension, and the unimproved, unheightened reality of those about him'. 'Those about him' were, of course, philistine, materialistic and hostile to the artist's dreamy ways. The modernist's response to this hostility had been to turn away from it and to become 'preoccupied with introspection sometimes to the point of insanity'. *The Waste Land* was seen by Wilson not as a vehicle for general wisdom but as 'a most distressingly moving account of Eliot's own agonised state of mind during the years preceding his nervous breakdown'.

It was this kind of bold biographising that marked out Wilson's criticism from the university mainstream, and much of the power of *Axel's Castle* comes from the sense we get that Wilson was writing not just about Joyce, Yeats and Eliot, but about himself. Two years before the book's publication, we now know, Wilson had had a breakdown of his own. He was thirty-three when it happened, but since childhood he had been haunted by the fear of going mad: his father, a brilliant lawyer who never lost a case, had also cracked up – or gone into what was then called 'an eclipse' – at thirty-three. With Wilson, the symptoms were panic attacks, trembling fits and phases of bottomless depression: 'The weeks when this was at its worst were the most horrible experience of my life . . . I felt I could not live through my crises of depression, when it seemed to me I was condemned, by some power I could not control, to destroy myself in some violent way.' At first, his doctors blamed the drink, for Wilson all his life was a prodigious drinker, but in the end settled for hot baths and electric shocks. Wilson curtailed the treatment and discharged himself from hospital but, according to Meyers, it took several years for him 'to recover from his manic-depressive mood swings, which would make him shudder and twitch, and fly into sudden rages. Fearful of losing control after his nervous breakdown, Wilson constantly tried to master himself and dominate others.'

With this knowledge we can see *Axel's Castle* as a first step towards self-mastery. We can also understand why Wilson's next move as a critic was to rush into left-wing politics, the realm of selflessness, of hopeful, useful action. In selling *Axel's Castle* to the publisher Max Perkins, Wilson came close to presenting the book's preoccupation with 'disillusion and resignationism' as, in essence, patriotic and progressive:

I believe that any literary movement which tends so to paralyse the will, to discourage literature from entering into action, has a very serious weakness; and I think that the time has now come for a reaction against it . . . we in America, in taking from Europe, as we have almost always hitherto taken, our literary standards and technique, have taken also, with the most recent consignments of artistic goods from Europe, a sea of attitudes and ideas . . . which have absolutely nothing to do with the present realities of American life and which are largely inappropriate for us. I believe – or rather, I hope – that the reaction of which I speak may come first in the United States. I seem to see certain signs of it: in another generation or two, we may be leading the world intellectually.

In this letter, the aim is to put some distance between Wilson the American sage and Wilson the unstable artist. And in some ways, this can be seen as Wilson's lifetime task. By the 1950s, few thought of the great rationalist as a closet Romantic. In the 1960s, books like *Upstate* and *A Prelude* were dark with misanthropy and gloom but by this stage Wilson's whole mood was elegiac, shot through with the fear that he was becoming a back number, that he was losing the authority his reason had toiled so hard to win. Now and then his poems bristled and seemed close to panic but Wilson the poet was always at his most comfortable in joky or satiric modes. Early on Allen Tate told Wilson: '*You have never spoken out.* There is an area of your sensibility that you have never completely come to terms with,' and Wilson suspected Tate was right. And perhaps at the same time he registered that *this* was why his poems, plays and stories – even at their best – seemed manufactured.

One of the most affecting passages in Wilson's life came in 1940, when his friend F. Scott Fitzgerald died. Wilson was forty-five and his first 'middle-aged' assignment, as he saw it, was to rescue his old Princeton classmate's reputation from oblivion. And this he did. It can fairly be said that, without Wilson's wonderfully skilful intervention, Fitzgerald's after-fame might not have been secured. For his Fitzgerald labours – he pieced together a text of *The Last Tycoon* and organised publication of *The Crack-Up* – Wilson took no money. The five hundred dollars he was paid went, at his insistence, to his friend's estate – which, in 1940, needed it.

The experience of editing Fitzgerald can be seen as a turning-point for Wilson. It forced him to take stock of his own eminence. Was it not dolorously fitting that he should find himself, at forty-five, serving the creativity of an old college-chum whom he had habitually viewed with condescension? Wilson was roughly the same age as Fitzgerald but he had always felt himself to be much older. And Fitzgerald had played along: he usually deferred to Wilson's judgements. In private, though, Fitzgerald was listening to other tunes, his own. When Wilson upbraided him for sloppiness, he tended to say Thank you and then sloppily work on. Wilson knew that he could never succumb to his intuitions in this way. As with the coins and mice, he liked to *know* how magic worked. All the same, even as he deplored Fitzgerald's recklessness, he could not help but envy it:

> And I, your scraps and sketches sifting yet,
> Can never thus revive one sapphire jet,
> However close I look, however late,
> But only spell and point and punctuate.

Around the time of his Fitzgerald labours, Wilson was brooding on the myth of Philoctetes, as dramatised by Sophocles. Philoctetes possessed a magic gift – he had a bow that never missed its mark – but he was unable to make use of it. He was the victim of an incapacitating wound, a wound so hideous and foul-smelling that he was forced to live in isolation from his fellow men. At the end of Sophocles's play, Philoctetes is nursed back to health by Neoptolemus. The Greeks need the sick man's magic bow and the plan at first is for Neoptolemus to steal it. The change of plan is crucial: 'It will not be enough,' Neoptolemus decides, 'for us to capture the bow without him. It is he who is to have the glory.'

Wilson's essay-collection of 1941 was called *The Wound and the Bow*. For him the plight of Philoctetes captured an important truth about the psychology of art and to ask why the myth affected him so deeply is to ask the question that beset him all his writing life. Should he identify with Philoctetes, the maimed creator, gifted but unable to deliver, or with Neoptolemus, the enabler, the imaginative go-between, the thoughtful man of deeds? Wilson was a magician, sure enough, but also – in World War One – he enlisted for army service as a nurse.

Jeffrey Meyers is inclined to see Wilson not just as a thwarted artist but as a thwarted human being – repressed and fearsomely eruptive. He recounts Wilson's drinking jags and calamitous sex-hungers with a kind of disapproving relish – drawing heavily, of course, on Wilson's own clinical disclosures in the diaries. Like the rest of us, though, he marvels at the strength of will that enabled this fine writer to keep his demons more or less at bay, and at the huge output he achieved in spite of a messy and uncentred private life.

As a biographer Meyers has some irritating habits. His sketches of supporting players tend to be school-of-identikit – 'a near-sighted, shy, intellectual artist' (Dos Passos), 'an intensely Germanic, beer-drinking, cigar-chomping man' (H.L. Mencken) – and his jokes are pretty awful. 'When Pushkin comes to shovekin' is perhaps the worst. Still, his task has not been easy. He has organised a mass of material with energetic competence and has not been at all fazed by his subject's intellectual range, nor by the rivalrous challenge of his multi-volume diaries. Meyers's productivity gets sniped at by reviewers – this is his twelfth literary biography – but he is seldom denounced as unreliable. For a writer who performs at hectic speed, he does seem to make remarkably few factual errors.

The same, I suppose, could be said of Edmund Wilson, whose bibliography lists nearly fifty publications. Nine of these were posthumous, and now we have a tenth. *From the Uncollected Edmund Wilson* brings together fifty or so fugitive reviews and articles from Wilson's early days as a full-time writer for the magazines: short pieces from his time with *The New Republic* and *Vanity Fair* (including his original *Waste Land* review) as well as slightly longer items for *The New Yorker* from the 1940s. Also included, I was glad to find, is his often-quoted 1959 interview with Henry Brandon, called 'We Don't Know Where We are'. Unhappily it now carries an amusing misprint that has Wilson comparing Britain's 'angry young men' with America's 'best generation' – which is not what he meant at all.

Edmund Wilson: A Biography by Jeffrey Meyers (Constable)

From the Uncollected Edmund Wilson selected and introduced by David Castronovo (Ohio University Press)

Times Literary Supplement, 1995

Harold Ross of *The New Yorker*

'How could a man who looked like a resident of the Ozarks and talked like a saloon bar brawler set himself up as pilot of a sophisticated, elegant magazine?' This was Ben Hecht's way of phrasing the Big Question about Harold Ross, the question that was asked repeatedly throughout Ross's twenty-five years in charge of *The New Yorker*, and is still sometimes asked today: how *did* he do it? Or rather (Ross loathed italics), how was *that* done by *him*? – 'that' being the last word in journalistic chic and 'him' being, well, just look at him: a Colorado bum.

Countless tales of Harold Ross's hayseed ways have now passed into legend. 'Is Moby Dick the whale or the man?', 'Willa Cather – did he write *The Private Life of Helen of Troy*?' Ross, it was said, hardly ever read novels and was suspicious of poetry that aspired beyond light verse. He called music and painting the 'two phoney arts'. He was contemptuous of all 'fancy college men'. 'Nobody's going to make me arty,' he would say. 'This isn't the old *Dial*.'

He had no politics to speak of. *The New Yorker* sailed through the Depression, nose in air, and managed to ignore most of the big issues of the Thirties. Instead of ideas, Ross had idiosyncrasies, phobias, taboos. 'Certain subjects' were understood to be banned from *The New Yorker*'s pages. For a time, 'the Jewish question' was outlawed; so too was the word 'cancer'. Homosexuality was an absolute no-no. Ditto all mentions of what Ross used to call 'the bodily functions'. He once complained over the telephone that a Hemingway book, so he had heard, contained a 'bathroom' word. When asked what the word was, he – whose speech was compulsively profane – refused to repeat it on an open line.

Although, at the outset, Ross announced that *The New Yorker* was not meant for the old lady from Dubuque, he always made sure that out-of-towners could read it without pain. It was, he'd say, a family magazine. According to Brendan Gill – a hostile judge – Ross's morality was shaped by 'the ugly commonplaces of almost a hundred years before'. His biographer describes him as 'classically laissez-faire in everything from war to income tax'. Nobody ever called him a progressive.

Even Ross's fabled editorial prowess is portrayed with condescension, sometimes by those who come to praise him. We read of his pedantry, his literal-mindedness, his mad grammarian's correctness. Thurber – who used to get off lightly – called Ross 'the most painstaking, meticulous, hair-splitting detail-criticiser the world of editing has known'. Both in Thurber's classic memoir and in this stylish new biography, we are given samples of Ross's handiwork, and some of these are indeed unnerving to behold. Their main feature is a kind of nagging, suspicious, utterly unembarrassed commonsense – sometimes impressively spot-on, sometimes dumbly reductive. One may not want to give Shakespeare's galleys to this man but at the same time it would be a pleasure to let him loose on X or Y.

1. The sentence at a. differs in nature from sentence at b. In the a. sentence you are writing from the viewpoint of the Bloodgoods, in the b. sentence you're the omnipotent author, knowing all about it. Seems to me wrong.
2. The *over their shoulders* phrase here give the right picture? Suggests to me *on their shoulders*, like a Greek maiden holding vase. (Small matter)
3. Very unexpected to learn at this late date that there's a bar in the place. Not mentioned before, and the definite pronoun has no antecedent.
4. Is it consistent that Mrs Bloodgood would be the repository for this confidence in view of the fact that she and her husband met the Spencers only two weeks before and have only seen them that once? And is it as clear as it should be *what* Dora whispered?
5. And same question here. Remember, Mrs Bloodgood has only

met the Spencers that one time, when she asked them to the party. How could she know?

It is clear from this why Ross had problems with some kinds of, shall we say, 'imaginative writing'. Thurber tells the story of coming upon Ross in his office, poem in one hand, dictionary in the other. 'I've got a poem here,' said Ross, 'that says "the leaves bronzen." Now "bronzen" is not a verb but an adjective, just as I thought. I know, I know, it's poetic licence – White has told me all about that. But I don't think there should be a licence, even in poetry, to get a thing wrong.'

Was this 'care for detail' Ross's way of taking revenge on the clever dicks he got to work for him: songbirds that needed bringing down to earth? Some of them thought so. Ross dreamed of a *New Yorker* style that would seem spontaneous and easy-going but he did everything he could to make his authors sweat for that ideal. Even as they indulged their delicious verbal fancies, he was along the corridor, deep in Fowler's *English Usage*, waiting for just one of them to make just one false move. During its most distinctive years – the late Thirties, early Forties – *The New Yorker*'s writers sounded as if they hadn't a trouble in the world. Ross knew that they had: big-trouble, Ross-trouble, the worst kind.

Ross's physical appearance was also the stuff of legend. The man who chose a monocled dandy as the logo for his magazine was famously unpleasing to the eye. To many, this connoisseur of cartoons seemed to have stepped out of a cartoon: the gap-tooth grin, the stick-up thatch, the all-over-the-place arms and legs. Ross's body resembled a huge questionmark, somebody said – perhaps too neatly. Thurber found it indescribable: those arms and legs were never still. 'He was always in midflight, or on the edge of his chair, alighting or about to take off.' Harpo Marx said that Ross looked like a cowboy who had lost his horse.

Cowboy, brawler, pedant: even before he started *The New Yorker*, even in Aspen, his home town, Ross was regarded as an oddball. Born in 1892, the son of an Irish silver-miner, he left school as early as he could. His aim was to become a newsman – he had worked on the local paper during his school holidays and caught the bug. His parents disapproved but even so they seem to have prepared him well. His mother, a frontier school-marm type, taught him to prize the essentials of good English grammar. They would parse sentences together and when Harold played truant, which he often did, he could usually be found in the public library: reading the novels of Bret Harte, we now discover. His father, when the silver-mining failed, set up as a storekeeper and by accident arranged for his son to enjoy regular slices of real life. The boy was sent to deliver groceries to Aspen's numerous brothels and saloons, and was not always in a hurry to get home – nor, after a time, was he to be found hiding in the library, or so we are led to presume.

In his teens, Harold began to make a habit of running away from home and when he did he would always get work as a 'tramp reporter', contributing short items to the newsheet of whichever town he happened to pitch up in. By the age of sixteen he really had left home and was flitting from rag to rag, from the San Francisco *Call and Post* to the Maryland *Appeal*, usually covering crime stories (throughout his *New Yorker* career, Ross nursed the idea of starting up a 'true crimes' magazine). Although most of these early writings were anonymous, his biographer has Ross, in his early twenties, writing for 'perhaps two dozen' different papers. On one occasion during those hobo years, Ross went looking for a New York job but was rebuffed. We don't need a biographer to tell us that this rejection would bear fruit in later years.

Ross's first big break came when he volunteered for army service during World War One. His interest in the European hostilities was strictly professional: as he saw it, war-reporters were the ultimate hobos. But he had also developed an interest in editing. At eighteen, on the Maryland *Appeal*, he had briefly been put in charge of the whole paper and done well. He knew he had a nose for a good story. Why not get others, now and then, to follow it? He founded a regimental magazine, *The Spiker*, and from there rose to become editor of the official army paper, the *Stars and Stripes* – a phenomenal success, this, with its captive audience, its guaranteed financial backing, its freedom from the need to play footsie with its advertisers. In no time at all, Ross was the best-known private in the American Expeditionary Force, turning down captains' poems by the dozen, despatching college men to hot-spots on the front, and altogether enjoying a doughboy-to-doughboy rapport with his trench readership. Says Thomas Kunkel: 'the paper, perhaps more than anything other than combat itself, coalesced the disparate, cobbled-together American units into an army.'

Although one of Ross's most effective ploys on *The Stars and Stripes* was to 'allow the enlisted men to speak for themselves' – in jokes, stories, cartoons, verses – he also knew a superior prose style when he encountered one. Later on, quite a few of his *New Yorker* contributors would be ex-colleagues on *The Stars and Stripes*: most notably Alexander Woolcott, with whom he would enjoy a career-long love-hate association. When Woolcott joined *The Stars and Stripes*, Ross asked him what he had done in civvy street. Woolcott told him that he had been drama critic on *The New York Times*. At this, Ross laughed a scornful hobo's laugh, causing Woolcott to reply: 'You remind me of my grandfather's coachman.' And this thoroughbred riposte seems to have stuck in Ross's mind, or gut. Here, surely, was big-city class of a high order. What it would be to have a magazine that could come out with lines like this week in, week out.

The Woolcott story, like so many others that have attached themselves to Ross, seems too good to be entirely true, but it was for New York that Ross headed as soon as he was out of uniform. His avowed aim was to find a way of continuing *The Stars and Stripes* in peacetime. *The Home Front*, a journal for returning vets, ran for two dozen issues but did not catch on, although it had ingredients – or 'departments' – that would later crop up in *The New Yorker*. And the experience of running it taught Ross the ins-and-outs of the magazine industry. It also, via Woolcott, brought Ross into contact with the then-embryo Algonquin network. In 1919, George Kaufman, Harpo Marx, Robert Benchley, Dorothy Parker and the others were in their twenties and unknown. But they were wits, albeit at each other's expense much of the time, and Ross watched with interest from the sidelines, every so often giving out 'teamster-like snorts' of appreciation or 'explosive, left-field interjections'. Several of the Algonquin group were journalists of a sort and they planted each other's names in any columns they had access to. Ross rather despised this log-rolling and was not altogether happy with the group's 'dissolute lifestyle', but he was all the time weighing up the likely talent. A magazine like *The New Yorker* would, he soon began to think, provide such talent with more useful employment than it would ever find at the Algonquin.

The New Yorker was partly funded with money put away for the purpose by Ross and his first wife, the journalist Jane Grant – a former singer whom he had met during his army years – but the bulk of the magazine's launch money came from a bakery-heir, Raoul Fleischmann. Fleischmann and Ross would remain enemies for years – and this is more of a sequitur than it may seem. Much of Ross's near-lunatic intensity of purpose was fuelled by his detestation of all those who, as he saw it, held his magazine in a financial stranglehold. Throughout his career, he saw himself as the victim of Fleischmann-like demons and hobgoblins, be they accountants, or admen, or majority stockholders. Ross hated being told what to do, even in areas where he was hopelessly at sea. And it was not just money-men who irked him: he had a way of delegating much of the magazine's administration to literary staff-members who, for a few weeks, he would revere as saviours and then turn on with savage and bewildering distrust. Thurber was one of these figures for a while and in his book he speaks amusingly, but bitterly, for a long line of puzzled sufferers.

At first there were no money-men. Indeed, had it not been for Fleisehmann's input, there would have been no money. *The New Yorker*'s first issues were resounding flops, rarely getting above a circulation of three thousand, and derided by the cognoscenti as feebly arriviste, would-be smart: the Algonquin circle looked the other way. For them, as for most others, it was not at all clear what Ross was playing at: was he sucking up to high society or mocking it? He was clearly aiming for a certain 'tone' – assured, off-hand, ironic – without knowing where to find it. It was a tone directly opposite to the one Ross was inclined to use when trying to define it. In the very first issues of *The New Yorker* – from 1925–6 – he tried to make a guess at what he meant, but nobody was fooled. As one critic put it – and this hurt – 'there is no provincialism so blatant as that of the metropolitan who lacks urbanity.'

It would not be long before this urbane critic, Niven Busch, was hired by *The New Yorker*. It took Ross about two years to find his feet – or rather, to find the people who knew where his feet should be. And chief among his rescuers was E.B. White. If this biography proves anything at all, it is that *The New Yorker* owed White almost as much as it owed Ross. White, arriving out of nowhere in 1927, had just the voice Ross had been straining for, and he could deploy it on demand, without seeming effort, in all departments of the magazine. As soon as Ross heard it, he knew why he would never have found it by himself: it was essentially good-tempered. White somehow made the superior tone likeable. It was as if he were saying to the readers: 'Sure I've seen it all, and on balance I think most of what I've seen is worth a smile, even the bits that are perhaps to be regretted.' Thomas Kunkel gives an apt illustration of what came to be treasured as White's 'magic touch'. In May 1927, the papers were full of Lindbergh's transatlantic flight and Ross 'fretted over what was possibly left to be said. White knew.'

> We noted that the *Spirit of St Louis* had not left the ground ten minutes before it was joined by the Spirit of Me Too. A certain oil was lubricating the engine, a certain brand of tires was the cause of the safe take-off. When the flyer landed in Paris every newspaper was 'first to have a correspondent at the plane'. This was a heartening manifestation of that kinship that is among man's greatest exaltations. It was beautifully and tenderly expressed in the cable Ambassador Herrick sent the boy's patient mother: 'Your incomparable son has done me the honour to be my guest.' We liked that; and for twenty-four hours the world seemed pretty human. At the end of that time we were made uneasy by the volume of vaudeville contracts, testimonial writing and other offers, made by the alchemists who transmute glory into gold. We settled down to the hope that the youthful hero will capitalise himself for only as much money as he reasonably needs.

This was it: the formula. Once it was set, Ross knew how to exploit it to the hilt. Within three years of White's arrival, the magazine's circulation had risen to six figures, and would continue to rise throughout the whole of Ross's reign, which ended with his death in 1951.

By then, of course, he had recruited other Whites, or would-be Whites, and driven some of them half-mad. White himself, together with his wife Katherine (*The New Yorker*'s long-serving and also hugely influential fiction editor), was always exempt from Ross's tyrannies. Once, when White left to work for *Harper's* – he felt like a change – Ross begged him to come back. If anyone else had dared to jump ship in this way, Ross would happily have seen him drown. As it was, White drifted back, but in his own good time. As Thomas Kunkel says, 'for Ross, getting out *The New Yorker* without the Whites was like trying to walk deprived of legs.'

'I am a monstrous person, incapable of intimate associations,' said Ross after, or during, the failure of one of three marriages. He married impulsively, because he liked a pretty face, but was soon back behind his desk, in hiding. After all, his first wife had stood up to him: he was not going to go through all *that* again. 'I'm married to this magazine. It's all I think about.'

And so it was. When Ross was out on the town, he was really looking for 'Talk of the Town' items. When he read the papers, it was in the hope that he would get a story-idea, or pick up a *New Yorker* 'casual'. When he made friends outside the magazine, he was usually firming up a contract. He hated the theatre, even though at least three of his friends wrote plays about him. The movies he could take or leave: every so often he needed to check up on his film critic. At one time, early on, he liked to eat, but *The New Yorker* gave him ulcers.

Kunkel's biography, it need hardly be said, is largely concerned with Ross-at-work. As an evocation of the man, his book could scarcely hope to rival Thurber's *The Years with Ross* or even Gill's *Here at The New Yorker* (both of which he censures as unfairly slanted). But he has trawled nobly through the records and taken pains to check out the various Ross legends – some of which remain sturdily uncheckable. He also provides an illuminating year-to-year account of *The New Yorker*'s somewhat protracted growing-up. His chapters on the magazine's impressive response to World War Two are certainly worth having. In many respects, Ross's wartime issues were his best: a *Stars and Stripes* for highbrows, so to speak. Certainly it was good to see the monocle mist up from time to time. As E.B. White – who else – remarked: 'We feel like a man who left his house to go to a Punch-and-Judy show and, by some error in direction, wandered into *Hamlet*.' And this, come to think of it, is not a bad way of describing what it must have been like to work for Harold Ross.

Genius in Disguise: Harold Ross of The New Yorker by Thomas Kunkel (Random House)

London Review of Books, 1995

The Buried Life: Elizabeth Bishop's Letters

For most of her writing life, Elizabeth Bishop was known for not wishing to be known. Where other poets muscled their careers to centre stage, she hovered in the wings. Where others importuned their audience with news of their private sorrows, she remained impressively tight-lipped. A near-contemporary of the so-called confessional poets, poets such as Robert Lowell and John Berryman, she once said of them: 'You just wish they'd keep some of these things to themselves.'

'Closets, closets and more closets' was Bishop's response to the gay liberation movement. Her friends knew that she was lesbian, and also that she was alcoholic, but she herself liked to believe that each of these dispositions was a secret. Certainly her poems gave no clues. And since Bishop spent most of her career outside the United States, mostly in Brazil, and took little part in homeground literary politics, there was not much word of mouth to go on. Her geographical self-exile seemed perfectly in tune with her habits and her demeanour as a poet.

Bishop died in 1979, aged sixty-eight, prize-laden and greatly respected by her fellow poets. 'A poet's poet's poet' was James Merrill's well-known tag. And yet she was still thought of as somehow marginal to the action. Austere and almost fiddlingly skilful, more interested in places than people, detached almost to the point of authorial invisibility, she was there to be invoked as a cool, neo-classical alternative to the various slacknesses and excesses of the moment: excessive avant-gardism, excessive self-exposure, excessive political engagement and so on. There was nothing excessive about Bishop. For her, it seemed, there was an active virtue to be found in self-forgetfulness, in saying 'look at that' instead of 'look at me'.

And now we have the letters, the biography, the 'oral testimony' of acquaintances, onlookers, colleagues, and they reveal a life filled almost to ruination by excess. Drink, sexual passion, sickness, suicides: Bishop, it turns out, had much to hide, or thought she did. At first, it is as if we've been given the low-down on the secret practices of some formidably righteous aunt. After a bit, though, we are glad that we have been told. Primary among Bishop's excesses was a yearning for the non-excessive, for the pleasures and the reassurances of the low-key, the repetitive, the known. In the light of what we now learn of her personal disorders, we can more widely respond to the obliquities of her determinedly well-ordered work. We can even conclude that the question of self-revelation (how much to tell and how to tell it?), far from not mattering to her, was almost always at the heart, or near the heart, of what she wrote.

Robert Giroux takes the title of his edition of Bishop's letters from a late poem called 'One Art', which ends:

> I lost my mother's watch. And look! my last, or
> next-to-last of three loved houses went.
> The art of losing isn't hard to master.
>
> I lost two cities, lovely ones. And, vaster,
> some realms I owned, two rivers, a continent.
> I miss them, but it wasn't a disaster.
>
> – Even losing you (the joking voice, a gesture
> I love) I shan't have lied. It's evident
> the art of losing's not too hard to master
> though it may look like (*Write* it!) like disaster.

Thanks to biography, we now know that this poem was written in delayed response to a catastrophe, a major turning point in Bishop's life: the death by suicide of Lota de Macedo Soares, with whom she had lived in South America for fifteen years. Knowing this, we can work out what Bishop means by 'two cities', 'three loved houses', 'a continent'. And the line about losing her mother's watch assumes a new forcefulness when we know about the poet's childhood. Bishop's father died when she was a baby. When she was five, her mother was moved to an insane asylum. Brought up by her grandparents, Bishop never saw her mother again (she died in 1934, when Bishop was 23).

Such knowledge indeed helps us to 'understand' the poem better. But we have not understood it at all if we fail at the same time to register how hard it was for Bishop to speak about these things in poems. She tells herself to '*Write* it!' but she has not, in this case, written it. She can't. Hence her employment of the villanelle, a form that encourages the jaunty-grim, but deals in general wisdom. As well as knowing the biographical background of the poem (written some eight years after Lota's death and sparked by the seeming failure of a new relationship), we also know, from Brett C. Millier's excellent new life, that the text went through seventeen drafts: '. . . each version of the poem', says Millier, 'distanced the pain a little more, depersonalised it, moved it away from the tawdry self-pity and "confession" that Elizabeth disliked in many of her contemporaries.'

She may have disliked it, but it made her think. Perhaps these sufferers who stared only at the mirror were closer to real poetry than she was. Robert Lowell, certainly, knew how to '*Write* it!' and also knew how to rise above self-pity; at his best, he was as accurate and intelligent as Bishop was. This worry about content was not new. When Bishop put together *North & South*, her first book, she fretted that in wartime, her precise, absorbed, descriptive sketches would seem disengaged, that she was strong on adjectives and nouns and weak on verbs. And later on, watching a sandpiper pecking at a beach, she only half-admires the creature's rapt certainty of purpose:

> The world is a mist. And then the world is
> minute and vast and clear. The tide
> is higher or lower. He couldn't tell you which.
> His beak is focused; he is preoccupied
>
> looking for something, something, something.

But what's the point of looking if you don't know what you are looking *for*?

Poor bird, he is obsessed!
The millions of grains are black, white, tan, and gray,
mixed with quartz grains, rose and amethyst.

For poets, sooner or later, there was always a 'So what?' – or so she feared.

In the beginning, though, for Bishop the joys and the skills of simple observation seemed sufficient. Her first literary mentor was Marianne Moore, herself famous as (in Moore's words) 'one of those who despise clamor about substance'. Bishop and Moore met in the substance-full 1930s, and each found an enjoyable delinquency in concentrating on the local, the miniature, the usually unnoticed. In a period dominated by vehemence and theory, they liked to cultivate an art of the curious specific. They kept smiling, or half-smiling, while everyone around them sported masks of doom.

When Bishop introduced herself to Moore, whose work she had admired in college ('Why had no one ever written about *things* in this clear and dazzling way before?'), there was an inevitable awkwardness on both sides. Bishop was in her early twenties, Moore in her mid-forties, and both ladies were well-buttoned-up. The ice was broken when Bishop offered to take Moore to a circus. 'I didn't know that she *always* went to the circus.' Together they watched 'bears on roller skates and a Chinese family who played cards and ate while hanging by their hair on hooks'. Soon after, they discovered that the circus was not the only offbeat interest they shared. They were both crazy about snakes, tattoos, semi-precious stones, exotic flowers and birds, dress-making, recipes. A friendship was launched that for five years would dominate the younger poet's idea of what poetry could be. As Moore saw it, poetry could be whatever it turned out to be: no more, no less. For the young Bishop, strong on visual detail, weak on subject matter, this news came as a relief, and a release.

Bishop's earliest letters to Moore are bouncy, chatty, eager to impress but lightly so. They are marked, really, by Bishop's sheer pleasure in having discovered a senior soulmate. Accounts of Bishop as a schoolgirl or undergraduate at Vassar present her as cagey, shrewd, aloof – witty but not cheerful. Mary McCarthy, a college-mate, spoke of envying 'the mind hiding in the words, like an "I" counting up to

100 waiting to be found.' At least something of the youthful Bishop 'I' showed through in her dealings with Moore, a mother-figure who lived with her mother. As David Kalstone has commented, 'What must it have been like . . . for a young woman who had not seen her mother since she was 5 to know an older poet who was inseparable from hers? And to have met Moore in the very year that Bishop's own long-absent mother died.' Whenever she visited Moore's 'otherworldly' apartment in Brooklyn, Bishop always felt 'uplifted, even inspired, determined to be good, to work harder, not to worry about what other people thought, never to try to publish anything until I thought I'd done my best with it, no matter how many years it took – or never to publish at all.'

Moore, though, was a natural eccentric. She really did prefer pelicans to people. Bishop's dottiness, not in the least faked but somewhat worked up for Moore's benefit, was never quite central to her personality. She was more of a dreamer, more of a worrier. And she was young, and far more ambitious for literary advancement than she made out; more, maybe, than she knew. Her methods and her aspirations could not for long be fashioned to Moore's model. And neither could her poems. Perhaps she came to feel that Moore's influence encouraged her in habits of detachment. But how to close the gap between the seer and the seen?

When writers of the 1930s worried about 'substance', their worry was usually to do with leftist politics – were they sufficiently engaged? Bishop was never attracted to the *Partisan Review* crowd (although she did publish in the magazine), and on certain key issues of the day – the Spanish War, for instance – she was indignantly right-wing. In 1936, when other writers were joining the International Brigade, she was in Spain as a tourist, and wrote to a friend: 'If you really want to see what the Communists are up to, what beautiful things they have ruined, you should come here.' (This letter is not printed by Giroux, nor is another letter, of 1956, in which Bishop writes about the Rosenbergs: 'I believe that the Rosenbergs were a wretched pair of dupes and traitors, and that the hysterical and hypocritical excitement whipped up by the Communist Party about their trial and deaths was just one more example, a particularly unsavory one, of the aims and methods of that Party.')

By the time Bishop settled in Florida in 1938 (she stayed there for nine years), the personality that she was accustomed to excluding from her poems had shaped itself in ways Moore would not approve. She knew she was lesbian, and she knew, too, that Moore was contemptuous of 'sodomites'. She knew that she was alcoholic and that in New York this could hardly be kept even semisecret. There had already been scenes, embarrassments, blackouts. She also suffered wretchedly from asthma, and needed to be in the sun. This last was a condition that she *was* able to disclose to Moore. In Florida for health reasons, she could enthuse about the scenery, the locals, the ins and outs of daily life. And Bishop is at her most likeable when she's allowed, when she allows herself, merely to chatter on:

Last week I found such a nice little house to "work in"; a tree on one side and a vine on the other almost hid it. The walls were lemon-pie yellow, and the doors were white with raspberry-pink panels. The woman who was going to rent it to me had it all fixed so nicely – a green table and three chairs, a whatnot with a bunch of wax roses on top, and lots of pictures of movie stars on the walls. But of course she didn't tell me there was a *machine shop* just across the lane.

I put off writing originally because I wanted to send you "something" – a sample, at least – when I did, but I have done NOTHING although I try hard every day, honestly . . .

The other day I caught a parrot fish, almost by accident. They are ravishing fish – all iridescent, with a silver edge to each scale, and a real bill-like mouth just like turquoise; the eye is very big and wild, and the eyeball is turquoise too – they are very humorous-looking fish. A man on the dock immediately scraped off three scales, then threw him back . . . I'm enclosing one [scale], if I can find it. Mrs A. is confronting a huge fish in the kitchen right now – Red Snapper, but it is gilt-rose. Oh how I wish that you and your mother too would sometime visit us, in the two-month Jane Austen style. There are so many things we'd like to show you – only of course we'd be *shown* so many more.

There is a revealing pathos in that 'I wanted to send you something', meaning a new poem. In fact, she *has* sent something. The description of the parrot fish is wonderfully alive – and all the more so for not being proffered as a poem, or as a piece of literary writing.

These letters to Moore from Florida will suggest to many readers that Bishop, without knowing it, had chanced upon the answer to her worries about substance, about human content, about involving the self in what is seen. This parsimonious producer of poems wrote several thousand letters. Only a 'fraction of her output', says Giroux, is included in this 600-page selection. She once wrote forty letters in a day.

It would be easy to say that letters don't matter, or that Bishop used letters to escape from the more rigorous requirements of her art. It is true enough that she preferred to burble on about parrot fish than face up to the 'so what?' of, say, 'Parrot fish: a Poem', and she was quite ready to confess that letter-writing was 'kind of like working without really doing it'. But this was how some poets felt about their poems. With Lowell's work, for instance, she could see that the distinction between poem and letter sometimes became blurred. And Lowell himself, now and then, treated the letters he received as though they were literary texts that he could borrow from, or assimilate into his poems.

When Lowell did this to Elizabeth Hardwick's letters, Bishop was famously outraged. Her reaction now seems odd. Her own letters are by no means as artless as she makes them sound. There is plenty of evidence that she was alert to the genre's literary possibilities: her library was full of collections of letters, and when she taught at Harvard in the 1970s she planned a seminar on 'Letters – Readings in Personal Correspondence, Famous and Infamous, from the Sixteenth to Twentieth Century', and had in mind to cover 'Mrs Carlyle, Chekhov, my Aunt Grace, Keats, a letter found in the street, etc.' Lowell spoke shrewdly when he predicted that Bishop's letters would one day establish her as 'not only one of the best, but also one of the most prolific writers of our century'. The shrewdness was in calling her 'prolific'. No one ever called her *that*.

Perhaps her fury against Lowell's treatment of the Hardwick letters (he quoted chunks of them in a poem-sequence that he wrote about the break up of their marriage) was a fury against his breach of manners – not just the manners owed to Hardwick, but also the manners on which the business of letter-writing hangs. For Bishop there was a decorum here, a code of conduct that had to be protected; otherwise the genre would lose everything about it that was precious. For Bishop, there *was* something precious about a form of writing that was both polite and intimate, that permitted self-revelation but was recognised as private, one-to-one.

In a letter, she knew whom she was addressing. She could exercise social prowess, vanity, charm, triviality of mind; she could manipulate and entertain. Much has been written about Bishop's crippling shyness, and most of the childhood witnesses assembled in *Remembering Elizabeth Bishop: An Oral Biography* testify to her separateness from the main drift: 'Elizabeth was kind of odd. She wasn't a girl that mixed very well'; 'She thinks for some reason, she is different from other girls'; 'Elizabeth was really different from everyone else'. In poems this shyness can issue as an icy reticence, a wish to divert attention from the self. In letters, though, Elizabeth could be one of the gang. She could giggle, exclaim, lecture, exchange recipes, enthuse about home furnishings. And when things got desperate, as they dramatically did for her after the death of her friend Lota, she could even cry:

> Oh WHY WHY WHY didn't she wait a few days? Why did I sleep so soundly? – why why why – I can't help thinking I might have saved her somehow – go over and over that Sunday afternoon but honestly can't think of anything I did especially wrong – except that I have done many wrongs all my life. Please try to keep loving me in spite of them, won't you? I am clinging to my friends desperately.

Bishop's fifteen years with Lota Soares were the best years of her life – well, the first ten were. The letters that she wrote from Brazil after settling there in 1951 are as vivacious as anything she wrote in verse. Her first book had appeared in 1946 and had done well enough to win her a few grants; she had a *Time-Life* commission to write a book about Brazil. Perhaps for the first time in her life, the way ahead seemed clear. Lota was a forceful protector, she had money, owned the house they lived in and had even built Bishop a study. She was heavily involved in local politics, but in the early years she saw it as her chief role to keep Bishop focused on her writing, to safeguard the poet's health and to restrain her from the bottle. According to a mutual friend, Lota believed that Bishop needed 'the affectionate protection of a home, a sense of belonging, the orderly consolations of habit and dailiness, the will to stay put. They became lovers, even if Lota more often acted the mother to Elizabeth the child.'

Another mother-figure. And there can be no doubt that for a long time Lota's programme worked. The letters poured out, some of them small joyous hymns to domesticity. Repeatedly Bishop's tone is one of buoyant gratitude, as if she had been rescued from a wreck: 'I must have died and gone to heaven without deserving to.' And there were poems too – poems more relaxed and rich in human content than anything she had attemped before. The old descriptive flair was still powerfully in evidence, but with a new, more distinctive zest. Landscapes became close-ups, locations became towns in which people live. The influence of Lowell was admitted, though cautiously. Something of his raw human eloquence can be heard in these Brazil poems, but it is always reined in by what Moore used to call Bishop's 'instinct against precipitousness':

> The sea's off somewhere, doing nothing. Listen.
> An expelled breath. And faint, faint, faint
> (or you are hearing things), the sandpipers'
>   heart-broken cries.
>
> The fence, three-strand, barbed-wire, all pure rust,
> three dotted lines, comes forward hopefully
> across the lots; thinks better of it; turns
>   a sort of corner . . .

In this new location Bishop also felt ready to recall episodes from her strange, puzzled childhood, episodes that she had for years kept at a distance. Much of Bishop's 'Brazil book', *Questions of Travel*, which appeared in 1965, is set in her birthplace, in Nova Scotia. Nova Scotia now seemed like the opposite of where she was – and not just in terms of climate and geography. Her childhood home had never felt like home. She had been shunted from one set of grandparents to

another; for a time she lived with her Aunt Maude. Then there was
boarding school. She was always a guest in other people's houses, and
her mother's absence had never been properly explained. For a long
time she had thought she was an orphan. Now that she had found
a home, she could afford to ask herself some leading questions. Had
she inherited her mother's madness? Why was she unable to give up
drink, even with Lota to watch over her?

The Brazil idyll began to fall apart as Bishop and Lota became
increasingly involved in their very separate careers. Lota was given
the job of designing and building a 'People's Park' in Rio, a huge
exacting job that left her with little time to supervise the management
of Bishop's writing life. Lota became rattier and bossier; Bishop more
mouselike and aggrieved.

In fact Bishop was not in the least mouselike when it came to the
running of her literary career. The notion that she cared nothing for
the baubles of Pulitzer and Guggenheim does not survive a reading
of these letters. She was well aware that her distance from the war
zone served her well. So, too, did her ingenuous demeanour. She
was the safe candidate, unsullied and above the battle. Even as the
prizes came her way, moreover, she continued to be thought of as
'neglected'.

This is not to suggest that her expatriation was strategic. The
idea of 'living as a poet' in America was, for her, entirely dreadful:
the teaching, the readings, the reviewing. And she knew that, if
the relationship with Lota failed, she would be dependent on the
goodwill of American universities and prize committees. Thus, when
the relationship did begin to falter, she held on to it, to the breaking
point. In 1966, the year before Lota's suicide, she wrote: 'The simple
truth is that my darling Lota, whom I still love very much if she'd
give me the chance to show it, has been simple hell to live with for
five years now – and I'm not exaggerating.'

After Lota's death Bishop returned to Brazil on two occasions. The
first time, she found to her horror that she was being widely blamed for
Lota's death, that some of her much-prized Brazilian friends were not
friends of hers at all; they had put up with her because of Lota. There
were ugly squabbles about property, and they were made worse when,
on her second visit, it was found that Bishop had a new companion, a

young American with whom she had been involved when Lota was still living. This new romance could not have been expected to survive Lota's suicide, and it didn't. Bishop's new lover (called by Giroux, a little chillingly, 'XY') was of psychotic bent, although at first she had seemed dominant, a masterful acolyte, a keeper. Bishop found herself having to play nursemaid, a role for which she was ill-equipped, as these letters painfully make clear. Bishop is at her least lovable in her descriptions of the strains imposed on her by her sick friend.

After Lota, and after the collapse of her affair with the unfortunate 'XY', Bishop's biography makes dismal reading: breakdowns, suicide-attempts, drinking jags, worries about money. Giroux prints several of Bishop's letters to her psychiatrist, so we can follow the decline in grisly detail. These letters, though affecting, are also somewhat evasive or self-serving. Looked at as literature, they are unlikely to find their way into the anthologies; but then after Brazil, there is a general falling-off in the quality of Bishop's letters. The ebullience, the straightforwardness seem just a little forced, as if she is trying to recapture her best form while fearing that it, too, has been lost.

Robert Giroux cuts or excludes several interesting letters referred to in Millier's biography, and in Lorrie Goldensohn's eager but absorbing *Elizabeth Bishop: The Biography of Poetry*. Perhaps he should have been stricter with Bishop's post-Lota miseries, and aimed for a more 'literary' coverage of her later years. From those years I would certainly like to have seen Bishop's letter to Lowell about his first sheaf of sonnets ('I am overcome by their sheer volume'). And I also quite like the sound of a letter quoted by Millier in which Bishop says that Diane Wakoski is 'writing the kind of poem that she herself had been fighting against all her life'. Giroux seems to want Bishop to sound nicer than she sometimes was.

Bishop's final port was Harvard, where – despite the ministrations of a small coterie of worshipful disciples – she felt herself to be neglected, inadequate and, by one or two of the faculty, despised. In her sixties the woman who cherished domesticity found herself lodging in cramped, dingy rooms in a student dormitory. By day, she steeled herself to teach 'Advanced Verse Writing' to 'all the usual nuts and freaks' – 'and yes, there *is* an Elementary or Beginners' or something Verse Writing, too.'

In Bishop's last short book, *Geographies III*, there are hints that, had she lived, she might have attempted to follow the instructions of 'One Art', simply to '*Write* it!' Poems like 'Crusoe in England', 'In the Waiting Room' and 'The Moose' seem melancholy worlds away from early poems like 'Roosters' or 'The Map'.

> I often gave way to self-pity.
> 'Do I deserve this? I suppose I must,
> I wouldn't be here otherwise. Was there
> a moment when I actually chose this?
> I don't remember, but there could have been.'
> What's wrong about self-pity, anyway?

It seems very doubtful, though, that she would ever have wished to break out into full-blooded candour. Her lifetime's worry about 'substance' would have stayed with her to the end. Even the one or two late pieces of hers that have been called 'confessional' or 'near-confessional' are essentially well-guarded, wry, rueful and resigned. This was how she came across in public, all her life. Letters, she believed, were different. Letters were private. All in all, we can be grateful that they weren't.

One Art: Selected Letters by Elizabeth Bishop, edited by Robert Giroux (Chatto, 1994)

The New Republic, 1994

The Sensitivities of Stephen Spender

My first meeting with Stephen Spender was in 1960, when I was president, chief executive, and general mastermind of the Oxford University Poetry Society. Spender had been asked up to Oxford to give a talk, and beforehand he was required to dine with the society's committee. This ritual was always an ordeal for everyone concerned, but the committee (that's to say, a couple of my friends and I) insisted on maintaining it, week in, week out. It was a chance for us to get a free meal out of the society's coffers, but it was also a means of enjoying some lively and informal contact with our visiting celeb. Best of all, it provided us with a rich source of superior chitchat for several months to come: 'Well, yes, but when I asked Eliot to clarify that very point, he said nothing. He just sat there.'

The week before Spender's visit, we had had dinner with W. H. Auden, and we were now in a position to spin tales of that master's irritability, his gluttonous drink intake, his astonishing complexion: 'It's actually much worse close up.' The week after, we would be getting Robert Graves. Why these grand figures put themselves to this inconvenience – no fee, no audience to speak of, and a dinner that few of them ever seemed to touch – remains a mystery to me. But it was rare for a poet, however famous, to turn down our invitation. One or two of them, unbelievably, came back for more.

In retrospect, I can see that this was my introduction to the limitless vanity of poets: they'll put up with anything, provided that they get to read their works. But I can also see how repulsive we must have seemed to them. Over dinner, we expected our guests to entertain. Our contribution was languidly interrogative. 'So. What are you up

to these days?' we would say, or 'Were you *very* upset by the reviews
of your last book?' And we were determined to be unimpressed. As
far as my buddies and I were concerned, these eminents had dragged
themselves to Oxford in order to be thought well of by the likes of
us. They were afraid of becoming back numbers. They wanted to
keep in with the young.

This was certainly the notion we had formed of Stephen Spender.
We planned to greet him with a special condescension. In 1960,
Spender was renowned as a figure from the past – a poet of the
1930s – and his work was deeply out of fashion. Indeed, the 1930s
were out of fashion, seen as a tragicomic literary epoch in which
poets had absurdly tried, or pretended, to engage with current
politics – one in which pimply young toffs had linked arms with
muscular proletarians in order to 'repel the Fascist threat' when they
weren't at Sissington or Garsinghurst for the weekend, sucking up
to Bloomsbury grandees. The Homintern, Cyril Connolly had called
them – 'psychological revolutionaries, people who adopt left-wing
political formulas because they hate their fathers or were unhappy
at their public schools or insulted at the Customs, or lectured about
sex.' Someone else had dubbed Spender 'the Rupert Brooke of the
Depression'.

We undergraduates liked to repeat these gibes. Most of us had
been told in school that of all the Thirties poets Spender was the one
whose reputation had been most inflated. He lacked the complexity
of Auden, the erudition of Louis MacNeice, the cunning of Cecil
Day-Lewis. He was the one who had believed the slogans – 'Oh
young men oh young comrades' – and, after the war, the one who
had recanted most shame-facedly. He was the fairest of fair game. I
remember my school's English teacher – an acolyte, I later learned,
of F. R. Leavis – reading aloud from Spender's 'I think continually
of those who were truly great' and substituting for 'great' words like
'posh' and 'rich' and 'queer'. The same teacher also had a scornful
party piece involving Spender's 'Pylons, those pillars / Bare like nude,
giant girls that have no secret.' 'Even you lot,' he would say, 'might
draw the line at girls who looked like *that.*'

My teacher was in line with current critical opinion. He usually
was. The late Fifties was a period of sceptical nay-saying. It was

modish to be cagey, unillusioned. The only brave cause left was
the cause of common sense, the only decent political standpoint
the refusal to be taken in. 'Look what happened in the Thirties!' was the common cry. And it was not just political wind-
baggery that was distrusted. There was suspicion, too, of anything
religiose, arty, or intense. 'A neutral tone is nowadays preferred,'
Donald Davie wrote in a mid-Fifties poem called 'Remembering the Thirties.' And Thom Gunn – the young poet we 1960s
students most admired – was preaching a doctrine of butch self-
reliance:

> I think of all the toughs through history
> And thank heaven they lived, continually.
> I praise the overdogs from Alexander
> To those who would not play with Stephen Spender.

It was better, Gunn said, 'To be insensitive, to steel the will, / Than
sit irresolute all day at stool / Inside the heart.'

Such tough talk was music to our ears. As we waited for Spender
in the olde-worlde Oxford pub that served as our bunker, our HQ,
we took bets on which beam he would knock his head against. Our
guest poet was notoriously tall. He tripped over things, we'd read.
As it turned out, he negotiated his entrance with discreet aplomb.
Almost before we knew it, he was there, stooping towards us with
an outstretched hand, and with an oddly mischievous half smile,
which seemed to say, 'Don't worry. It's entirely *my* fault that I'm
six foot three.'

He was not at all like the Spender we recalled from the Thirties
photographs: the open-necked, simpering young zealot just back from
the cafés of Vienna and Berlin and about to lurch off to the Spanish
Civil War. Nor did his appearance accord with his contemporaries'
descriptions: 'an immensely tall, shambling boy of nineteen, with
a great scarlet poppy-face, wild frizzy hair, and eyes the violent
colour of bluebells.' This was Christopher Isherwood's description
of a fictional character based on Spender (named Stephen Savage)
in *Lions and Shadows*. Isherwood had been one of Spender's closest
friends, and his book was our chief source of Thirties knowledge. And

John Lehmann, another key associate, had written about Spender's 'demoniac look' and his 'huge pantomime grin'.

We had been half-expecting our man to show up in cap and bells, but the Spender who now shook our hands was snowy-haired, and stably benevolent of mien. He looked like the sort of headmaster we had never had, the sort for whom my satirical English teacher would no doubt have uprooted his forelock. The handshake was a trifle limp, but there was no sign of the poppy face. Spender seemed to be sporting a Florida suntan.

When he spoke, it was in a sheepish semi-whisper, eyes averted or downcast. He wanted us to tell him about *us*, about the student literary scene, which magazines we wrote for, which poets we admired. On this last we were sturdily evasive, and although he looked sorrowful, he did not press. At dinner, it was pretty much the same. He encouraged us to have our say, soliciting our opinion of *Encounter*, the magazine he edited in London. *Encounter*, he said, was always on the lookout for new Oxford talent – why didn't we send him some of our unpublished work?

Through all this, Spender's demeanour was impossible to fathom; there was in it a strange fusion of attentiveness and deep preoccupation. Again, the memoirists seemed to have let us down, with their stories of his ludicrous garrulity, his mad compulsion to tell all. John Lehmann called Spender 'the most rapidly self-revealing person I had ever met,' and Virginia Woolf, after dining with him in the Thirties, noted that he 'talks incessantly' and would one day turn into a 'prodigious bore'. According to Isherwood, his voice (that is, the voice of Stephen Savage) 'would carry to the farthest corners of the largest restaurant the most intimate details of his private life.' In Oxford, it was we who burbled on. Was he hanging on our words or was he miles away? We couldn't tell.

Over coffee, though, things changed. We'd had our say; now it was his turn. What was he doing these days? Did he care about reviews? With each question, Spender winced, as if he had been prodded with a fork. But his eyes seemed to have brightened, and, for the first time that evening, his total attention was engaged. He was earning his keep, he said, lecturing at American universities – usually on Auden and the Thirties. Also, in connection with *Encounter*, he attended a lot of congresses in Europe. And, yes, he did care about reviews – so much so that he had stopped publishing his poems in book form. Young people didn't know how wounding reviews could be. 'They think we don't mind it, but we do.' He sounded close to tears, but when we looked he wasn't. He was staring straight at us, and again there was that glint of mischief. We fell silent and took to studying our cups. No further questions. We had been comprehensively disarmed.

Later on, after Spender had left and we had recovered our accustomed cool, we tried to sort out our impressions. Our critical weaponry had been routed – of that there was no doubt. For the first time, we had met a name poet we felt sorry for, a poet who had chosen us as his confessors. And yet we also felt pretty sure that Spender had manipulated the entire event. He had somehow made us warm to him; he'd made us drop our guard. After all, what had we learned? Not very much. And the same could be said about the talk he gave that night: none of us could quite recall its substance, but the presentation had been winning – shy, apologetic, I-could-well-be-wrong. The audience – an unusually large one, as it happened – seemed mightily impressed. One woman, on the way out, was heard to remark upon his 'aura'.

Spender's departure was courtly but abrupt, as if, having delivered, he were suddenly anxious to return to base. We watched him take off along the High Street. Even from the back, he looked hesitant, but he seemed to know where he was going. Was he bound for some vexing encounter with the Muse, or for late brandies at All Souls? It could have been either; it could even have been both. Or was it just that he had had enough of us? If so, we couldn't blame him. Whatever it was, we were left feeling both humbled and perplexed.

I have since learned that ours was a fairly typical response to Spender's charm. Throughout his career, he has given rise to several varieties of puzzlement. A saint or a schemer? A victim of fashion or a skilful self-advancer? A talent neglected or a small gift made too much of? These are the familiar questions about Stephen Spender. Everyone asks them, but no one seems to know quite where they came from. The answer is: they came from him. In his numerous volumes of poetry, fiction, autobiography, diaries, and letters, Spender has had one predominating subject: Who am I? To which, in each book, there has usually been one reply: I wish I knew. If Spender has become an enigma, it is not because he has shown us too little of himself. On the contrary, he has given us more than we can easily digest – a surfeit of self-exploration.

To judge from his writings, the Spender self can be explored by way of three paramount, lifelong preoccupations: fame, sex, and politics. In each of these areas, irresolution struck early and struck deep, so that studying his life story is rather like studying a map on which all roads lead you back to where you started. The signposts are timidity, guilt, vanity, remorse. The cartographer is Stephen Spender.

Another signpost – some would say the one that really matters – is personal publicity. In his 1951 autobiography, *World Within World*, he recalls a formative childhood embarrassment. His father, Harold Spender, a well-known Liberal journalist, decided in 1923 that he would stand for Parliament in the General Election. He became the Liberal candidate for Bath, and he recruited the fourteen-year-old Stephen and his younger brother to serve as his campaign aides. The two children were trundled through the streets of Bath in a donkey cart. Around the donkey's neck was hung a placard: 'Vote for Daddy'. Harold, on the hustings, introduced them by exclaiming to the audience, 'I have brought up my reserves!' He lost the election.

This incident, among others, had two effects on Spender: it made him ask questions about Daddy, whom he was accustomed to revere, and it instilled in him a sharp appetite for popular attention. In *World Within World* he tells us, 'Even today it often disgusts me to read a newspaper in which there is no mention of my name.' And in his published journals he reveals that a word such as 'spring,' seen on the page, will always cause his heart to 'stop a beat'. A nicely poetic impulse, you might think, but no: the heart stop is what happens when he sees 'the printed word "Spender" or even – now I am getting a bit astigmatic – any conformation of letters like it. ("Spring", for example.)'

Spender himself claims to regard this trait as 'repellent and odious'. He says, 'I obviously have a secret craving for very vulgar publicity. At the same time I despise this.' This is very Spenderesque – to name the flaw before we do, and then speak of it more harshly than we would. Still, it was there, and it probably had much to do with his choice of vocation. As an earnest adolescent, he wanted to channel his odious self-love into realms higher and nobler than the ones his father moved in.

Even at fourteen, Stephen knew himself to be more sensitive than Harold. Certainly he was more easily embarrassed. Perhaps this sensitivity came from his mother, Violet, who died when he was twelve. A semi-invalid, she had kept her family on tiptoe. She painted, wrote verse, and was given to hysterical frenzies and protracted sulks. Violet's chaise-longue dramatics counterbalanced Harold's man-of-the-world shallowness, and later on Spender seemed to wish that he could remember her more fondly. The truth was, she got on his nerves: 'If I felt the death of my mother at all, it was as the lightening of a burden and as a stimulating excitement.'

But she did write verse. And an uncle, J. A. Spender, was the editor of the *Westminster Gazette*, a friend of Henry James and Oscar Wilde, and a heeded voice in Victorian intellectual circles. A grandmother, Lily Spender (née Headland), had been a noted novelist; her *Parted Lives* was once bracketed with *Middlemarch*. Compared with these, Harold was a Grub Street hustler. By the time Stephen went up to Oxford, in 1928, he had declared that his own fame would not be cheaply won. He would pursue it as a Poet.

No doubt, Harold would have been appalled by his son's declaration: his attitude to modern verse was rudely philistine. But Harold died in 1926, and Stephen, with the small private income left to him by his maternal grandfather, was suddenly free to be a rebel, to reject his father's Victorian work ethic. An orphan, he could remake himself without fear of reprisals. The prospect seemed thrilling, but facing it close at hand put Spender into a deep panic. Fame was the spur and poetry the vocation. But how on earth did one begin?

When, in years to come, Spender told T.S. Eliot that he wanted to 'be a poet', Eliot responded, 'I can understand your wanting to write poems, but I don't quite know what you mean by "being a poet".' Nor, at twenty, did Spender. The affectation was what mattered, and, for this, Oxford in the 1920s was the place to be. The so-called Brideshead Generation had moved on by the time Spender enrolled at University College, but much of its legacy remained. People still painted their rooms pink, wore monogrammed silk shirts, and threw outrageous parties: lobster Newburg served in dustbins, blood-coloured soup, and so on.

Although neither rich nor posh enough to set up as a thoroughgoing dandy and poseur, Spender was swift to present his credentials as a budding aesthete. In those days, there were aesthetes and hearties, and you had to be one or the other. Hearties drank beer, chased girls, played sports, despised the arts. 'Affectation is an aping of hidden outrageous qualities which are our real potentialities,' Spender wrote in his autobiography. 'I aped my own exhibitionism, effeminacy, rootlessness and lack of discipline.' He announced himself to be 'a pacifist and a Socialist, a genius'. He wore a red tie, hung reproductions of paintings by Gauguin, van Gogh, and Paul Klee on his walls, and 'on fine days, I used to take a cushion into the quadrangle, and sitting down on it read poetry.'

This was enough, it seems, to bring him to the attention of W. H. Auden, who had already achieved legendary status in the university by promoting an alternative to the old Brideshead styles of affectation. Where the standard Oxford aesthete of the 1920s had been showily dissipated, full of wild talk about decadence and beauty, Auden was preaching a new gospel of icy austerity and self-control. A poet, he would say, is like a chemist, a clinician. His own work was full of obscure words drawn from psychology and science, and it eschewed all traces of emotional excess. He also insisted on the need for expertise in traditional metres and verse forms. He wore a monocle and always kept his curtains drawn. If you wanted to see him, you needed an appointment.

Spender, who had been shaping up as an apprentice Blake or Shelley, was entranced. It was not that he wanted to write poetry like Auden's – he already suspected that he couldn't – but he did want to be allowed to join his gang. Auden, it turned out, had already decided on the shape of things to come. Over the next decade, he would be the Top Poet, and Christopher Isherwood would be Top Novelist. He spoke of these matters as if they were already settled. Spender instantly offered himself as a candidate for one of the vacant lower ranks: Poet No. 2, perhaps, or No. 3 or

4? When Auden eventually gave him a qualified thumbs-up, he was elated:

> Once I told him I wondered whether I ought to write prose, and he answered: 'You must write nothing but poetry, we do not want to lose you for poetry.' This remark produced in me a choking moment of hope mingled with despair, in which I cried: 'But do you really think I am any good?' 'Of course,' he replied frigidly. 'But why?' 'Because you are so infinitely capable of being humiliated. Art is born of humiliation,' he added in his icy voice – and left me wondering when *he* could feel humiliated.

In *World Within World* Spender presents this as a purely literary transaction, but membership in Auden's gang had other implications. Both Auden and Isherwood were committed homosexuals, and Spender, typically, was not sure what he was. He had had sentimental attachments to both boys and girls, but neither had been strikingly successful. When he met Auden, he was hopelessly in love with one of his fellow-students – a hearty he calls Marston, who met his 'fussy and old-womanish' advances with not always tolerant disdain. Spender was 'repelled' at times by his own conduct in this matter but could not break free of 'that sore and flaming wheel I must live by'.

Auden and Isherwood were in no doubt that Spender was *comme ça*, or T.B.H. – two code names of the day. (T.B.H. meant 'to be had'.) For them, there was no other way to be. Once, when Spender had a falling-out with Isherwood and then suggested, 'If we're going to part, at least let's part like men,' Isherwood replied, 'But, Stephen, we *aren't* men.' For Spender, part of the attraction of the Auden gang was that, unlike him, they were sexually decisive. They liked being naughty boys. They even made jokes about it. Now and again, Spender was the subject of those jokes.

In 1920s Oxford, it was 'chic to be queer', according to Isaiah Berlin, and 'many students who weren't had to pretend to be, if they wanted to be socially successful.' Spender longed to be chic, but could detect no affectation in his love for Marston. In the so-called Marston poems, he comes across as howlingly fixated. As Auden recognized, these are guilt poems rather than love poems. They want to sound exalted, but they're too sickly with self-hatred. In his autobiography

Spender speaks of his 'search for the identification of my own aims with those of another man,' and there is a near-comic pomposity in his analysis of sexual definitions:

> I suspect that many people feel today that a conception of friendship which can be labeled homosexual, on account of certain of its aspects, excludes normal sexual relationships: and conversely that the heterosexual relationship should preclude those which might be interpreted as homosexual. As a result of this tendency to give themselves labels, people feel forced to make a choice which, in past times, was not made. It also follows that since a relationship of the highest understanding can be between two people of the same sex, some who have experienced this relationship renounce a normal way of life.

Spender did not altogether want to 'renounce a normal way of life', but neither did he want to abandon his search for male relationships 'of the highest understanding'. Post-Oxford (he left in 1931, without taking a degree), he seemed to most observers to have made a decision – at least, for the time being. Isherwood was by then living in Berlin and was mailing back accounts of the rich pickings, or pickups, to be had there. The German Boy, he reported, was not like the English Boy. On summer vacation in Hamburg before his last year at Oxford, Spender had liked what he saw. Young Germans were guilt-free, adventurous, and proudly physical. They sunbathed in the nude. He wrote in his journal, 'Now I shall begin to live.'

And live he did, although not in the louche way of an Isherwood. His Ernsts and Helmuts were not to be located in boy bars. In Spender's novel *The Temple*, which he began writing at this time but didn't finish, the drippy, repressed English hero discovers in Germany 'a new attitude toward the body': once 'sinful', it has now become 'a source of joy'. Not that *The Temple* is a joyful book; far from it. Whereas Isherwood's accounts of Germany between the wars are full of a sly, sexy relish, Spender's are always dolefully high-toned. German bodies are lovingly gaped at, but, as soon as they begin to move, our hero breaks out into an English sweat.

As with sex, so with politics. Where Isherwood, in his Berlin stories, gets a perverse thrill out of the encroaching atmosphere of social menace – the decadence before the storm – Spender's first instinct is to plunge into lengthy ruminations about his own role in the coming conflict. Was he a poet or a political activist? Could the quest for personal fulfilment be reconciled with a commitment to the public good? Was it possible for politics to be personal, intense, good for the soul?

This self-questioning carried on throughout the 1930s. From 1930 to 1933, Spender divided his time between Germany and England, and during that period he acquired a reputation as one of the new poets. There was much praise for his attempt to inject political concerns into his essentially self-centered lyrics. There was praise, too, for his 'sense of pity'. Auden, whose first book had appeared in 1930, was hailed as his generation's satirist and prophet. Spender's role was to provide soulfulness and passion. Critics were ready to overlook the details: the archaic diction, the confused syntax, the wild apostrophes to Time, History, and Freedom. Apart from the odd pylon or express train, Spender's Thirties poems were thoroughly old-fashioned, but there was perhaps a timeliness in this. Auden, after all, was often forbiddingly cryptic and oblique.

Spender was not, of course, a poet of the people, although he sometimes wrote as if he were. His books of verse sold about a thousand copies each. His compassion for the victims of history was savoured mostly in literary circles. And in these circles fame was to be measured in terms of reviews in highbrow quarterlies and invitations to dinner at the Woolfs', or to Ottoline Morrell's salons, or to T.S. Eliot's club. Spender was gleeful when such invitations started to pour in. He seemed to find it easy to keep his politics separate from his social life. And he was well liked by the pacifists, monarchists, and aesthetes who controlled the London literary scene. They found him engagingly impulsive and confused. In his autobiography, there is more reverence for the great hostesses of the day than there is for any of his left-wing political associates:

> Living in their small country houses, their London flats, full of taste, meeting at week-ends and at small parties, discussing history, painting, literature, gossiping greatly, and producing a few very good stories, they resembled those friends who at the time of

the Plague in Florence withdrew into the countryside and told
the stories of Boccaccio.

Spender's opponents would say that his struggle against Fascism was
in reality a struggle to safeguard these small parties and weekends.

On weekdays, though, he was busily living up to his new reputation
as a fervent Socialist. He set up house with a proletarian ex-soldier,
Tony Hyndman. He wrote articles and pamphlets, addressed meet-
ings, signed petitions. He wrote anguished poems about poverty and
unemployment, slums and factories. He even wrote a prose book,
called *Forward from Liberalism*, in which he argued that old-style
Liberals, of the sort he had grown up with, 'must accept the methods
which it might be necessary to use in order to defeat Fascism' – in
other words, the methods of Communism.

This was Spender's bid for status as a hard-nosed political thinker.
The Communists took his unfeeling treatise at face value and offered
him a Party card. Out of politeness, almost, Spender accepted. His
membership, he said later, lasted for a month. The Party wanted
him to go to Spain. 'Go and get killed, Comrade,' the CP leader
is said to have told him. 'We need a Byron in the movement.'
They wanted him to write propaganda, to toe the Party line on
Moscow. He was fiercely upbraided for having expressed doubts
about the treason trials.

This contact with real politics was enough to send Spender scu-
rrying back to his home ground. He had come to recognise, he said,
that he could support no political 'method' that prohibited personal
dissent – or, in his case, personal confusion. And a couple of comic and
disastrous trips to Spain confirmed him in this view. His real subject,
he now saw, was what it had always been: the private self. And in
1936 that self was urgently in need of some repairs. His relationship
with Hyndman was foundering. Like real politics, real proletarians
could become boringly restrictive. 'I stifle in a bugger's world,' he
wrote. It was time for him to come up with a new analysis of his
sexual 'ambivalence':

I could not develop beyond a certain point unless I were able to
enter a stream of nature through human contacts, that is to say,

through experience of women. Yet I never lost the need for camaraderie also, my desire to share my creative and intellectual adventures with a man, whose search was the same as mine.

The two needs, while existing side by side, seemed to some extent to be mutually exclusive.

Spender's immediate solution to this impasse was a hasty marriage to one Inez Pearn, a student of Spanish poetry, whom he had met a few weeks earlier. 'If I did not act on impulse I decided nothing' was his plea. This betrayal was greeted with astonishment all around, and not least by Tony Hyndman, who at once volunteered for action in the Spanish Civil War. After a brief taste of front-line duty, Tony declared himself a pacifist, and a remorseful Spender, already in Spain, rushed to his aid. Not surprisingly, the marriage to Inez soon collapsed, and Spender was back, more or less, where he began.

By 1939, with the outbreak of war, many of the delusions of the 1930s lay in ruins. When Auden and Isherwood fled to the United States, Spender stayed put in London – adrift, as he saw it, in the wreckage of his Thirties enterprise. He was now wifeless and companionless and, in the eyes of many, a symbol of the decade's follies. He had become a well-known ex-poet of the Thirties. On the day war broke out, he wrote, 'I feel as if I could not write again. Words seem to break in my mind like sticks when I put them down on paper. I cannot see how to spell some of them. Sentences are covered with leaves, and I really cannot see the line of the branch that carries the green meaning.'

Now eighty-five, Stephen Spender is still answering questions about the Thirties. He has been doing so for fifty years and more. His career since 1939 has brought him numerous honours and awards. There have been lectureships and professorships and, in 1983, a knighthood for his 'services to literature'. But the Thirties tag persists, and he has not done much to remove it. Many of his books have been Thirties-linked: *World Within World*, *Letters to Christopher*, *The Thirties and After*. He has tinkered endlessly with his poems of the period, toning them down, wising them up. In 1988, he finally brought out *The Temple*. He has given countless interviews and broadcasts on the

Thirties, and in recent years, with the deaths of Auden, Connolly, Isherwood, and others, he has been in demand for TV obituaries and tributes. Not long ago, he was on the cover of a Sunday-paper supplement, cosying up to a young actress. This was to mark a new London production of *Cabaret*, the show based on Isherwood's stories of Berlin. Although some might see the Thirties as a cross that he has had to bear, others would say that he has milked that 'low dishonest decade' for rather more than it is worth.

In the early Forties, Spender joined the London Fire Brigade – he served with it throughout much of the war – and helped Cyril Connolly start up the magazine *Horizon*. (*Horizon's* first editorial proclaimed, 'Our standards are aesthetic, and our politics are in abeyance.') In 1941, he married again; his second wife was the pianist Natasha Litvin. The daughter of the musicologist Edwin Evans and the actress Ray Litvin, Natasha was brought up on the fringes of the 1930s left-wing intellectual scene and was introduced to Spender at a *Horizon* lunch, in September, 1940. 'I thought Horizon was a pub,' she told me, which suggests that she knew little of her husband-to-be's literary status, and she added in a letter:

> Thereafter we were courting through the Blitz – coming out of restaurants to see ARP workers shovelling up broken glass and other bomb debris – we were oddly unconcerned for safety – foolhardy. (I must write it up some time – Erika Mann and Brian Howard sheltering exuberantly under the piano I was playing at [a] party during an air raid – very curious times they were.) Stephen and I married in April, 1941 – lived for some weeks chez the A. J. P. Taylors in Oxford . . . We then lived in London in the top flat of the Ernst Freuds' house in Maresfield Gardens – Lucian had a studio full of dead birds in our flat – and I played concerts and when pregnant learned 'babycraft' at the Anna Freud wartime nursery for which we campaigned to raise money . . . The Stephen I met in 1940 . . . had the qualities he's never lost in fifty-three years. Apart from being the most generous and forgiving person I had ever met, . . . he was – and is – the most truthful.

In this marriage, each of them promised, there would be 'no question of blame'. They are still together, and have two children: Matthew, a painter, sculptor, and writer, and Lizzie, an actress and writer, who, to Spender's great delight, is married to the female impersonator Barry Humphries, better known as Dame Edna Everage. Nowadays, at parties, the Spenders rarely fail to catch the eye – and not just because they are both fairly tall. Handsome, young-looking for their years, they must have been – well, knockouts in the 1940s. No wonder Edith Sitwell wrote to them, in the forties, 'You and Natasha with whom all parties of mine begin. I mean you are the centre and then I spread outwards.'

After the war, Spender joined UNESCO as Counsellor to the Section of Letters, and this marked a new phase of his celebrity: a twenty-year-long stint as a kind of globe-trotting cultural emissary. The postwar years were good years in which to be an intellectual. The civilised world had to be rebuilt, but thoughtfully: this time, we had to get it right. Huge congresses were organised at which famous thinkers debated the big questions: 'Freedom and the Artist', 'The Role of the Artist', 'Art and the Totalitarian Threat'. Spender was in regular attendance at such gatherings in Europe, and was soon in demand for trips to India, Japan, even Australia. These 'junketings', as he described them, were usually paid for by the Congress for Cultural Freedom, based in Washington, as part of America's hearts-and-minds offensive against Communism. In 1953, he was approached by the congress to edit the literary side of a new monthly, *Encounter*, which would be 'anti-Communist in policy but not McCarthyite'. (He was told that the money for it came from the Farfield Foundation, a supposedly independent body.) Spender, it had been noted, contributed to the much discussed 1949 anthology *The God That Failed*, a collection of contrite essays by six of Europe's most prominent ex-Communists. His 1936 flirtation with the Party was no longer to be laughed at: he had experienced that of which he spake, and could thus be seen as a Cold Warrior of high potential.

As Spender saw it, there was nothing at all warlike in the politics he'd settled for – a politics that transcended immediate East-West disputes, that dealt not in power plays but in moral absolutes. 'I am for neither West nor East,' he wrote in 1951, 'but for myself considered as a self – one of the millions who inhabit the earth.' Freedom of speech, the pre-eminence of the individual conscience

– in short, the mainstream liberal verities – would from now on be the components of his faith.

He had by this time become the Spender who disconcerted us in Oxford. No longer the holy fool of Thirties legend, he was transmuting into an itinerant representative of liberal unease. During the late Fifties and throughout the Sixties, Spender was perpetually on the move, sometimes as troubled ambassador for Western values, for the congress, for International PEN, or for the British Council, an agency for promoting British culture abroad, and sometimes as hard-up literary journeyman, lecturing on modern poetry at Berkeley or Wesleyan or the University of Florida – wherever the fees were sufficiently enticing – or dreaming up viable book projects, such as *Love-Hate Relations*, a study of Anglo-American literary relationships, and *The Year of the Young Rebels*, an account of the 1968 upheavals in Paris, Prague, New York, and West Berlin.

In 1970, Spender's English friends tried to get him to slow down, to settle. At the age of sixty-one, he was appointed professor at University College, London – not bad going for an 'ineducable' (his word) Oxford dropout, but, as it turned out, a big mistake. Frank Kermode, who fixed the job for him, is full of fond stories about Spender's bumbling ways, and says, 'He is cut out to be the sort of visiting poetic professor rather than a run-of-the-mill teacher'. In 1975, Spender retired and was at once back on the United States circuit – Florida, then Cornell, then Vanderbilt. In between, he was to be found once more in Seoul, Tokyo, Teheran – back in the old PEN routine.

During these years, Spender produced little poetry. *The Generous Days* appeared in 1971, and was his first new volume of poetry since 1949. It was reviewed with kindliness by some, dismissively by others. ('A Generous Daze' was the title of one harsh review. Hardly anyone treated the publication as a significant event.) Meanwhile, the Poetry of the Thirties had become a hot subject in the universities: books and articles were beginning to pour out in which Spender – the young Spender – was treated as a centrally important figure. It was as if he were savouring his own posterity. Sometimes the taste was bitter: 'I imagine the young reading nothing of me but the bad notices other young critics write,' he wrote. 'Poets today are simply critics' guinea-pigs – at any rate their poems are. The so-called "science" of modern criticism has been invented specifically for performing vivisection on poets.'

These remarks, and others of similar import, are recorded in Spender's *Journals 1939–83*, which was published in 1985 and welcomed by reviewers with a warmth that no other recent book of his had enjoyed. Here was a man who had been everywhere, known everyone. The critics quoted with appreciation his tales of Eliot, Auden, Forster, Sartre, Aragon: there were few twentieth-century literary celebrities whom he had not at least had lunch with, or sat next to on a panel, or shaken hands with at a cultural reception. According to Spender's friend David Plante, famous people have more 'credibility' for Stephen than those who are unknown. And musicians and painters and sculptors figured in the *Journals*, too. Bacon, Hockney, Henry Moore were all close friends – closer, in fact, than most of the literary big names. These friendships were remarked on with near-abject reverence by one or two reviewers, as if they were appraising not a book but an address book. But there was admiration also for Spender's numerous good deeds over the years, and for his commitment to the journal *Index on Censorship*, his eagerness to speak out, in letters and petitions, whenever free speech seemed to be imperilled, his modesty, his candour, his paternal conscientiousness, and so on.

Some commentators marvelled that Spender had ever managed to find time for writing. He had always seemed to be out and about. In addition to his working of the cultural networks, there was the matter of his friendships with the Astors, the Rothschilds, the Glenconners. Big-money names like these pepper the pages of his diaries. When he is not lodging at Michael Astor's Oxfordshire estate, he is cruising the Mediterranean on Hansi Lambert's yacht. In America, he hobnobs with Anne Cox Chambers and Drue Heinz. On his seventieth birthday, the claret is laid on by Philippe de Rothschild. 'Stephen has always been interested in knowing grand people,' Kermode says. 'But not in any odious way.' And, clearly enough, grand people have a weakness for Stephen. 'He is so amusing and has such wonderful stories about such interesting people,' David Plante attests. 'After all, he has been a witness to so many great events.

He is very charming, and also these people are flattered to have a
famous poet as their friend.'

According to Plante, Spender does not go looking for these
glittering contacts – they simply happen, or one leads to another. And
Spender, Plante says, has no time for an unamusing toff. He requires
his millionaires and aristos to have style – to be smart enough to be
amused by him. In the dourer zones of literary London, Spender's
socialising is frequently jeered at: here he is, the ex-Communist, this
voice of the downtrodden, spending all his holidays and weekends as
a kind of court jester, or court conscience, to the rich. Such killjoys
also speak mockingly of his 'great house in Provence'. This French
residence, I am assured by those who have visited, is no château. On
the contrary, it cost the Spenders five hundred pounds when they
purchased it, in 1960, and was then a ruin. Many comic tales are
told of Spender's refurbishing exploits, his tree planting and weed
plucking. All in all, the whole thing sounds more like Peter Mayle
than like Philippe de Rothschild, although when Spender needed
electricity in 1960 he *was* able to get André Malraux to phone the
local prefect on his behalf.

Among his friends, Spender has a reputation as a wit, and he himself
has well described his circle at the dinner table: 'frivolous descendants
of Bloomsbury who make a game of passing the ball of conversation
from one to the other, feeling the cuff of rebuke if anyone tries to
introduce a note of world-suffering into the conversation.' 'Passing
the ball of conversation' usually means gossip about absent or dead
friends, and in this genre Spender is reputed to excel. His style can
be 'malicious even but not malignant', Berlin says. 'Mischievous but
not *méchant*', David Plante says. He possesses a rich stock of slightly
sneaky anecdotes – about Auden, Evelyn Waugh, John Lehmann –
and will repeat them word for word, seeming to have plucked them
from the air. And then there is the giggle. After delivering one of his
feline thrusts, Spender is likely to splutter in helpless merriment, or
in delight at his own naughtiness. 'He thinks of himself as a great
comic turn,' one friend says. 'He almost knows he is a fraud. Well,
not a fraud exactly – a performer. And the giggle is part of his great
charm – it is his way of signalling that he, too, finds Stephen Spender
a bit silly.'

In the *Journals*, there is not much wit, but there is plenty of self-deprecation. And there is also a deep-running vein of disappointment – a recognition that for all his fame, for all his hard-won virtue, he has fallen short, sold out, preferred the warmth of social bustle and quick plaudits to the cold solitude of the genuine creator. Whose fault is that? His, or the hurtful critics'? One day, Spender will castigate himself for feebleness: 'I wonder whether I am so mild through weakness, timidity, conviction, perversity or what. I think it is a mixture of these things,' and 'I'm struggling at the end to get out of the valley of hectoring youth, journalistic middle age, imposture, money making, public relations, bad writing, mental confusion.' On other days, he will whimper about getting a raw deal. On some days, he'll do both: the two are absurdly interlocked. Reading the book through in 1985, I could have been back at that Oxford dinner table: half liking him, half wondering what he was trying to pull.

But has Spender been given a raw deal? On the face of it, the proposition seems ludicrous. He is now ranked as one of Britain's most venerable poets, yet hardly anyone can remember more than a line or two from his entire œuvre, and the lines they can recall are always taken from his Thirties work. Even people who profess to like his poems can never quite bring to mind *which ones* they like. They mumble about his 'sincerity', or they 'vividly recall' reading 'The Pylons' or 'The Landscape Near an Aerodrome' at school. And it is this discrepancy, this gulf between repute and demonstrable achievement, that has led critics to go at him with vehemence.

One can see their point, but this doesn't mean that there hasn't been an injustice. In my view, Spender is not really a poet of the Thirties. Temperamentally, he belongs in the following decade, in the company of neo-Romantics like Dylan Thomas and George Barker. He may have been impressed by Auden's doctrines of impersonality, but he never actually knew what to do with them. In the Forties, the fashion was for the irrational, the dark unconscious, the deep vat of the self. With Auden gone, Spender was able to relax into his true element. And yet he did so with Auden still lurking at his elbow – an influence that, on the whole, kept him at one remove from the willed incoherence that became the Forties norm. Spender's war poems are pretty dreadful – 'scalding lead anxiety', 'wild seas / Of chafing despairs.' Even so, one feels that, but for Auden, they would have been much worse. After the war, the work that matters is all personal. The faults persist: the bardic posturing, the dead adjectives, the weedy self-absorption, the vein-popping effort for magniloquence – 'I, who stand beneath a bitter / Blasted tree, with the green life / Of summer joy cut from my side.' Now and again, though, as in sections of Spender's elegy for his sister-in-law, an attempt is made to prune away the affectations, and when this happens an authentic lyric tenderness does struggle through:

> 'How far we travelled, sweetheart,
> Since that day when first we chose
> Each other as each other's rose
> And put all other worlds apart.'

Since the 1940s, Spender's strongest work has been 'occasional': 'Remembering Cincinnati, 1953', 'Auden's Funeral', 'Late Stravinsky Listening to Late Beethoven', 'Louis MacNeice'. By setting his sights lower, he has achieved a decent competence. The language, pared down, purged of the old luridness, still fails to sparkle, and the rhythms are too often inert, but at least he seems now to have a sensible measure of his gifts. This explorer of the self turns out to be at his most effective when exploring his memories of other people; the prophet's best insights come, in the end, from looking back.

When I visited Spender last December at his home in North London, I was determined to make at least some of my questions present tense. He was about to publish a new book of poems, his first since 1985, and two or three of them, it seems to me, are as good as anything he's done. These, too, are elegies, in memory of a young American, Brian Obst, who died three years ago, from AIDS: 'Letter from an Ornithologist in Antarctica,' 'Farewell to My Student', and 'Laughter'. I would ask him about these.

And so I did (Obst was 'one of the best people I have ever met,' Spender said, and he went on to talk of him at length, with evident affection), but there was no avoiding the old topic: Spender in the Thirties. This time, it was he who brought it up. During the week before I called, he had been in the throes of legal action against the novelist David Leavitt and his publisher to halt the British publication of Leavitt's *While England Sleeps*. The charge was that Leavitt had made fiction out of Spender's life as Spender himself recounted it in *World Within World*. The central relationship in Leavitt's novel is clearly based on the Spender-Hyndman liaison of the Thirties, and the main action has to do with the Spender figure, Brian Botsford, chasing off to Spain to rescue his lost lover, Edward Phelan. In Leavitt, the hero is a novelist, not a poet, and went to Cambridge, not Oxford, and Phelan is a ticket-collector on the London Underground, but the resemblances are unmistakable. For long stretches, Leavitt's book reads like a dutiful response to some college writing assignment: fictionalise your favourite nonfiction; liberate into explicitness a coy text from the past. There is an earnest, mugged-up quality to the whole enterprise, although the intention, one suspects, was to register admiration, by empathy, for Spender's 1930s love quest.

World Within World is achingly discreet on sexual matters. It had to be: in 1951, the homosexual act was still a crime in England. Leavitt, though, lets rip; he has page after page of lingering physical description, and it was these pages that I expected Spender to object to. Botsford, although he has moments of Spenderish 'ambivalence', is 100 per cent gay. He thinks about marrying a girl, to please an aunt whose money he depends on, but in the end he doesn't. His real treachery is social: he keeps Phelan away from his smart friends.

I put it to Spender that the reams of gay sex in Leavitt's book must have been – well, peculiar to read. Spender agreed that the book is 'pornographic', but he said, 'What I really object to is that Leavitt has no sense of history. The Barcelona he describes is based on his experiences of the city in the Eighties. In 1936, Barcelona was not at all as he describes it. I blame the publishers. Publishers get their young writers into a great deal of trouble.'

Later, I asked friends of Spender's why he was making such a fuss about the Leavitt book, and why, a year and a half earlier, he had gone to great lengths to stop the publication of Hugh David's 1992 biography *Stephen Spender: A Portrait with Background*. In his campaign against David, he sent letters to the directors of Heinemann, the book's publisher, wrote articles, gave interviews, drew up detailed lists of the book's factual errors. The friends' verdict was that neither of these well-publicised dramas had been of Spender's making. 'He has been steamed up by Natasha,' Isaiah Berlin told me. And Frank Kermode agreed, saying, 'All these crises in his life are reflected off Natasha in a way. If Natasha is very upset, that sort of stands for Stephen being upset, in a way. I don't think Stephen is very upset about the Leavitt book. And we had it all a couple of years ago with the Hugh David book. I think that must have happened many, many times in their lives. When things go wrong, she does the worrying, and Stephen goes on in his usual passive way.'

According to Kermode, Natasha was also a central figure in another well-known Spender *crise*, when, in 1967, he discovered that *Encounter* had for many years been funded by the CIA. This news came as no great surprise to those who had noted the magazine's reluctance to discuss Vietnam – or, indeed, any of America's more dubious foreign-policy involvements. Spender had heard rumours, and asked questions, and had been lied to by his contacts at the Congress for Cultural Freedom. When the news broke, he was famously outraged. Or, at any rate, Natasha was outraged. By 1967, Spender was no longer editing *Encounter*. He had handed his job over to Frank Kermode two years earlier. But all the publicity centered on *his* wounds. 'He was upset,' Kermode says. 'But he has a kind of calm that is made possible by the fact that Natasha takes the strain, I think.'

David Plante's assessment is more subtle. 'Stephen can be mischievous. One thing he loves doing, not only to Natasha but to others, as well, is to make them jealous. For example, I would be with him and Natasha and a few others, and Stephen would come up to me and say in a stage whisper, "Are you free for lunch tomorrow?" which of course Natasha would hear. A sweat of embarrassment would come over me, and I'd go to Natasha and say, "Oh, Stephen and I are having a secret lunch tomorrow," and she'd laugh. So it was his fault for creating this mischief.' Plante is full of admiration for Natasha and her various 'accommodations', and he is not at all convinced that it is she who stirs things up. 'He'll say, "Oh, Natasha's very upset," but I sometimes suspect that he's the one who's making her upset. But she is heroic in her intentions. I wish I could just give her a cup of warm milk and get her to go to sleep for ten or twenty hours.'

It seems doubtful that Plante's wish will be granted. Natasha certainly sees herself as Stephen's round-the-clock protector. 'I'm not by nature at all militant,' she writes. 'But I do sometimes see that Stephen's trustfulness will not avail him, and truth will not be served. He is incapable of dissembling or concealing, or even of keeping the secret of what he's going to give you for Christmas. Equally, it never occurs to him that others may be devious. This explains the *Encounter* row (though other, more perspicacious people, like Isaiah, were also taken in). Since it was simply not in Stephen's repertoire of expectations that colleagues of many years' standing could give solemn assurances that were systematically misleading.'

About her role in crises such as the Leavitt matter, she wrote to me: 'The record may never be put straight unless one takes steps. And also it's upsetting to see the toll of stress and the waste of energies in Stephen's declining years. He shouldn't have to be dealing with tiresomeness when he could be working at his own writing.' And she told me earlier, 'What I really think is that there are pressure groups in America now, and that in a way it's rather like McCarthyism. If you remember how we in Europe felt about McCarthyism – we thought America would never get out of it. Well, it *did* get out of it and there was extraordinary moral courage on the part of people who actually lived in America, which you didn't see through the newspapers. Well, now it seems to me a similar thing is going on. I mean witch-hunting by the gay-rights movement. Outing, they call it, I believe.' Was she saying that Leavitt's book was part of that? 'I don't know what Mr Leavitt's position is at all. But we shouldn't really talk about it at all, because of the case.'

'But Stephen *is* out,' David Plante says. 'Just by being himself. The gayrights people see him in a limited way – simply in terms of his homosexuality. They say, "He's married, he's lived with a woman for over fifty years." So they are simplifying Stephen. All they see is the stereotype: a homosexual man married to a heterosexual woman. So they say Stephen is false to the marriage, false to homosexuals. But they haven't looked at the marriage closely. Make no mistake: the most important person in Stephen's life is Natasha. There is no question that they love one another. They had to love one another in order to be able to get through difficulties. And Natasha is right

to object to the gay-rights sort of stereotype. She's also right to feel
excluded. She's right to object to the view that she has stopped
Stephen from expressing the fullness of his homosexuality, which
is the kind of thing they might think. But these gays don't know
the marriage – they don't know anything about it.'

Does Spender himself object to being outed? I asked him how he
felt about gay rights. 'Well, when my novel *The Temple* was published
in America, a few years ago, my friend Brian told me that I had
become a hero of the gay-rights movement,' he said. 'I was quite
pleased – quite amused, really. I am very loyal to homosexuals. A
lot of the best people I know are homosexual. Some of the very best
relationships I've ever known are homosexual. They seem to me
rather heroic relationships, some of them.' Why did he think they
were heroic? 'Well, the way in which such people live out their lives
quite fearlessly, openly, and so on. I think it does have a rather heroic
aspect.' He paused, thought for a moment, and then added, 'Maybe
that's because I am old-fashioned. I don't suppose nowadays it does
require much heroism. But I dread the mutual bachelor household.
And yet there are men who can live together and have a thoroughly
domesticated life. They can make an art out of their life together. I
don't think I could do that with a man. If I were sharing this house
with a man, it would be an absolute shambles.'

It is certainly not that, in spite of the crosscurrents. The Spenders
have lived in the same rented house in St John's Wood for nearly fifty
years, and its interior captures the spirit of their marriage rather well.
The drawing room is spruce and elegant, ready to take on the world.
The poet's study is amiably cluttered, a retreat, and Spender wasted
no time getting back to it as soon as his interviewee's chores were
done. This ground-floor study is littered with the usual literary man's
debris: review copies, old periodicals, press cuttings, galley proofs.
An unexpected touch was the Spender word processor, which he
seemingly knows how to use.

But then he still has to earn his living as a writer. His private income,
he says, is now about ten thousand pounds a year, which 'doesn't take
one very far these days'. I didn't ask about his fabled cellar, said to be
piled high with minor works by the several distinguished artists he
has known over the years. According to legend, there are Hockneys

and Bacons down there, or perhaps a drawing by Cocteau, a statuette by Henry Moore. Nobody knows. My own hunch is that the cellar is stacked with back numbers of *Encounter*. But the Aladdin's-cave fantasy fits well with the image of Spender that his friends like to promote. On the one hand, he is so innocent and otherworldly that he seems to have no idea what his property is worth; on the other, he pretends to be a lot poorer than he apparently is. And when you ask which is the real Spender, the answer will be: both.

'He's in the clouds, but he has radar,' the writer T. C. Worsley is reputed to have said, and Cyril Connolly once proposed that there are actually two Spenders: one is an 'inspired simpleton, a great big silly goose, a holy Russian idiot, large, generous, gullible, ignorant, affectionate, idealistic – living for friendship and beauty'; the other is 'shrewd and ambitious, aggressive and ruthless, a publicity-seeking intellectual full of administrative energy and rentier asperity.' In a homelier way, Frank Kermode goes along with some of this: 'If you're walking with Stephen in London, you always feel he doesn't know where he is, and yet he always seems to know the shortest way. The not knowing is the sort of thing Auden patronised him for. But Auden saw the appearance rather than the reality. Stephen wasn't quite sure what he was doing at any particular moment, but then he always was doing it.'

I asked Natasha if Stephen really did know all the London shortcuts. She thought the idea was laughable. 'Perhaps he just does it on automatic pilot.'

I left the Spenders to their war on David Leavitt, whose book has now been withdrawn by the publisher; a revised version will come out later this year. As I left, Spender reminded me of a 'not very kind' review I wrote some years ago of his *Collected Poems 1928–1985* and two other Spender works – a review that provoked a loyal outcry from his friends. I had been hoping that he wouldn't bring this up and had readied myself for a reproach. But, no, he was wearing that mischievous half smile – his 'Oxford smile', as I now think of it. 'Usually,' he said, 'when critics say negative things about a work of mine, I cast the work aside. I can't bear to look at it again. I dismiss it from my mind. In your case, I was grateful.' Grateful for what? 'Well, you said very nice things in your review about those 1940 poems. No

one had ever remarked on them before. I looked them up again quite
recently, and you were right: they are quite beautiful.'

The New Yorker, 1994

Auden's Juvenilia

W.H. Auden once revealed his 'life-long conviction that in any company I am the youngest person present.' This confession, made when he was fifty-eight, perhaps raised a shifty smile among those of his acolytes who had grown used to the crotchety, old-womanish persona of his later years – the early nights, the carpet slippers, and so on. Old when young and young when old: the ageing of our most-wrinkled-ever poet has always seemed a somewhat mysterious process.

Most people who knew Auden when he really was 'the youngest person present' were struck by his air of being much older than his years. Memoirists of his schooldays speak of him as having been almost spookily unboyish. Even Christopher Isherwood, who later on would enjoy noting his friend's 'stumpy, immature fingers' and 'babyishly shapeless' ankles, found it hard to view him with full-hearted condescension: 'I remember him chiefly for . . . his smirking, tantalising air of knowing disreputable and exciting secrets.' This was at prep school, when Auden would have been nine or ten years old. And Isherwood was not the only one to be impressed by little Wystan's 'self-assurance', his 'clinical detachment', his 'air of authority'. Among his schoolfellows, says Isherwood, he had the 'status of a kind of witch-doctor'.

This talk of clinics and doctors mainly had to do with Auden's precocious know-how about science – and not just the smirking kind of science he had picked up from studying 'anatomical manuals with coloured German plates'. Where other boys collected stamps and conkers, the young Auden liked nothing better than to potter around

factories, machine-shops and power-stations. He also had a big thing
about limestone and derelict lead mines. His nursery library, as he
would later report it, included works like *Machinery for Metalliferous
Mines*, and *Lead and Zinc Ores of Northumberland and Alston Moors*.
Another of his boyhood favourites was *Dangers to Health*, a Victorian
treatise on plumbing.

These curious interests were sparked by Auden's father. George
Auden was a medical doctor by profession but he was also a Classicist,
linguist and all-round heavy reader. He had what used to be described
as 'an enquiring mind': there was nothing much he didn't know,
or want to know. But he did not confine his son's reading to the
merely knowable. Auden's nursery library was also stocked with
Beatrix Potter, Edward Lear and Harry Graham. And George had
a passion for Norse legends, believing as he did that the Audens could
themselves be traced back to the land of Thor: 'In my father's library,
scientific books stood side by side with works of poetry and fiction,
and it never occurred to me to think of one being less or more
"humane" than the other.'

For a long stretch, though, of his childhood and early adolescence,
Auden liked to present himself as the icily preoccupied boy-boffin,
his playbox 'full of thick scientific books on geology, metals and
machines'. He disliked games and was contemptuous of most of his
teachers – 'hairy monsters with terrifying voices and eccentric habits'.
When he 'grew up', he said, he would become a mining engineer.
He would go underground.

His mother had more elevated plans for him. Both of Auden's
parents were the children of vicars, but so far as Wystan was concerned, it was Mother who took charge of matters spiritual. George
was a burrower, Constance was disposed to soar. She tried to
counterbalance her son's passion for the subterranean by directing
him towards the airy stuff of music and religion. And by all accounts,
she was a formidable teacher – domineering and possessive. For
Auden, Father stood for 'stability, commonsense, reality', Mother
for 'surprise, eccentricity, fantasy'.

In 1914, George Auden joined the Army. 'I was seven,' Auden
recalled, 'the age at which a son begins to take serious notice of
his father and needs him most . . . and I didn't see him again until

I was twelve and a half.' During these years, Auden 'spent a great deal of my waking hours in the construction and elaboration of a private, sacred world, the basic elements of which were a landscape, northern and limestone, and an industry, lead mining . . . my sacred world contained no human beings.' In this way, he could keep faith with Father while succumbing to the sacralising influence of Mother. Mother, meantime, was becoming 'very odd indeed. When I was eight years old, she taught me the words and music of the love-potion scene in *Tristan*, and we used to sing it together.'

By the time George returned from war, Auden had become his mother's boy. Although he continued to draw on George's stock of knowledge, the father-son relationship had stalled: the two 'never really came to know each other'. Later on, Auden would remember his father as 'hen-pecked' and 'too gentle'. In Auden biographies, George now tends to be a pallid background presence. Constance, on the other hand, is usually portrayed as a key source of unease. 'Mother wouldn't like it' would become the mature Auden's pat way of ramming home some moral point. In his adolescence, though, what Mother wouldn't like became for him the thing to do, the thing to fear. In 1942, he told a friend: 'You would be surprised how unpleasant too much parental love and interest can be, and what a torture of guilt it makes breaking away.'

Auden was fifteen when his schoolfriend Robert Medley suggested that he might try his hand at writing poems.

> Kicking a little stone, he turned to me
> And said, 'Tell me, do you write poetry?'
> I never had, and said so, but I knew
> That very moment what I wished to do.

At fifteen, Auden knew, too, that he was homosexual – indeed, Medley was the then-object of his ardour. He was careful, though, to keep this side of things out of the verses he began sending home to mother. Binding a small sheaf of his early work into a notebook, just for her, he added the following inscription:

To Mother
from her son, the author

You too, my mother read my rhymes
For love of unforgotten times
'And you may chance to hear once more
The little feet along the floor.'

R.L.S.

The showdown came when Mrs Auden discovered a 'suggestive' poem of Auden's about Medley, as seen in the school swimming pool. George was assigned to lecture both boys on the proper boundaries of male friendships, and from now on Constance would view her son's writings with suspicion. Their appearance had coincided also with the seeming collapse of his religious faith. With touching ineptitude, Auden got one of his friends – not Medley – to intercede on his behalf. The friend obligingly explained to Mrs Auden that her son was a genius and thus had little further need for 'a personal God – or for a Mother'.

Most adolescent verse is full of Self, and the teenage Auden had plenty of self-problems to get off his chest, it may be thought. But poetry was never for him a vehicle for personal emotion – not even at the start. Boys, God, his confused feelings about Mother: these subjects are all touched on, or are present, in his early work but without Katherine Bucknell to assist us, we would be hard pressed to locate them, let alone make out a case for their huge personal significance. Auden trained himself as a poet as he might have trained himself to be an engineer. Now and then he worried that he was not feelingful enough to make the grade, or that his poetical toolbox might be short of some important spiritual component, but such anxieties did not run very deep. Emotions could wait, he seems to have decided. What mattered was to master the technique, to find out how poetry was made, and how it could be mined. Ever the boffin, he set himself to analyse and replicate the strange alchemies of English Verse.

Juvenilia covers the years 1922 to 1928, and is really a kind of laboratory log-book, the record of an apprentice's experiments, or of the progress of a pasticheur. Almost every 'poem' is an exercise in imitation. First it was the Romantics (Katherine Bucknell is particularly good at spotting Wordsworth echoes), then a few

Georgian big-names of the day, then Thomas Hardy. As imitations, the boy Auden's efforts are dutiful and dull. One never feels that there is anything of his own, by way of rhythm or vocabulary, pressing for a point of entry. As de la Mare, he can 'see the fairies dancing in the ring'; as Housman, he exhorts 'Take up your load and go, lad / And leave your friends behind'; as A.E. – the Irishman – he thrills to the 'sweet unforgettable ecstasy of sound / Of leaves drinking the young dew'. Or was this meant to be like W.H. Davies? The submission to Hardy, while it lasts, is almost comically abject: 'Who'd have dared to say / There would come a day / When, passing this spot, / I should not stay / But go on my way'; 'For little we sensed of the delight / Hid in the laughter / Yes, little we recked of things that we / Would prize hereafter.'

Even with Hardy, where there was admiration for the poet's personality as well as for his skill (Hardy's looks reminded Auden of his father's), the pasticheur is more interested in fathoming how the tone and rhythms work than in making use of them for his own purposes. From time to time, Auden's 'own purposes' show through, but rather wanly. The author's temper, so far as we can make it out, tends to the mournfully inert, yearning for silence and solitude but thrilled from time to time by sudden movements or sharp noises. Disturbance is both sought and fled. Up to 1926, the words 'silence' or 'quiet' appear in almost every poem, whatever the current model. 'Silence is best,' 'I will be silent, Mother Earth,' 'Silent thoughts, so sweet, so deep', 'Beauty's silent quiet attack', 'Silence more achieves than singing may,' 'Silence and Beauty sit enthroned, alone!', 'This is the place for you if you love quiet,' 'O there is peace here,' and so on. 'Silence' can stand for sexual isolation (voluntary or involuntary) or for spiritual equilibrium, depending on who does the reading. Auden still liked to show his work to Mother but he also liked to pass it round among his friends. The cryptographer of later years can perhaps be glimpsed here as practising the rudiments of authorial evasion. More likely, though, he just didn't have the words. Not yet.

One of the few early poems that we know to have been based on a specific personal experience is 'The Old Lead-Mine' – a feeble piece about dropping a stone down a mine-shaft:

> I peered a moment down the open shaft
> Gloomy and black; I dropped a stone;
> A distant splash, a whispering, a laugh
> The icy hands of fear weighed heavy on the bone
>
> I turned and travelled quickly down the track
> Which grass will cover by and by
> Down the lonely valley; once I looked back
> And saw a waste of stones against an angry sky.

Many years later, in *New Year Letter* (1941), Auden describes this same stone-dropping moment as (in Dr Bucknell's words) 'the seminal moment of his life as a civilised human being and as an artist':

> There
> In *Rookhope* I was first aware
> Of Self and Not-self, Death and Dread:
> Adits were entrances which led
> Down to the Outlawed, to the Others,
> The Terrible, the Merciful, the Mothers;
> Alone in the hot day I knelt
> Upon the edge of shafts and felt
> The deep Urmutterfurcht that drives
> Us into knowledge all our lives,
> The far interior of our fate
> To civilise and to create
> Das Weibliche that bids us come
> To find what we're escaping from.

In 1924, the boy-poet had to make do with 'the icy hands of fear', the 'angry sky'. The experience was his; the words, though, had to come from stock. And there was no point in calling on his usual masters – as he discovered a year later, when he had another try; this time with an assist from Robert Frost:

> Like other men, when I go past
> A mine shaft or a well,
> I always have to stop and cast
> A stone to break the spell

Of wondering how deep they go;
    And if the clatter end
Too soon, turn grieved away as though
    Mistaken in a friend.

In 1925, Auden went to Oxford and there discovered *The Waste Land*. 'I now see the way I want to write,' he told his tutor, Nevill Coghill, a year later. He had, he said, torn up all his early poems 'because they were no good.' There would be no further sub-Georgian trysts with Mother Nature. 'Man's got to assert himself against Nature . . . I hate sunsets and flowers . . . I loathe the *sea*. The sea is formless.' The poet had a choice between Nature and Geometry. From now on, Auden would be geometrical, a Modernist, an individual talent who, by his apprenticeships, had already digested a fair dose of the tradition. Not only that: he was a scientist. In his first year at Oxford he read Natural Sciences and in literary circles he was once again able to parade his 'clinical' credentials. As Isherwood amusingly recalled, he 'was peculiarly well equipped for playing the *Waste Land* game'.

> For Eliot's Dante-quotations and classical learning, he substituted oddments of scientific, medical and psychoanalytical jargon: his magpie brain was a hoard of curious and suggestive phrases from Jung, Rivers, Kretschmer and Freud. He peppered his work liberally with such terms as 'eutectic', 'sigmoid curve', 'Arch-Monad', 'gastropod'; seeking thereby to produce what he himself described as a 'clinical' effect. To be 'clinically minded' was, he said, the first duty of a poet. Love wasn't exciting or romantic or even disgusting; it was funny. The poet must handle it and similar themes with a wry, bitter smile and a pair of rubber surgical gloves. Poetry must be classic, clinical and austere.

Auden's sub-Eliot period – as Isherwood suggests – is by far the most irritating stretch of his development, and is made even more so when he begins mixing in elements from Edith Sitwell. But it is also the first phase of his liberation, the phase that shows him beginning to itch for his own authoritative tones. His earlier enslavements induced pallor, correctness and humility. Eliot, though, taught him how to strut.

Eliot's direct domination lasted for about a year and when it was over Auden was ready to step out on his own. By 1928, he had left Oxford where – he said – he would never have 'found my own voice . . . as long as I remained there I would remain a child.' He had read Anglo-Saxon, he had been to Berlin, he had dabbled in psychoanalysis and briefly been enchanted by the later Yeats – the style, not the ideas. These were some of the ingredients: the recipe remains unknown. What we do know is that, some time in 1927 to 1928, Auden suddenly discovered Audenesque. His privately-printed *Poems* (1928), reprinted here as juvenilia, was not altogether free of Eliotic affectations, nor of other echoes, but it was in essence unmistakably his own. The Auden landscape was more or less in place and so too were the telegraphese, the admonitory rhetoric, the throat-grabbing opening lines: 'Consider if you will how lovers stand'; 'Taller today, we remember similar evenings': 'Control of the Passes was, he saw, the key.' Many lines, fragments and whole poems from the 1928 book would soon reappear in Auden's *Poems* (1930) – one of the century's most weirdly original first books. Thanks to Katherine Bucknell, we can now ponder in detail how he got there by way of what must be one of the century's most rigorous and self-humbling trainee schemes – a five-year commitment to the second-hand. And in the end the mystery is still happily intact. Auden's boy-poetry is good to have, and Dr Bucknell has edited the book with exemplary thoughtfulness and skill, but there is nothing at all in it to bring cheer to a boy-poet.

Juvenilia: Poems 1922–28 by W.H. Auden, edited by Katherine Bucknell (Faber)

London Review of Books, 1994

The First Life of Salman Rushdie

In Salman Rushdie's *Midnight's Children*, Amina Sinai is persuaded to consult a soothsayer. She is about to give birth to the main character of an important novel, and she wants to know what to expect. The soothsayer tells her that the child will be a son – and 'such a son!' The boy will 'never be older than his motherland', and one day he will be very famous. The soothsayer continues to peer into the future and gets more and more worked up. He launches into a mad dance: 'Crowds will shove him! Sisters will weep; cobra will creep . . . Washing will hide him – voices will guide him! . . . Spittoons will brain him – doctors will drain him – jungle will claim him – wizards reclaim him! Soldiers will try him – tyrants will fry him . . .' The rhymes accumulate, the dance speeds up, and Amina begins to wish she'd never asked. And then the magic man achieves his climax: '*And he will die . . . before he is dead.*'

Salman Rushdie has a taste for ominous nativities. When he looks back now on the soothsayer's words, Rushdie smiles a shrugging smile. In 1989, he was condemned to death, but he is still alive. Alive and yet near posthumous. 'For many people, I've become an issue, a bother, an "affair".' For Rushdie, there is the life he led pre-*fatwa* and the life he has led since.

His own birth – on June 19, 1947 – came just two months before India's first day of independence, India's birthday, and he has always made much of the coincidence: baby Rushdie, baby India, twin destinies, linked fates.

As far as we know, the infant Ahmed Salman Rushdie arrived in pretty good condition: the first, long-hoped-for child of Anis Ahmed

Rushdie and Negin Rushdie, née Butt – the father a barrister turned businessman, from Delhi, and the mother a teacher, from Aligarh, in northern India. According to family legend, the new child was unusually good-looking. Little Salman caught the eye. Mary Manezes, a worker in the Bombay hospital where he was born, took one look at him and decided that she would become this baby's ayah: in effect, his 'second mother'.

The Rushdies were a wealthy Muslim family – a notch down from India's super-rich, but rich enough. They called themselves upper-middle-class. Their money came from a leather-and-cloth business started by Anis Rushdie's father (who was also something of a poet), and by the mid-1940s the family owned real estate in northern India, including a grand colonialist folly on Westfield Estate, in Bombay, where they lived. The Rushdie residence was called Windsor Villa. It was a house fit for kings.

Down below, off Warden Road, were the shops: Chimalker's Toyshop, Reader's Paradise, and the confectioners Bombelli's, with their delectable One Yard of Chocolates. There was also the Breach Candy Swimming Club, even after Independence a segregated hide-away for Brits: 'where pink people could swim in a pool the shape of British India without fear of rubbing up against a black skin.'

Baby Rushdie was not pink, but he was strikingly light-skinned, and his parents were by no means anti-British – not publicly, at any rate. Anis Rushdie was a Cambridge man and proud of it. He had practised as a lawyer before dedicating himself full time to the family business, and in Bombay he had status as a Europeanised sophisticate, a scholar of international range.

It is not entirely clear that this status was deserved. Anis had an impressive library, which may have been purchased in toto from a British colonel. In Salman Rushdie's *Shame* we read of a sham scholar whose books 'all bore the *ex libris* plates of a certain Colonel Arthur Greenfield, and many of their pages were uncut,' and in an interview published this year in the literary magazine *Brick* Rushdie speaks of having 'had the feeling of growing up in quite a philistine house':

> I mean, my grandfather who was a very minor Urdu poet and essayist, was already dead before I was born, so I never knew him.

My father had certainly studied English literature and Oriental literature in Cambridge, but that was a long time ago and he had since forgotten most of it, and certainly it is true – it's a terrible story to tell about my father but I will tell it since he's dead and can't answer back – that he bought a library. So a lot of the books at our house had once been collected by someone else. He just decided he needed books on the shelves so he went out and bought someone's library. So I lived in this house with a stranger's books, not my father's.

Was Anis Rushdie a sham scholar? Sameen Rushdie, the eldest of Salman Rushdie's three sisters, believes he wasn't: 'He was within his field a very learned man. He knew a lot of classical Arabic, a lot of classical Persian. People would come to him as an authority if they had questions to ask.' Even so, he seems never to have completed the one scholarly task that people knew about: editing for publication one of his own father's manuscripts – an interpretation of some part of the Koran, Sameen thinks.

Anis did have one invaluable gift – and on this brother and sister are agreed. He knew how to tell a story. 'My father,' Rushdie has written, 'was a magical parent of young children,' and Rushdie regularly acknowledges the influence of his father's bedtime tales. 'I grew up in a literary tradition,' he once told Günter Grass. 'That's to say that the kind of stories I was told as a child, by and large, were *Arabian Nights* kind of stories . . . It was accepted that stories should be untrue . . . That horses and also carpets should fly.' In Windsor Villa, the nightly story was a precious ritual. As Sameen recalls, Anis would sprawl out on 'this huge big bed' and let the children climb all over him:

We never had a 'story a night.' The story never ended. I remember begging for more but he'd say, 'No – you just have to wait until tomorrow.' One story fell into another story. Some of them were rooted in the *Arabian Nights*, but he would embellish them and some he would tell straight, probably depending on how imaginative or tired he was feeling. That they never ended is what I remember.

In Rushdie's *Haroun and the Sea of Stories*, written for his own son, we read of Rashid Khalifa, a renowned storyteller whose 'never-ending stream of tall, short and winding tales' earned him two nicknames: to those who admired him, Rashid was 'the Ocean of Notions'; those who didn't called him 'the Shah of Blah.' Haroun, Rashid's son, often referred to his father as 'a Juggler, because his stories were really lots of different tales juggled together, and Rashid kept them going in a sort of dizzy whirl, and never made a mistake.'

Rushdie's mother also had a way with narrative, but her tales were rooted in real life. It was she, according to Rushdie, who was 'the keeper of the family stories': she had 'incredible genealogical gifts'. The children had only to mention a name and she would be ready with the lowdown: 'She would tell you who their mother had married or who their fourth cousin was or the terrible scandal that had happened to the grandparents.' She was 'a kind of encyclopedia of stories'.

One story seems to have been missing from Negin's compendium: her own. Her first name had not always been Negin. She began life in Aligarh as Zohra Butt, and when she met Anis Rushdie she was already married. It seems that she and Anis began seeing each other before she eventually made the break from her first husband. The Butt family, though Muslim, was progressively inclined, but even so there was a need for some fairly delicate negotiations.

Salman Rushdie always speaks with warmth of his maternal grand-father, and Dr Butt does seem to have been unusually enlightened for the time. A medical doctor, he had seen to it that his daughters got an education, and he never required them to observe purdah. When Zohra divorced in order to marry Anis (who was himself a divorcé), the arrangements were handled by her father. It was his idea that her new marriage contract should give her the right to divorce: a practice normally enjoyed only by the husband.

When Sameen and her brother were children, they were not told of these first marriages. The topic is still sensitive today. Sameen says:

I was over thirteen before I knew that either of my parents had been married before. I remember feeling a great sense of shock. My mother finds it very hard to speak about her previous marriage – even now. She says, 'You mustn't ask me about these things.'

In *Midnight's Children* Salman Rushdie does speak about these things, but in his fictional telling the first marriage of Amina Sinai takes place, literally, beneath the ground. Thus a secret chapter from his mother's genealogical storybook gets published in the manner of one of his father's *Arabian Nights* fantasies – a cunning ploy.

Rushdie's books are full of such tricks: time and again, autobiography is re-experienced as fairy tale. Sometimes the intention is celebratory and fond; sometimes it is lavishly delinquent. Rushdie's 'pell-mell' imagination is crowded with what-ifs: What if his father could be turned into a character in one of his own bedtime stories? What if all supposedly true-life experience could be fabulously re-imagined? The wilder the fictional conjecture, the more gleefully energised Rushdie becomes. As he has said, his books have a spirit of connection with real life. But the spirit is mischievous. Readers who try to tease out links between Rushdie's life and Rushdie's fiction are likely to end up feeling teased.

Although the Rushdies were Europeanised and secular-progressive, they were still Muslim, and after Independence and Partition they had to tread with care. 'From a very young age, we were conscious of being a Muslim minority in India,' Sameen says. 'There were certain things our parents never said out loud, certain things we knew we mustn't mention to anybody.' Anis Rushdie's business and properties came under threat from both the Hindu mobs and the new post-Independence courts. Sameen says:

> There were questions about my family's loyalty to India: as Muslims who hadn't left. There were court cases. The government took over my father's properties, as being evacué properties. He had to prove that he hadn't left and then come back, that he had always been Indian. 'Because he had all these cases against him, no Hindus were to be trusted, really, although my father's best friends were Hindu.

In *The Satanic Verses* Salman Rushdie refers to the 'lackadaisical, light manner' with which Bombay Muslims treated their religion. The Rushdies called themselves religious; they observed the Muslim festivals and sometimes they fasted during Ramadan, but on the whole their observances were lax.

The children were 'never encouraged to play with Muslim children', and the Bombay school that Salman attended, the Cathedral and John Connon School, was more British than Indian; the prayers were strictly Church of England. Rushdie has recalled:

> We were obliged to say these Christian prayers – 'Our Father,' and so forth. It was very bizarre. Here was a school of maybe a thousand boys of whom maybe two per cent were Christian and we were obliged every morning to recite the 'Our Father'. None of us knew the words. We all knew the beginning but as we went through the 'Our Father' everybody sort of ran out. And by the end of it there was just this mumble which had the right rhythm. I didn't know what 'World without end' meant at all.

Salman's sister remembers him as 'every parent's dream child'. A year younger, and a girl, she envied him his golden status in the household. He was thoroughly adored: studious, obedient, 'no trouble'. He loved to read, he had to be persuaded to go out to play, and at school he mopped up all the prizes:

> In his school, we went every year to prize-giving. They had a prize for each subject and then they had an over-all prize. And he got *every* prize. He went on and off that stage, every year – it was just boring. History prize, Geography prize, English prize; and people would just laugh because it would be Salman who came on and off the stage. And then he came up and got the class prize. He must have got every prize every year he was at school.

Not surprisingly, Rushdie was not 'street popular'. If his parents had a worry, it was perhaps that he was *too* studious, *too* bookish. And maybe he agreed with them. He had no wish to be reviled as the school swot, and he would probably have traded at least some of his prizes for a single triumph on the sports field. 'He was bad at sports. He'd kick the ball and fall over,' Sameen says, and she believes that this failure hurt. 'He never talked about it that much, but I think he minded. He was always a very keen spectator.'

Readers of Salman Rushdie's fiction would suspect a substantial vein of mischief in his makeup, but as a child, at least, he was noted for his caution: 'He was a *good child*. He never did what he shouldn't do.' According to Sameen, this caution sprang not from a feebleness of spirit but from an excessive attachment to the truth. 'He's very straight,' she says. 'In some ways too straight. I think it's this honesty that leads him to do the things he does.' She remembers in particular a time when the Rushdie parents would send the children to the local club, with permission to sign a tab for any snacks they had – burgers, fries, ice cream:

> Then our father would get the bill and he would say: 'You mustn't eat so much' or 'You're only allowed to have' – whatever – 'a Coke, some chips,' or whatever the rule was. And Salman would have only what he was allowed, and I would continue to have whatever I wanted, really. We'd come home and they would say 'What did you have?' and I would mention just one of the three things I'd had. But Salman would eat only what he could admit to. My memories of him are not of him being a rule-breaker.

Luckily, there was no vetting of the children's literary intake; in fact, the rule was that they could read whatever they wanted – comic books, movie magazines, trash fiction. Low culture was not perceived to be a threat. The little Rushdies were let loose on Reader's Paradise, with no restraints. Sameen says, 'They thought, As long as they read, that's terrific. Let them find what they want.'

It seems to have been much the same with films, if we can judge from Rushdie's habit of peppering his books with allusions to American B movies and to local 'Bollywood' extravaganzas. As a child, he was a glutton for the Bombay talkies. He admired their unsubtle all-inclusiveness. Aimed largely at a village audience, the Hindi hit movie had to have something of everything – comedians, villains, fight sequences, music, dance, romance. It aimed for 'total entertainment'. The last thing it tried to be was true to life. Salman's Sunday-morning outing to the cinema was the high point of his week, and it is no surprise that the first story he attempted, at the age of ten, was movie-based. Its title was *Over the Rainbow*, and it featured 'a talking pianola whose personality is an improbable hybrid of Judy Garland, Elvis Presley and the "playback singers" of the Hindi movies.'

For Salman Rushdie nowadays, the most painful consequence of his predicament is that he may never again see Bombay. For most of us, the place we belong to is where we spent our childhood, or so we tend to say. In Rushdie's case, though, the attachment to Bombay is more than just nostalgic; it is an essential component of his talent. And for Rushdie, as a child, India meant, first of all, Bombay. Whenever he describes his native city, it is as if he were describing the books he likes to write, the sensibility he wants to cultivate or keep intact: multicultural, plethoric, zany, bristling with weird beliefs, weird disbeliefs. 'People from Bombay,' he has said, 'think of themselves as being unlike people from elsewhere.'

At the age of thirteen, in 1961, Rushdie was sent 'elsewhere' – to England, to an English public school. And he was thrilled. When he was told that he was bound for Rugby, the home of Tom Brown, Flashman, Dr Arnold, 'it felt as exciting as any voyage beyond rainbows.' For middle-class Indians of Rushdie's parents' generation, the English public school was 'the acme of educational possibility'. The Cathedral School's star pupil had landed the biggest of all prizes. At home, he was much envied. 'We were quite jealous of Salman,' Sameen recalls. 'He'd gone off to England in this great big airplane and we'd think, You *must* love him best, because you've sent him to England, to boarding school. It was very glamorous.' His leaving was a tearful occasion. '[My mother] really didn't want me to go,' Salman has said. 'I was her darling, her first-born.' It is also possible that Negin had her doubts about the English, whose bathroom habits were known to be, well, a little unhygienic: 'They wipe their bee tee ems with paper only. Also, they get into each other's dirty bathwater.'

For Anis, this should have been the moment he had been waiting for, the moment when his fair-skinned, brilliant boy would be transformed into a proper English gent. By the time the two of them reached London, however, the proud father seems to have deflated. Anis, it was known, enjoyed a drink, and 'he was also prone to explosions, murderous rages, bolts of emotional lightning.'

In Bombay, these rages came and went and could be seen as features of his paternal grandeur. He was the boss; he told the stories; he laid down the law. In London, though, there was a crumbling, an abdication, that is still remembered with some fury by his then bewildered son.

Just what happened between them is unclear. On arriving in London, they checked into a double room at the Cumberland Hotel, at Marble Arch. They had some days before the Rugby term began, and during this time Salman seems to have discovered what Anis was really like. In *The Satanic Verses*, Changez takes his son Salahuddin to England to attend a public school. The two of them stop off in London and check into a hotel. At this point, the father hands his son a walletful of cash and tells him, 'Now that you are a man, it is for you to look after your old father while we are in London town. You pay all the bills.' The boy is terrified; this is his first day in a foreign city. But Changez is in earnest and for two weeks 'never put his hand into his own pocket once'. The son has to buy food and school clothes. There are no movies, no restaurants, and no glimmer of the magic that had been dreamed of: it is all 'pounds shillings pence'. For their entire stay, Changez sits in his room watching cartoons on TV.

The son, meanwhile, experiences 'the birth of the implacable rage which would burn within him, undiminished, for over a quarter of a century'. This rage 'would boil away his childhood father-worship and make him a secular man, who would do his best, thereafter, to live without a god of any type.'

For Rushdie, in real life, the Cumberland Hotel episode was an important severing ('He drank too much and became abusive – it was the first time I saw him like that, the first time he was drunkenly abusive to me'), and he still speaks of it with feeling. It was a huge relief, he says, to leave his father for his English public school. As for Anis, it should perhaps be kept in mind that in 1961 his life was at a turning point. Should he continue living in Bombay, where his business was failing, or should he make the move to Pakistan, where some of his relatives already lived? Or should he move to England? Perhaps he envied his son's English prospects. Perhaps the boy's starry-eyed excitement was getting on his nerves. Or maybe it was just the drink.

★　　★　　★

On the train to Warwickshire, Salman registered the greens and greys, the patchwork fields, the 'winter-naked trees'. In India, he had once calculated, you could not travel on a train for fifteen seconds without spotting at least one human being – and, most likely, dozens. In England, you could go for several minutes and see no one. How could a country so tiny be so empty?

And then there was the school. In interviews, Rushdie has portrayed his time at Rugby as one of torment. He was, he has said, repeatedly the butt of racist taunts. His Indian-English way of speaking was laughed at, his essays were torn up, he was forever being made to feel alien, a misfit – he, who thought he was so British. On one of his first days at school, Rushdie was given a kipper for his breakfast. He had no idea how to eat it and classmates watched unhelpfully as he struggled to find out:

> He sat there staring at it, not knowing where to begin. Then he cut into it, and got a mouthful of tiny bones. And after extracting them all, another mouthful, more bones. His fellow-pupils watched him suffer in silence; not one of them said, here, let me show you, you eat it in this way. It took him ninety minutes to eat the fish and he was not permitted to rise from the table until it was done. By that time he was shaking, and if he had been able to cry he would have done so. Then the thought occurred to him that he had been taught an important lesson. England was a peculiar-tasting smoked fish full of spikes and bones, and nobody would ever tell him how to eat it. He discovered that he was a bloody-minded person. 'I'll show them all,' he swore. 'You see if I don't.' The eaten kipper was his first victory, the first step in his conquest of England.

This kipper story appears in *The Satanic Verses*, but Rushdie has said that it is 'absolutely true', and that 'it's one of the very few stories I've used in fiction which needed no embellishment at all.'

Another Rugby story that Rushdie has told more than once describes him catching one of his study-mates crayoning 'Wogs Go Home' on a wall. The slogan, he thought, clearly was aimed at him. 'I went insane. I grasped that boy by the collar with my left hand and by the belt with my right hand, and I banged him as hard as I could against the wall he was writing on.' Rushdie has called this a determining moment in his school career – indeed, in his whole attitude to life in England. It was the moment when he learned how to strike back.

When Rushdie's former Rugby classmates are asked about these stories – the kipper and the wall – they profess ignorance. They remember Rushdie's 'strong accent', his ineptitude at sports, his premature beard growth, his 'wonderful yarns of life in India', but none recall any racist bullying. Even the 'Wogs Go Home' scribe named by Rushdie has no recollection of the incident. All of them thought that Rushdie was 'clever'; some thought that he was 'good fun'. One fellow-pupil recalls Rushdie's turning in divinity-class essays that were studded with fake quotes: 'Salman couldn't be bothered to do the research, so he used to make them up. He had this authority called Professor I. Q. Gribb. I think eventually the chaplain caught on, but I don't remember what happened.' When, for a scholarship exam, Rushdie was required to write a general essay – typical subjects were 'My Most Exciting Holiday', 'My Bicycle' – he elected to discourse on 'Mediocrity'. His classmates were impressed. 'I didn't know what the word meant,' one says. 'I had to look it up in the dictionary. And Salman had written a whole essay on it.'

Another Old Boy remembers Rushdie as 'a great debater – he could argue black was white,' and the school's Debating Society records cite several contributions from 'A. S. Rushdie'. In one debate, Rushdie argued against the motion that 'this House would abolish Fagging' (the practice of treating younger students at school like servants) and is reported to have said that 'without fagging . . . Rugbeians would be snobbish, self-centred and foppish.' Other contributions were less frivolous. On the motion that 'this House would never build another Empire,' Rushdie 'spoke of the Indian civilisation and culture that Imperialism had destroyed, and the degradation of Indians under foreign rule.' And in another, on the motion that 'there are no good, brave causes left,' he took the line that 'peace was a good, brave cause.'

On top of his debating skills, A. S. Rushdie also showed some promise as an actor, appearing in at least two productions: Friedrich Dürrenmatt's *The Physicists* and Arthur Watkyn's *Not in the Book*. In this March, 1964, production, Rushdie played Pedro Juarez and 'proved an excellent South American', evincing – according to the school's Play Annals – 'the necessary suave aplomb . . . His heart attack and death may have been slightly overacted but they were certainly effective.'

These jottings suggest that Rushdie was having a reasonably good time – or, at least, a cheerier time than the one he presented later on. So do his school reports, although in his second year it is noted that 'either English food or English climate doesn't suit him.' His over-all academic record shows him more often than not in one of the top three places in his class, and the verdict on his final school year reads, 'He has made excellent use of what Rugby has to give.' He won a Queen's Medal for History – the highest school prize in that subject – and was offered a scholarship at Balliol College, Oxford: but he turned it down. 'I think I'm the only person ever to turn down a Balliol scholarship.' The difficulty was that he had already been offered a scholarship at King's College, Cambridge, which was his father's old college. Anis insisted that he go to King's.

Rushdie himself did not want to go to any English university. He had had enough of England. His schoolmates' memories have faded, but incidents that they recall now as boyish rough-and-tumble were for Rushdie memorable confrontations. There was, for instance, one debate – a mock General Election – in which he attacked a right-wing 'candidate' who was urging stronger immigration laws. Rushdie asked if, as a black, he himself would be excluded under the proposed new rules. 'You are not black,' came the reply. 'You are a peculiar brownish colour. But yes, you too would be denied entry to this country.' And in an end-of-term 'satirical' revue during his final year Rushdie heard himself lampooned:

What is this shape 'midst the nebulous fog?
Merely the resident Bradley House wog.

Rushdie had fathomed the mysteries of kippers, he had learned how to speak 'goodandproper' English, he had passed his school exams. He had even turned down a scholarship at Balliol. His conquest of England was complete, and he had no wish to consolidate the spoils. He was ready to go home.

But where *was* home? For Anis Rushdie, in Bombay, things had been going from bad to worse. His business was in ruins, and daily life in India had become increasingly precarious for Muslims. His drinking problem had got worse. In 1962, Anis and his family had followed Salman to England, become naturalised British citizens, and set up house in a flat in Kensington. In a short story called 'The Courter', Rushdie portrays the move as typical of his father's authoritarian impulsiveness: 'I had been at boarding school in England for a year or so when Abba took the decision to bring the family over. Like all his decisions, it was neither explained to nor discussed with anyone, not even my mother.'

From Kensington, Anis was able to keep a close eye on his son's academic progress. When Rushdie failed chemistry at O level, Anis refused to speak to him until he had apologised. Sameen remembers the explosion:

> Salman's results came. Salman had failed! This man who never failed anything! Complete shock. And what my father said to him – I still remember – 'You did it deliberately. You did it to spite me.' I'm sure he meant that, because Salman had said that he didn't want to do Chemistry and my father said, 'You have to.' Salman said, 'Couldn't I do a subject called Physics *with* Chemistry,' and my father said, 'No, you have to do a Physics paper and a Chemistry paper. You have to do them both.' And there had been this big row. Then Salman failed it. My father couldn't believe that Salman couldn't pass Chemistry at O level if he wanted to.

There was a similar eruption when Rushdie announced to his parents that he did not want to go to Cambridge. 'He begged them. He really didn't want to go,' Sameen recalls. 'But they said: "That's what it's been *for*. You *must* go."' Apparently, Salman had never told his parents, or his sister, of his unhappiness at Rugby. 'Never, never, never,' Sameen says. There was a now lost work of Rushdie fiction about Rugby life, a short novel called *Terminal Report*, but no one was allowed to read it at the time.

The Cambridge altercation took place in Pakistan. After dithering in England for two years, Anis had at last decided to 'shift location' to Karachi (even though he was now the holder of a British passport).

'As usual,' according to 'The Courter', 'there were no discussions, no explanations, just the simple fiat.' Worst of all, from Rushdie's point of view, Anis had sold the family's Bombay home. Sameen says, 'When they broke the news to him that they had sold the house, he wept.'

The choice, then, was no longer Cambridge or Bombay, England or India; it had become Cambridge or Karachi, England or Pakistan – and for Rushdie Pakistan was 'a stain on the face of India'. The India he dreamed of was the opposite of everything that Pakistan stood for. It was secular, multiplicitous, tolerant, hospitable. He could never forgive Karachi for not being Bombay. But where did he belong now: India or Pakistan? In August, 1965, the two countries went to war over Kashmir. Rushdie had gone 'home' to Karachi for the summer at a time when both India's and Pakistan's Armies had claims on him. He had to make a choice – to which country did he owe his allegiance – and the pressure of making that choice almost undid him. 'I didn't particularly feel India was my enemy, because we'd only very recently come to Pakistan. And yet if somebody's dropping bombs on you, there is really only one reaction that you can have toward them, which is not friendly.' In the end, his parents more or less forcibly threw him on a plane to England.

In October, 1965, Rushdie arrived at King's College, Cambridge, to read for a degree in History. In Pakistan, students were demanding 'a stricter, more Islamic society . . . more-rules-not-less.' In England, students wanted sex, drugs, and rock and roll. Rushdie's Cambridge career ran from 1965 to 1968 – the life span, some would say, of the authentic 1960s. 'It was a very good time to be at Cambridge,' he has said. 'I ceased to be a conservative snob under the influence of the Vietnam War and dope.' He saw himself as having been 'radicalised' by his experience at Rugby, and, by his own account, he fell for the whole Sixties package:

> In those days everybody had better things to do than read. There was the music and there were the movies and there was also, don't forget, the world to change. Like many of my contemporaries I spent my student years under the spell of Buñuel, Godard, Ray, Wajda, Welles, Bergman, Kurosawa, Jancsó, Antonioni, Dylan,

Lennon, Jagger, Laing, Marcuse, and, inevitably, the two-headed fellow known to Grass readers as Marxengels.

While there is no record of Rushdie's having been arrested at anti-Vietnam demonstrations, there were signs of his now notorious spikiness of manner. Professor John Dunn, of King's College, recalls his former student as 'very self-assured, independent, uncompromising, not overwhelmed by modesty. I vividly remember the sense of personal confrontation I had with him. He was not staggeringly clever by Cambridge standards – just clever. We have lots of clever people here.'

Arthur Hibbert, another King's tutor, has a vague memory of his former student. Hibbert it was, though, who set Rushdie on a path that ultimately led to *The Satanic Verses*. In his final year at Cambridge, Rushdie had chosen a special subject: Mohammed and the rise of Islam. But only five people turned up, and the lecturer cancelled the course. Rushdie persisted and went to see Hibbert, his director of studies. According to Rushdie, Hibbert said, 'I'm not a career specialist in Islam, in early Islamic history, but I am a medievalist and I do know quite a lot about it, so if you would be happy for me to supervise you, I'll supervise you.' Rushdie ended up being the only person in the university studying the course. 'I remember coming across the Incident of the Satanic Verses, thinking, that's interesting, there's something there, you know . . . and put it away in my head.'

Cambridge in the Sixties, although it had its leftist pockets, was still a contented seat of privilege. There were more hearties than hippies, and the posh ex-public-school boys could effortlessly keep themselves aloof from the down-at-heels students from state schools. The gentlemanly traditions still flourished: private dining clubs, May Balls, the Boat Race, Twickers. Rushdie himself once recalled, 'It was a very strange time at Cambridge. There was a mixture of the old and the new. There were a lot of chinless wonders in blazers who threw people into the river at night. I'm sure they're still there – they endure like the earth.' And yet Rushdie, as a well-off Rugbeian, may have felt some affinities with the university smart set. Simply because of his

school background, he is likely to have been more at ease with the
wealthy sons of Eton, Harrow, and the like than with working-class
boys from the state-aided grammar schools. One King's contemporary
has said:

> He was rather pompous and we always felt that he was trying to
> have it both ways – be a representative of the oppressed people
> of the Third World and yet also glory in the public-school gloss
> around him. A lot of us were grammar-school lads and, however
> he has tried subsequently to present himself as the outsider, we
> actually felt alienated from him by his education.

Another Cambridge contemporary, not from King's, speaks of
Rushdie's 'radical chic'.

Like many bright students, Rushdie approached his subject not in
any kind of methodical way but accidentally, haphazardly, in the way
of someone who likes to read. He went to the cinema five times
a week and developed a more than passing interest in the occult.
Unsurprisingly, his academic record showed a distinct falling off
from his straight-arrow performance at school. He ended up with
a 2:2 – a degree well below the average, low enough certainly to
have barred him from postgraduate research. Not that he gave any
sign of wishing to become a Cambridge don: by the time he took his
Finals, Rushdie – who had played in student productions of Ionesco,
Brecht, Ben Jonson, and others, and had been, as well, 'a tiny bulb in
the Footlights' (the famous Cambridge revue) – had been bitten by
the theatre bug.

If he had been asked in 1968 what career he had in mind, he would
have said that he planned to be an actor. 'Actor', it seems, was easier
to say than 'writer': 'I knew even then that I wanted to write, but I
kept quiet about it. I was afraid to say it for a time, even to myself.'

Rushdie the would-be actor, the secret writer, finally returned to
the confines of Karachi, his new Oriental home. He went there, he
says, because, among other reasons, he had a return air ticket. (As it
happens, he ended up driving overland.) And he had nowhere else to
go. The visit was a failure on all fronts. Anis had embarked on a new

business venture, a towel factory, and had high hopes that his returning son, B.A. (Cantab.), would run it. Sameen recalls, 'My father would take him to see the towel factory and Salman used to go there gritting his teeth, saying "I'm not going to do this." "But I'm setting it up for *you*." "Well, please don't, because I'm not going to run it."'

Instead, Rushdie took a job with Pakistan's new television service. He persuaded Karachi TV to let him produce and act in Edward Albee's *The Zoo Story*. The play is short, it has a cast of two, and the only prop required is a park bench. The proposal was accepted. Before production could begin, though, there had to be a series of 'censorship conferences'. An Albee remark about the disgustingness of pork hamburgers was seized on by the censors. 'Pork,' they said, is a 'four-letter word'. Rushdie argued that Albee's hamburger remark was 'superb anti-pork propaganda' and should stay. '"You don't see," the executive told me . . . "The word 'pork' may not be spoken on Pakistan television." And that was that.' He also had to cut a line about God being a coloured queen who wears a kimono and plucks his eyebrows.

The same kind of thing happened when Rushdie agreed to write an article for a small magazine about his 'impressions on returning home':

I remember very little about this piece (mercifully, memory is a censor, too), except that it was not at all political. It tended, I think, to linger melodramatically, on images of dying horses with flies settling on their eyeballs. You can imagine the sort of thing. Anyway, I submitted my piece, and a couple of weeks later was told by the magazine's editor that the Press Council, the national censors, had banned it completely. Now it so happened that I had an uncle on the Press Council, and in a very unradical, string-pulling mood I thought I'd just go and see him and everything would be sorted out. He looked tired when I confronted him. 'Publication,' he said immovably, 'would not be in your best interest.' I never found out why.

In Pakistan, he discovered, censorship was 'everywhere, inescapable, permitting no appeal'. There was 'no room to breathe'. So it was back to England and the 1960s, or what was left of them. In London,

Rushdie set up as a struggling artist. A struggling actor or a struggling writer? 'A struggling both,' he says. It seems that he was now ready to come clean about the writing.

Sameen was studying in London, so it was agreed that she and her brother – together with some Cambridge friends of his – should rent a house in Fulham. Here, for a time, a jolly-commune atmosphere prevailed. Jenny Richards, one of the Cambridge friends, recalls the house as 'chaotic and great fun. There were lots of arguments – who cleans the bath, who shops. And about partners. We had dinner parties all the time. Salman was a great raconteur and bon vivant. Great wordsmith. There were parlour games, and he was brilliant at things like "the worst movie titles": *The Second Man*, *Around the World in Eighty-nine Days*.'

Back in Karachi, Anis was not thrilled to learn that his son was living like a Western hippie. Sameen says, 'He thought it was a disgrace that Salman should be living on the dole, but he refused to support him while he did this thing called writing. I think Salman always held that against him – for not supporting him, even emotionally.' In the Fulham house, Rushdie began writing his first novel. 'When he told my father that he wanted to write, my father said, "What on earth would *you* write about? You should get a job like everybody else. These are all excuses for not wanting to work."'

In fact, Rushdie did have a job of sorts, appearing now and then as an actor in productions at the Oval House, in Kennington. Dusty Hughes, an old Cambridge friend, was then directing shows but was not particularly encouraging about Rushdie's career. In *Viet Rock* – a play about the Vietnam War – Rushdie was cast in a variety of roles, including that of a Vietcong soldier: 'It would be unkind to say that he was totally without talent – perhaps that's the best way to put it.' In a multimedia rock show, *Rainy Day Woman*, Rushdie played a drag queen, but evidently refused to shave off his John Lennon moustache. 'I think that may have been the beginning of his prima-donna phase. I don't think it did him any good. So far as I know, that was the end of his theatrical career.'

Dusty Hughes, it turned out, had a superior career plan. During the day, he worked for the J. Walter Thompson advertising agency. Hughes remembers, 'Salman visited me and saw this plush office, the desk covered in telephones, and learned of my "huge salary," as it seemed then, and he said, "How do you get *this*?"' Hughes advised him that all he had to do was 'take the test,' which meant – in Rushdie's case – writing a jingle about the merits of car seat belts. Rushdie set his text to the music of Chuck Berry's 'No Particular Place to Go'.

Rushdie failed the test, or so he says (Hughes thinks that he passed), but he had heard the chink of easy money and soon afterwards found work with a small agency called Sharp MacManus. There he seems to have spent most of his time sitting at the feet of a 'voluptuous' (his word) colleague, Fay Coventry (who later married Rushdie's future publisher at Jonathan Cape, Tom Maschler). 'Fay moved in bookish circles' and would depress Rushdie with her tales of 'the smart literary weekends she'd attended'. He was envious but knew that the only way he would ever get his hands on some of *that* would be to complete the book he was working on.

Rushdie quit Sharp MacManus and resumed work on his novel. Completed in 1971, it was entitled *The Book of the Pir* and featured a Muslim guru, in some unnamed Eastern land, who gets taken up by a military junta and installed as the figurehead President of its corrupt regime. It was a strong enough plot, but it was written in what the author calls 'sub-Joyce'. After being rebuffed by various literary agents ('It couldn't even achieve *that!*' Rushdie says of it), the book was set aside, and Rushdie decided to go back to advertising. The same year, he joined Ogilvy & Mather as a copywriter. His immediate superior was Keith Ravenscroft. Ravenscroft recalls:

> My boss said to me, 'You're getting this new man. He's a bit unusual but I think he'll be all right.' By unusual I think he meant that Salman was black and he was Cambridge and that he was long-haired and more intelligent than most people. Ogilvy & Mather was known as the Ministry of Advertising. It was a big, reputable, quite solid sort of place and has spawned some good people, like Fay Weldon.

Other Rushdie colleagues included Jonathan Gathorne-Hardy (the author of *The Rise and Fall of the British Nanny*), the poet Edwin

Brock, and Franc Roddam, who later directed the film *Quadrophenia*. Brock says, 'Most copywriters then were writing novels or poems under the desk.'

One of Rushdie's tasks was to prepare a weekly commercial for the *Daily Mirror* – a thirty-second scenario built around the *Mirror's* big story of the week. 'Salman was very good,' Ravenscroft says, 'very instinctive and cerebral, although he was probably too bright to be doing it. You have to reduce yourself to a middle-range sensibility because that's what your consumers have, largely.' Rushdie did manage to reduce himself from time to time, coming up with catchphrases like 'naughty but nice' (for the Milk Marketing Board's promotion of cream cakes) and 'irresistibubble', for Aero chocolate bars.

In 1970, Rushdie had met his future wife, Clarissa Luard, a 'very well-bred English-rose type', says an acquaintance from those days, and the model, presumably, for Pamela Lovelace in *The Satanic Verses*. Readers of Samuel Richardson will remember that in *Clarissa* the heroine is ruined by the merciless rake Lovelace, and that *Pamela* is another Richardson narrative of virtue under siege:

> Saladin Chamcha met Pamela Lovelace five and a half days before the end of the 1960s, when women still wore bandannas in their hair. She stood at the centre of a room full of Trotskyist actresses and fixed him with eyes so bright, so bright. He monopolised her all evening and she never stopped smiling and she left with another man. He went home to dream of her eyes and smile, the slenderness of her, her skin. He pursued her for two years. England yields her treasures with reluctance.

Clarissa Luard remembers Rushdie telling her that he first saw her at a rally at the Albert Hall. She – in 'purple bell-bottoms and with flowers in my hair' – was working with a group that was 'raising consciousness about Biafra'. According to Clarissa, it was a year after the Albert Hall sighting that the pair finally met face to face:

> We saw each other at a party, and he asked a mutual friend to

give a dinner party for me. Then we had a date and went to a Santana concert. Then we saw each other once a week. I had a boyfriend and he had a girlfriend. It was clandestine for about two years. He was pursuing me. I was very flattered because he was this very clever person, a bit awe-inspiring. If I was being analytical . . . My father committed suicide when I was sixteen, and I suspect I was missing a father figure. He knew a lot and could talk a lot and could teach me a great deal about literature. I was very uneducated.

Clarissa's family was – or had been – wealthy. They were upper-middle-class and very British. 'Salman is marrying the Raj,' a friend would later say. In 1973, Clarissa's mother emigrated to Spain, leaving her daughter, Rushdie, and a female lodger to occupy her Lower Belgrave Street flat, next door to what had been the Luards' family home. Rushdie's new residence was just off Eaton Square, an address of stunning grandeur.

It was in Lower Belgrave Street that Rushdie wrote *Grimus*, his first published work of fiction. Liz Calder, who had just begun working as an editor at Victor Gollancz, happened to be the lodger in the Luard flat, and she remembers that she first heard of the novel when Gollancz announced a competition for the best new science-fiction novel. She says:

I knew Salman was writing things, and I was trying to ignore it. It could only be a source of embarrassment, I thought. But when he heard about the competition he said, 'I'm going to enter it.' And my heart sank. Anyway, he finished it and showed it to me, and I liked it. I responded to its extraordinary use of language. I mean, it was just wild. I hadn't read anything like it. And although it was barmy in some ways, all over the place, I thought it was amazing. So he entered it. There were three judges: Arthur C. Clarke, Brian Aldiss, and Kingsley Amis. Kingsley violently disliked it. So it wasn't going to win. But I thought, Well, I'll try and get it published anyway. We offered Salman some paltry sum.

To celebrate, Rushdie and Clarissa took a five-month trip to India

and Pakistan. The proofs of *Grimus* reached him in Karachi. He
also, on this trip, saw Bombay again, and Delhi and Kashmir, the
places of his childhood. 'I loved India!' Clarissa exclaims. 'The
people, the smells, the colours, the history, the architecture!' She
was less thrilled by Pakistan, where on at least one occasion she
and Rushdie had stones thrown at them. 'I wasn't dressing badly,'
Clarissa says. 'I knew about the country and I was wearing long
skirts. But I wasn't wearing the *dupatta*.' In one town, a driver tried
to run them down. However, she was given a warm welcome by
the family:

> There I was, a strange English person, unmarried, travelling with
> their precious son. We were chaperoned heavily. We were never
> alone in the same room for an instant. I didn't like Pakistan, but I
> liked them and their house, which was huge, grand, magnificent.
> They lived in some style: a lot of servants, swimming pool in the
> garden. It was a bit shabby, though. Salman's father was not as well
> off as he had been.

She was aware of the tension between son and father: 'There was
a lot of bad feeling. Salman's father adored him but had difficulty
showing it. That's the impression I got as an outsider. And I don't
think Salman picked up on that. But he'll probably say that I am
wrong.'

Returning to England for the publication of *Grimus*, Rushdie may
already have known what was wrong with his first book. He has
called it 'a kind of fantasy novel set in an imaginary island, out of
space and time', and so it is, but it is also laboriously mannered.
Esoteric knowhow is exhibited throughout – hypnosis, numerology,
time travel, black magic, pseudo physics. In the cast of characters,
wordy weirdos abound: seers, gnomes, and so on. The novel has a
few good jokes: I. Q. Gribb, of Rugby fame, makes an appearance
as the author of an All-Purpose Quotable Philosophy, and there is an
amusing Wild West bore called One-Track Peckenpaw. In a brothel
called House of the Rising Son, the prostitutes have funny names like
Boom–Boom de Sade, Kamala Sutra, and Lee Kok Fook, but the sex
scenes are inept. It seems unfair to go on, especially since Rushdie

has more or less disowned the book, but if *Grimus* had *not* failed we might never have had *Midnight's Children*.

After all, despite its flamboyant self-display, *Grimus* was a forbiddingly anonymous affair: one could deduce from it almost nothing about the author's background. 'I must try and write something from much closer to my own knowledge of the world,' Rushdie decided after India. 'Something which is – where I know what's happening and where I know the place and time.' In 1974, he asked Ogilvy & Mather to let him work part time. He needed time to write, he said. The agency was not entirely happy with the deal, but Rushdie, according to Ravenscroft, stood firm: 'It's very simple. You pay me good money and I do my best work for three days a week and then I do other things. That's the only basis on which I am prepared to work.'

We get a hint here of what Ravenscroft calls Salman's 'very, very strong sense of self. Quite unshakable. Work and dignity. The right to be as he is and to say what he says.' From Clarissa Luard's point of view, this aspect of his personality was sometimes hard to understand:

> Salman is very explosive. When we were first living together, I never knew how long we'd be staying at any dinner party. There would always be these violent arguments and out we'd be storming, yet again. It didn't occur to me not to storm out with him. I thought my role was to support my man, to do whatever he did. They were ridiculous arguments. He was quite shouty . . . He didn't drink. Salman hates drink, because his father drank so much. It was just pure belief in himself: a conviction and determination that certain things *are*. I remember a long-standing relationship with a dear friend ending because Salman suddenly said, 'You can't stay in my house if you don't like such-and-such a writer.'

In April, 1976, Rushdie and Clarissa Luard married, in London's Caxton Hall, and soon afterwards they bought a house in Kentish Town, in North London. The house was spacious, but semi-derelict. 'There were holes in the roof,' Rushdie later told a columnist. 'Dry rot and damp everywhere and it had electricity on the ground floor only.'

He set to work. Friends were astonished to discover a new Rushdie talent: he knew how to 'do up' houses. 'They never thought I could do anything practical, but I learned as I went along.' He converted two of five bedrooms into a workroom for himself. He restored fireplaces and cornices, sanded floorboards, repainted the walls. 'Once I got into it, I became quite manic.'

No. 19 Raveley Street was not quite Windsor Villa, but it meant a lot. And he was through with upper-crust Belgravia. In Kentish Town, Rushdie the immigrant found himself living in a different sort of London, a London whose 'race problem' he had read about but had rarely witnessed close at hand. In this London, citizens who hailed from Pakistan or Bangladesh, or even India, were strictly second class and made to know it. On the subject of race prejudice Rushdie had sometimes had to bite his tongue. He had kept silent when a jingle was rejected because the singer 'sounded black', or when black children had been excluded from feel-good commercials about sweets. 'I found the prejudice of senior executives in British industry quite appalling,' he wrote later, and in *The Satanic Verses* Hal Valance, a top adman, is portrayed as a bigoted grotesque.

In 1977, Rushdie became involved in a local North London project to create jobs for Bangladeshi immigrants. The experience revealed an England that had forgotten all about 'fair play, tolerance, decency and equality'. Racism, he came to believe, had 'seeped into every part' of British culture. Britain had 'imported' a new Empire, a community of subject peoples. He found that in certain areas, like Camden, Southall, and Brixton, there was no point in blacks calling in the law. The law was white. The police offer the immigrant 'threats instead of protection, and the courts offer small hope of redress,' he wrote. 'Britain is now two entirely different worlds, and the one you inhabit is determined by the colour of your skin.' Rushdie's own skin, of course, was not dark enough to be targeted by street thugs or by racist cops. 'I have this accidental fair skin, speak with an English accent, and don't go around in Nehru topees.' His own persecutions were subtle, middle-class, well meant:

The phrase that really gets me angry is this thing about being 'more English than the English'. It is used as if it should be offensive. I point out to these people that if there was an English person living in India who adopted Indian dress, who had learnt to speak Urdu or Hindi or Bengali fluently without an accent, nobody would accuse him of having lost his culture. They would be flattered and pleased that the language had been acquired so efficiently. And they would see it as a compliment to themselves. But they wouldn't accuse him of having betrayed his origins.

It would be several years before Rushdie tackled these British matters in his fiction. In 1977, his 'writing self' was living somewhere else – in India. His next book, he had vowed, would be rooted in personal experience. He would go back where he had come from.

His first effort was entitled *Madame Rama*, and its main character bears some resemblance to Indira Gandhi, whose state-of-emergency repressions had left Rushdie disillusioned and indignant: Nehru's legacy betrayed by Nehru's daughter. He offered *Madame Rama* to Gollancz, but, to his surprise, Liz Calder turned it down. 'It had some great stuff in it,' she concedes, and points out that 'he plundered it for *Midnight's Children*.'

For a while, Rushdie floundered. But something about India had been in progress ever since his trip there. 'I spent many months trying simply to recall as much of the Bombay of the 1950s and 1960s as I could':

> I found myself remembering what clothes people had worn on certain days, and school scenes, and whole passages of Bombay dialogue verbatim, or so it seemed; I even remembered advertisements, film-posters, the neon Jeep sign on Marine Drive, toothpaste ads for Binaca and for Kolynos, and a footbridge over the local railway line which bore, on one side, the legend 'Esso puts a tiger in your tank' and, on the other, the curiously contradictory admonition: 'Drive like Hell and you will get there.'

He knew that he was tapping 'a rich seam', but he was blocked. The breakthrough came when he switched from the third person to the first person. 'I've always remembered this as the moment I became a writer,' he says. *Midnight's Children* was completed in June of 1979, two weeks before the birth of Rushdie's son, Zafar.

According to Clarissa, 'it was a race between us to see who would produce first.'

By this time, Liz Calder had moved from Gollancz to Jonathan Cape, then London's most prestigious house for literary fiction, and she wanted to take Rushdie with her. As a newcomer, Calder thought that she needed backing from within the firm. The first report she got on *Midnight's Children* was scathing: 'this fat ramble round Indian Rushdie's mind.' Subsequent opinions, though, were powerfully in favour of the book. 'So we took it on,' Calder says, 'and Tom Maschler read it and told us all we didn't realise what we had got: this was a work of genius.'

In spite of Maschler's enthusiasm, Cape printed only 1,750 copies of the book, and at the firm's 1980 Christmas party Rushdie had no sense of being the focus of a 'buzz'. No one knew who he was. When he approached Martin Amis, a Cape celebrity, Amis, he says, 'just turned his back'. (Amis, by the way, has 'no memory of snubbing Salman', and says, 'It feels doubly improbable to me, because I seemed to be the only person on earth who admired his first novel, *Grimus*. It is easy to imagine him feeling vulnerable and sensitive at that stage in his life. Shiva Naipaul used to consider himself snubbed if he glimpsed you from the top of a bus on Regent Street and you neglected to jump on board.')

Midnight's Children was published first by Knopf in the United States, and here Rushdie, on a short visit – paid for by himself – enjoyed his first taste of literary glamour. Bob Gottlieb, his editor at Knopf, who took him to the ballet, remembers Rushdie on this visit as 'enthusiastic about everything, interested, charming, hopeful – he knew he had written a wonderful book.' Most of the reviews were rapturous. *The New York Review of Books* called *Midnight's Children* 'one of the most important [novels] to come out of the English-speaking world in this generation.'

In Britain, there was a blizzard of superlatives – 'major,' 'magical', artistic', 'brilliant', and 'fantastic'. Although Rushdie acknowledged as his forebears some pretty hefty Western names – Cervantes, Sterne, Grass, Melville, Kafka – most Western readers were dazzled by the book's sheer foreignness. Or, rather, they were astonished that material so alien could be delivered with such Westernised panache.

This is how the book begins:

I was born in the city of Bombay . . . once upon a time. No, that won't do, there's no getting away from the date: I was born in Doctor Narlikar's Nursing Home on August 15th, 1947. And the time? The time matters, too. Well then: at night. No, it's important to be more . . . On the stroke of midnight, as a matter of fact. Clock-hands joined palms in respectful greeting as I came. Oh, spell it out, spell it out: at the precise instant of India's arrival at independence, I tumbled forth into the world. There were gasps. And, outside the window, fireworks and crowds. A few seconds later, my father broke his big toe; but his accident was a mere trifle when set beside what had befallen me in that benighted moment, because thanks to the occult tyrannies of those blandly saluting clocks I had been mysteriously handcuffed to history, my destinies indissolubly chained to those of my country. For the next three decades, there was to be no escape. Soothsayers had prophesied me, newspapers celebrated my arrival, politicos ratified my authenticity. I was left entirely without a say in the matter. I, Saleem Sinai, later variously called Snotnose, Stainface, Baldy, Sniffer, Buddha and even Piece-of-the-Moon, had become heavily embroiled in Fate – at the best of times a dangerous sort of involvement. And I couldn't even wipe my own nose at the time.

V.S. Pritchett, reviewing the book in this magazine, described the author as 'a master of perpetual storytelling', but also seemed to have difficulty reconciling an Indian novel with what seemed to be a novel so *not* Indian: 'There are strange Western echoes, of the irony of Sterne in *Tristram Shandy* – that early nonlinear writer . . . This is very odd in an Indian novel!' Indian readers had no such difficulty. For them, the book was like a gift from Heaven. Anita Desai has described the Indian novel's predicament, pre-Rushdie. With Independence, she believes, English-language novelists in India felt irrelevant. How to be 'post-colonial' in genres bequeathed by the colonial oppressor? Rushdie, she says, showed them the way forward. In the summer of 1981, Desai was at a reading that Rushdie gave at the India International Centre, in New Delhi, a reading in a 'small auditorium that drew a crowd so unexpectedly large that it spilled out under the trees and loudspeakers had to be set up to broadcast his voice, a voice that everyone present recognised instantly as being the voice of a new age: strong, original, and demanding of attention.' There was, she says,

> a kind of euphoria in the air to greet him. For the first time an Indian writer had found the language to say things which we had all been through but had still not found the words for. After that, I think every young Indian writer tried to write like Salman. The whole next generation of Indian writers started off by writing their own *Midnight's Children*. The effect his writing had on Indian writers was somehow to loosen their tongues.

A similar experience occurred in Cambridge, Rushdie's alma mater, and the site of his first reading. He was warned beforehand by the organiser not to expect much of a turnout; after all, he was an unknown writer. But when they reached the art gallery where the reading was to be given it was packed – with Asians. At one point, the organiser has recalled,

> a woman in a sari stood up. Her voice cracked as she spoke: and she wanted to express her gratitude to Salman Rushdie for writing India; that was the actual construction she used. 'No one,' she said, 'has written about India as you have. You have written my India. I will always be grateful to you.'

Mukul Kesavan, a student at the time, described the reading as 'a religious experience'. Fourteen years later, Kesavan was to publish his own *Midnight's Children*-inspired novel, *Looking Through Glass*.

Midnight's Children was less happily received by the author's family in Karachi. Anis was shocked by his son's scornfully freewheeling way with family secrets. Rushdie had taken incidents and personalities from the Rushdie family history and mischievously re-imagined them. Anis found himself portrayed as Ahmed Sinai, 'a man over whom, even in his moments of triumph, there hung the stink of future failure, the odour of a wrong turning that was just around the corner, an

aroma which could not be washed away by his frequent baths.'
Ahmed is a ludicrously inept businessman, inadequate in marriage,
a drinker, a bully, and a self-deceiver. It is a savage portrait –
fiction as revenge. 'They were all shocked,' Rushdie says. His father
more or less 'disowned' him, even at this moment of his Western
triumph.

The triumph was made official, so to speak, in October of 1981,
when *Midnight's Children* won the lucrative Booker Prize, Britain's
top award for fiction. Rushdie was overjoyed. Liz Calder has talked
of his 'un-British' manner, 'excitable, passionate, outspoken'. Rushdie
had been given what he wanted. Life had changed.
    According to Clarissa, 'it changed hugely. Hugely. We'd always
had a very sociable life but it became crazy':

> Our life just went haywire. We were fêted – well, I wasn't fêted,
> but I was brought along, too. It was extraordinary to see the
> extent to which that sort of thing comes into action, as soon
> as you win ... Salman revelled in the success. [His writing]
> mattered so much to him, and it was being recognized. But we
> were very young ... I probably didn't see what was happening
> very clearly.

Even the intensely loyal Keith Ravenscroft detected troubling devel-
opments:

> I remember going to a dinner party at his house, not long after
> *Midnight's Children*. There were all these people who revered him.
> I'm not saying they weren't genuine. They were literary folk, and
> he was holding forth on something and everyone was listening
> reverently. I thought it was crap and said so. I said, 'Come on, you
> silly old tart, that's rubbish.' And there was this horrified silence
> round the table, that someone they'd never heard of, who – so
> far as they knew – hadn't written anything, was laying into the
> maestro.

Midnight's Children was translated into more than a dozen languages,
and by the time Rushdie paid a return visit to his homeland – or

homelands – he was a world name. He told the *New York Times Book Review* that he had been nervous about returning:

> In Pakistan there is suspicion because I'm Indian and in India because I'm Pakistani. Both sides wish to claim me. Both sides find it hard that I don't reject the other side. So I was expecting hostility or fear, and instead what happened was an extraordinary emotional event. It wasn't just that the audiences for my lectures were very large, but that there were these great waves of affection. Mostly from young people. The book was written as a way of reclaiming India and this was like India and Pakistan doing the same thing back.

Increasingly, over the next year or so, Rushdie came to see himself in public terms. Polemics that had previously been the stuff of dinner-table bust-ups were now expressed in magazines or on TV. Rushdie had no doubts about the writer's role: it was essentially subversive. He summed it up in an essay about Günter Grass: 'Go for broke. Always try and do too much. Dispense with safety nets. Take a deep breath before you begin talking. Aim for the stars. Keep grinning. Be bloody minded. Argue with the world.'

In *Midnight's Children* Rushdie enjoyed toying with the private lives of public figures. When Indira Gandhi was reported to be planning a libel action against the book, Rushdie was pleased that she had read it. Normally, he had said, she 'subsists on a diet of Mills & Boon romances'. In the event, Mrs Gandhi won her libel action but was assassinated before a new, expurgated text could be printed.

Also buoyantly lampooned in *Midnight's Children*' are various high-up Pakistani politicos and generals, and in Rushdie's next book, *Shame*, published in 1983, it was their turn to occupy centre-stage. The tone is different, though. In *Midnight's Children*, even the most wounding thrusts are tempered by an antic inwardness; there is a sense of We're-in-this-together, this madhouse, this abundance. In *Shame*, there is no love of Pakistan: 'a failure of the dreaming mind.' And in Rushdie's skewering of the country's leaders there is no sense of disappointed affection. His version of Zia-ul-Haq ('Old Razor Guts') has no redeeming features: Zia's 'Islamisation programme' is a front for workaday repression. Zulfikar Ali Bhutto comes off slightly better: he at least has brains. Bhutto's daughter Benazir – 'the virgin Ironpants' – represents the future: a future of 'arrests, retribution, trials, hangings, blood, a new cycle of shamelessness and shame'. *Shame* was quickly banned in Pakistan. (When Zia met his death, in August of 1988, Rushdie was reported to have said, 'Dead dictators are my speciality. I discovered to my horror that all the political figures most featured in my writing – Mrs G, Sanjay Gandhi, Bhutto, Zia – have now come to sticky ends. It's the grand slam, really. This is a service I can perform, perhaps. A sort of literary contract.')

In September, *Shame* was short-listed for the Booker Prize. Nobody had won the Booker twice, and Rushdie had reason to believe that he might pull off this coup: none of the other titles on the short list had brought reviewers to their knees. Yet the prize went to a little-known South African, J. M. Coetzee, for *Life and Times of Michael K*, a spare, drab, realistic novel about race relations. Rushdie and his supporters were dismayed, and there were stories of spilled wine and angry words at the ceremony. There may have been some kind of scuffle. This Booker night of *Shame* has now passed into legend, by means of a Rushdiesque process of telling and retelling. Nobody seems to know for sure what happened. Whatever it was, Rushdie was perceived to be uncool, undignified, un-British.

That same year, the Rushdies moved. Their new home was unequivocally splendid: a massive five-storey house in Highbury Hill, one of Islington's smartest areas. Clarissa had given up her job, and set about refurbishing their 'super' house. Rushdie was now in demand worldwide, for festivals, conferences, symposiums. Clarissa envisaged a new life for herself, as Salman's consort:

> My grandmother was still alive, my mother was around, we weren't frantic for money, so I thought it was better to be not working, to be daughterly or granddaughterly or wifely, and go on trips with Salman. And I liked that very much – although of course I didn't go on any trips.

In 1984, Rushdie attended the Adelaide Festival's Writers Week,

in South Australia, and afterwards toured the outback with Bruce
Chatwin, who was gathering material for his book *The Songlines*.
Rushdie seems to have found himself out-Rushdied by the garrulous
Chatwin: 'In Bruce's company, I don't manage more than a few
interruptions.'

Rushdie left his friend in Alice Springs and headed off to Sydney,
equipped with a few contacts. One was Robyn Davidson, the author
of *Tracks*, an account of a 1,700-mile camel ride across Australia.
Rushdie describes his first meeting with Davidson as 'a thunderbolt
. . . love at first sight'. And Davidson seems to have felt much the
same. In her novel *Ancestors*, the heroine describes her first encounter
with Zac Appelfeld, a theoretical physicist from New York:

> We talked until our bones ached with cramp and cold, peeling away
> layers of conversation, becoming more and more personal, laughing
> helplessly at each other's jokes like children, both of us opening up
> with excitement. We marvelled at our uncanny ability to finish
> each other's sentences. There was something disquieting about it,
> this entangling of thoughts, as if we had a previous knowledge of
> each other.

On his return to England, Rushdie told Clarissa that he had met
someone he 'liked as much as me':

> I didn't understand what he meant. I just said, 'That's nice. I
> look forward to meeting her.' Something like that, something
> really stupid. It eventually became clear what he meant. Then
> he went back to Australia and saw her again, and it didn't work
> out. But he couldn't bear being away from her. So I said, 'Go for
> six months and then we'll decide what happens.' But then he was
> back. Never wanted to split up with me again. Make a go of it –
> blah, blah, blah: you know, all this stuff that one gets. Then, lo
> and behold, after another three months he'd gone again: finally.
> It was eighteen months between him coming back from Australia
> the first time and us actually splitting up. It was miserable, moving.
> It was just a nightmare.

Rushdie says that his marriage to Clarissa had 'gone flat' eighteen months before he met Davidson, and that before that he had never considered himself 'available' for love affairs. Clarissa's sense of how it was is rather different:

> It is very difficult when one person achieves greatness, has all the fame, because you're suddenly not an equal partnership any longer. And I was desperate to have another baby, but I just kept miscarrying and stuff. So I was going through my own personal bad time and I suspect that if I'd had the baby it would have been more equal somehow. I didn't feel quite included in it all. People used to say, 'Gosh, is it all right?' and I'd say 'Yes, it's fine' but I wasn't always happy. But I did always feel that it was strong underneath. I didn't think that bond would break.

The Highbury Hill house was sold in 1985. Clarissa bought a new house for herself and Zafar. When Robyn Davidson agreed to live in England for a time, she moved into Rushdie's new house, in St Peter's Street, also in Islington. It was a provisional arrangement. As if to underscore the point, Davidson brought along her camel saddle.

Rushdie's two-year relationship with Davidson has been described as 'nuclear'. 'Volcanic' is how a friend of theirs described it: It was always exploding and subsiding. It was an exciting combination: the chemistry was potent. Pauline Melville, a Highbury Hill neighbour of the Rushdies and a close friend of Salman's, believes that Davidson's literary ambitions may have been a problem. She recalls:

> They had one of these rows, which were quite frequent. He would mainly come to me and she would go to Sameen. One time, she said, apparently, 'I don't know what it is, but we have one of those rows and he can go straight upstairs and I can hear the typewriter. He just goes on writing. I'm wandering around in a state, unable to do anything.'

In *Ancestors*, the moody and possessive Zac often disappears into his study, a 'holy shrine' from which Lucy, the book's heroine and now Zac's wife, is barred. In fact, the *Ancestors* portrayal is not at all vindictive. Nor is Rushdie's of Robyn Davidson in *The Satanic Verses*. (The mountaineer Alleluia Cone seems to be based on her.) Each of these fictional accounts of the affair – if such they are – is essentially self-blaming.

Rushdie's leftism of the Sixties was steadily resurfacing as his fame grew. Asked to speak out, he spoke out, and he was often to be found in the company of London's so-called 'champagne socialists' – anti-Thatcherites like Margaret Drabble and anti-Americans like Harold Pinter. Rushdie was invited to Nicaragua, and he went there in July of 1986 for three weeks. A guest of the Sandinista Association of Cultural Workers, *el escritor bindú* felt a natural sympathy for the Sandinista cause but had no wish to be branded as its tool. Even so, he went, and was colourfully entertained by members of Ortega's famous Cabinet of poets. People who ran countries were not *meant* to be like this. 'For the first time in my life, I realized with surprise, I had come across a government I could support.'

Just before Rushdie's arrival, the government had shut down an opposition paper, *La Prensa*, on the ground that it was financed by the CIA Rushdie warned his Sandinista friends, 'Censorship is very seductive . . . I don't like it. Not because of what you are but because of what, if this goes on, you might eventually become.' By his standards, this was a muted, kindly protest, more in sorrow than in anger. On being asked later to compare Nicaragua's state of emergency with Mrs Gandhi's clampdown in the 1970s, he said that the two situations resembled each other 'very slightly'. In India, there had been no outside threat, no American aggressor: 'I can see why [the Sandinistas] have a state of emergency. The problem is when to lift it.' Rushdie did his best to see Nicaragua with his own eyes, and in the end he came out solidly in favour of his hosts. He wanted this government to work:

> It was a disorienting realisation. I had spent my entire life as a writer in opposition, and had indeed conceived the writer's role as including the function of antagonist to the state. I felt distinctly peculiar about being on the same side as the people in charge, but I couldn't avoid the truth: if I had been a Nicaraguan writer,

I would have felt obliged to get behind the Frente Sandinista, and push.

Prior to setting off for Central America, Rushdie had begun writing *The Satanic Verses*, and he was reluctant to break off from it. But, he said later, 'when I came back I found that I had become a Nicaragua bore. I couldn't stop talking about what I had experienced. I wrote *The Jaguar Smile* as a way to shut up.'

The Jaguar Smile appeared in January of 1987 – a short book full of arresting on-location yarns, more travelogue than tract. The reviews tended to be divided along party lines. The left usually took the book's politics for granted and praised Rushdie for providing a new, 'vivid' slant. The right mocked him for his naïveté, calling the book 'fawning', 'mesmerised', and superficial. *The New Republic* derided it as a 'snap book': in snap books, 'war and revolution serve primarily as backdrops against which star writers can shine.' Rushdie liked to call himself a political animal and was no stranger to political controversy, but he must have been disappointed by the reception of *The Jaguar Smile*, which was treated mainly as straight reportage. The novelist's transforming powers, his truthful lies had no function in this cause-serving genre. *The Jaguar Smile* is dedicated to 'Robbie'. Rushdie recalls that when he told Davidson this she said, 'You mean your new novel *won't* be dedicated to me?' Such is the cryptology of literary romance.

But Davidson was right. Shortly afterwards, she flew back to Australia – this time, for good. At a Thanksgiving dinner in 1986, Rushdie had met another strong-willed writer, an American, Marianne Wiggins, who was the author of several works of fiction. Rushdie had recently read and liked one of her short stories, 'Herself in Love'. Wiggins later told a reporter, 'At the end of dinner, he said I should call him up.' Again, it was Salman's 'brilliance' and 'wit' that did the damage: 'He is a really funny man . . . The brain is clearly the central erogenous zone for me, and he's got a big one.' She moved into Rushdie's house in St Peter's Street early in 1987.

Marianne Wiggins, like Robyn Davidson, found it difficult to live with Rushdie's fame, or so some friends of his now say. Some friends say that Rushdie is simply difficult to live with. Others believe that

Wiggins used Rushdie to advance her own career. The novelist William Styron had known Wiggins 'quite well' on Martha's Vineyard in the mid-1980s and was struck by her determination to 'get ahead in the literary world'. He felt that she wished to 'cultivate' him but that, 'being married, I could not offer her sustenance'. He added, 'When I heard that she had taken up with Salman, I gave an inward groan. She was very attractive, very seductive, but I felt that she was really trouble.' Like the relationship with Davidson, Rushdie's relationship with Wiggins was turbulent, but among Rushdie's friends Davidson's explosions get a better press than Wiggins's 'manipulations'. Davidson is spoken of as a 'free spirit' who could not be tamed. Stories about Wiggins now tend to portray her as a schemer. It is possible that she is the model for Uma, in Rushdie's latest book, *The Moor's Last Sigh*, who, like Wiggins, seems to come 'out of nowhere', and who 'would invent long, elaborate personal histories of great vividness, and would cling to them obstinately, even when confronted with internal contradictions in her rigmaroles.'

By all accounts, Wiggins's long, elaborate personal stories were similarly stylish. And Rushdie was swiftly taken in: the two were married in January of 1988. Why did he do it? A clue is perhaps offered in *The Moor's Last Sigh*: 'How much longer did I have? Ten years? Fifteen? Twenty? Could I face my strange, dark fate alone, without a lover by my side? What mattered more: love or truth?'

The previous summer, Rushdie had spent several weeks in India, compiling a film essay for Britain's Channel Four. This, it turned out, gave him his last look at the places of his childhood before the *fatwa* put them out of reach.

The film was called *The Riddle of Midnight*, and it set out to look at India through the eyes of Rushdie's own, forty-year-old generation – 'the real-life counterparts of the imaginary beings I once made up. Midnight's real children.' These were people who, like Rushdie himself, had been born the year that India was born. The question he pondered was 'Does India exist?' His trip coincided with an upsurge of Hindu-Muslim clashes following the occupation of the disputed Babri Masjid, a mosque in Ayodhya. The country was being torn apart by 'the politics of religious hatred'. Rushdie's dream India, 'based on ideas of multiplicity, pluralism, hybridity', now seemed profoundly fanciful, quixotic.

The film was finished in the autumn of 1987, and Rushdie dedicated it to his father. During the editing, back in London, news reached him that his father was ill and close to death. In *The Satanic Verses*, Salahuddin is summoned to the deathbed of his father. The two are reconciled. 'I came because I didn't want there to be trouble between us any more,' the son says. Changez replies, 'That doesn't matter any more. It's forgotten, whatever it was.' And the son reflects:

> To fall in love with one's father after the long angry decades was a serene and beautiful feeling; a renewing, life-giving thing, Saladin wanted to say, but did not, because it sounded vampirish; as if by sucking this new life out of his father he was making room, in Changez's body, for death . . . Cancer had stripped Changez Chamchawala literally to the bone; his cheeks had collapsed into the hollows of the skull, and he had to place a foam-rubber pillow under his buttocks because of the atrophying of his flesh. But it had also stripped him of his faults, of all that had been domineering, tyrannical and cruel in him, so that the mischievous, loving and brilliant man beneath lay exposed, once again, for all to see. *If only he could have been this person all his life*, Saladin . . . found himself wishing. How hard it was to find one's father just when one had no choice but to say goodbye.

The son says goodbye in Urdu.

Rushdie, in a 1988 interview, acknowledged that 'like the character in the book, my father and I did in fact work it out, in the end,' and he went on to talk about his own changed attitude towards India, as if the one were connected to the other:

> I am no longer Indian in the way that I would have been if I hadn't left. I'm another thing. For a long time I would try and tell myself that that wasn't so, and that somehow *that* was still home, and *this* [England] was still away. When I went back there I was going home. It's true that even now I feel 'at home' in Bombay, in particular, in a way I don't feel anywhere else in the world, really. But I came to feel that I had to stop telling myself that:

that there was a sense in which it had become a fiction that was
no longer useful to me: it was a way of not looking at the real
things about my life, which were that *that* isn't home, that *that* is
away. *This* is home. In a way, you can't go home again.

Rushdie's film had a similarly elegiac tone. When *Midnight's Children*
was first published, 'the most common Indian criticism of it was that
it was too pessimistic about the future.' Six years later, the book's
conclusion seemed 'absurdly, romantically optimistic'. Rushdie was
now an exasperated exile. A father's death, a homeland that no longer
felt like home: these were life-alerting upheavals. And Rushdie had
turned forty.

In 1987, he seems to have been in the mood for severings, fresh starts.
On June 19th, there was a birthday lunch for him at Bruce Chatwin's
house in Oxfordshire. One guest was the New York literary agent
Andrew Wylie. For some time, Wylie had been courting Rushdie,
but Rushdie was committed elsewhere. His British agent, Deborah
Rogers, was a friend. So, too, was his British publisher, Liz Calder,
his discoverer and longtime ally. The year before, Calder had left
Cape in order to help found a new publishing house, Bloomsbury,
and Rushdie had promised to move with her. *The Satanic Verses* would
be Bloomsbury's big title for the coming year.

Evidently, Calder had made an offer for the book: £50,000 for the
British hardcover rights. On June 18th, an elated Rushdie conveyed
the news to Wylie. Wylie's response, it has been said, was to advise
Rushdie to reject the offer: 'You mustn't do it.' The following
day, everyone – Rushdie, Calder, Rogers, and Wylie – gathered at
Chatwin's house, and feelings ran high. Rushdie's next move was
to fire Deborah Rogers, break with Calder, and sign up with Wylie.
Wylie's conduct was, says Calder, 'the most blatant and unfeeling piece
of daylight robbery I've ever seen.' She sent Rushdie an angry letter,
which she now somewhat regrets; it was, she says, 'too angry'. He
did not respond. Rushdie's new agents, meanwhile, set to work and
sold the novel abroad first – to a German and an Italian publisher – to
establish the book's value in the marketplace. Only then was it offered
to English-language publishers. It was bought by Viking Penguin for

850,000 dollars, and, while the deal entitled the firm to publish the book in both Britain and the United States, it was still a staggering sum for a literary novel.

The Satanic Verses was published on September 26, 1988. Prepublication comment in London suggested that the British were quite ready to concede that large parts of this long novel were not meant for them. Mark Lawson wrote, in the *Independent Magazine*, 'There must be a question about the ability of even the willing Western reader to migrate mentally to the book's space.' He wished that Rushdie had provided a 'course of running instruction' for his non-Islamic readers.

When the reviews appeared, they were, on the whole, a touch bemused. There were grumbles about Rushdie's lack of structural control. In the *TLS* Robert Irwin wrote of an 'alarming increase' in Rushdie's 'inventive powers', and in *The New York Review of Books* D.J. Enright called *The Satanic Verses* 'a thousand and one nights crammed into a week of evenings . . . A book that nobody else in Britain (at least) would have wanted to write, or could have written.'

This notion that in *The Satanic Verses* Rushdie's true audience was elsewhere meant that few Western critics picked up on the book's 'offensive' elements: calling the Prophet Mahound (a name used by medieval Christian theologians); suggesting that the Koran was not the direct word of God, that a scribe might have been 'changing verses'; the naming of whores in a Mecca brothel after the Prophet's wives. Not much notice was taken either of jokes about camels that spoke in the voice of the Prophet or of Rushdie's numerous Art-versus-God asides. Nowadays, some of the book's passages leap from the page with irony:

> 'A poet's work . . . To name the unnamable, to point at frauds, to take sides, start arguments, shape the world and stop it from going to sleep.' And if rivers of blood flow from the cuts his verses inflict, then they will nourish him.

The furore began in India. In September, a Muslim MP, Syed Shahabuddin, protested that *The Satanic Verses* was 'an indecent vilification of the Holy Prophet' and that 'no civilized society should permit it.' On 5th October, the book was banned. Rushdie wrote an open letter to Prime Minster Rajiv Gandhi, accusing him of kowtowing to Muslim extremists, and explaining that the so-called offensive passages of the novel were the dream of a fictional narrator – 'an Indian movie star, and one who is losing his mind, at that. How much further from history could one get?' To this the Muslim MP responded, 'You are aggrieved that some of us have condemned you without a hearing and asked for a ban without reading your book. Yes, I have not read it, nor do I intend to. I do not have to wade through a filthy drain to know what filth is.'

When news of an impending Indian ban reached Britain, photo-copies of the book's 'offending passages' were sent to Islamic organ-isations, and to the London embassies of the Islamic nations. On 8th October, a London-based Saudi newspaper denounced Rushdie, and soon after a Muslim magazine published provocative selections from the book. There was no immediate outcry, although Viking Penguin received letters of protest and, in the New York offices, a few bomb scares and death threats. Such rumblings went on until December, and then there was a burning of the book in Bolton, Lancashire, attended by a large gathering of Muslims, but it was not much reported in the press.

It was not until January 1989 that the British Muslims' campaign began to hit the headlines. A book-burning in Bradford, Yorkshire, was covered by national TV, and two weeks later 8,000 Muslims marched in London. Rushdie tried to reason with his foes: his novel was not 'anti-religious'; it was an attempt 'to write about migration, its stresses and transformations' – a subject that his Bradford critics, his fellow-immigrants, should know something about. But it was too late for reason. In Islamabad, Pakistan, sections of *The Satanic Verses* were being read out on street corners. On 12th February, an inflamed mob stormed Islamabad's American Culture Centre and was fired on by police. Five demonstrators died. The next day, there was rioting in Kashmir: one dead and more than sixty injured. Scenes from these riots were shown on Iranian TV and, according to one account, were watched by Ayatollah Khomeini. Khomeini summoned a secretary and dictated the *fatwa:*

I inform all zealous Muslims of the world that the author of the book entitled *The Satanic Verses* – which has been compiled, printed and published in opposition to Islam, the Prophet, and the Qur'an – and all those involved in its publication who were aware of its content, are sentenced to death.

I call on all zealous Muslims to execute them quickly, wherever they may be found, so that no one else will dare to insult the Muslim sanctities. God willing, whoever is killed on this path is a martyr.

As Khomeini dictated, so the story goes, Rushdie was attending a party in London to celebrate his wife's new novel, *John Dollar*. Gillon Aitken, now Rushdie's British agent, was at the party, and recalls that the atmosphere was 'strained':

I remember that evening the news of the deaths in Pakistan was in the air. There was a kind of excitement that this was happening: people dying in Pakistan because of Salman's book. And this of course overshadowed Marianne's book. It was an uneasy evening; uneasy, too, because, a couple of days earlier, Salman had said that he was definitely going to extricate himself from the situation with Marianne. Things were very bad. She was badmouthing him to friends. I think he really did want to be shot of her. At the same time, he really was caught up with her. There was something very powerful there still.

The next morning, Wiggins phoned Gillon Aitken to inform him of the *fatwa*. Rushdie was in the middle of a television interview (in which he expressed the wish that he had written a 'more critical' book). It had previously been agreed that, as soon as he was done, he and Wiggins would take a cab to Aitken's offices in Chelsea:

They arrived at around 11 a.m. At 2 p.m. – each of us had the date in our diaries – there was a memorial service for Bruce Chatwin, who had died a few weeks before. The service was in the Greek church in Bayswater. We had sandwiches brought in. Salman and Marianne did not say very much. The telephone rang ceaselessly. The world's press . . . people asking, Is it true? Has he gone into hiding? I can't remember how I responded to the calls. I was picking up the receiver, speaking, putting it down. Then another call would be put through – on and on and on. They were both sitting on the other side of my desk, rapt as I was by this astonishing performance of the telephones.

Before the Chatwin memorial service, the press was gathering outside the church. Aitken shepherded the Rushdies to their pew:

> The church was packed. Paul Theroux was sitting behind us and he said something like 'We'll be here for you next, Salman. Watch your back!' By the time we left the church, the press coverage had increased. Some reporters were actually inside the church. Someone from the *Telegraph* approached us and I remember saying to him, 'Look, just fuck off, will you?' Salman has always treasured that. And the man from the *Telegraph* said, 'Don't you talk to me like that. I went to public school, too, you know.' It was very funny.

After the service, Aitken took Rushdie and Wiggins back to his offices and spent the rest of the afternoon fielding calls. Eventually, Rushdie and Wiggins were transported to Islington – not to the St Peter's Street house but to a nearby basement flat that Wiggins kept for her writing. A friend who saw the couple just after the *fatwa* was announced described Wiggins as 'excited, clinging seductively to Salman'. The tabloid *Sun* later told the world that 'VENGEANCE VOW SAVES ROCKY MARRIAGE.' Not for long, as it turned out. Wiggins and Rushdie separated a few months after he went into hiding (provisionally at first, and then, the following year, definitively). Later, she said to the press, 'He's not the bravest man in the world, but will do anything to save his life.'

At Wiggins's flat, Rushdie was told to stay put. 'Police officers on short patrol watched over me that night. I lay unsleeping and listened out for the angel of death.' The next day, he was offered Special Branch protection and, when he accepted, was taken into hiding. He believed that the whole business would be solved in a matter of days. The police thought so:

> So off we went, not to any deep-secret safe house, but to a hotel in the countryside. In the room next door to mine was a reporter

from the *Daily Mirror* who had checked in with a lady not his wife. I kept out of his way. And that night, when every journalist in the country was trying to find out where I'd gone, this gentleman – how shall I put this? – missed his scoop.

Yes, we all thought that it was going to be over in a few days. But this was almost seven years ago: for Rushdie, the start of a new life, his second life, post-*fatwa*. When I first discussed with him the idea of a biographical essay, he said that he would co-operate, provided that I did not pursue my researches beyond what was for him the final day of his first life: Valentine's Day, 1989. The story of his second life, the life he is living now, cannot be told just yet: there are too many prohibitions. And when it *is* told he will do the telling – when he is able to. In 1990, on the first anniversary of the *fatwa*, he wrote:

> I feel as if I have been plunged, like Alice, into the world beyond the looking-glass, where nonsense is the only available sense. And I wonder if I'll ever be able to climb back through the mirror.
>
> Do I feel regret? Of course I do: regret that such offence has been taken against my work when it was not intended – when dispute was intended, and dissent, and even, at times, satire, and criticism of intolerance, and the like, but not the thing of which I'm most often accused, not 'filth', not 'insult', not 'abuse'. I regret that so many people who might have taken pleasure in finding their reality given pride of place in a novel will now not read it because of what they believe it to be, or will come to it with their minds already made up.
>
> And I feel sad to be so grievously separated from my community, from India, from everyday life, from the world.
>
> Please understand, however: I make no complaint. I am a writer. I do not accept my condition. I will strive to change it; but I inhabit it, I am trying to learn from it.
>
> Our lives teach us who we are.

The New Yorker, 1995–1996

Note

The foregoing essay needs a note of explanation. It was commissioned by *The New Yorker* as an experiment in biography. The idea was that, just for once, the subject of a biographical narrative would be given the opportunity to answer back. It was agreed that Salman Rushdie would annotate my version of his early life – annotate it on the page, as it unfolded, so that there would be a running dialogue, my facts versus his. For one reason and another, stage two of the experiment – Rushdie's footnotes – was not achieved. This seemed, and seems, to me a pity. The results could have been significant. Still, the narrative remains and, I would say, it does have documentary value. After all, it was Rushdie himself who gave me the bare bones, the important leads, the access. That he should do so was part of the experimental plan. It was also part of the plan that I, the biographical tale-teller, would seek to adopt a wholly neutral stance. Hence, no dominant 'interpretation'. Is biographical neutrality achievable? I doubt it. My expectation that Rushdie would respond certainly influenced my tone and presentation. And once or twice, I ought to say, the tale was set up for him to make reply.

Ford Madox Ford: Who Am I?

In 1915, Ford Madox Hueffer became Ford Madox Ford – by deed poll. Around the same time, at the age of forty-one, he enlisted for active service in the British Army: 'I have never felt such an entire peace of mind as I have felt since I wore the King's uniform. It is just a matter of plain sailing doing one's duty, without any responsibilities, except to one's superiors and one's men.'

People close to him were not all that surprised when he joined up. As they saw it, this was just Fordie's latest bid for a clear-cut identity: a uniform, a rank. No longer would he need to wonder who his 'superiors' really were. Nor would he have to worry about keeping his underlings in line. The Army was not literary London. In the military scale of things, the likes of General James and Colonel Conrad would, of course, look down on him. At the same time, salutes were guaranteed from Privates Lawrence, Pound and Eliot; even from Lance-Corporal Lewis. And in the Army, you got paid: paid every week, not just when you happened to get lucky – which, in Ford's book-writing life to date, had not been very often.

By 1915, Ford had published more than forty books – novels, poems, historical romances, propaganda, local history, lit crit – but he was still waiting for a windfall. Even his just published novel *The Good Soldier*, praised on all sides as his best, had earned him next to nothing. Worse still, he was getting the feeling that English Letters thought they could get by without him: without his books, his deeply-felt art-worship, his editorial acumen, his messy life. Only five years ago, he had been kow-towed to as the 'Olympian' editor of the *English Review*, dispensing mysterious 'instinctive' judgements from on high, holding court in his Holland Park Avenue apartments. Now his authority was on the wane. Had he ever been truly valued 'for himself'?

But then, what was this self that he called his? And where did it belong, in Literature's great call-up? Was he a left-over Pre-Raphaelite – a *post* Pre-Raphaelite? The grandson of Ford Madox Brown, he had spent his childhood trying to fathom the Rossettis. He was named after his maternal grandfather, and Brown had been the subject of his first grown-up publication, a homage-ful biography. His imagination, however hard he tried, might never quite be free of pale lost lilies. Or was he a proto-Modernist, the wised-up decoder of rebarbative new talent? Where did the best of his own writing fit? Was his 'impressionist' aesthetic a throwback to the Nineties or a blueprint for *les Imagistes*?

Ford cared about such definitions. James and Conrad condescended to him as he himself now wished to condescend to Pound and his weird Modernist disciples. In Ford's version of his own career, he had served a long apprenticeship to excellence – not least in his tense partnership with Conrad – and, in his late thirties, had much to offer the aspiring young. But neither the old guard nor *les jeunes* quite saw him as 'the real right thing'. Conrad made use of him but never really thought that he belonged in the big league. James, if pressed, would have called him slapdash, unreliable, too vulgarly worried about money. Lawrence, though always grateful and affectionate, reckoned that his discoverer would, in the end, turn out to be too stuffily insistent on technique. Only mad Ezra, the American, seemed certain of Ford's worth.

This feeling of forever being somewhere in-between was Ford's ongoing curse, or so he would have said. And of course the more he pondered it, the worse it got. The either/ors piled up, sometimes to breaking-point. Was he English or German? Pre-1914 he could take his pick, and did – but now, in wartime, a Hueffer could only be a spy. Another spur, this, to enlistment. And if he really was British, where did he fit in the class set-up? Was he a clubland gent up from the shires or was he a big-city chancer, all airs and no substance? Ford's fictional heroes are usually well-acred but unworldly and he would certainly have wished to be like them. In the matter of money, was he a giver or a taker? Ford was hugely generous when in funds but/therefore frequently in need of bail-outs and cash-in-advance. By 1915, he was more or less bankrupt.

Ford – called many-modelled by a waggish friend – was always popular, but never quite knew why. In society, he came across either as too lordly or too keen to please. His tall stories, though, were passed around with ribald glee – indeed, some of them still are. Was he a liar or a dreamer? At the time, his fabulations were widely indulged. Sometimes they were based on fact – at other times: well, nearly. In any event, he seemed – or needed – to believe his own big talk: talk about the great figures he had been so chummy with, or about how he had influenced this or that turning-point in literary history. Nowadays the big talk does him harm: he infuriates critics and biographers by leading them down false trails and blind alleys, and they are inclined to punish him as a result. In 1915, quite a few people looked forward to hearing his News from the Front – and so did he.

Ford was of course famously popular with women – as they were popular with him. And this was a key either/or. Was he – this plump bookman, rabbit-toothed, short of breath, with moist eyes and straggly lemon-coloured hair – in truth a vile seducer, as so many of his primmer associates believed, or was he just too gullibly anxious to be love-struck, *all* the time? In Ford's novels, a bumblingly polygamous male hero is constantly having to explain himself to some vengeful, manipulative shrew – or, if the shrew won't listen, to her rather pretty, sympathetic friend:

> For, whatever may be said of the relation of the sexes, there is no man who loves a woman that does not desire to come to her for the renewal of his courage, for the cutting asunder of his difficulties. And that will be the mainspring of his desire for her. We are all so afraid, we are all so alone, we all so need from the outside the assurance of our own worthiness to exist.
>
> So, for a time, if such a passion comes to fruition, the man will get what he wants. He will get the moral support, the encouragement, the relief from the sense of loneliness, the assurance of his own worth. But these things pass away; inevitably they pass away as the shadows pass across sundials. It is sad, but it is so. The pages of the book will become familiar; the beautiful corner of the

road will have been turned too many times. Well, this is the saddest story.

A lot of Ford's best writing comes packaged as doleful apologia, and so does some of his worst. In the best, though, his eloquence is masterful, unerring. And it is also knowingly seductive. He once said that, in his fiction, he aimed for 'a limpidity of expression that should make prose seem like the sound of someone talking in rather a low voice into the ear of the person that he liked'.

The above 'saddest story' speech from *The Good Soldier* is delivered by the book's artless American narrator, John Dowell. 'I know nothing of the sex instinct' is Dowell's general line but we are not sure that we believe him. He knows more than he is letting on; or he wants to know more – and quite soon. When he comes to assess the adulterous Ashburnham – the seducer of his, Dowell's, wife – he hopes that he has not 'in talking of his liabilities, given the impression that Edward was a promiscuous libertine. He was not; he was a sentimentalist.'

And so was Ford, we think. Sentimentalists get into muddles; libertines move on. Ashburnham, Dowell assures us, was a good man: a sort of feudal saint, in fact, always looking to reduce his tenants' rents, helping drunks and prostitutes go straight, subscribing to hospitals, handing out prizes at cattle shows. Was it surprising that such a man, so open, so large-hearted, so alive, should find it hard to rein back his emotional largesse? In *The Good Soldier*, Ashburnham is not allowed to have his say, which sometimes means that Dowell has to elucidate on his behalf. If this also means that Dowell has to slip out of character for a few paragraphs, so be it. Ashburnham – Ford, with some vehemence, believes – ought to be given a fair hearing:

> As I see it, at least with regard to man, a love-affair, a love for any definite woman – is something in the nature of a widening of the experience. With each new woman that a man is attracted to there appears to come a broadening of the outlook, or, if you like, an acquiring of new territory. A turn of the eyebrow, a tone of the voice, a queer characteristic gesture – all these things, and it is these things that cause to arise the passion of love – all these things are like so many objects on the horizon of the landscape that tempt a man to walk beyond the horizon, to explore. He wants to

get, as it were, behind those eyebrows with the peculiar turn, as if he desired to see the world with the eyes that they overshadow. He wants to hear that voice applying itself to every possible proposition, to every possible topic; he wants to see those characteristic gestures against every possible background.

Is this what Ford really meant by 'impressionism'? Maybe so. As a novelist, he celebrates conditions of alert passivity. He strives – begs, even – for a seeing of all points of view, 'an exhaustion of aspects': a recognition, in short, that one woman's libertine may be another's noble-spirited self-giver. More than with most writers, Ford's art pleads for an understanding of Ford's life. And in consequence, if we wish to deal kindly, it pleads, too, for an understanding of each human life, its many-sidedness, its susceptibility to erroneous interpretation. If, on the other hand, we're feeling – in our many-sidedness – a bit hard-nosed, we might complain that his novels were too often damaged by having to serve as silvery-tongued back-ups to whatever life-muddle he happened to be engaged with at the time of writing.

Ford hated having his intimate life talked about and, in his public persona, he liked to strike postures of fierce reticence. Some hope. According to the tenets of the day, he was a pretty shocking fellow, with his love-affairs, his breakdowns, his lawsuits, his 'wrecked friendships', his cash-flow. There was always a Ford scandal on the go. Chief among these, in the period covered by Max Saunders's first volume, was his liaison with the writer Violet Hunt, with whom he lived as man and wife – or wife and man – after deserting Elsie Martindale, the legal spouse he had newsworthily eloped with in his youth. Elsie, a Roman Catholic, refused Ford a divorce and when Hunt began calling herself Mrs Ford (well, Mrs Hueffer) a much publicised libel case ensued. Ford – in a complicated offshoot from the case – was sent to Brixton for ten days and, as with the Army, he took prison in his stride. 'The apostle in bonds', Pound – of all people – called him, rather shrewdly. For ten days, Ford was able to see himself as a martyr in the cause of many-sidedness. He also, for ten days, knew who he was: a humble convict.

Max Saunders's first volume ends with Ford setting off for war. *Parade's End* is yet to come, and we should really defer judgement, on both Ford and Saunders, until each of them gets to grips with that strange, haunting, self-indulgent work. Saunders, in this immensely scholarly book, tracks in detail and with ardent empathy the links between Ford's muddles and Ford's fiction, and to this end digs up a number of forgotten texts. On the matter of life-art connections, *Parade's End* should test him to the full.

So far, so good, though. Saunders's fifty-plus pages on *The Good Soldier* do justice to Ford's celebrated 'time-shifts' and happily concede the influence of James. Their real interest, though, is biographical. Saunders has found a real-life model for John Dowell and argues persuasively (with biographical support) that Ashburnham's suicide was forced on him by the knowledge that Nancy was actually his daughter.

Has this theory been proposed before? Not that I know of. All in all, Saunders's *Good Soldier* chapter had the effect of altering my reading of a book I thought I knew – a book I thought was marred by Ashburnham's implausible exit – so I, for one, am grateful. And, in consequence, all the more eager to read Saunders's next volume. And after that, I will, I hope, propose that Saunders prune his two volumes into one – if only to allow the narrative some air. At the moment, the life is somewhat buried by the work: a Fordian irony, indeed.

To date, there have been six biographies of Ford, the two best-known being Arthur Mizener's and Alan Judd's. Mizener still stands up pretty well, although Saunders would say that he was too heavily influenced by his conversations with Ford's daughter. Judd's is flashily readable, with no footnotes, and ridiculously overrates Ford's verse. On all the evidence so far, Saunders's is likely to become the standard Life. But then, Ford himself would surely, and touchingly, have reckoned that six Lives were far too few.

Ford Madox Ford: A Dual Life. Vol. I: The World before the War by Max Saunders (Oxford)

London Review of Books, 1996

Louis MacNeice: Anxious and Aloof

Why did Louis MacNeice have to wait thirty years for a biography? He died comparatively young – aged fifty-five – and was outlived by almost everyone he knew: wives, girlfriends, classmates, colleagues. He led an active public life, had two careers – in universities and with the BBC – and was well known as a poet from quite early on. He was a pub-dweller, he travelled a lot, and through his radio work was in contact with many talkative celebs: actors, musicians, singers as well as literary types. For a quick-off-the-mark chronicler, there might have been rich pickings.

Certainly, MacNeice himself would not have objected to a prompt post-mortem. In 1940, anticipating a biography, he sent his friend and mentor E.R. Dodds a list of what he called 'the best authorities' on his life so far, 'though each only from a certain angle'. He was thirty-three at the time and half-joking but a year earlier he had begun work on an autobiography, *The Strings Are False*. He had also recently won fame with *Autumn Journal*, which – for all its documentary vividness – is hugely self-absorbed.

The letter to Dodds was sent in wartime, when everybody was writing a will, but with MacNeice the disposition to self-scrutiny ran deep. He called it his 'personal fixation' and from time to time he tried to shake it off, or rise above it, but 'the pulse keeps thrumming.' 'None of our hearts are pure,' he would lament, his grammar gone, 'We always have mixed motives.' *Autumn Sequel* (1954) is tirelessly preoccupied with the day-to-day climate shifts of the MacNeice interior, and even in his oblique and metaphoric pieces we can usually detect an underlying – and sometimes undermining – interrogation of the Self: what kind of human being should I/could I be? How much, if any, virtue has my self-questioning laid waste? Is the quest for honesty in truth – in all honesty – a cover-up for never quite knowing what to do? But then 'if you analyse it, public-mindedness itself can be a form of escapism,' can it not? *The Strings Are False*, we notice, opens with the words: 'So what?' We also notice that that book was shortly set aside, and never finished.

And perhaps this authoritative fretfulness has been part of the problem for would-be MacNeice biographers: they may have felt that the territory had already been well mapped by its original proprietor. They may also have feared, from consulting the one or two memoirs put out by MacNeice's acquaintances, that there was too daunting a gap between MacNeice the poet and MacNeice 'as we remember him'. Those who had social dealings with MacNeice tended to scratch their heads and remember nothing very much. They spoke of him as a 'dark horse' and recalled his lack of warmth, his silences, his impenetrable moods. He was forever in the pub, they'd say, but not really *of* the pub. He kept himself not just to himself but for himself. For, that's to say, the poems.

It has also been observed, though, that his aloofness in fact carried over into the way he proceeded as a poet; he was always to one side of the fashionable drift – he was of the swim, it might be said, but never in it. Thus he was a Sitwellian sparkler in the 1920s but, being Irish and dark-visioned, could never settle for the merely jewelled phrase. At Oxford he was an apprentice dandy but too 'irredeemably heterosexual' (in the words of his schoolfriend Anthony Blunt) to fully enjoy the jokes that mattered. In the 1930s, he tried hard to turn himself into a socially-conscious poet but was too riven by self-doubt, by the awareness that 'If it were not for Lit. Hum. I might be climbing/A ladder with a hod.' Post-war, he wanted to be a fire-tongued sage and seer, like his BBC colleague Dylan Thomas. MacNeice worshipped Thomas and did not, we trust, live to read Dylan's description of his work as 'thin and conventionally-minded, lacking imagination and not sound in the ear'.

MacNeice may not have known for certain that this was how Thomas rated him (Thomas also described MacNeice as 'a very good chap') but he probably sensed it, and may not have disagreed. Being

MacNeice, he may have feared that hard work – and how he worked:
600 pages of close-packed *Collected Poems*, numerous now unreadable
verse-plays – could never compensate for an essential absence in his
make-up, for a lack of that creative magic which poets like Dylan
Thomas assumed that they were full of, head to toe. MacNeice did not
know that he would die of pneumonia at fifty-five, but his last poems
are his best: in them, laborious self-scrutiny has hardened into horrified
self-knowledge. When MacNeice assembled what turned out to be his
final book, *The Burning Perch*, he was 'taken aback', he said, by the 'fear
and resentment' it evinced, 'by the high proportion of sombre pieces,
ranging from bleak observation to thumbnail nightmares . . . I am not
sure why this should be so.' He may not have been sure, but he had a
pretty good idea. After a lifetime of asking himself large, convoluted
questions, he was starting to come up with a few crisp replies.

Bad news, then, for biography, or so it may have seemed. What
to do with a writer who knew himself too well? Another reason for
the delay in preparing a MacNeice Life might be deduced from Jon
Stallworthy's Introduction to the book we are now offered:

> In 1976, as an editor of the Clarendon Press, it was my good fortune
> to oversee the publication of Professor E.R. Dodds's autobiogra-
> phy, *Missing Persons*. Acquaintance ripened into friendship when he
> found me a house close to his own in the Oxfordshire village of Old
> Marston. Over many midnight glasses of Irish whiskey, we spoke
> of the famous friends of his 'missing persons' (his own past selves)
> – Yeats, Eliot, Auden and MacNeice. The last and least-known
> of these was closest to his heart: he had given MacNeice his first
> job and after a lifetime's friendship had, as his Literary Executor,
> edited his 'unfinished autobiography' *The Strings Are False*, and his
> *Collected Poems*. He was concerned that MacNeice's reputation still
> bobbed – as it seemed to him unfairly – in the wake of Auden's and,
> concluding that it would take a biography to initiate a revaluation,
> invited me to write one. I declined, regretfully, unable to imagine
> myself having time to write a prose book while publishing books
> by other people.

After Dodd's death in 1979, Stallworthy was approached again – this
time by the OUP's Dan Davin, another of MacNeice's friends, and

Dodds's successor as literary executor. 'Having by then exchanged a publisher's office for a professor's, I accepted and, with Dodds's ghostly presence at my elbow, went back to his editions of the *Collected Poems* and *The Strings Are False*.'

The mention of Dodds's 'ghostly presence' is surely meant to be remarked on. Dodds was indeed an industrious executor. He edited the works; he monitored the fame; he sifted the biographical remains. He knew MacNeice for many years, but 'from a certain angle' – the angle of a father-figure whom the poet looked up to and was keen not to disappoint. His best memories of MacNeice were of the early 1930s, when he appointed the poet to his first job as a Classics lecturer at Birmingham University. MacNeice was just down from Oxford, newly married, and writing his first poetry and fiction. Dodds and his wife adopted the young couple and rejoiced in MacNeice's 'rich flow of fun and fantasy, the mercurial gaiety, the warm vitality and love of life which endeared him to the friends of his early days'. Dodds introduced MacNeice to Auden, put him in touch with Eliot at Faber, accompanied him to Ireland to take tea with Yeats. When MacNeice's first wife ran off with an American footballer, it was the Doddses who knew what to say. There were, though, other, later angles on the poet's life, and Dodds would have encountered these in the course of his commemorative labours.

Even so, says Stallworthy, 'no father could have done more for his son's memory.' And one of the things Dodds did, of course, was to ask Stallworthy to write MacNeice's Life. In 1976, when the first approach was made, Stallworthy had just published a conscientious and determinedly well-mannered life of Wilfred Owen. Dodds may also have recalled that MacNeice, just six months before he died, reviewed an earlier Stallworthy book on Yeats, describing its approach as 'on the whole, perhaps, just a shade too reverential (but that is a good fault)'. Dodds understandably wanted a biography that would honour his own warm feelings for MacNeice, and that would direct posterity towards those areas of the poet's experience which seemed to him to matter most.

If we suspect that Louis MacNeice is not altogether Stallworthy's kind of chap, there is no doubting the biographer's regard for Dodds. This *Louis MacNeice* is dedicated to the memory of Dodds – 'an

Irishman, a Poet and a Scholar, who knew more about all this than I do' – and Stallworthy's narrative is studded with gratuitous tributes to 'this most temperate of men'. We hear of Dodds's 'high intelligence', his 'rock-like integrity' (also his 'granite-like integrity'), his 'moral courage', his 'passionate commitment to teaching and the pastoral care of his students'. More than once we get the feeling that Stallworthy would rather be writing about Dodds. On that subject his reverential disposition would have been able to let rip.

This does not mean that what we have here is a whitewash, or a hush-up. The facts of MacNeice's often ramshackle private life are presented in exhaustive detail: names are named. What we do get is a tendency to replicate, in biography, something of the 'steadying influence' that Dodds applied in life. There is a wish to smarten MacNeice up a bit, to cut down on his drinking (which, during his BBC years, became something of a legend), to make his black moods more creatively purposeful, his love affairs more considered and considerate than perhaps they were. MacNeice's twenty years of writing for radio are sometimes perceived as having wrecked his talent, directing him towards drawn-out, pretentious allegories when his true gift was for delighting in the small, surprising detail. And the BBC milieu of the early Fifties, with all its beery self-importance, has been blamed for pitching this donnish introvert into some pretty noisy company. Stallworthy does not really penetrate this BBC ante-world of pubs and clubs, this salaried suburb of Fitzrovia. He would much rather lead us through the plot of *The Dark Tower* than prop up the bar with Reggie Smith. For this it's hard to blame him.

Still, perhaps something is missed here that might have accounted for the deep 'resentments' of MacNeice's final phase, the sense we get from his last poems of lost time and irremediable error. There is an essay by Geoffrey Grigson on MacNeice, in which this is said: 'He could be embarrassingly silent. A conversation came to a halt. Who was going to break the silence and bridge the silent interruption? His lack of usual reticence, too, could be sudden, startling and improbable, rather like his appearance, dark, handsome, tall, well-dressed; then, looked at more closely, almost squalid.' 'Squalid' seems a bit extreme. What is Grigson hinting at? He goes on to reveal that MacNeice 'had, as a rule, the dirtiest of fingernails' and that his dog 'bent slowly and gracefully around the corners of tables and chairs, but goodness, how dirty that Betsy was underneath, what brown matted curls she had, and how she stank!' Could this be *all* he meant by 'squalid'? Stallworthy does not say, or ask. When he comes to paraphrase the Grigson essay, only the dog's dirt gets a mention: 'Grigson was intrigued by the contradiction of the sceptical romantic (so well matched by the stinking elegance of his attendant borzoi), the melancholy and the wit, the confidence and the reticence. Much though he liked MacNeice, he never felt he knew him.' This may seem to be a smallish smoothing-over but it does typify Stallworthy's meliorative bent. And I'd still quite like to know more about that 'squalid'.

If the Dodds influence has been sanitising, it has also – on the whole – been shrewd. Dodds reckoned that MacNeice was all his life haunted by certain 'images, incidents and motifs' to do with his strange Irish childhood and that the key to his personality was to be found not in the English public schools he was sent to from the age of ten, nor in the literary and political influences that bore in on him during the Thirties and thereafter, nor in the BBC. The real shaping of MacNeice, as the poet himself so often and so mournfully acknowledged, was accomplished at the age of five, when he saw his mother removed to an asylum, leaving him in the care of a sorrowingly prayerful father ('intoning away, communing with God') and a busily puritanical housekeeper. His mother's 'agitated melancholia' had struck suddenly, following a hysterectomy (for which MacNeice contrived to take the blame). 'Almost overnight', she changed from 'the mainstay of the household – serene and comforting, the very essence of stability – into someone who was deeply unhappy and no longer able to make decisions'. MacNeice's last 'memory-picture' of his mother was of her 'walking up and down the garden path in tears' just before her removal to hospital. She died two years later of tuberculosis.

'When I was five the black dreams came/Nothing after was quite the same,' he wrote in his poem 'Autobiography', and his biographer believes him, as Dodds did. The early chapters of Stallworthy's book, from the Irish rectory garden (MacNeice's father was a Church of Ireland vicar) through to the collapse of the Birmingham idyll, are by far the strongest. When MacNeice's first wife abandoned him (and their one-year-old child), the old wound was re-opened. When it healed over, he was set in the ways of dispirited self-scrutiny. From then on, the 'rich flow of fun and fantasy, the mercurial gaiety' would be glimpsed but intermittently, or after a few drinks. And it would be twenty years before he would come close to recapturing the lyric forcefulness of his best poems of the Thirties. When he joined the BBC in 1940, at the age of thirty-three, he spoke of his past life as 'dead'. He craved anonymity, he wanted to be one of a crowd, one of the boys. As for his poetry: it may as well do something useful. He wrote propaganda and developed a taste for mass-communication, and for 'collaborative' creativity. By the end of the war, he was well prepared for the lofty solemnities of radio verse drama, for the Trials of Everyman, the Quest for the Dark Tower:

> Such was our aim
> But aims too often languish and instead
> We hack and hack. What ought to soar and flame
> Shies at its take-off, all our kites collapse,
> Our spirit leaks away . . .

Louis MacNeice: A Biography by Jon Stallworthy (Faber)

London Review of Books, 1995

Edward Upward: It's No Joke

In the title story of Edward Upward's new collection, a forgotten Marxist author of the 1930s dreams that he is approached by a present-day admirer, a 'lecturer at a Yorkshire polytechnic'. At first Stephen Highwood is suspicious. He doesn't expect people to know who he is. His books have long been out of print and are not to be found in public libraries. In surveys of modern literature, his name barely rates a mention. 'Are you some kind of high-class tout?' he asks. 'Which books of mine have you read?'

But this dream fan is for real, or so it seems, and the two of them fall to discussing the reasons for Highwood's neglect. The reasons, they agree, are obvious: because of his unflinching left-wing views, Highwood has been evil-eyed by 'dominant opinion in Establishment circles'. 'There was a time,' the fan suggests, 'when it would have been quite in order to refer to your work dismissively or disapprovingly but that time has passed. They've decided now that you are to be obliterated permanently.' Highwood accepts this analysis, but adds: 'I don't doubt that the people who would like to obliterate me would like even more to obliterate the political ideas I have supported in my writings.'

This sour-smug note can be heard throughout the linked stories of *An Unmentionable Man*. Time and again, Highwood is presented as a figure of adamantine integrity who has paid a high price for his faith. When publishers take him to lunch and offer to sex up his image – to 'put an end for ever to the idea people unfortunately have that you are boringly old-fashioned and over-serious' – he recoils with indignation. 'You are really little better than prostitutes,' he cries.

On the other hand, he is by no means indifferent to the trappings of literary success. All the evidence suggests that he has monitored the downward curve of his career with zealous rage. Meeting, in his dream, a contemporary who now earns his crust by penning self-serving memoirs of the Thirties, Highwood says to him: 'I may not have read every article you've written or television talk you've given about the Thirties, but I have read and heard more than a few, and there wasn't one that didn't completely ignore me.'

At moments like this, we might be tempted to diagnose a straight-forward case of back-number paranoia. For Highwood read Upward, and so on. Upward is now in his nineties and, in spite of these homageful reissues by Enitharmon, his work has in recent years been given a rough ride. Nowadays, by those readers who know of him, he is likely to be thought of as a once-vaunted star of Thirties legend who disappeared into Marxist politics and never quite returned – or, rather, who did return but who had in the meantime transmuted from vivacious satirist to plodding bore.

Upward's major work, *A Spiral Ascent*, came out in three parts between 1962 and 1977, breaking a silence that had lasted since the early Forties, when he joined the Communist Party (he left it in 1948). The trilogy presents the saga of its artist-hero's joining and leaving of the Party and ends with him solemnly recommitting himself to the 'poetic life' – by which he means the writing of a political literature that will put art first and politics a tenaciously close second. In terms of Upward's own career, we are seemingly meant to value the trilogy as the outcome of a long, brave effort to negotiate a truce between two vital but conflicting loyalties: the author's still-unwavering Marxism and his deep-seated notion of himself as a free-range creative spirit.

On publication of Parts One and Two, *A Spiral Ascent* was widely scorned by reviewers. Like Stephen Highwood, it was found to be 'boringly old-fashioned and over-serious'. Even Samuel Hynes called it 'arid, unimaginative and unreadable'. And Upward had trouble finding a publisher for the third section. The overall suggestion was that his laborious rephrasings of the Art v. Politics dilemmas of his youth had added nothing much to what had already been chewed over in numerous memoirs and studies of the Thirties. Nothing, that

is, except an insistence that those dilemmas were still very much alive
– or ought to be.

By the Sixties, when the trilogy started to appear, there was an
impatience with conflicts that could not easily be solved. There was
a weariness, also, with big talk about 'commitment': a topic of earnest
discussion during the middle to late Fifties. And the Thirties, though
popular as a source of anecdote, were mainly thought of with fond
condescension. Auden and Spender had lashed themselves with twigs
and been forgiven, and their 'politics' had come to be viewed as
something of a pose – an interesting pose, with some painful and
marvellous offshoots, but in essence a bit silly.

With Upward, though, there was no sense that he even knew that
this was how some people spoke about the epoch that had shaped
him. In *A Spiral Ascent* we find no god-that-failed shamefacedness.
As Upward saw things, the failure of the Thirties was in those who
had merely pretended to believe. His earnest, striving characters make
mistakes from time to time. They can be too trusting and naive, too
purist in their attachment to the sacred texts. But not one of them is
allowed even the tiniest of self-deprecating chuckles. It was perhaps
this absence rather than the menace of its politics that led critics to
'obliterate' his book.

And yet Upward, when he started out, was highly regarded as a joker.
In Christopher Isherwood's *Lions and Shadows*, he appears as 'Allen
Chalmers', the brilliantly mischievous co-inventor of Mortmere, 'a
sort of anarchist paradise in which all accepted moral and social values
are turned upside down'. Isherwood and Upward went to the same
school, Repton, then to Cambridge, and in both places formed an
alliance against what they called 'the poshocracy'. Teachers, vicars,
hearties, dons: all of these feature in the Mortmere tales as lunatic
grotesques, representative of privilege and authority gone mad. The
idea, said Isherwood, was to induce in the reader sensations of 'disgust'.
He planned one day to publish the tales in a very limited edition, 'as
a volume containing oil paintings, brasses, intaglios, pressed flowers,
mirrors and harmless bombs to emphasise points in the story'. The
dialogue would be spoken by a concealed gramophone and the pages
'would smell, according to their subject-matter, of grave-clothes,
manure or expensive scent'.

The Mortmere stories are of interest now chiefly as documents, although they do have some nice inspirations: the Rev Casimir Welken, for example, who breeds angels in his belfry. And it is easy enough to see why they made their adolescent readership sit up. As well as exhibiting a tense familiarity with the habits of the English upper-middle class – the village fête, the rectory tea party, 'the damp beehive in the summer-house' – they were themselves impeccably well-bred: Joyce, Kafka, Baudelaire, a dash of Conan Doyle. In the late Twenties these were fashionable names. Best of all, though, the stories were so smuttily school-boyish: in those days, saying rude words in front of nanny took a lot of nerve. Shit features quite a lot in Mortmere – as it does, curiously enough, in *An Unmentionable Man*.

When samples of Mortmere reached Oxford, the court of Auden was spellbound. Stephen Spender later on recalled that 'just as Auden seemed to us the highest peak within the range of our humble vision from the Oxford valleys, for Auden there was another peak, namely Isherwood, whilst for Isherwood there was a still further peak, Chalmers.' And much the same message reached John Lehmann, whose Hogarth Press would eventually publish Upward's first novel: 'I heard with the tremor of excitement that an entomologist feels at the news of an unknown butterfly sighted in the depths of the forest, that behind Auden and Spender and Isherwood stood the even more legendary figure of . . . Edward Upward.'

For Upward, this was quite a load to carry, and it was all the heavier perhaps because he could not be sure of anyone's praise except Isherwood's. Only Isherwood knew who, in these Mortmere tales, had written what. In later years, Isherwood would say that Mortmere mattered more to Upward than it did to him but maybe all he meant by this was that Upward always took things more solemnly than he did. Or did he mean that Upward's attachment to these boyish fantasies was more unhealthily neurotic than his own? In the third part of *A Spiral Ascent*, Upward equips his schoolboy-narrator Alan Sebrill with a Mortmere-like dream-realm he can retreat to when he's feeling glum, which is quite often. The dream-realm is called Eitna ('Auntie' spelled backwards) and in it terrible Old Testament-style punishments are visited on 'men of evil character' – all of whom are based on

Sebrill's various school-foes, boys as well as teachers. As described in the trilogy, Eitna was by no means played for laughs.

It is not until Sebrill teams up with his friend Richard Marple (who 'did not dislike the poshocracy quite as deeply' as he did) that the fun and games begin. 'We began to write stories together with titles such as *The Leviathan of the Urinals, The Horror in the Tower* and *The Loathly Succubus* . . . Our intention was to make these stories as bluntly and ludicrously disgusting as we could: obscene farce was our answer to the kind of namby-pamby delicately indelicate pseudo-pornography . . . which was fashionable with some members of the poshocracy.'

This may have been Sebrill/Upward's intention but the flighty Isherwood had no such worthy aims. For him the cultivation of Disgust was just a giggle, an escape from the boredom of institutional life and from a fear of his own 'puritan priggishness'. Isherwood was the nimble pasticheur, Upward the glowering introvert. For a time, the two supplied each other with useful ammunition – Isherwood was witty, Upward was well-read – but they were fighting very different wars. Upward envied Isherwood's cabaret slickness of expression; Isherwood was in awe of Upward's ideological vehemence. The liaison could not last.

Indeed it was the coming war against Fascism that broke up their partnership. For Upward, the poshocracy was a horrific foreshadowing of Fascism, and he would find it necessary to refocus and intensify his opposition. For Isherwood, war was an imminent romance, a Test that he already knew he'd fail. 'I wonder how I should have reacted to the preaching of an English Fascist leader clever enough to serve up his "message" in a suitably disguised and palatable form?' he asked in *Lions and Shadows*. 'He would have converted me, I think, inside half an hour – provided always that Chalmers hadn't been there to interfere.'

Upward's first novel, *Journey to the Border*, appeared in 1938, the same year as *Lions and Shadows*: in other words, late in the day. By 1938, Isherwood had published three novels, including *Mr Norris Changes Trains*, and had probably already written his Berlin stories. For him, Mortmere was the stuff of coolly amused reminiscence. It had served a purpose: traces of it can be found in Auden's *The Orators* (1933) and in the Auden-Isherwood verse-play, *The Dog beneath the*

Skin (1935). By the time of Upward's 'long-awaited' fictional début, the joke was all used up.

But for Upward it had never been a joke. This much was made clear by *Journey to the Border*'s fervid mix of Mortmere-style fantasy with firm-jawed political resolve. The book's narrator is in the process of becoming as mad as the mad characters he dreams about. His sanity is imperilled by a surfeit of Mortmerian hallucinations. In the end he saves himself by resolving to quit the murky enticements of literary fantasy in favour of the healthy, useful comradeship offered to him by the Internationalist Workers' Movement: 'His decision to join it would not make life easier for him. But at least he would have come down to earth, out of the cloud of his irresponsible fantasies; would have begun to live. He had already begun.'

After Cambridge, while Auden and Isherwood were turning into celebrities, Upward worked quietly as a schoolmaster, distributed leaflets for the Party, and kept out of the literary swim. His one-time admirers tended to avoid him; he was a reproachful presence, a reminder to the lads of what political commitment really meant. Also, he was not part of the homosexual scene. He may even have thought queers were 'decadent'. Apart from *Journey to the Border*, he published nothing much until 1948, the year in which he left the Party because of its 'expedient' support for Attlee's post-war 'socialist reforms'. And in 1948, the best he could come up with was yet another slice of Mortmere. 'The Railway Accident' (written in 1928) appeared under the name 'Allen Chalmers', with a note by Isherwood explaining that 'Chalmers' hated his own story and believed that 'the kind of literature which makes a dilettante cult of violence, sadism, bestiality and sexual acrobatics is peculiarly offensive and subversive in an age such as ours – an age which has witnessed the practically applied bestiality of Belsen and Dachau.'

Even so, Chalmers/Upward allowed the story to be published, and it was reissued, under Upward's name, in 1969 – complete with Isherwood's disclaimer. It also appears in this comprehensive new collection of *The Mortmere Stories*. Mortmere, it seems, will not let Upward go. Or is it the other way around? In *An Unmentionable Man*, there are some weird Mortmere-like set-pieces, and in his use of a dream-structure for his tales, Upward does seem to be harking back to his old manner. But the fantasy-flights come across as effortful, interrupting the main thrust, which – as in the trilogy – is earnestly political and argumentative. And in any case, the committee-meeting prose is always likely to clog up the works. Without an Isherwood at his elbow, Upward can't help keeping the straight face he was born with.

An Unmentionable Man and *Journey to the Border* by Edward Upward (Enitharmon)

The Mortmere Stories by Christopher Isherwood and Edward Upward (Enitharmon)

London Review of Books, 1995

R. S. Thomas – Frown by Frown

R.S. Thomas's four autobiographies (four memoir-essays, really) were written in Welsh, and the most substantial of the four – first published in Wales a dozen years ago – was titled *Neb*, which means 'nobody': as in 'a nobody' or 'nobody very special'. And this fits with our uncertain view of Thomas these past four decades. Has this poet been too humble? Or has he been too proud? Is he to be admired for self-effacement or chastised for self-absorption? Over the years, Thomas has asked himself such questions many times, and his replies have been as non-definite as ours.

According to Thomas's eccentric but industrious biographer, Justin Wintle, a complete tally of the R.S. Thomas oeuvre would add up to some 1,200 poems, not all of which appear in his 500-page *Collected Poems*. These figures come as a surprise. Thomas, after all, has never been thought of as abundant. Nor is he. The truth is that for long stretches – and the work does divide neatly into stretches – he has written the same poem over again, several times. First there were the startlingly sour Prytherch poems – still for me the ones that matter most – then the Welsh Nationalist phase, then the deus absconditus prayer-bout, then the vague musings about God as cosmic scientist, then the poems inspired by paintings, and so on. The drift throughout has been away from the carefully wrought individual poem towards a kind of open-ended ruminative jotting.

Thus, faced with this huge *Collected Poems*, we are hard pressed to name single Thomas poems that succeed as others of his don't. There are very few star items. The impact is by way of dogged, frown by frown, or prayer by prayer, accumulation. The work comes at us in clumps. And in this we can perhaps identify a genuine effacement of the self. As with their author, each poem is proffered as a nothing very special, a not quite. Spare, colourless and repetitious, Thomas's work has made up for its lack of vigour by the unembarrassed steadiness with which it focuses on this or that obsession, so long as the obsession lasts. Again just like the author, as self-presented in these memoirs, here is an art that simply goes about its business, nothing fancy. The business has been humble, sometimes dismal, often futile, but – as Thomas might in certain moods retort – somebody (a nobody-somebody) had to do it.

But then again, perhaps somebody didn't have to do it. Thomas's attitude to his own verse-making, as to several other aspects of his life and personality, and to most aspects of the modern world, has rarely been far from the reproving. This much we can gather from the verse, but there is a powerful strain of misanthropy in these curt and candid memoirs, especially in those composed in the third person, with Thomas referred to as 'R.S.' or 'the rector' or 'the vicar'. If these essays were fictions, we would surely reproach the author for his ungenerous, and superficial, treatment of the hero. Does the poor rector have to be so dreary and resentful, we might ask, and so hard on himself?

For R.S. Thomas, the poetry of R.S. Thomas has never been able to shape up to requirements, could never quite be work that he might publicly take pride in. After all, it is 'in English', and Thomas has time and again insisted that all Welshmen worthy of the name should write in Welsh. His own inability to do so (he has tried, he says, and failed) has been for him a constant discomfiture – a source, sometimes, of shame. And, sure enough, we can detect a grudgingness in his deployment of the English tongue, the tongue – as he would say – of his political oppressor.

And yet this grudgingness, we English will contend, has served the poet pretty well. The bare simplicity of Thomas's poetic speech has, we'll affirm, been one of his great strengths. For him, though, 'bare and simple' has been as close as he could get, in English, to honouring his anti-Englishness. Even the faintest tremor of luxuriance might give the folks back home the wrong idea: the idea that here is a writer who relishes linguistic treachery. Thus Thomas gives his English foe the minimum, and we applaud. We say: if only D. Thomas had been similarly grudging now and then! But D.T. was, of course, South Wales. The South, as viewed by R.S. and his allies in the North, has long ago, and irredeemably, sold out to English money and machines.

Over the years, Thomas's language guilts have had a central, undermining influence on his career – or, rather, his careers: as poet, as Welshman and as priest. In poetry-career terms, certainly, he has staked out a kind of no man's land, or call it a 'nobody's land': he has felt obliged, it seems, to stand aloof from his 'in English' contemporaries, as if he might be tainted, further tainted, by their anthology-companionship, their co-poets' appreciation of his plight. He is talked of as frosty and austere. And only rarely has he felt able to indulge the full range of his responsiveness to the 'in English' poetry of the past. Usually, when he has revealed links to the English past, there has been some Christian-vicar or nature-study slant: he has edited selections from Wordsworth and George Herbert and compiled a *Penguin Book of Religious Verse*. Out of church, he has kept fairly silent, confining his enthusiasms to co-Celts like Yeats and MacDiarmid and to the odd American, like Wallace Stevens. Thomas's favourite Larkin poem, he says, is 'Faith Healing'. (Larkin, of course, referred to Thomas as 'Arse' or 'Arsewipe'. The two of them met once, and Thomas – said Larkin – 'stood there without moving or speaking: he seems pretty hard going. Not noticeably Welsh, which is one comfort.')

In politics, although Thomas has been vehement in his attacks on the loathed English, he has never quite won over the most hardline of his nationalist comrades. OK, some of these will say, he has to write his poetry in English, but why has he not rejected all those English prizes, in particular the Queen's Medal? Why has he seemed to nurture his English reputation with appearances on radio and TV, and in English periodicals? Why, when he speaks English, does he sound so thoroughly non-Welsh? Why did he choose to educate his son at English schools? And why, if the Welsh language means so much to him, has he not spent more time translating the great English poets into Welsh – or, come to that, the great Welsh poets into English?

Thomas has, of course, been well aware of such critiques –
sometimes he has levelled them against himself. The trouble is
that, although Thomas loves Wales and its language, he finds it
hard to scrape up much affection for the Welsh. His anti-English
ravings of the late Sixties, early Seventies were presumably sincere
but they always sounded a bit forced and shrill – not least because, as
Thomas saw it, the Welsh themselves bore a large slice of the blame
for their own subjugation:

> I have walked the shore
> For an hour and seen the English
> Scavenging among the remains
> Of our culture, covering the sand
> Like the tide and, with the roughness
> Of the tide, elbowing our language
> Into the grave that we have dug for it.

'That we have dug for it'. Is it the 'we' more than the 'they' that angers
Thomas? From Prytherch onwards, he has found it hard to conceal his
contempt for Welsh stupidity and feebleness, as evidenced by most of
his parishioners. But is it their unculturedness that irks him rather than
their political inertia? After all, the Prytherchs rarely showed up at his
church, and they knew nothing of George Herbert. In later years, the
rustics who used to stare blankly at their mountain livestock can be
found staring blankly at TV, or listening to 'pop'. In several of his
poems, and repeatedly in his memoirs, Thomas acknowledges his
own 'affectedness' and bookishness, and tries his best to warm to
other people. But these compatriots of his, whose souls are in his
charge, get on his nerves: they don't respond with sensitivity to the
glories of Welsh landscape, they allow themselves to be denatured by
a barbaric Anglo-US culture. Even if Thomas did write his poems
in Welsh, who would read them? How, in truth, can such sunken
creatures be expected to 'Rise up, you Welsh!' Most days Thomas
would rather go bird-watching or whisper imprecations to an absent
God than attempt to stir such oafs into the 'direct action' called for by
the nationalist cause. Not that Thomas himself altogether approves of
the bombing of EIIR postboxes: after all, he is a pacifist from way

back – a Welsh Nationalist pacifist. It's not easy being R.S. Thomas, as he keeps reminding us.

Really, though, it's other people he can't stand. Reflecting on his often solitary boyhood, Thomas writes in *Neb*:

> He was yet to discover Maeterlinck's story, describing how, while descending from a mountain in the Alps, he saw below him a glorious valley under the summer sun. And to crown everything, there was a crowd of people out in the fields harvesting the hay. But as he came within earshot of the people, he found that they were quarrelling amongst themselves, using the dirtiest and most unseemly language. An extremely relevant parable, as the boy later learned.

Thomas's memoirs are full of types – yokel types, squire types, country-cottage types, low-church types and so on – but there are hardly any individuals. When individuals do appear they tend to represent a type. Thomas admits that he was never a greatly 'distinguished' parish priest. He visited the sick, went through the Sunday motions, had scant patience with the ritual and abhorred the hymns. He knew himself to be disliked by many of his flock – or flocks, since he moved churches several times, ostensibly in search of a Welsh-speaking parish but usually to suit his personal convenience: as he has pointed out, his moves kept edging him closer and closer to the Llyn peninsula, where he grew up and where he now lives in retirement. Thomas, though, seems to have rather thrived on his unpopularity: why else would he paint his church pews black, drive slowly in the middle of the road, tick off locals he caught ordering their groceries in English? Wintle's biography is not short of spooky-vicar anecdotes, and we often get the feeling that for Thomas the only good church is an empty one.

Thomas was, it seems, attached to his merchant-sailor father, who became deaf in old age (Wintle acutely makes a link between the boy Thomas attempting to talk to his deaf father and Thomas the priest attempting to 'get through' to God), but the parent who really interests him is his mother: an anxious, over-bearing shrew, as he describes her. In fact, Mother comes in for several lashes, both in the memoirs and in certain of the poems: she killed her sailor husband's sense of romance, she failed to teach her son Welsh and then sent him to theological college for reasons more to do with status and money than with faith. She is to blame, finally, for Thomas's 'in English' poems and for his probably wrong choice of a career. As a boy, even as a youngish man, Thomas seems to have been scared of her. When, at the end of her life, she could no longer take care of herself, Thomas refused to take her in. He tells us this unblinkingly, as if he's sure that we will understand.

On the whole, though, we have to search long and hard here for symptoms of soft-heartedness. Thomas speaks fairly coldly of his only son and says nothing much about his wife, to whom he was married for some fifty years. He once addressed a poem to this wife, telling her

> because time
> is always so short, you must go by
> now without mention, as unknown
> to the future as to
> the past, with one man's
> eyes resting on you
> in the interval of his concern.

In the memoirs, there are few such intervals. Indeed, there is one somewhat chilling sequence when Mrs Thomas, a painter by profession, falls seriously ill and loses her sight. Her husband writes:

> While she was in hospital in London, in order to raise her spirits and give her something to look forward to, R.S. arranged a vacation for both of them in Mallorca in October 1972. They went under the auspices of a company that arranged bird-watching holidays, and the two had to take a night-flight from Heathrow. What a new experience it was to look down on the Continent at night through the small window of the aeroplane!

What do we make of a wordsmith, Welsh or English, who can speak at such a time of 'looking forward' to a bird-watching holiday, who can tell of what a thrill it was to peer down at the Continent by night? The trip to Mallorca is described in full by Thomas, with acerbic side-reflections on the Spaniards' bird-threatening use of pesticides, but we wait in vain for news of his sightless wife's reaction to her treat.

In fact, the strongest pages of these memoirs are those that have to do with Thomas's bird-watching. This really is a passion – and once again Wintle seems on the mark when he connects Thomas on the look-out for rare birds with Thomas the God-seeker on his knees. In each case, it is a long and passive quest, not always worth it, but for Thomas patience and faith can come to seem like virtues in themselves. Best of all, though, watching out for God and praying for just one glimpse of a tawny owl are each of them deeply solitary undertakings: no craven Welshmen, no all-conquering tourists, no TV, no pop, no wife, no child, no mother, no poems to be written in a foreign tongue. On bird-watch or on God-watch, true happiness for Thomas is when he can say, with all his heart: 'Nobody's here.'

Justin Wintle's biography was not authorised by Thomas: indeed large chunks of it are given over to accounts of Wintle's rebuffed overtures. Wintle did not expect Thomas to co-operate, but – being a bouncy kind of guy – he was not to be put off. And this opposition of temperaments does give his book a plot: the upbeat, with-it, 'seven-eighths English' biographer pitted against the unworldly Welsh curmudgeon. Friction ensues (at any rate in Wintle's head) and by the end there is a truce, with Wintle settling for liking the poems far better than he likes the poet. And, as I've said, he comes up with some worthwhile insights. He does have the habit, though, of over-exhibiting his 'intellectual' credentials. If the topic is religious doubt, say, we can be sure that Wintle will soon be zapping us with five pages of A-Level rundown on the 'background'. Thus we get, repeatedly, this kind of thing: 'Hume may be regarded as the father of philosophical atheism. His assault on religion was twofold. First he sought to show that . . .' Also, running through the book, there is a too determined jokiness, an insistent watch-my-speed: 'This is not an address to Chloe or Amaryllis in the shade (or, these days, the shed).' Still, Wintle has done a great deal of research and trudged more than a few Welsh mountainsides, and on the whole his book is far more entertaining than might readily have been expected, given its dour subject. Certainly in terms of readability, *Furious Interiors* has the edge on Thomas's own telling of the Thomas life. But then Thomas, we feel pretty sure, would not at all object to this disparagement, however much he might object to Wintle's book.

Autobiographies by R.S. Thomas (Dent)

Furious Interiors: Wales, R.S. Thomas and God by Justin Wintle (HarperCollins)

Collected Poems 1945–90 by R.S. Thomas (Phoenix)

London Review of Books, 1997

3

'These are Damned Times': Two Victorians

Tennyson: Two Lives

October, 1992, was the centenary of Tennyson's death, and in England the anniversary was greeted with a nonchalance that would have astounded his Victorian admirers. There was no ten-gun salute at Buckingham Palace, no minute's silence in the House of Lords. Nationwide, the tributes amounted to not much more than a few localized murmurs of respect. There was a small flurry of activity in academia – *Tennyson and the Text, Tennyson: Seven Essays* – and the *Times Literary Supplement* came through with a cover picture and a two-page spread on which twelve current literary figures offered short assessments of Tennyson's 'achievement and influence' in the twentieth century. The *TLS* feature was, I believe, the nearest anybody got to formal eulogy, but even this could hardly be thought of as full-hearted. 'I grew up on "The Lady of Shalott" and "Morte d'Arthur,"' said A. S. Byatt. Gavin Ewart said, 'I had Tennyson, willy-nilly, when I was nine or so, at my prep school.' Each spoke as if in mitigation: Tennyson was fed to them when they were too young to resist. Others on the *TLS* panel also told sad tales of Tennyson abuse. Most of the twelve seemed ready to rank Tennyson as one of the great English poets; few, though, were able to sing his praises straightforwardly, without some foot-shuffling parenthesis. A weakness for Tennyson still needs to be accounted for, explained.

Two recent biographies, both called *Tennyson* – one by Michael Thorn and the other by Peter Levi – were presumably commissioned with the centenary in mind. Thorn's effort is competent but full of those pat linkages which are such a feature of routine biographese

('Tennyson's mind was taken off his ghosts and irritations at the beginning of June by a visit from the vivacious Miss Gladstone'). Levi's is more showy and eccentric, and makes a parade of its author's command of the minutiae of Victorian intellectual life. A classical scholar and a former Professor of Poetry at Oxford, Levi sometimes sounds like a Monty Python caricature of the high-table don: Arthur Hallam's poetry, he says, 'is not negligible, being about as good as Moore's, intellectually stronger than much of Campbell's, and technically at least as able as Bishop Heber's, abler for example than Archbishop Trench's.'

Neither book has much to add, in the way of information, to Robert Bernard Martin's massive and elegantly written life, *Tennyson: The Unquiet Heart*, published in 1980. And in the way of critical perceptiveness neither is in the same league as Christopher Ricks's masterly study, *Tennyson*, which came out in 1972. Ricks and Martin between them rescued Tennyson from long years of neglect – neglect bordering on hostility – but even they could not achieve for him full reinstatement. For this, it seems, Tennyson still needs the passing years: nowadays we are inclined to measure a writer's standing by the length of the 'books about' section of his bibliography, and according to this reckoning the Thorn and Levi contributions can be seen as a good thing. There is – can we say? – a *need* for unnecessary volumes about Tennyson. In the *TLS* centenary issue, there was a review article on T. S. Eliot in which eighteen studies of the poet were discussed – a year's crop, so it seemed. Few of us will read these Eliot publications, but we like to know that they are there – that Eliot, by sheer weight of scholarly toil, is getting to be unassailably 'canonical', impossible to shift. After all, Eliot is our twentieth-century Great Poet. By comparison, Tennyson's centenary booty seemed niggardly, or hesitant – as if the powers that be were still making up their minds.

A hundred years ago, the death of Tennyson was regarded as a national calamity: a vital part of England, people felt, had breathed its last. And, as far as the status of poetry was concerned, it surely had. Since Tennyson, no poet has enjoyed his measure of celebrity, or been so admiringly identified with the so-called temper of his age.

In mid-Victorian England, the temper of the age was to deplore the temper of the age, and in this department Tennyson excelled. Yet his melancholia usually left room for spiritual manoeuvre – enough, anyway, to leave his readers feeling both lowered and uplifted:

> Sleep sweetly, tender heart, in peace:
> Sleep, holy spirit, blessèd soul,
> While the stars burn, the moons increase,
> And the great ages onward roll.
>
> Sleep till the end, true soul and sweet.
> Nothing comes to thee new or strange.
> Sleep full of rest from head to feet;
> Lie still, dry dust, secure of change.

In gratitude, they hailed him as their laureate, who could voice their deepest fears, their proudest boasts. One of the Victorians' proudest boasts was that they knew how to grapple with their deepest fears. Tennyson showed them the way.

Simply at the level of cash takings, Parnassus will never see his like again. For the larger part of an extremely long career – his first book came out in 1830 – the author of *In Memoriam* and *Idylls of the King* was a regular, and spectacular, best-seller, outstripping most fiction writers of his day. *Enoch Arden* sold 40,000 copies within weeks of publication and netted him £8,000 pounds – in 1865, huge money. (Once, when he read this work aloud, he begged his audience 'not to go into hysterics.') Near the end of his life, he was offered $50,000 for a lecture tour of the United States. For twelve lines on a Christmas card he could have asked a thousand guineas. His toenail clippings, he once reckoned, might do a brisk trade were he to put them up for sale.

He never needed to, any more than he needed to give lectures or write book reviews. Although his first two books were cruelly panned, his third scored a great success. He was made poet laureate at forty-one. On the proceeds of his verse, Tennyson acquired two mansions, and lived in them like a lord. But then he *was* a lord – made so in 1883, by Gladstone and Queen Victoria, who were his friends. He was also viewed by many as a god: his utterances were believed to be not of this world. Tourists would climb fences at his Isle of Wight retreat, hoping to see him eat his lunch. This was not a pretty sight, by some accounts, since Tennyson was rough-mannered, and at table he regularly downed two bottles of port. 'He did things which were just not done,' says Michael Thorn, who also speaks of the poet's 'utter lack of any sense of social decorum'. Levi is less reproving, on the whole, but even he can sound a bit sniffy on the subject of Tennyson's nicotine intake. For nine hours of every day, Tennyson could be found puffing on a 'small, blackened clay pipe'. According to one contemporary, he favoured the 'strongest and most stinking tobacco'.

Although Tennyson often seemed graceless in his ways, he was a gregarious spirit and was much in demand at social gatherings. At the height of his fame, he hobnobbed with aristocrats and high-up politicians. Queen Victoria admired his work and now and then summoned him to court. When, at dinner parties, his host asked him to read aloud from one of his new works, he usually complied, setting to with great stamina and powers of emphasis. And when he sallied forth on country walks he looked the part: the wide-awake hat, the flowing cloak, the straggly beard. And was not his un-English swarthiness a sign that he had issued from afar? He was also tall, and intriguingly short-sighted. When he ran into old acquaintances, he sometimes looked through them or asked who they were. This, too, could be taken as a guarantee of his inspired unworldliness. Both Levi and Thorn recount a famous and perhaps true story of Tennyson's introduction to James Russell Lowell. He asked Lowell, then America's Ambassador to England, 'Do you know anything about *Lowell*?'

Like several of our own celebrities, Tennyson pretended that he wanted to be left alone, yet monitored his fame with angry vigilance. He had grown used to adoration in his early twenties and could easily be thrown off track thereafter by even the mildest disparagements. 'Don't abuse my book,' he wrote to his candid and usually admiring friend Edward FitzGerald about his *Poems* of 1842. 'You can't hate it more than I do, but it does me no good to hear it abused; if it is bad, you and others are to blame who continually urged me to publish.' Even at the height of his fame, he was looking over his shoulder, ever ready for the back stab, the betrayal. When critics spoke ill of his works, as now and then some did, he was cast into the depths. Why should his name be 'Shot like a racketball from mouth to mouth/And bandied in the barren lips of fools,' he asked in an unpublished poem of 1839. For him, the pain of being attacked was 'thrice keener than delight from duest praise'.

Worldly praise was never quite enough – it fell short of the highest validation. But then, for Tennyson, what didn't? Life itself was meaningless, he used to say, unless he could be *certain* that there was an afterlife. And the same went for literary celebrity. 'Modern fame is nothing,' he once said. 'I'd rather have an acre of land. I shall go down, down! I'm up now. Action and reaction.'

In his final years, Tennyson was able to pick up one or two intimations of posterity's likely 'reaction'. There had been a slight falling off from his great peak of the 1860s, and if he listened hard enough (and we can be pretty sure he did) he would have been able to detect the faintest of faint murmurings against him from the young. There were Tennyson parodies, and the term 'Tennysonian' was sometimes used in fun. But the gibes were generally respectful. As Swinburne said, 'I allow no one to laugh at Tennyson except myself.' When Tennyson died, his reputation and his popularity were solidly intact, and they remained so for thirty years longer.

It was not until after World War One that Tennyson, along with many another icon of his period, came under serious assault. As an 'eminent Victorian', he was lumped in with the old men who had sent their sons to slaughter in the war. His 'The Charge of the Light Brigade,' which in 1854 had been one of his biggest hits, was now reviled as the ultimate imperialist battle hymn. His Arthurian idylls were laughed at as typical Victorian escapism. Even the racked miseries of *In Memoriam* were patronised as facile, metronomic. By the 1930s, the decade in which loathing of the Victorians was at its fiercest, he had become Alfred Lawn Tennyson. The sally was copyright James Joyce, who was by then revered as being all that Tennyson was not. To be Tennysonian in the 1930s was to be sentimental, bogus, a state lackey, a reactionary dud. And the fact that his work was thought by the very old to be 'real poetry' made matters worse, as Kingsley Amis has explained:

> When I first noticed Tennyson, some time in the 1930s, he must have been at or near the nadir of his reputation among those starting to read poetry. He had not only been Poet Laureate all those years and written 'The Charge of the Light Brigade'; he was popular with antiquated persons like Mr Oakley, who taught me Latin and above all he was a *Victorian* and therefore intolerable. The young and youngish of today can hardly imagine the extreme pejorative force of that label at that time.

Tennyson's very giftedness was held against him: his ear was too perfect, and his productivity and range were sure indications of an eagerness to please. He was expert, yes, but slickly so. A consummate self-parodist, he could turn on the quality at will. The vandalistic drives of modernism found in Tennyson a monument that *had* to be pulled down. Discredit the Tennysonian, said Ezra Pound, and you will expose the hollowness, the mediocrity of British taste. Only then will you be free to 'make it new'. It was as if nothing of the new – the new morality, the new atheism, the new frontiers staked out by Marx and Freud – could be properly developed or explored until poor Tennyson was given the heave-ho.

From a distance of sixty years or so, the treatment of Tennyson seems philistine and thuggish. There was an awful wilfulness about it, as if everyone were determined to read the jacket, not the book. Still, the tide gradually turned, and biography can take much of the credit for this. Tennyson often railed against biographers. The 'lives of great men', he said, should not be treated 'like pigs to be ripped open for the public'. In an effort to protect himself, he recruited his son Hallam as his authorized-life writer. Not only that but he assisted Hallam in his research – destroying or censoring letters, advising on points of interpretation, suppressing negative reviews, glossing over ancient quarrels. Anything that smacked of 'intensity of feeling' was suppressed. Hallam got the message and set to with the scissors. The result, five years after the poet's death, was an anodyne two-volume

Memoir that would soon enough be ridiculed as further evidence of its subject's pitiable hunger for respectability. 'A smooth bust of rosy wax', one critic called it.

Hallam's memoir stood for fifty years as *the* Tennyson biography, and it did his father's cause no good at all. In 1949, though, another family-approved Life was published, this time by the poet's grandson Charles. Charles had access to the family papers – what was left of them – and, with Hallam dead, he was under no pressure to safeguard the family name. After all, he was addressing a hostile audience, for whom the name Tennyson had been made risible, a byword for rectitude and cant. His job was to introduce some darker hues, to rattle a few skeletons.

This he did, and with a vengeance. When Charles Tennyson's biography appeared, the world was ready to take another look at Tennyson. In Charles's presentation, the family tree bristled with neurosis, and in the light of his revelations the poems somehow became stranger, more disturbed, more genuine. Even *Idylls of the King*, once thought of as a pretty tapestry, now appeared to be simmering with sexual thwartedness and with the nervous strain of trying to live up to an ideal. 'The Charge of the Light Brigade', it could be seen, dispatched its warriors to certain death. 'Maud' was re-read as a psychological case study. In other words, Tennyson was rediscovered as that most 'modern' of literary animals: the deep-divided yearner. When T. S. Eliot called Tennyson the saddest of all English poets, and when Auden described him as a connoisseur of melancholia, there was in each of these judgements a distinct whiff of condescension, of reproof. The music of Tennyson's despair was far too easy on the ear. And how had that despair been earned? Charles Tennyson's book made questions of this sort seem cheap, and paved the way for Ricks and Martin – and, indeed, for the generally relaxed respectfulness of the new biographies.

The Tennysons, it transpired, were victims of 'black blood': a disposition towards melancholia, sometimes bordering on madness. Drink and drugs were used to keep the malady in check. In the poet's immediate family, three brothers were afflicted with some kind of mental illness. One of them became an opium addict; another ended up in an asylum. And the boys' father, George, was famously unbalanced – a drunk, given to titanic rages and pitch-black depressions. George had a bitter grievance: the eldest son of a rich man, he had been disinherited in favour of his younger brother and forced to seek a living in the church. Nobody ever told him why. It was the whim, seemingly, of his black-blooded father. As a result, his own black blood went on the boil. For a dozen years, his rectory was a mad-house, with the whole family living in dread of George's regular 'attacks'. Levi speaks of the rectory's 'doom-laden and bottle-strewn atmosphere', Thorn of the 'prevailing atmosphere of savagery in the house'. In the end, Tennyson's mother had to remove herself and her children from the scene, and leave George to it. He died, still furious, in 1831.

Throughout Tennyson's adolescence, it seems, barely a week passed without some agonising psychodrama. By the time he escaped to Cambridge, to make friends and write poems, he was well established in the fear that he, too, was marked for lunacy. Then came a further blow – for him more cataclysmic than any of his family tragedies, though, as he saw it, part of the same pattern. Arthur Hallam, his best friend, his most admiring critic, and the fiancé of his sister, died – of a stroke, it was said – at twenty-two. Tennyson was devastated by this loss, and over the next two decades he wrote *In Memoriam*, the long sequence of heartbroken elegies, which he at first intended not to print. It was published anonymously in 1850. That year, he married Emily Sellwood, after a lengthy and frustrating courtship. His wife-to-be kept him waiting because she suspected that his soul was not at peace. She had presumably scented the black blood. Tennyson's most powerful work – poems like 'Ulysses' and 'The Lotos-Eaters' – spoke of inertia, of exhaustion, of not really wanting to go on.

When they married, Tennyson was famous, about to be made poet laureate. Emily saw it as her duty to provide a well-ordered ambience in which his genius might flourish – and in which, she hoped, he would find God. She became his secretary, business manager, and spiritual counsellor, and the around-the-clock supporter of his self-esteem. Some of Tennyson's friends believed that her solicitude was stifling – that she encouraged the respectable in Tennyson and steered him away from the darker sources of his inspiration. Both Thorn and Levi, though, speak well of her: she handled him 'most perfectly', Levi says, and in Thorn's view 'Tennyson's marriage was good both for his work and for his temperament'. Even so, Emily's wifely tasks exhausted her, and she herself fell victim to a never diagnosed lassitude that kept her more or less bedridden for the last eighteen years of their long marriage. But Tennyson did not go mad. Edward FitzGerald was one of those who hinted that his poems might have got better if he had, but even FitzGerald would probably have shuddered at the thought of what might have become of him if Emily had not set herself to do battle with his demons.

There are questions about Tennyson that will almost certainly not be answered. How important was his early, pre-Emily infatuation with Rosa Baring, an upper-crust, coquettish heiress, who spurned him around the time of Hallam's death? Christopher Ricks believes that the pain of this setback was 'deep and abiding', that Rosa was the inspiration of several well-known poems, most notably the anguished 'Maud'. ('Cold and clear-cut face, why come you so cruelly meek,/Breaking a slumber in which all spleenful folly was drowned . . .') Levi dismisses the whole episode as 'an insignificant flirtation or hardly even that'. What was the 'true nature' of his relationship with Arthur Hallam? Why, really, did his engagement to Emily drag on for so long?

And then there is the Tennysonian black blood. How much of it did Tennyson actually inherit? Levi refers to the idea that the black blood was a form of epilepsy, and that Tennyson himself may have been subject to epileptic fits, but he dismisses this theory with fine bedside scorn: 'impossible for medical reasons,' he declares, without quite saying why. Thorn refloats the old notion that Tennyson may have been hooked on opium, like his brother Charles, citing 'the popular perception during his own life'. This perception, he says, 'was more widespread and lingering than the effort to brush it aside has implied.' Thorn also wants to make out that Tennyson was more of a rake than we had known: 'On the Isle of Wight . . . you can still hear off-the-record (and off-the-wall) saloon-bar theories about the poet's amatory exploits. They are probably as wide of the mark as the more sedate fabrications enshrined in Tennysonian legend.' Do we detect here a new legend in the making – Alfred Porn

Tennyson, sex fiend of Farringford? Well, action and reaction. Who can tell?

Tennyson often yearned for easeful death, but more hungrily he yearned for life. He wanted more of life, not less; he already knew what less felt like. 'So various, so beautiful, so new' was how Matthew Arnold described *his* land of dreams. No more than Arnold did Tennyson like being a Victorian. And yet he also yearned for stability and reassurance, a deep sense of duty done. To serve or to escape? To do or to dream? Such themes could hardly be thought of as not 'modern'. Once forbiddingly well groomed, Tennyson in the 1950s could be seen as excitingly unkempt. In the age of Dylan Thomas, it even became possible for him to be regarded as a bohemian at heart. Biography had done the trick – or, at any rate, had set in motion a willingness to think again. By forcing a new reading of the man, it had also forced a reappraisal of the texts. Readers were free once more to marvel at his music, and not have to say of it, Oh, how Victorian:

> There lies the port; the vessel puffs her sail:
> There gloom the dark broad seas. My mariners,
> Souls that have toiled, and wrought, and thought with me—
> That ever with a frolic welcome took
> The thunder and the sunshine, and opposed
> Free hearts, free foreheads – you and I are old;
> Old age hath yet his honour and his toil;
> Death closes all: but something ere the end,
> Some work of noble note, may yet be done,
> Not unbecoming men that strove with Gods.
> The lights begin to twinkle from the rocks:
> The long day wanes: the slow moon climbs: the deep
> Moans round with many voices.
> Come, my friends,
> 'Tis not too late to seek a newer world.

And yet, of course, the music *is* Victorian. It plumbs the depths, it reaches for the heavens, and it doesn't know for certain which is which. We are used to not knowing things 'for certain', but Tennyson was not. We must therefore be careful when we seek to rescue him from history, or to reclaim him as a modern, one of us. Much of

Tennyson's power to touch us springs from sources that we know he would rather have kept hidden – hidden from Emily, from England, from himself. Seen like this, even his official mode can strike us as a near-heroic style of recompense, a making up for not being the kind of Victorian he seemed and wished to be, and loathed.

For some readers, Tennyson's acts of recompense – if such they were – need not have been conducted at such length. It takes a rare sort of devotion to plough through the two hundred or so pages of *Idylls of the King* in the hope of encountering the real man behind the tapestry. Similarly, *In Memoriam* is best read in selections that eschew its more ponderous stretches of 'philosophy'. Even 'Maud', the most jaggedly 'modern' of his works, goes on and on.

New readers, then, need guidance, but when it comes to Tennyson – once we have picked out the best of the bleak early lyrics, or 'Ulysses', or 'Tithonus', or bits of the 'Morte d'Arthur' – it is not easy to know where to point. As Gerard Manley Hopkins famously opined, Tennyson wrote well even when he was untouched by inspiration: he wrote well when he wrote badly. With Keats or Wordsworth, say, we can readily distinguish the inspired works from the duds, but the duds in Tennyson are pretty good: skilfully made, sonorous, and ever likely to throw up something we would not have wished to miss – a wave of pathos, a glintingly accurate description. He is thus both the most skippable and the least skippable of poets. To know him is to know that there is far too much of him; there had to be. From most overproductive poets we salvage what we like, and put the rest on ice, for scholars to pick over. Not so with Tennyson. In his case, the very bulk of his collected works has an important meaning. Chiefly, and most movingly, it means that the 'real Tennyson' can never be set free.

Tennyson by Michael Thorn (St. Martin Press)
Tennyson by Peter Levi (Scribners)

The New Yorker, 1994

Arnold's Letters, Finally

A few years ago, I had the idea of trying to write a biography of Matthew Arnold. The ambition sprang chiefly from an interest in the poems, and in biographical questions relating to them: there were, it seemed to me, a number of intriguing puzzles. Chief among these, of course, was the much-pondered Marguerite. Who was she: a dream-girl, an invention born of too much exposure to the novels of George Sand, or a real person met in Switzerland in 1848? Then there was Dr Arnold of Rugby: a devitalising ogre or an inspiration? And, overarchingly, there was the question of Arnold's attitude to his own gifts as a poet: why did he abandon the 'poetic life' and settle for three decades of drudgery as an inspector of elementary schools? Was it a fierce love of duty that took him down this path, or was it, rather, that he all along had insufficient faith in his own talent? And this, of course, led to the question that matters most of all: how much faith do we/should we have in that talent?

There were other aspects of the Arnold life that seemed to be worth looking into: his marriage, his relationship with his older sister, his friendships with Arthur Clough and other Oxford contemporaries, his youthful self-assertiveness and foppery, his fluctuating feelings about God, his Tennyson-phobia, the steady, slow-drip sadness that seemed to underly even his most elegant and amiable sermons. In the best of Arnold's poems – 'Dover Beach', 'The Buried Life', 'Empedocles', 'The Scholar Gipsy', some of the pieces about Marguerite – the deepest impulse is towards repudiation: repudiation, often, of those very elements in his own nature which urged him towards poetry in the first place.

When Arnold got married and became an educationist, he also turned himself into a didactic neo-classicist; the age, he said, needed the kind of large-scale, objective, architectonic verse-constructions which he himself, he came to learn, had no real gift for. Or, to put it another way, what the age didn't need were more poems of the kind that Arnold did have a real gift for, and had indeed already written: lyric poems of the self – that Arnold self which, as he came to see it, had or should have had more important things to do than, well, write lyric poems.

Thus most of my lines of inquiry seemed to be focusing on Arnold's early life; his poetic life – such as it was. I soon enough abandoned plans for a cradle-to-grave Life. For quite a time, though, I did some serious dabbling in Arnold Studies: serious enough, anyway, to make me wonder why certain areas of the terrain still seemed to have been under-tilled. A sizeable amount of the material lodged in libraries had yet to be edited and published. This seemed strange, given Arnold's generally acknowledged eminence. After all, who of his epoch had not been thoroughly worked over by the scholars?

The first question biographers tend to ask of any likely subject is: where are the Letters? In Arnold's case, I found, the answer was not at all straightforward. When I began my Arnold chores, more than a century after the poet's death, there was still no Collected edition of his correspondence. Most other things had, as it were, been seen to: the poems, the pocket diaries, the prose works (in eleven volumes). The letters, though, were scattered: Yale, Balliol College, Leeds, the Bodleian, and elsewhere. Several non-collected items had been quoted or referred to in biographies or in Kenneth Allott's fine edition of the poems; some had appeared in learned periodicals. There were book-length gatherings of 'special interest' letters: for instance, Arnold's correspondence with his publisher, post-1867, had been brought together in a single volume. To get the whole picture, though, Arnold enthusiasts would need to spend at least a year in libraries, full time.

In other words, there appeared to be a need for high-level academic action. By the time of my involvement, it transpired, such action was already well in hand. Cecil Y. Lang, the hero of Swinburne's Letters, and of Tennyson's, was said to be working on the case. And so he was.

And here now are the first two volumes of what will be a six-volume publication. And it is entirely clear from Volumes One and Two that Lang has pulled off yet another triumph of industry, wisdom and precision. Volume One (1829–59) covers Arnold's schooldays at Winchester and Rugby, his years as a bantering young Balliol dandy, a kind of anti-Arnold, so to speak, and then – in 1842 – his father's sudden death, at the age of forty-six. For a period, Matthew's response to this life-altering event was to opt wholeheartedly for the poetic life, but he was soon enough brought down to earth. The Arnold inheritance – he was the oldest son – proved inescapable. After a short spell of employment in the office of the Whig grandee, Lord Lansdowne, Arnold married in 1851 and became a school inspector – and would remain one for the rest of his working life. He died in 1888. By the end of Lang's Volume Two (1860–65), he is forty-three, has served as Professor of Poetry at Oxford, and has written all of his best poems. Two decades and four volumes of his letters lie ahead: decades of public service, literary criticism and social theory, with Arnold's poetic life safely in the past. It's not much of a story, told in its barest outline – or rather, it's a story that needs detail, fleshing-out. Which is, of course, why we have been waiting so anxiously for these *Letters*. The question lingers, though: why did we have to wait so long?

And this question, Lang happily concedes, is well worth asking – if only for the light it seeks to shed on the curious processes of literary conservation, and (in this case) on the personalities involved. Lang tells the story well, and wittily, in his introduction to Volume One. It all began, as have so many Victorian literary mysteries, with a flurry of scissors and blue pencils. Not long after Arnold's death in 1888, his widow – Frances Lucy – and his youngest sister – Fan – commissioned a two-volume Letters, to be edited by G. W. E. Russell, a clever young Arnold disciple who felt honoured to be given the task. Russell's edition appeared in 1895, but, as he later explained, it was by no means his own work: 'in reality my functions were little more than those of the collector and the annotator. Most of the letters had been severely edited before they came into my hands, and the process was repeated when they were in proof.'

And these were just the letters which Arnold's family considered suitable, or partly suitable, for publication. Hundreds of others, we can reliably surmise, were burned. In Russell's edition, there are seventy-odd letters from Arnold to his wife. The Arnolds were married for thirty-seven years, and for long stretches of those years Matthew was away from home, school-inspecting in the provinces or travelling in Europe. It was his habit, when away, to write daily letters to his wife. As Cecil Lang points out: 'No estimate about the total number written can even be attempted, but for nearly two dozen of those thirty-seven years no letter is known.' In addition to Russell's seventy-odd, only a further five have since been found and, out of the sum total, only eight holographs survive.

These holographs afford a revealing glimpse of Mrs Arnold's editorial methods, and the spectacle is most depressing. Anything at all personal, in a husband-and-wife way, was suppressed. Even Arnold's none-too-frenzied expressions of affection ('Dear darling'; 'Your own most terribly attached') were primly set aside. To Arnold's wife, Lang groans, 'the slightest endearment seemed an indiscretion, gossip an abomination, the trivia of personal relations almost unclean'. Helped by her equally determined sister-in-law, Mrs Arnold was able to make sure that the 1895 *Letters* raised no eyebrows, and especially not her own. Arnold was presented to the world as an amiable, nature-loving family man, but also as an uncomplaining martyr:

> qualified by nature and training for the highest honours and successes which the world can give, he spent his life in a long round of unremunerative drudgery, working even beyond the limits of his strength for those whom he loved, and never by word or sign betraying even a consciousness of that dull indifference to his gifts and services which stirred the fruitless indignation of his friends.

This, from Russell's introduction, was surely Mrs Arnold speaking. We now know, of course, that Arnold did complain, quite often, and not just about the boredom of his working life. He also complained about the dreariness of the domestic round, about his children and his in-laws, about money. What else did he complain about, we have to ask, in those hundreds of lost letters, or in those paragraphs scissored by his widow?

★   ★   ★

Russell's edition of the *Letters* did the job that was intended: it made Arnold out to be a safe and saintly man of duty. By printing no letters prior to 1848, it gave no sight of him at Rugby, or at Oxford, or – post-Oxford – wandering romantically in Europe ('un Milton jeune et voyageant', according to George Sand). As presented in Russell's volumes, Arnold's life began at the age of twenty-six, a year or two before he met his wife. It was in order to marry Frances Lucy that he took employment as a school inspector, gamely telling her after his first day at work: 'I think I shall get interested in the schools after a little time.'

It was not until 1932 that the young Arnold was revealed, in Howard Foster Lowry's *The Letters of Matthew Arnold to Arthur Hugh Clough*. This collection of sixty-two letters, spanning a period from 1845 until Clough's death in 1861 but at their most intense and voluminous in 1847–8, transformed the general view of Arnold. All at once, the cold fish was shown to have been edgy and excitable, affected and verbose. His poetry, which in Russell features as rather a side-issue, was here utterly central to his thinking, to his idea of his own future. Vigorous, playful, argumentative, even a touch bawdy here and there, these letters to Clough would surely have shocked Mrs Arnold, had she known of them. Perhaps she did know of them, although this seems improbable. Certainly, she knew the Arnold who wrote them rather better than she wanted to admit. There was a bossy side to him, when young, and this can scarcely have just disappeared with marriage.

Arnold did not keep Clough's replies to his letters, and this perhaps makes him sound more imperiously pedagogic than he really was, or meant to be. For one thing, he wins all the arguments. Still, when one remembers that Clough was his senior and had been Rugby's star pupil during Matthew's adolescence, there is a striking absence of the tentative in Arnold's manner. He talks down to Clough as to a muddled and too-impulsive younger brother. This also means, though, that Arnold felt free to speak his mind, to ramble on – and ramble on he did, sometimes confusedly but usually with dandified panache. It is in these letters that we find his now well-known denunciations of the mid-century *Zeitgeist*, set forth in terms which later on, when he had become famous for sweet reason, he would surely have judged to be intemperate. 'My dearest Clough, these are damned times – everything is against one – the height to which knowledge is come, the spread of luxury, our physical enervation, the absence of great *natures*, the unavoidable contact with millions of small ones, newspapers, cities, light profligate friends . . .'; 'God keep us from aridity – Arid, that is what the times are!'; 'How deeply *unpoetical* the age and all one's surroundings are. Not unprofound, not ungrand, not unmoving – but *unpoetical*.'

Intemperate, perhaps, but Arnold meant it, and this voice was rarely heard again, post-1851, the year in which he married and took work as an inspector. Fittingly, it was Lowry's edition of Arnold's letters to Clough that set in motion the great hunt for Marguerite. In a letter of September 1848, Arnold confided to his friend, from Switzerland: 'Tomorrow I pass the Gemmi and get to Thun: linger one day at the Hotel Bellevue for the sake of the blue eyes of one of its inmates: and then proceed by slow stage down the Rhine to Cologne, thence to Amiens and Boulogne and England.' On the strength of this small clue, Lowry, accompanied by the intrepid Chauncy B. Tinker (of Boswell papers fame), set off for Thun, only to find that the Hotel Bellevue's register for the years 1848 and 1849 had been destroyed. (Cecil Lang, it should be reported, has unearthed no further letters about Marguerite and, unlike Lowry, is inclined to see her as a fiction: Arnold's Laura, his Beatrice, his Rosa Baring. And there, for now, the matter rests.)

The publication of Lowry's edition did wonders for Arnold's then uneasy reputation – and for Clough's, which was in even worse shape at the time – and one might have expected it to prompt swift action on the Letters. And in a sense it did. For the next thirty-five years, the story of Arnold's correspondence became, as Lang somewhat tartly testifies, the story of one man: Arthur Kyle Davis (1897–1972), a member of the Department of English at the University of Virginia from 1923 until his death. Davis it was who, in the mid-1930s or perhaps earlier, set himself to assemble records of all known Arnold letters, including photocopies, microfilms, typed and handwritten transcriptions. Even letters which Davis hadn't seen copies of but which had been mentioned in sales catalogues and auction records were added to his lists.

By 1968, Davis had compiled a huge inventory, totalling more than 2,500 items of Arnold correspondence. Copies of 1,600 of these were housed in Virginia's Alderman Library. The others were described in detail: addressees, number of pages, dates, present whereabouts, etc. Thanks to Davis, Charlottesville, Virginia, became the world centre of Matthew Arnold Studies. If scholars did not insist on consulting the originals, they could save themselves journeys to Oxford, Yale or Leeds by viewing Davis's extraordinary Virginia trove. As Lang here comments: 'It is no exaggeration to say that as much as any other single archive [Davis's] reanimated scholarly work on Matthew Arnold.'

On the other hand, it could be said that Davis took his time. For much of the late 1930s and throughout the war years, his project was often 'in abeyance'. After the war, it was interrupted more than once by 'intervals of relaxation'. It was also interrupted by Davis's other scholarly obsession: collecting old Virginia folk-songs. Year after year, from 1950 onwards, the great Davis Checklist was announced in PMLA's 'Work in Progress', and during those years scholars kept up a steady flow of articles announcing the discovery of this or that new cache of Arnold correspondence: 'Matthew Arnold and W. E. Gladstone, Some New Letters', 'Three Matthew Arnold Letters', 'Three New Letters of Arnold', 'Matthew Arnold and Percy William Bunting: Some New Letters'. During the years between Davis's first announcement of his Checklist and its publication in 1968, almost thirty such discoveries were reported in the journals.

The bulk of these discoveries belonged to the 1950s, the decade in which – thanks to Lionel Trilling's 1949 biography – critical interest in Arnold hit something of a peak. Another good moment, one might think, for academia to demand a full-scale edition of the letters. But no: as Lang points out, although Arthur Kyle Davis was in many ways a highly admirable presence in the field, he was also its all-powerful ruler. Everybody who knew about Arnold knew about the Davis Checklist and supported it. It was thought of as 'preliminary' to an actual printing of the letters, which Davis himself would presumably take charge of. And in the meantime, of course, scholars had endless scope for scoops. It was a cosy arrangement, and could have dragged on for even longer than it did. Thus, paradoxically, the scholar who made an edition of the letters seem feasible was also the scholar who, in Lang's words, 'made progress improbable. He presided over this well-defined turf for nearly half a century, by which time his presidency, virtually unchallenged, was effectively unchallengeable. He was deposed only by mutability.'

In 1972, with the Davis Checklist at last published and applauded, sixty Arnold scholars were summoned to an MLA seminar entitled 'The Sesquicentennial Celebration of the Birth of Matthew Arnold' (Arnold was born in 1822). The purpose of the event was to pay tribute to Davis's labours and 'to discuss the future of Arnold scholarship'. The question of the letters would be raised. Unhappily, though, Davis died shortly after the invitations were sent out. The seminar went ahead (although not everyone invited managed to attend), and 'in due course' an approach was made to Cecil Lang, a colleague of Davis's at the University of Virginia. 'The rest is history', says Lang, 'but it is a history somewhat murkier than has been allowed in previous accounts.'

'Murky' seems rather strong, although I suppose we do have to wonder if Davis ever really wanted to bring his inquiries to a close. After all, he was over seventy when his 'preliminary' Checklist finally appeared. Still the upshot is not at all to be lamented. Arnold never wanted a biography, and would presumably have recoiled from the idea of posterity getting at his private letters. How he would have viewed his widow's efforts in this line we can but guess. If there had to be a Letters, though, he would surely have settled for something like the present outcome. Enough of his correspondence has gone missing for certain privacies to be thought of as unbreachable – in perpetuity, it seems. On the other hand, enough has been preserved for us to carry on feeling somewhat thwarted. Knowing a little, we want to know much more. And the letters that do survive have now been edited respectfully but not pedantically, and with a light touch that Arnold would have relished. Footnotes are used sparingly, but are usually there when we need them. Arnold altogether, we feel sure, would have approved of Cecil Lang. Indeed, Lang, it could be said, is something of an Arnold-figure. He rails against *his* 'damned age' as vigorously as the young Matthew did in 1848 ('Philistinism has become a virtue, anti–intellectualism a badge of honour'), but he also likes to be seen as well up on the enemy's resources: Dr Arnold is at one point here described as 'no Darth Vader'.

Lang also has a touch of Arnold's vanity. He enjoys flaunting his scholarly exactitude: 'no detail is too niggling,' he writes, 'no nuance too nice, no mite of pointing or mote of orthography too puny for the dainty appetence of what Carlyle called the "Able Editor".' Indeed, Lang's exactitude is such that he can even find fault with Lowry's celebrated edition of the *Letters to Clough* – an edition which, in Arnold circles, has for decades enjoyed the 'status of Holy Writ'. Lang picks up quite a few incorrect transcriptions – 'on the moon' for 'on the moors', 'longueurs' for 'longness' – and in general seems disinclined to grant Lowry more than his minimum deserts. On one occasion, he scolds Lowry for not knowing that 'the schools', in Oxford parlance, means 'B.A. examinations'. But Lowry's note to the letter in question (Letter 23) shows that he did know. It is simply that his reading of the text does not accord with Lang's (though Lang's reading, I should say, does seem to be the right one). A friendlier commentator might not have made so much of this small disagreement.

More seriously – and here perhaps we have a source for Lang's animus – a question mark is raised against Lowry's personal integrity. Since the question also touches on Arnold's all-important 1848 letter from Switzerland (the 'pair of blue eyes' letter), Lang could scarcely have ignored it. Even so, the interrogation is mounted with some vigour. Lowry, we are reminded, said of Arnold's letters to Clough that 'the manuscripts of all but two are now in the possession of the Sterling Memorial Library at Yale'. He did not say which two, nor did he say who held the manuscripts (we presumed some private dealer). Lang tells us now that the two letters are Nos 1 and 22 (22 being the 'blue eyes' letter), and he further notes that these two, as printed by Lowry, have a peculiarity in common: they are the only two letters in the volume with ellipses. These ellipses, Lang concedes, could have been Arnold's, but (and the italics here are Lang's): '*there is only one other ellipsis, verifiable by manuscript, in the entire range of Arnold's letters in these several volumes!*'

The question, therefore, seems to be: did Lowry himself own the two letters, and did his transcriptions (which are Lang's sole holograph source) omit lines so as to sustain the market value of the manuscripts? 'One is driven to the conclusion,' says Lang, 'unpleasant but hardly avoidable, that Lowry himself owned them and sold them at some point to a collector knowledgeable about Arnold and Arnold scholars.' The 'blue eyes' letter may not be, as Lang contends, 'perhaps the best letter Arnold even wrote', but it is certainly one of the most valuable, given the Marguerite connection. Where then is the original? If Lowry really did sell it, more than thirty years ago (he died in 1967), who owns it now, and will we ever get to see it?

Lang takes a dim view, as well he might, of letter-owners who for money reasons refuse to release their property for publication, and he is perhaps hard on Lowry here. It is not impossible to think of other ways of explaining the ellipses and the missing manuscripts. Perhaps Lang's supposition will be challenged; one rather hopes that it will be. In another instance, though, Lang does seem to have safe grounds for editorial resentment. In his introduction, he refers to a certain collection of Arnold letters which he had been 'unable to include' in his edition. This collection, he says, is the property of one Roger L. Brooks, professor of English at Baylor University and director of the Armstrong Browning Library, Waco, Texas. Brooks, we are told, is 'a collector as knowledgeable about Arnold and Arnold scholars as any man'. But let Lang tell it in his own words:

> Brooks has provided photocopies of several Arnold letters in the Armstrong Browning Library for inclusion in this edition, and, though he several times expressed his willingness to send copies of those in his private collection, they have not been forthcoming. I inquired about the possibility of remunerating him for the *use* (not the purchase) of his 'twenty-five unpublished letters' and he replied (I quote from his handwritten letter, April 13, 1989, before me): 'Now arriving at a fair price is difficult, but considering the depreciation of the value of the collection, I would think $10,000 would be fair and reasonable'. 'And when I heard this thing', as Ezra says, 'I rent my garment and my mantle, and plucked off the hair of my head and of my beard, and sat down astonied.' I replied (I quote from a copy of my letter, April 29, before me): 'Before I can go any further, I will have to have a listing of the letters, dates, addressees, and number of pages.' No reply has been received.

Lang, as we can see from this, is something of a humorist, and – to use one of his own words – his humour is often tinged with the 'subacid'. I'm not sure, though, how humorous he is being when, in his Appendix A to Volume One, he painstakingly prints the dates on which, in 1845–7, Arnold chose to annotate his pocket diaries with crosses. In Arthur Kenny's *Oxford Diaries of Arthur Hugh Clough*, certain dates in Clough's journal are similarly marked – but with asterisks. With Clough, the asterisks indicate those days on which he fell victim to the 'wretched habit' of masturbation, 'the worst sin'. Lang believes that Arnold's crosses have the same significance: they denote his surrenders to 'the coercions of the postpubertal, premarital libido'. Well, maybe. But do we need two pages itemising every Arnold lapse? Are we meant to match days-marked-with-crosses to days on which he wrote this letter or that poem? But if so, to what purpose? For the record: only one Arnold letter was written on a day-marked-with-a-cross, of which there were more than 200. The letter is to Clough, it so happens, and in it Arnold comes out with the unArnoldian 'Goly what a !!!Shite's!!! Oracle', but – let us be clear on this – he was writing about Clough's poem, 'The Questing Spirit'.

Arnold's diaries for 1847–50 have not before been published – not because of the tell-tale crosses but, as Lang suggests, because they were 'not manifestly worth the effort' of transcription, being even more terse and uninformative than those which had seen print. Arnold used his pocket diaries for reading-lists and quotations which caught his interest, for appointments, train-times, financial calculations and the like. Rarely did he comment on his state of mind, and when he did, there was no lingering: 'Miserable day with toothache', 'Dreadfully tired and languid'. Lang here prints the texts of Arnold's hitherto unpublished diaries for 1851 and 1859, but he has been unable to locate the 'missing diaries' for 1848–50, the years of Marguerite. The crosses, by the way, do not appear in Arnold's diary for 1851, the year of his marriage, nor thereafter.

In addition to Arnold's letters and these diaries, Lang prints for the first time a number of most useful 'background' items: letters from Dr Arnold, to Matthew and to certain of his other children, letters from his sister Jane (or 'K', as she was known) to brother Tom, from Tom to Jane, and so on. Volume One is particularly strong on Arnold's early years – years in which, of course, the child Matthew wrote few letters. Not only do we get letters to Matthew from his parents (letters which show Dr Arnold to have been more lenient than his wife on the subject of Matthew's schoolroom failures), but there are letters too from members of the grown-up Arnolds' social circle – in which, of course, the nine Arnold children were frequently discussed.

Thus, there are interesting contributions here from William and Mary Wordsworth, the Arnolds' close neighbours at their lakeland house, Fox How – a house which Wordsworth himself helped design. When the Arnold children were growing up, Fox How was their school-holiday haven, and after Dr Arnold's death it became the Arnold family home and a kind of monument to Dr Arnold's 'values'. Certainly for Matthew, in later years, images of spiritual contentment and emotional spaciousness usually had their roots in memories of his childhood at Fox How. It is good, therefore, for us to see the place and to feel its significance, during those years in which Matthew was too young to describe it.

Matthew's brothers and sisters feature strongly in these first volumes. His eccentric older brother Tom (Dr Arnold's favourite in childhood) comes through as an engaging minor character, with his excruciating, almost comic, conscientiousness. Tom, who fled to NewZealand and was constantly changing his religion, serves as a reminder of what Matthew might well have turned into if he had been his father's favourite. The most compelling (and for Matthew the most influential) presence, though, is sister Jane. We have known for a long time of Matthew's high regard for his older sister, but she herself has always been a little shadowy – not least because she too was a great burner of her correspondence (as was Matthew, it would seem). 'There is no-one,' Arnold wrote to Jane in 1850, 'and never will be any one who enters into what I have done as you have entered into it, dearest K, – and to whom I so want to communicate what I do.' He wrote this on hearing of Jane's surprise engagement, but in other letters he is similarly reverential: she was the one figure in Arnold's life whom he could see both as moral exemplar and as intellectual equal. Lang, by printing one or two of her letters alongside those which her brother wrote to her, now makes it possible for us to grasp why Arnold rated her so highly: she was kindly, sweet and wise, but she was also fearsomely strict in her defence of 'Arnold values' – she was indeed her father's daughter.

Jane aside, Lang's decision to print 'family letters' – letters in which Matthew is mentioned or discussed by brothers, sisters, parents – does seem wholly justified. This 'background' material gives the whole enterprise as rich a narrative as one might look for in an orthodox biography. As Lang says, the Arnold family letters will be 'the valve pumping the life-blood' of his six volumes. Already, we can see what he means. And, of course, we would gladly have more of them. But this is the feeling we get with most Victorian literary archives: however keen our curiosity, however many master-sleuths like Lang are set to work, the best we'll ever get is a half-picture pieced together from whatever evidence managed to escape those dreadful bonfires. Lang, it must be said, gives us as whole a half-picture, so to speak, as we could reasonably hope for. At least – and at last – we can stop yearning to know more about Arnold than is (officially) already known. We can: but will we? And will Cecil Lang? I somehow doubt it.

The Letters of Matthew Arnold Vol. One: 1829–1859; Vol. Two: 1860–1865, edited by Cecil Y. Lang (University of Virginia Press)

Times Literary Supplement, 1997

4

Sports and Pastimes

On Being a Soccer Bore

For years – since boyhood, really – I've seen myself as an above-average soccer bore. At my peak, I would happily hold forth for hours about the rugged terrace-time I'd served, at Feethams, White Hart Lane, the Manor Ground. And when it came to the archival stuff, if you could spare the time, well, so could I. 'Name three of the Spurs' double side's *reserves*,' I'd say, or: 'How many of the 1964 West Ham cupwinning team had names beginning with a B?' Or it would be: 'Pick an XI in which every position is taken by a Gary. I will start you off. Gary Bailey in goal. Gary Stevens right back. Now you carry on.'

Yes, truly boring. But in those days soccer-mania was dark and lonely work. Outside my small circle of co-bores, most people I knew just didn't want to know. From time to time, I'd cut a prole-ish dash in pubs or quell some terrace skinhead with a deft statistic but there were few other social benefits, so far as I could tell. Soccer scholarship cut no ice in the examination halls of Life and it helped not at all with girls. 'I thought you were supposed to be a *poet*,' they would say. 'But soccer,' I'd protest, '*is* poetry – well, at its best, it can be, or it nearly is . . . Take Jimmy Greaves. The Man United game.' And that, usually, was that.

Those were the days. Now everything has changed. Over the past five years or so, soccer has moved to the very centre-circle of our culture. Books, magazines, TV shows have been sprouting on all sides. Nowadays everybody wants to be a soccer bore. And, what's worse, everybody seems to have found it pretty easy to become one. Trivia I once treasured as peculiarly, eccentrically mine are now revealed to be the dreary stuff of common knowledge. Faced with my archival fire-power, these new young soccer bores don't even blink: 'Who *doesn't* know of Bovington, Boyce, Brabrook, Bond et al,' they say. 'And as for all those Garys you're so keen on, why not make up *two* teams of them, plus subs? Let's see now: Ablett, Bennett, Brookes . . .'

These past few years, these years of rampant soccer cred, have been a slow torment for the antique soccer bore. In the old days we were friendless and perhaps despised but we enjoyed a steady faith in our own expertise, our strength-in-depth: we knew the lot. The depressing thing about these new-wave chaps is that they know it too, and then some. For instance, quite a few of them were ten-year-olds when England played Brazil in the 1970 World Cup but mention that Jeff Astle miss and they will shed real tears. And they go further back than that. Tell them about the first Wembley Cup Final, the one with the white horse, and they will talk as if they had had a seat in the front row: actually, the horse wasn't white, they'll say, it was dark grey – it just looks white in that over-exposed snapshot you keep showing me.

Where did they get this stuff? From Sky TV, from *Fever Pitch*, from Skinner and Baddiel? Or did they get it from their fathers, old soccer bores with nobody to talk to except their captive kids? 'Once upon a time there was this big white horse.' Another dismaying feature of the new 'soccer-literacy' is that its exponents tend to be Lit-literate as well. They can zap you with fantasy-league teams of big-name authors: Borges and Márquez up front, Kundera in midfield, Sam Beckett 'in the hole'. They like to assure you that Gunter Netzer's hairdo belongs in the same world as Gunter Grass's prose. They know all about Nabokov and Camus, and not just because the pair of them kept goal. A recent new-wave soccer-book gives something of the flavour:

> Albert Camus, Algerian goalie and French Existentialist, never took a penalty but it would have been interesting to watch him try (if, say, a penalty shoot-out against a Structuralist XI went all the way to the respective goalkeepers during sudden death). Would Camus have beaten an upright and non-diving Russian

Formalist like Vladimir Propp? And if a penalty shoot-out is inherently meaningless and absurd, would Camus have exercised his will effectively by scoring, thereby bringing individual meaning to the experience? Or would he have deliberately ballooned the ball over the crossbar, thereby defining himself through negative action? And what would he have made of that old Romantic bourgeois Hamish McAlpine, the Dundee United keeper who used to take all of his side's penalties whenever one was awarded during regular 90-minute matches? Come to think of it, Camus taking a penalty at Tannadice doesn't bear thinking about. He'd probably have stood over the ball for thirty agonising seconds, before whipping out a revolver and shooting a suspiciously dark supporter in the George Fox Stand (since United fans are known colloquially as 'Arabs').

This muddle of transdisciplinary pretentiousness comes from a book called *Not Playing for Celtic: Another Paradise Lost*, and yes, the paradise in question is indeed John Milton's − or Big John's (as he is called here):

Beating Airdrie in this year's final has hardly sent warning shock-waves reverberating around the football giants of Europe, but having witnessed the emotional scenes which followed, it seems appropriate to quote Milton once again:

Some natural tears they shed, but wiped them soon;
The world was all before them, where to choose
Their place of rest, and Providence their guide:
They hand in hand with wondering steps and slow
Through Eden took their solitary way.

A 'lack of pace' might seem to be the problem with this dual strike-force, but happily the author − David Bennie − does not say so.

Nick Hornby cannot be blamed for writing of this kind, although *Fever Pitch* has helped to set the tone. In some ways, Hornby has links with the old school. He knows and cares that there is something 'moronic' about his passion for the game, and about his Arsenal-fixation. Old-style bores used to keep quiet about this aspect of their calling; Hornby has had the nerve to make a book out of it − and a most unmoronic book, at that. A terrace Holden Caulfield, he doesn't even *like* Arsenal, for Chrissake, but he knows that he is stuck with them, just as he is stuck with pop music, junk lit crit, trash TV, just as he is stuck, really, with himself – a self shaped not by action or direct experience but by a kind of bombed-out cultural passivity, a wry/glum putting up with what's on offer, what's served up to him, week in, week out.

Soccer fans are nothing if not passive. The games they go to hardly ever turn out as they would wish, as they have dreamed. Football is nearly always disappointing. Epic confrontations turn out to be tepid stand- offs; celebrity performers are forever going through 'lean spells' or getting injured. If a star actor were to turn in a succession of substandard performances – forgetting lines, appearing onstage at wrong moments, tripping over during sword fights – he would soon enough not be a star. With soccer, the spectator is conditioned to expect the second-rate. He gets to like it; he gets even to prefer it. As with Nick Hornby, the new soccer bore's most vivid memories tend to be drawn from adolescence, that stretch of non-life when everything is less than it should be. TV at the moment is obsessed with soccer of the 1970s: the soccer watched with maximum intensity and thwartedness by the now-thirty-somethings who decide what is broadcast on TV. For types like these, supporting, say, Watford is remembered as a kind of pimply rite of passage, like going out with the wrong girl, the only girl who would have them in those days.

To be a new-style soccer bore, then, it is not enough merely to know about the soccer. It is what you muddle the soccer up with that wins marks. For Seventies adolescents, all of life's dramas were enacted to the sound of music, the music that just happened to be there, as Watford – and that girl – just happened to be there. Thus, the new soccer bore is expected to be as knowledgeable about chart-placings as he is about league tables and cup-runs. He has to be able to come on (more or less) as follows:

Abba's 'Super-Trouper' got to Number One on the Friday before the Luton game. I remember hearing it on someone's tranny on my way to Vicarage Road. I'd just split up with Sue, partly because I'd missed her birthday the week before; it was the same day as Wolves away. That was a crap game, nil-all, but I suppose it served me

right. Anyway, Abba at the time were spot-on, so I thought: 'I
was sick and tired of everything/When I called you last night.'
And I was reading Philip Larkin, where he says about nothing like
something happening anywhere. The next Saturday it was West
Brom at home.

Puppy love, pop tunes, A-level poetry, crap soccer. This seems to be
the recipe. Old soccer bores don't really stand a chance.

Even so, it has to be confessed that soccer-writing is a lot livelier
these days than it used to be. Even the lowest forms of soccer-lit –
the star player's ghosted Life, for instance – have become noticeably
more candid and style-conscious. For one thing, not all players choose
to hire a ghost. David Platt's *Achieving the Goal* is, we are told, all Platt's
own work. Unluckily, in this case, the author seems to have modelled
his prose style on soccer books that *have* been ghosted, so not a lot is
gained. As a player, David Platt always seems over-anxious to project
himself as the 'model professional', and on the page he evinces a similar
unease. When in doubt, he falls back on backpage soccer-speak, as if
believing this to be a model of correct procedure.

Still, now and then he does come close to speaking his own mind,
or so it seems. He admits that the goal he scored against Belgium in the
1990 World Cup changed his status overnight from 'eager-midfield-
runner' to 'man-capable-of-magic-moments'. Without that goal, Platt
might not have been so lucratively pursued by the Italians. He might
not even have lasted in the England team.

Graham Taylor, though, was always a Platt fan, and Platt owes a
lot to Taylor. One of the most strenuous sections of Platt's book is
devoted to repairing Taylor's reputation: a forlorn task, but rather
touching to behold. Taylor, we learn, is 'one of the best observers
of people I have ever met', whatever that might mean. Platt never
quite praises his old boss as a tactician but he makes no mention of that
foul-mouthed video and manfully condones Taylor's notorious substitution of Gary Lineker during the 1992 European Championships:
'I know Graham well, and can state categorically that the substitution
was tactical and not vindictive. If we had equalised in that final twenty
minutes Gary would have worn his number ten shirt in the semi-final.
Quite simply, it wouldn't have been his last game.'

This anodyne generosity of spirit is in evidence throughout. Even Ron Atkinson, who long ago 'released' Platt from Manchester United's youth squad – released him to Crewe Alexandra – comes in for a few words of praise. The only time Platt shows even a flicker of unwholesomeness is when he comes to describe his unhappy season with Juventus. Juventus, he says, never got the best out of him because they played him in the wrong position. One suspects, though, that Platt's experience of the Italian big time was more sharply humbling than he makes it out to be. In Turin, he may well have come to recognise that he was not, and never would be, quite the equal of his reputation. He would never improve on that heart-stopping Belgium goal – but then, who could?

A few years ago, David Platt's book would have been an altogether thinner, shoddier affair – aimed cynically at a fan readership not used to reading books. This is not to say that he does not incline towards the shoddy: 'You can only take people as you find them'; 'confidence is a funny thing'; 'an old cliché says that time flies,' and so on. All the same, Platt does from time to time make a real effort to analyse the mechanics of a footballer's career. He is no good at describing what the soccer itself feels like but on the subject of what the papers call 'personal terms' – cars, contracts, houses, perks – he is enthusiastically informative. For access of this sort, we should be grateful. Platt even reveals that his own Access card was once withdrawn because he had strayed into an offside position. This disclosure – from an England captain – would have been unthinkable in the old days.

Ghosted lives still have a market, though. This season has already brought us Gary McAllister's *Captain's Log* ('with Graham Clark') and *Blue Grit* by Glasgow Rangers' John Brown ('with Peter Watson'). Would Brown reveal some juicy Gazza tales or give us the dirt on Graeme Souness? Not a chance. Gascoigne is not mentioned (perhaps he arrived too late) and as for Souness: 'I haven't got a bad word to say about Graeme. I don't know if he was appreciated the way he should have been in Scotland. He had an arrogant streak, but he knew what he wanted and was a winner.' Would McAllister provide some inside dope on Eric Cantona? No, not a drop. These footballers write about their teammates as if they had never met them, as if – like us – they get their information from *The Sun*. Take McAllister on Cantona:

'But Eric, on and off the pitch, is different, and you have to live with that. His biggest problem is undoubtedly his temperament. We never saw too much of the dark side of that when he was with us, but it has reared up time and time again since he left. I think it must go with the territory of being something of a genius, even if that in no way excuses some of his excesses.' Cantona 'was a great guy any time we went out'; 'he had simple tastes and wasn't at all materialistic'; 'he spoke what is basically a football language and gelled immediately with the rest of the lads'; 'Lee Chapman was particularly pleased to see him.'

For all I know, the real-life Gary McAllister is as boring and pious as this 'log' makes him seem. I doubt it, though. And one day we may find out. Television's current soccer-madness has engendered a fashion for 'oral testimony' and already a few tongues have been loosened – usually the tongues of players who no longer play, but even so. *Kicking and Screaming*, the edited text of BBC TV's recent 'oral history of football in England', has several splendidly unbuttoned sound-bites. The book covers all of soccer history's important milestones – the Matthews final, the Hungarians at Wembley, the Munich disaster, the various World Cup campaigns – and offers intelligent close-ups of individual players, clubs and managers. It also covers most of the big soccer 'issues' – the maximum wage, hooliganism, bungs, all-seater stadiums. Altogether, the ideal 'how to' book for the aspiring soccer bore. But there are also rich pickings for the fan who knows it all: *Kicking and Screaming* is particularly good on English soccer in the early post-war years, when star players were paid next to nothing and, on top of that, were treated with crass condescension by the suits and bowler hats at the FA. There are several sardonic contributions here from members of the 1947–8 England team that beat Holland 8–0, Italy 4–0 and Portugal 10–0. For such triumphs the England players got a £10 appearance fee and a third-class train ticket home. And maybe a 'well done'. Just around the corner lay the 1953 defeat by Hungary, and a new epoch for English soccer: more money, higher status, fewer wins. *Kicking and Screaming* is admirably undecided on the matter of which epoch it prefers.

Less useful is Tom Watt's *A Passion for the Game*, which pokes about 'behind the scenes' of week-to-week league soccer, interrogating the game's faceless servants, from club secretaries to groundsmen to tea-ladies. Watt says that his book is modelled on Studs Terkel's *Working* but his tape-recorded informants are less interesting and much less articulate than Terkel's. A ticket-office clerk, a press-box assistant, a programme editor: Watt does his best to heroise these worthy toilers but most of them are deadly dull, and so too are their jobs. Some of Watt's workers are humble volunteers: 'They don't do it for the money. For them, it's Mark Bosnich calling them George or Steve.' Others view their tasks as inherited family traditions: Brentford's chief steward, for example, is the son of a Brentford turnstile operator and already has two daughters selling Brentford programmes. For several, though, the 'soccer industry' is just a job, and involves no special loyalty to the employer. These hard men tend to belong in merchandising or match-day hospitality. Thus, Liverpool's commercial department is staffed by Evertonians, and Manchester United's away strips are the brainchildren of a fugitive from Irving Scholar's Spurs. Hmm. Is that so? How boring. I must take a mental note.

London Review of Books, 1996

Tel's Tale

'I feel like the man who shot Bambi,' said Alan Sugar in May 1993, shortly after sacking Terry Venables from his job as manager and 'chief executive' of Spurs. Sugar presumably meant Bambi's mum. Bambi, as everybody knows, is still alive, still kicking, and now manager of England.

For a crack shot like Alan Sugar, it must be galling indeed to see his quarry frisking on the fabled Wembley sward: no longer wet-nosed and shaky-legged, perhaps, but still thoroughly adored. And all the more adored, it seems, each time *Panorama* or *The Sunday Times* unearths a new pile of dodgy paperwork. Sugar is normally a somewhat angry-looking chap but every so often over the past eighteen months he has seemed puzzled and upset. Why, he may have been wondering, does everyone so unthinkingly, so unaccountably, prefer this guy to me? Is there something so very wrong with my Bambi-like chin stubble? Don't these people want my kind of money – that's to say, real money, not the sort Tel likes to shift around? What *do* they want?

In 1992, it was Sugar's real money that saved Tottenham Hotspur from extinction, but somehow Terry Venables got all the credit (in more ways than one). As the fans saw things, it was Tel who persuaded Sugar to chip in, and it was Tel who, by stretching his own limited 'resources' to breaking point and maybe well beyond, made up the crucial shortfall – enough, anyway, for him to secure for himself a number two spot on the board and a power-sharing deal with Sugar, his new chairman. It was announced at the time that Venables would look after the XI on the field and Sugar would

take care of the XI at the bank: Spurs owed about eleven million,
rumour said. Venables, though, made it seem as if the success of the
whole enterprise depended on his business skills – or rather, on the
unique way in which those skills were interfused with his deep soccer
know-how. Thus, when Sugar turned on him, it was as if the host
had been evicted by the guest.

For a few weeks after the sacking, there were demos and petitions.
Sugar's home was picketed, his Roller vandalised. When Venables
sued for wrongful dismissal, crowds of his admirers gathered at the
High Court to barrack his oppressor. Sugar pretended to take these
shows of fan-power in his stride, predicting that by the beginning
of the new season Venables would be just another name at White
Hart Lane. He recruited Ossie Ardiles, a one-time terrace favourite
(now also fired), as Venables's replacement, headed off a rather feebly
threatened player strike, and let it be known that his cheque-book
would soon be available for glamorous new signings.

Sugar then set about trying to persuade the fans that Venables did
not deserve their love, that his record as a businessman was speckled
with illegal stratagems, most of these designed to pretend that he was
much richer than he really was. According to Venables: 'a relentless
newspaper campaign continued against my associates and me. They
dumped so much garbage that while I was answering one set of false
allegations, another load would be heaped on me from a different
direction. I was so busy defending my goal that I could not mount
any attacks of my own.'

Like the team he used to manage, Venables is not at his nimblest
when obliged to 'funnel back', but Sugar's pursuit of him since the
original bust-up does seem to have been fuelled by something other,
something deeper and fiercer, than mere business indignation. To
most fans, though, the details of Sugar's allegations seem unreachably
arcane: lots of stuff about buy-backs and bungs, about money that
is not money, loans that are not loans, pubs that might be made
of paper, and so on. On *Panorama* last month, a Lustgarten-style
presenter throbbed with gravitas as, sheet by sheet, he led us through
Tel's funny-money moves: invoices, loan agreements, letters of intent,
guarantees that had gone missing, signatures Tel claims are forged.
And yes, we supposed, it did look bad. But not *that* bad. As one fan

pointed out to me, whatever it was Tel did, he did it for the love
of Spurs.

And it is this kind of thinking that Sugar and his allies at the BBC
seem not to grasp, and certainly won't shift, however many bits of
paper they produce in evidence. After all, the fans will say, what are
they doing *their* whatever-it-is for? Why has the BBC's main current
affairs programme twice rearranged its schedules in order to bring
us the latest on Venables's long-ago financial juggling? According
to *Panorama*, they have a duty to get Venables dumped from the
England job because he is unfit to serve as our game's ambassador
abroad. Why then did the BBC only a few weeks before offer him a
long-term contract to continue as one of their chief soccer pundits?
If Tel is looking dodgy, so are some of his pursuers. And anyway,
since when has the England manager seemed, or wished to seem,
ambassadorial?

If Alan Sugar really does want to be loved as Tel is loved, he had
better change his tactics. He could begin by studying the fans he's
trying to win over. At White Hart Lane, the stands are full of wide
boys, artful dodgers, cheeky chappies of one sort or another. On
match days it's like a great army of the self-employed. Somebody
once reckoned that if you shouted 'Taxi!' at the Lane about a third of
the West Stand would want to know 'Where to?' And if you were to
yell 'VAT' another third would start making for the exits. You could
spend all day showing these lads off-colour invoices. Most of them
would marvel that *anything* had actually been put on paper.

For fans like these the worst that might be said of Tel is that he
got a bit above himself, out of his depth. But then again: so what?
He had a dream; he had a go. And now he's back doing what he's
good at: playing games. The really laughable idea is that, because of
the money, he should be kept from doing the football. The other way
round, maybe. Even here, though, surely some tribute should be paid
to the boy's chutzpah. Who else in football would have invented the
Thingummywig (for putting on over your curlers), or written a book
called *They Used to Play on Grass* shortly before installing a plastic
pitch at QPR, or marketed a soccer board-game called *The Manager*,
in which *everyone* starts out with a million pounds?

When Venables was at Tottenham in the late Sixties, he was viewed with deep suspicion by the fans. He liked himself too much, he put on airs, he had too many 'outside interests'. At the same time, though, there was a residual affection, an irritated sense of fellow feeling. The fans got at him, called him Vegetables, but they knew who he was: a chancer, a flash git – in other words, what they would be if they were him.

One particular incident sticks in the mind. Spurs had a throw-in just in front of where I was standing and Venables ran over to collect the ball. It had disappeared into the crowd behind me and was not instantly returned. For a few seconds, Venables stood facing his audience head-on, the audience that had been booing him all afternoon. What would he do? Glare back at us, go deadpan, turn away? Not Tel. After a tiny hesitation, he broke into a huge grin, shifted his eyebrows up and down, went down on one knee, then topped it all with a cheesily mimed '*Please*.' This did it. The ball shot from the crowd at brutally high speed and caught him, splat, full in the face. And along with it came a tumult of abuse. 'Flash fucker', 'poofter', 'cunt', 'Get on with it, you fucking ponce.' For a moment, Tel – all muddy-faced – looked utterly bewildered, close to tears. He picked the ball up, threw it in, and for the rest of the game did all he could to keep clear of the action.

And this was pretty much what might have been expected. The comedian had misread his audience-appeal, overrated his own charms. What happened next, though, was not quite so easy to explain. During the remaining half-hour of the match, whenever Venables did get the ball, the people around me, the ones who had just been calling him a ponce, now took to murmuring 'Nice touch, lad', 'Lay it off, son' – stuff like that. Was this remorse; a wish to make amends? Or was it simply that these fans now felt they owned a piece of him? He had in some way become theirs. They'd seen him flinch; they'd *made* him flinch. And now it was 'Good lad', 'Tel-mate', and all the rest of it. Sickening, yet it revealed plenty about fan psychology, about the vast impotence they feel most of the time. It also showed how little in the way of real-life power they'll settle for.

Tel knows all this; he learned it the hard way. Nowadays his cheeky-chappy routine is seasoned with just the right amount of 'you-tell-me' humility. He's still cocky but he plays up the imperilled look – the Bambi-look, as Sugar would describe it. Venables's new book is steadily boastful, in the way of most sports 'autobiographies', but lays on some extra blushes now and then. His triumphs are retailed as if they were not of his making, accidents that could not have happened to a nicer, abler bloke, perhaps, but accidents – the first English footballer to represent his country at 'all levels', the first to turn himself into a limited company, the first to take a foreign team to the final of the European Cup. Tel's tale is full of firsts. For a short time he was the first manager to own (well, semi-own) the club he managed. This prize, though, was snatched from him by Alan Sugar.

On the matter of Sugar, Terry shows his fairmindedness by confessing to one or two shortcomings of his own. Here and there he lets slip an admission that maybe his trusting nature plus his love of soccer plus the underhand ways of his opponent caused a brief slackening of his customary shrewdness:

> For the first few board meetings . . . both Jonathan Crystal and I decided to save time and avoid embarrassment by just assuming that the minutes would be accurate and agreeing them without studying them first, and the first four or five sets slipped through on that basis. It was a serious error of judgment on my part, but I was not then aware of the real nature of Alan Sugar, nor the use to which those minutes would later be put.

'I never bear grudges,' says Terry early on, and he does his lovable best to rein back his hostility to Sugar. All the same, the bile keeps seeping through. About a quarter of the book is given over to Venables's Tottenham power struggle and throughout there are too many bruised asides. Sugar even gets a mention on Day One: 'The house in which my Mum had been living before I was born was bombed flat the night she left to stay with my grandparents. Had she stayed twenty-four hours longer or the Luftwaffe arrived twenty-four hours earlier, Alan Sugar's future life might well have been rather less complicated.'

Another Venables bogey-man is Sugar's predecessor, Irving Scholar: 'Irv the Swerve', with his 'well-polished front' and his 'tangled web of secret and irregular loans and deals'. Scholar's own autobiography,

Behind Closed Doors, was anti–Tel, so this is Tel's moment for revenge. Again he strains for the soft-pedal with irregular success. 'I'm not bitter but a fact's a fact' is more or less the way it turns out. But it is hard going on the way, having to sit through Venables's not-very-bright rebuttals of Scholar's not-very-damaging put-downs.

One barb of Scholar's does, it seems to me, require an answer. In his book, Scholar accuses Venables of 'turning the key' on an already wound-up Gascoigne, just before the 1991 Cup Final, the game in which Gazza wrecked his knee. On this, Venables supplies the following:

> Irving Scholar's . . . suggestions that I had hyped Gazza up before the game are laughable and I think the players who were in the dressing-room would say the same. Gazza never needed anyone to hype him up, and all my conversations with him before any game, and the Cup Final in particular, were designed to calm him down, not wind him up . . . I do not know whether he was angry or what the reason was, but he did himself no favours.

Well, we know *that*. Gascoigne has not been the same player ever since. But what about those pre-match 'conversations'? Why doesn't Venables get us in there, show us something of what actually went on? Gazza's mad-bull conduct in that final still needs to be explained – or, shall we say, fleshed out. Venables, the player's number one mentor in those days, must surely know more than he is saying.

But this is the way it goes with sports books. They rarely tell the things you want to know. Unless, re Venables, you are hungry for more Sugar. Perhaps – with this ungripping book – Terry will feel that he has had his say, and get on with the serious business of saving us from humiliation in the forthcoming European Nations Cup. I doubt it, though. Just as Sugar wants the fans to love him, so Tel wants them to admire his business brain. There will be extra time.

Venables: The Autobiography by Terry Venables and Neil Hanson (Michael Joseph)

All Our Yesterdays:
Remembering the 1966 World Cup

The other day, just for a laugh, I asked a thirty-year-old soccer fan
to give me his 'memories' of England's 1966 World Cup victory. He
didn't laugh. On the contrary: within seconds, he was reeling off a list
of the 'key moments' of the match – the moments that 'mean most
to me, you understand'.

He itemised Hurst's thundering third goal, then spoke with eloquence of those 'heart-stopping' few seconds when the ref went over
to consult the Russian linesman. And he 'could not forget' the sight of
Bobby Moore, on the shoulders of his valiant team-mates, holding the
World Cup aloft. The fan's expression, as he reminisced, was wistful,
quietly proud. He'd been there and had lived to tell the tale.

And yet, of course, he hadn't. In 1966, this stripling had been
nowhere. Nonetheless, no detail of that famous July afternoon had
managed to escape him. He also had a point of view on all the
'talking points'. Hurst's controversial second goal, he reckoned, was
'legit – well, just about'. The ball *did* cross the line. And Alf Ramsey's
wing-back policy had, in his view, been 'justified, in the event'. There
was, he added, rather more to Ramsey than had met the eye.

Whose eye, one had to ask. Again, the jest fell flat. So far as
this fan was concerned, his memories were just as good as mine.
His were synthetic, mere hand-me-downs picked up from soccer
books, TV nostalgia shows and bar-room word of mouth. Mine
were authentic, on-the-spot: I'd been there and he hadn't. And
yet the sad truth is that if he had asked *me* to name *my* World
Cup magic moments, I would almost certainly have come up with:

'Well, I suppose Hurst's thundering third goal, the Russian linesman, Bobby Moore.'

There was a generation gap, and no doubt every other kind of gap, but for twenty years or so, it seemed, we two had been glued to the same re-runs, dipping into the same tub of soccer lore. The myth of the 1966 World Cup, as sanctioned by time and the media, was ours to share. My yesterdays were his.

Well, maybe. The first law of mythogenesis is to eliminate the fuzzy bits. There are people who like to be told what they should remember and sometimes, with big historical events, 'real' memories queue up to be subsumed by legend. And the legend of our World Cup victory will live, no doubt, until we win the thing again – which could take quite some time. Lots of other things happened in the world in 1966. In China, for example, the Cultural Revolution's infamous first Fifty Days overlapped with the Twenty Days of our World Cup. France pulled out of NATO. The Soviets landed a spacecraft on the moon. *Star Trek* premièred on NBC TV and in Florence there were ruinous floods. In Vietnam, the 'American presence' was quadrupled; by the end of 1966, it was close to 400,000, with more to come. The average Briton, though, remembers one set of statistics from that year: England 4 West Germany 2 (after extra time).

For three decades now, we have been sipping from that 1966 World Cup, finding in it some important sustenance or comfort. Political historians mention the Cup win as a significant feature of Harold Wilson's populist New Britain. Pop analysts connect it to the Beatles, swinging London, the whole chirpy Sixties thing. At last, they say, England had something to sing about; the grey days of the Fifties were outlived. And cultural iconographers continue to pore over those photos of Bobby Moore's obeisant encounter with the Queen.

Moore, it will be remembered, wiped his muddy hands before accepting the trophy from the gloved fist of his ruler. Dave Hill, in his new book, *England's Glory*, has described the moment rather well: 'Moore's later explanation for this was prosaic – he was worried about soiling Her Majesty's white gloves. But some now see in his gesture evidence of a finer era long demolished, a kind of Wembley Stadium of the national spirit, with chivalry and deference as its twin towers, with the monarch as its blameless guardian and Moore representing the dauntless decency of the English working class. Add Nobby Stiles doing his wacky lap-of-honour war-dance and perhaps a Spitfire doing a victory roll overhead, and you have enough raw material to keep romantic patriots in reveries for years.'

I'm not sure about the Spitfire, but Hill is right to identify a strain of war-hero nostalgia in the World Cup myth. After all, it was Germany we beat. He might also have mentioned the 'patriotic' T-shirts worn by English soccer fans on European away-trips in the Seventies. They spoke of blitzkriegs and invasions. 'Two World Wars and One World Cup' was a slogan which, presumably, did not survive West Germany's subsequent near-ownership of the Jules Rimet trophy, but it still leaves a nasty taste.

During the Falklands War, it was widely recalled that Alf Ramsey, after England defeated Argentina in the 1966 quarter-finals, had called his opponents 'animals'. Ramsey's remark, considered ill-considered at the time, became – just like his wing-backs – 'justified, in the event'.

'Then we were up yelling and stamping, and slapping one another as Hurst shot the last staggering goal. The sky had been overcast all afternoon, but now the clouds split and the sun glared down on the stadium. Maybe those fellows were right when they said God was an Englishman.'

This was Hugh McIlvanney, writing in *The Observer* the day after England's win. God an Englishman? McIlvanney, a fierce Scot, presumably meant by this that England had been very fortunate. And so they had. Hurst's second goal (the one given by the Russian linesman) actually *didn't* cross the line. And as for his marvellous third strike, the German defenders had stopped playing. Like the fans who were already invading one corner of the pitch, they believed the referee had blown the final whistle. They, too, thought it was all over. And then, suddenly, it was. England, to be sure, were lucky; they got all the breaks. But if I had said such a thing to my underage fan-friend, he would have said: 'So what?' And I would happily have left it there.

Even so, 'real' memories should sometimes have their say. For one thing. I am sure I didn't 'yell and stamp' when Hurst blasted his third goal. And nobody I knew waved any flags when Bobby Moore went up to meet the Queen.

To tell the truth, so far as I can now exhume it, most of my friends and associates – poets, literary critics, academic long-hairs and the like – spent that 30th July half-hoping that England would get thrashed. A well-merited defeat, I think we all agreed, would be a good thing for English soccer, good for England, good for literature, art, culture, good for us.

We had our reasons. As trainee soccer-intellectuals, we were duty-bound to despise the patriotic hype: the rubbish about World Cup Willy, the dog Pickles, and all that. And we had an obligation to despise Alf Ramsey, whose press-conference syntax was a mess and whose taste in footballers seemed contemptibly utilitarian. In my circle, soccer was thought of as akin to poetry, and in poetry we thinkers much preferred brief lyric surges to, let's say, the drudgery of epic. As we perceived it. England had a deeply prosy team. Apart from Bobby Charlton and perhaps the goalie Banks, not one of Ramsey's men could plausibly be thought of as world-class. But then Ramsey, we believed, was the arch-enemy of individual talent. If he ever watched *us* play, he wouldn't pick us. This we knew.

Some weeks before the World Cup tournament got going, Ramsey had announced, to general mirth, that England would emerge victorious. Now all he cared about was saving face. Our line was: if a Ramsey line-up were to capture soccer's biggest prize, we would be in for at least three decades of nervous mediocrity. And this was to say nothing of the impact such a victory might have on English verse.

In 1966, I was in my middle to late twenties, a Spurs fan and, in particular, a fan of Jimmy Greaves. For me – and for most of my soccer-playing literary pals – the chief, if not the only, point of World Cup '66 was that it offered a stage on which to show the world what we at Spurs already knew – that here was genius: high-speed, instinctive, deadly, off-the-cuff.

And it was not just that Greaves scored lots of goals. We also wanted the world to know something of the man. Greaves, we contended, had unusual human qualities: wit, warmth and – probably – much wisdom. You could divine this from the way he played: it was as if he didn't *care*. He scored goals without looking, without ever seeming to take aim. He just did what he did, as if by magic.

Needless to say, Greaves knew nothing of defence. He never tackled, never fouled. When Spurs were pinned back on their own goal-line, frantically trying to protect a one-goal lead, our hero could be found at the other end of the field, chatting with the opposition's keeper. And he would always be forgiven. If anyone reproached him, he would smile, stir himself and score another goal. A two-goal lead was much more easily defended.

Alf Ramsey never fathomed Jimmy Greaves. Everything about this player was a kind of insult to the conscientious pre-planning that the England manager most prized. Greaves quite liked to win. Ramsey was terrified of losing. Also, Greaves came from Dagenham, Ramsey's own home town. Where Ramsey had struggled to better himself, taking elocution lessons so that he would come over on the telly as a diplomatic-official type of guy, Greaves was unashamedly the Cockney imp. It was also rumoured that Greaves liked a drink. Ramsey, of course, didn't.

All the same, as long as Greaves kept scoring, Ramsey had to pick him for the England team. In the group game against France, though, Greaves was injured, and Ramsey replaced him with Geoff Hurst, a willing plodder, in our view. Hurst shocked us by scoring in the Argentina game and was selected once again, for the semi-final against Portugal. Greaves was almost fit but not quite, so we let this pass. He would be ready for the Big One, which – by now – we were quite keen should come to pass. The Final would be Greaves's finest hour.

As it turned out, England – in a thrilling match – beat Portugal 2–1, and for the first time in the competition, they played pretty well. Hurst did nothing much, but he was competent – and he was *there*, one of a winning team. I remember us all sitting in a Wembley pub after the Portugal game. Everyone was celebrating: England had reached a World Cup final for the first time, and were looking good. All we could do was wonder: would Ramsey choose this moment to strike back at Greaves and all he stood for?

And he did. Greaves was left out of the England team, left out of history, annulled. If someone had told us before the final that Hurst would score a hat-trick, we would probably have wept. After the game we did – well, sort of – weep. Greaves, we were told, had not shown up for the celebration banquet at the Royal Garden Hotel. He was somewhere else in London, getting drunk. And so were we.

You'll think we were absurd. Perhaps we were. But maybe not entirely. The truth is that Ramsey's 1966 triumph has had plenty of negative outcomes: the obsession with 'work-rate' and defensive ruggedness, the lingering belief that English soccer really is world-class, the hooligan phenomenon, with all its National Front tie-ins. And, thanks to Ramsey, it is now thoroughly acceptable for managers to turn their noses up at an unstable individual talent. Great players are described as 'luxuries'.

Since Jimmy Greaves retired, it seems to me that only two English players have come close to matching him: Glenn Hoddle and Paul Gascoigne (as it happens, both ex-Spurs). Each of these splendid talents has had his career dogged by managerial suspicion. Neither Ron Greenwood nor Bobby Robson really 'trusted' Hoddle's gifts and it took Robson two seasons to make up his mind about Gascoigne. As it transpired, Gazza more or less saved Robson's reputation with his performances in the 1990 World Cup, but I doubt that Robson even now could bring himself to say so.

And so to the European championship, the first international tournament to be held on English soil since '66. No wonder we are apprehensive. The omens, though, are somewhat brighter than they were thirty years ago. The manager, Terry Venables, is more of a Ramsey man than he likes to pretend, but at least he has no reservations about Gascoigne. And his successor is to be Glenn Hoddle, finally certain of his England place.

Under Venables, England have become expert at low-scoring draws and one-nil wins, and Shearer is no Greaves, but this time I really will, full-throatedly, be rooting for the lads. And I'll no doubt be telling anyone who'll listen that the whole thing takes me back – back to the great days of '66: Hurst's thundering third goal, the Russian linesman, Bobby Moore. Ah yes, I remember it well.

The Times Magazine, 1996

Cups and cups:
Chelsea, the Boro, Alan Hudson

Saturday's FA Cup Final [May, 1997] has been billed as something of a connoisseur's delight. The question being asked is not so much 'Who will win?' as 'Who will blow it?' Which of the two contestants will jettison a handsome half-time lead or snatch an ingenious own goal in the last minute? Which of them will come out of it more poignantly? Chelsea and Middlesbrough have this season been the soccer aesthete's dream teams: bristling with Italo-Brazilian flair but inconsistent, full of attacking wizardry but suspect in defence. In other words, too good for their own good. No wonder we like them, as Kingsley Amis used to say, though not of course re soccer.

On paper, certainly, with their expensive foreign stars, both teams ought to have done better in the Premiership contest, what we used to call the League. Chelsea, as I write, are in sixth place and Middlesbrough are still candidates for relegation. It has been a feature of their charm, though, that they have always seemed a cut above the dreary labour of accumulating Premiership points. To win the Cup you need to win six games. You need to get it right six times in a season of, say, fifty matches. Cup teams, the story goes, are those which thrive on the high tension of kill-or-be-killed. League teams, on the other hand, are those which know how to deliver, points-wise, on a weekly basis. Cup teams win 'famous victories'; League teams 'grind out results'. Chelsea and Middlesbrough are, assuredly, cup teams. Even in the Cup, though, they have each enjoyed leaving too much to chance. For instance, neither would be in the final but for two spectacular refereeing blunders.

At the same time, neither would be there without flashes of wondrously un-English brilliance from Zola and Juninho. These players – Zola for Chelsea, Juninho for Middlesbrough – have injected a new interest into our post-Gascoigne soccer scene, a new possibility of unexpectedness. Would we have loved them, though, if they had played for teams that did the business every week? Much of their appeal has been to do with the uncertainty, the recklessness they seem to generate: in their opponents but also in their team-mates. In the presence of a Zola, average players tend to get above themselves. Now and then this can pay off: above themselves, they play accordingly. More often, though, they end up forgetting what it was that made them average – no left foot, slow on the turn, weak in the air – and forgetting, too, the safety ploys they had developed in order to disguise their averageness. And this can make for some weird and wonderful defensive cock-ups. Still, who would rather be watching Leeds United?

For Middlesbrough, their current glamour-team status must have taken some getting used to. For more than a century, they have been one of football's least intriguing also-rans, shuttling contentedly between the First and Second Divisions, with one or two spells in the Third. A hundred years is a long time to go without even a whiff of the game's major prizes – no League titles, no FA Cups, not even a cup-run to speak of – but Boro fans have never seemed to mind. Mid-table mediocrity (preferably in Division One) has always been the most that they'd allow themselves to hope for. Reaching, say, the fifth round of the FA Cup would, in the old days, have been reckoned to be somewhat pushy.

I used to watch Middlesbrough from time to time in the early Fifties, when they were heading for one of their sojourns in Division Two. They finally went down in 1954, along with Liverpool, who – ten years later – were back at the top as League champions, then Cup-winners, and then kings of everything. Middlesbrough ten years later were tenth in Division Two and were relegated a couple of years afterwards. Nobody on Teesside, so far as I recall, appeared to think that Boro might have emulated Liverpool's revival. The two teams were – and so they were – 'in different leagues'.

Before Bryan Robson's arrival as manager and his signing, not long afterwards, of Juninho, Emerson and Ravanelli, Middlesbrough star-names had been names from the distant past: Wilf Mannion, George Hardwick, Brian Clough. For a brief period in the mid-Seventies, under Jackie Charlton, the team looked as if it might be going places, but not for very long. Players like Graeme Souness, Bobby Murdoch and David Armstrong got them to the sixth round of the Cup, the semi-finals of the old League Cup, and to seventh in Division One, and this was thought to be a peak achievement. But the upsurge swiftly fizzled out. Indeed Souness, who the Boro fans believed was 'too big for his boots', was steadily barracked throughout his final game at Ayresome Park and at the end 'tore off his shirt and hurled it at the crowd'. Souness, according to his biographer, 'hankered for the bright lights, the glamour, the bigger stage. Middlesbrough was a minor repertory company, what Souness wanted was the National Theatre.' So, too, says this same chronicler, did Jackie Charlton – who, in fact, quit before Souness was sold to Liverpool. 'Even Charlton would have acknowledged that Middlesbrough was a club that was never going to go very far.'

If Middlesbrough, over the years, could have loved themselves a little more, Chelsea could surely have loved themselves a little less. No doubt because of their upmarket location, Chelsea have always been thought of as a showbiz team: i.e. according to their enemies, all show and not much business. Early on, we're often told, they were the constant butt of music-hall comedians (something to do, this, with George Robey who was apparently on Chelsea's books once, as an amateur). There was even a popular ditty – 'The day Chelsea went and won the Cup' – which was taken to encapsulate the club's special brand of dreamy ineffectiveness. 'No club,' says one Chelsea historian, 'had, for so long, possessed the ability to be brilliant or pathetic without reason, to excel or disappoint without warning.'

Chelsea's record, since they started out, is actually not unimpressive, but there has always been this feeling about them that they were too wetly narcissistic for the serious big time. And that image seemed to be confirmed, in the mid-Sixties, when Chelsea players took to hanging out in the King's Road boutiques and hostelries of Swinging London. Chelsea's team of that decade – the team of Venables, Tambling, Bridges and so on – was often wonderful to watch, but you could see what was meant when people sneered at Chelsea's preening. The lads were just a bit too likely – too suntanned, too winsomely well-coiffed, too playboy.

On form, though, they could play. Being Chelsea, they were not consistently on form but even on bad days they were pretty good. For four years Venables and Co kept coming close. They were Cup semi-finalists in '65 and '66 and losing finalists in '67, by which time Venables had left for Spurs, the victors in that final. Venables, we understood, had had a 'clash of personalities' with manager Tommy Docherty – he who, when asked to describe one Chelsea star's non-soccer interests, said: 'That's simple. He has two: wanking and comics.' Docherty, it seems, had envied Tel's smooth metropolitan charisma, as well he might have done.

For all their flash, or maybe because of it, the Venables side never seemed likely to upset the general dominance of Leeds and Liverpool. And much the same was true of their successors, the also fun-to-watch Chelsea of the Seventies, the Chelsea of Osgood, Cooke and Hudson. But this side did manage to deliver, especially in cup competitions. Chelsea won the FA Cup in 1970, the European Cup-Winners' Cup in 1971, beating Real Madrid in the final. They could never quite hack it in the League, though. Some weeks they seemed unbeatable; others they seemed, well, bleary-eyed, somewhat unsteady on their boots. As with the Venables team, and perhaps with more justice, there was talk of too much King's Road booze, too much of the old showbiz. You could not read about Chelsea in those days without getting a list of their 'growing array of support from the entertainment world, including Terence Stamp, Michael Crawford, David Hemmings, Lance Percival, Tommy Steele and Marty Feldman' – and that was just the defence. (Nowadays, of course, it's Banks up-front, Major on the bench and Mellor for the early bath.) For a time, Richard Attenborough was club chairman. Viewed from the bleak kingdom of Don Revie up in Leeds, these 'Southern softies' never stood a chance.

It was Leeds, though, who lost – narrowly and unluckily – to Chelsea in that 1970 final. According to Alan Hudson, Don Revie was so incensed by the defeat that when he became England manager he took his revenge by not picking Chelsea players. Hudson relates this story in his newly-published autobiography, and it is one of several in which Hudson features as the injured party. His grievances are many and run deep. Like several of his admirers at the time, he wants to know what happened to his early promise. What spoiled it? Who's to blame? In the Chelsea first team at nineteen, Hudson was widely tipped for greatness. In his book, he provides numerous impressive testimonials to his precocious gifts – and accompanies each of them with his own heart-felt personal endorsement. What went wrong? By his mid-twenties, Hudson was burnt out, an England discard, ex-Chelsea, ex-Arsenal, ex-Stoke, seemingly doomed to play out what was left of his career with the Seattle Sounders. After Seattle, there were one or two come-back attempts, but none of them worked out. Even a brief return to Chelsea was, he says, 'a nightmare'. Hudson had trouble holding down a place in the reserves. In the end, Stamford Bridge, home of his early triumphs, had turned into 'a rancid meat pie, crawling with maggots'.

There are many explanations for what happened to Alan Hudson – an early leg injury, a weakness for the bottle, a tendency to put on weight – but in his book the real blame lies with Revie-like managerial conspiracies, the eagerness with which mediocrity seeks to destroy genius. At every stage of his career, says Hudson, his giant talent was envied and undermined by 'lesser mortals' – coaches, managers, club chairmen, sometimes even team-mates. Sir Alf Ramsey, he tells us, 'once said of me: "There is no limit to what this boy can achieve." He was wrong. There were limits put on the parameters of my career by the confederacy.' (Yes, you've guessed it. Hudson now works as a sportswriter.) Not only was Hudson's soccer genius a marvel to be envied by the second-rate: there was also the problem of his general classiness – his looks, his fashion sense, his up-West restaurant sophistication, his glittering contacts in the worlds of stage and screen. Hudson's book is full of contempt for less than top-notch footballers, but when it comes to even the most minor showbusiness celebrity, his prose suddenly begins to drip with adoration. Indeed a whole chapter is given over to 'all the great and famous people I have come across'. One of Hudson's biggest all-time thrills was being spoken to by Elton John.

How can a man who has been thus honoured take orders from

a joyless frump like Dave Sexton? As Hudson remembers it, the brightest soccer talents of his day – Alan Hudson, Stan Bowles, Tony Currle, Charlie George – were systematically sidelined by soulless FA apparatchiks in the Sexton mould, men who treated Rolls-Royces as if they were minicabs. Undervalued as players, such figures now find themselves barred from top jobs in management and coaching. (Hudson has, it seems, been turned down for several coaching jobs.) 'I call them the Reservoir Dogs – a huge lake of talent waiting to be passed on, yet treated like rabid dogs by the establishment that strangles the game.'

If Alan Hudson really does want a job in soccer management, this book will scarcely serve his cause. On the one hand, he tries to promote himself as a sobered-up, deep-thinking soccer sage. On the other, he can't help inflating his own superior-soul tragic plight: the wounded late-night loner, the 'scarred soul', the My Way pilgrim of dead dreams, and all the rest of it. Worst of all, though, he can't resist settling old scores. His book is full of petty digs and sneers: all of them retaliatory, as it turns out, but masquerading as considered judgements. It's a sorry, sour performance: not to be read by nostalgic Chelsea fans until after 17 May. [Chelsea won 2–0].

The Working Man's Ballet by Alan Hudson (Robson Books)

London Review of Books, 1997

Three Managers: Busby, Shankly, Stein

Next weekend [March, 1997], BBC TV's *Arena* will be screening three hours of homage to a trio of Scots soccer bosses: Matt Busby, Bill Shankly and Jock Stein. The three had much in common: each rose from a less-than-comfortable upbringing in the Lanarkshire coalfields – their childhood homes were only a few miles apart – and each achieved consistent and spectacular success in soccer-management: Busby with Manchester United, Shankly with Liverpool, Jock Stein with Glasgow Celtic. Their successes belonged largely to the late 1960s/early 1970s but their memory is certain to live on. Most soccer-folk today would place these three among the all-time greats.

Even so, a few non-soccer-folk – if such there are – will maybe feel that three hours of screen biography is rather much. Aware of this possibility, *Arena* is at pains to let us know that something more than soccer-greatness is at issue here. Busby, Stein and Shankly are presented as three bona-fide heroes of our time, three titans who just happened to express their genius through sport. A study of their lives encompasses reflections on the decline of industry in western Scotland, the folly of religious sectarianism, the once vital and inspiring power of the trades union movement, and – most of all – the still-perplexing enigma of 'Scottishness'. In other words: don't get the idea that you'll be watching yet another laddish laugh-in about footie.

Luckily, each of *Arena*'s trio had a gripping television-presence: Busby the benign, all-knowing patriarch; Shankly the cocksure, perilously-tense obsessive; Stein the shrewd but ever-anxious Scottish chieftain. Using old interviews, clips from big games and yards of reminiscence from a cleverly-assembled pack of 'living witnesses',

Arena interweaves the three biographies with even-handed skill. There are contributions from surviving relatives of the big three, from friends, colleagues and ex-players. Busby in particular is well served by these memoirists: in one entertaining sequence, John Stalker (a close friend of Busby's) takes us on a tour of Manchester, where he himself used to be Chief Constable. Busby, before managing United, played for City. There are tours too of abandoned coalfields, and of disappeared pit villages. And the whole thing is assisted in its bid for general depth by an emotional, first-person script by Hugh McIlvanney, known to us all as sportswriting's most sonorous and stylish rhetorician.

A Scot from Lanarkshire himself, McIlvanney knows from experience how hard it was for these three local heroes to do what they did. In consequence, his phrasing sometimes veers towards the grandiose. And his contrived exchanges with his brother William, the 'poet and novelist', are steadily adrip with Celtic self-congratulation. For McIlvanney, Matt, Bill and Jock were soccer-saints: tough, wise, emotional and deeply 'moral'. Successful men, they were no strangers to misfortune. Busby survived the Munich air crash that wiped out half his team. Shankly was forced out of the game prematurely. Stein suffered a fatal heart attack while watching a highly-charged Scotland World Cup game in 1985. On the whole, though, the *Arena* trilogy provides a record of accumulated triumphs. Each of the three took from his mining ancestry some secret, primal gift that perfectly equipped him for the burdens and excitements of strong public leadership. Each possessed, in William McIlvanney's words, 'an instant ability to command respect. You knew this was not a person to mess about with, or to be glib and silly with. They could laugh, but there was an innate, instinctive, dignified seriousness about them and their purposes.'

The world of coal-mining and the world of soccer, we are told, are not so very different. 'Hard places' both, they ask for deep reserves of courage, mental strength and camaraderie: a sense of one-for-all and all-for-one. Busby, Stein and Shankly brought these miners' qualities to all their soccer-dealings – plus, thankfully, a fair knowledge of the actual game. *Arena* in fact tells us very little about how the mining ethos was made to pay off on the field of play. None of the three managers under discussion was greatly distinguished as a player. Their characters were best expressed through other people's skills. But how, in practice, did this work? *Arena*'s efforts to explain are unimpressive. A clip of some deft interpassing movement is used to illustrate the importance of team-spirit. This is then followed by a swift cut to the pithead, where it all began. Well, thanks a lot. But then, to be fair, most of us are pretty ignorant when it comes to assessing the performances of soccer bosses. In the end, we judge according to results. And certainly, by this criterion, *Arena*'s men were peerless. All three of them delivered, in abundance: League Championships, FA Cups and, in the case of Stein and Busby, the long-yearned-for European Cup. Celtic, in 1967, became the first British club to conquer Europe; a year later, Busby's rebuilt side magnificently followed suit. And Liverpool – though Shankly retired in 1974 – went on to win the European Cup four times. On *Arena*, Joe Fagan (who briefly managed Liverpool himself) testifies, with warmth, that it was Shankly who laid the foundations for these record-breaking victories.

The statistics, then, cannot be quarrelled with. All the same, we are left wanting to know more about just how this soccer-management thing works. In today's game, managers are more heavily glamourised than all but the starriest of their star players. No longer do we talk merely of Everton or Aston Villa; nowadays, it's 'Joe Royle's Everton' or 'Brian Little's Aston Villa'. Thirty years ago, managers were acknowledged as important, and the best of them were heroised, but mostly they were thought of as vague backroom presences. Nowadays, even a mediocre soccer-boss is guaranteed his spot at centre-stage. For some fans, the fate of the manager has become almost more engrossing than the fate of the team: the team is there to stay, the manager is always on the brink. When things go well, the bosses preen themselves on touchlines, in their matchday haircuts and their snazzy suits, as if they were pop stars. A few setbacks, though, and they are skulking in the stands – dowdy and ashen-faced, like *Private Eye's* Ron Knee.

For pressmen, it would seem, there is a special thrill in studying a line of work that makes their own seem safe as houses. The papers are constantly reminding us that no manager can be sure that he'll survive the season, however impressive his curriculum vitae, however many cups he won last year. The question always is: when will he get the sack? Not will he? but *when* will he? A mis-hit shot, a handball, a deflection and it's curtains for Ron Knee. Or, if such misadventures go the other way, it's curtain calls. Looked at from this standpoint, there can be no such thing as a dull nil-nil draw.

Television coverage is similarly manager-fixated. Thus, an extra *frisson* has been added to our viewing pleasure. A goal goes in, or doesn't. Within seconds, a camera leaps to the touchline dug-out, which has suddenly become a site of top-grade human interest: joy, bewilderment, despair – or, if it's Chelsea, studied cool. The commentator spells it out: 'Joe's job is safe!', he yells. And then: 'Or *is* it?', as the opposing team mounts an attack. And so it goes, week in, week out – a whole new ball-game. Players no longer strive for personal glory; they are now said to be 'doing it' or 'not doing it' for Joe. And afterwards it's Joe we want to hear from: especially if we happen to be writing for the Monday papers, which would be quite lost without at least one paragraph per game of managerial debriefing.

These post-match interviews are handled with an almost comic guardedness. In a style seemingly borrowed from *Newsnight*, the managers treat every question as if it bore some hidden threat to their integrity, or livelihood. Quite simply, they don't trust 'the media'. Too many of their fellows have been wooed, then knifed. On the other hand, they need the coverage. Hence, on Mondays, we are fed with crumbs: '"It's early days", said Bassett, "and we mustn't get carried away, but the players responded well and kept going, and if we continue to show this sort of ability and belief we've got a chance."' In other words: get lost, sir, if you please.

In recent years, three big-name managers have voluntarily quit their jobs because they were suffering, they said, from nervous stress. Kenny Dalglish relinquished his post at Liverpool because the 'pressure' had become too much for him. Kevin Keegan suddenly walked out on Newcastle, the club he had 'single-handedly' rescued from long years of dismal failure: again, pressure was said to be the reason. (Keegan's job was taken by Dalglish.) Steve Coppell resigned from Manchester

City after only a few days at his post. He too, he said, had been engulfed by 'stress'.

There are, of course, rumours which suggest that other factors might have been behind these resignations. 'Pressure', though, does have a certain glamour – evoking, as it seems to, heroes driven to the edge. And yet, oddly enough, this stress epidemic has coincided with an overall reduction in the powers of soccer managers. The Terry Venables/Alan Sugar power struggle, the George Graham bung disclosures, the regular press hints of an upcoming – and bung-related – showdown with the Inland Revenue: all of these, together with soccer's growing awareness of itself as a big business, have lately persuaded quite a few club owners to stay closer to their money than they used to. In the past, managers ran everything: players' transfers, bonuses, new contracts, even ticket distribution. Nowadays they are being told to leave the money side of things to those who know how money works. Their job, they are reminded, is to supervise the soccer.

As if to underscore this edict, club chairmen are now looking to Europe for their managers – or 'coaches', as they would prefer them to be called. In Europe, a coach is just a coach, and proud of it. He wears elegant tracksuits and brainy-looking spectacles and bristles with mysterious strategic know-how. Arsène Wenger is already at Arsenal; Ruud Gullit at Chelsea – and there are more to come. Soccer-thinkers of this calibre don't *want* to be distracted from their soccer tasks by balance-sheets and stock-market flotations.

For Busby, Stein and Shankly, this new development would have been an unacceptable demotion. All three were heavily involved in every aspect of the clubs they managed. Matt Busby in fact pioneered the executive-box scheme. Some of today's bosses, schooled in the old ways (and influenced, no doubt, by the example of *Arena*'s fabled trio), have found it hard to give up money-tasks which they regard as central to team supervision: the buying and selling of players, for example, and the fixing of wage-levels – these, they would say, bear weightily on team performances. The players themselves tend to be money-mad, forever eyeing each other's salaries. Dressing-room politics, we're told, are ruled by money rivalries. It is the manager's job to stabilise these things. And how better to motivate a disaffected star than to threaten him with a wage-freeze? Gaffers who run the till get more respect than those who don't.

Responsibility without power: a stressful combination, to be sure. But with some managers the stress comes from within – from that intensity of soccer-passion that Busby, Stein and Shankly were brought up with, and shared with the fans. Perhaps those three were lucky not to have been top-rank players. They never expected too much from their teams. Great players who turn to management rarely live up to their own expectations. One thinks of Bobby Charlton, Liam Brady – and even Stanley Matthews. For such as these, watching from the touchline and powerless to intervene, each mis-hit pass can be a kind of aesthete's agony. As they remember it, inch-perfect passing was dead easy.

The England manager, Glenn Hoddle – in his day a player of the highest quality – seems to have found a way of, so to speak, adjusting his high standards downwards. For others, of less sanguine temper, the management of not-quite-perfect teams can be, well, super-stressful. You can sometimes see it in their faces (courtesy of Sky TV). And sometimes, after ninety minutes of internal seething, their frustration bubbles over. Take the recent behaviour of Coventry's Gordon Strachan – not a great player, maybe, but certainly a notch or two above most members of the side he is currently struggling to save from relegation. After a big Coventry defeat the other day, Strachan let fly at his own players: 'All the best players,' he fumed, 'have good desire. All the best players have the desire to win. There are loads of people, and I'm not just talking about my players, for whom to be a great player is too much hard work. Desire is with the great players.' This is not the first time that Strachan has seen red, and one can sympathise, to some extent. At the same time, one fears for this manager's job prospects. Is this really the way to rally a disheartened team?

Even the dictatorial Bill Shankly was incapable of publicly dispraising his own team, in spite of his belief that players who 'cheated the public' by not trying should be jailed – 'put oot the way of society'. He made his players proud, he said, to play for Liverpool. He gave them something important to live up to. 'He treated us like grown-ups': this, or something like it, is said more than once in the *Arena* trilogy, when players are asked to analyse Shankly's success. And the same too is said of Stein and Busby. A sensitivity to players' vanities seems to be a first requirement for good soccer management. 'I always wanted to treat the players the way I expected to be treated myself,' says Matt Busby in *Arena*. Stein agrees: 'I don't treat them just like players. I'm part of them and they're part of the club they play for.' And Shankly gives the sentiment his own distinctive spin: 'It's the study of human nature, that's the main thing. Every player who comes here, the minute he steps in here, he's being watched, he's being *scrutinised*. We're reading him like a book. Then, in a month's time, we know everything about him – all his weaknesses and all his strengths. We study them and I could write a book about every player here. I could tell you the colour of every one of their eyes. So, this is the thing.'

This paternalistic zeal, alas, did not extend to players' wages. Busby, Stein and Shankly grew up in the old maximum-wage, retain-and-transfer era, when players were treated like club chattels. In that context, a spot of fatherly goodwill was more than welcome. But when, in 1963, the ceiling on players' wages was removed, Busby and Co were in no hurry to distribute the ensuing benefits. Manchester United in the 1960s were notoriously poor payers, and Liverpool were not much better. And Jock Stein at Celtic found it hard to come to terms with a new breed of money-hungry stars – stars ready to leave Celtic in search of English gold. Club loyalty had been easy to insist on in the old days, when everyone was paid the same – i.e. not very much. Stein himself was poorly-paid but didn't mind. He was still better off than his old mining friends. He never got above himself and could not bear it when young players put on affluent new airs. 'What do *you* want with a prawn cocktail and a fillet steak?', he asked one of them at a club dinner: 'What's wrong with fish and chips?'

The third section of *Arena*'s trilogy is perhaps the most affecting of the three. In it the miners' strengths which took these three men to the top are shown to have worked against them in the end. 'They were forward-looking men,' says McIlvanney, 'but they could not escape the baggage of their upbringing in the game.' Strength turned into stubbornness, a dour unwillingness to change. At Manchester United, Matt Busby eventually retired but could not bring himself to walk away: his several successors felt overshadowed by the Busby myth, and Matt himself seems to have somewhat revelled in their nervousness. Jock Stein was not given the chance to stick around at Celtic. Believing him to be in decline, the Celtic board decided to appoint a younger man – one of Stein's former protégés, Billy McNeill. Stein was offered an obscure fund-raising role: an offer which the board knew he could not *not* refuse. And Shankly's end now seems the saddest of the three. Having resigned because of some recondite mix-up about his pension (a mix-up which has yet to be explained), he spent his retirement hanging around the Liverpool training ground – in case he was still needed. After a while, this erstwhile hero of the Kop was asked to keep his distance, and he did. Soon after that he died: 'a broken heart' is the diagnosis of one former colleague.

Arena's narrative ends on a sombre note. Its purpose, though, is celebration: and on this line it surefootedly succeeds. Three hours, after all, is not too much. Certainly, we fans end up well fortified against any temptation to exaggerate the charismatic power of soccer's current, over-hyped supremos. Compared with McIlvanney's hefty three, quite a few of them seem vulnerably lightweight.

Sunday Telegraph, 1997

Glenn and 'Glenda'

Spurs fans used to call Glenn Hoddle 'God'. They also called him 'Glenda'. The God tag was not difficult to fathom: as a player, Hoddle often seemed superhuman. He created space. He pulled the strings. He made opponents disappear. And as for his long passes – pinpoint forty-yarders – these were routinely called 'sublime'.

Why then the Glenda slur? To answer this, you need to know something about soccer fans – and, in particular, the Spurs fans of the mid-Eighties, with their just-turning-sour nostalgia for the club's great triumphs of the Sixties. Hoddle was a classy act, such die-hards would agree, and firmly in the Spurs tradition of elegant ball-players, sure enough, but when-oh-when would he *deliver*? Why, in spite of his magician's gifts, did Spurs still languish mid-table?

Another player might have been forgiven, on account of the sheer size of his talent, or even been thought of as a victim of his team-mates' mediocrity. With Hoddle, though, there was a persistent impulse to reduce, to undermine, to pull the poseur down a peg. Glenn didn't really care about the team, his critics would complain, nor even about victory. He was, they said, a solo self-indulger. He rarely tackled, never liked to head the ball and, when his team got pinned back in defence, he was inclined to stand and watch.

At moments such as these, the mob would have happily jettisoned his subtle feints and body-swerves in favour of some honest aggro. But Hoddle always appeared a disdainful cut above the hurly-burly. When fouled, he rarely made a fuss. At ease with his own brilliance, he instinctively steered clear of combat zones: such areas, he seemed to think, were meant for lesser souls. The deeply lesser souls who lined the terraces at White Hart Lane were not impressed. Indeed, they felt themselves rebuked by Hoddle's nonchalant superiority.

When things were going well at Spurs, the crowd purred with delight as Hoddle strolled upfield in search of an unusual opening. When things were going badly, as they often were, the chorus would be: 'Fairy', 'Ponce' and 'Where's your handbag?'

One fateful year, Glenn turned out for Tottenham's first game sporting a new, luxuriantly crinkled perm, to go with his intense, close-season tan. We who adored him inwardly despaired. Looking like *that*, Hoddle would just *have* to play like God. Mostly he did, of course – thank God – but Spurs continued to drop points. Then Hoddle had one less-than-godlike game and, all at once, the hairdo, which had been ignored when he was playing well, was the focus of enraged mass-mockery. 'Who is the queen of White Hart Lane?' jeered the fans. Poor Hoddle hung his curly head. A week later the perm had disappeared, but it was never quite forgotten.

Looking back, I tend to think of Hoddle's perm as a turning point in his relationship with the Tottenham supporters. 'These people,' we could almost hear him think, 'will never really love me – but why not?' And he had similar thoughts, seemingly, on the matter of his international career – a career which, most soccer folk agree, was 'unfulfilled', although he did play more than fifty times for England. Throughout the early to mid-Eighties, the football mags staged frequent debates regarding Hoddle's usefulness to England's hopes of recapturing old Sixties triumphs: the Spurs scenario replayed, Glenn may have thought, and, once again, it was God or Glenda. Even supposedly enlightened managers, like Ron Greenwood and Bobby Robson, were inclined towards the Glenda point of view. Hoddle was the best, they agreed, but would he pull his weight; was he not something of a 'luxury'?

Arguments such as these were at their fiercest just before and after the 1982 World Cup, in which Hoddle's involvement turned out to be, well, intermittent. For his full-time admirers – like myself – there was no need for debate. England should pick Hoddle every time. Indeed, they should build a team around his skills. For others, the Glenda factor was decisive. 'Superman or Mickey Mouse?' and 'Is Genius a Curse?' were typical headlines, summing up a long-standing English prejudice against free gifts from heaven. Even the great Jimmy Greaves, who had himself been involved in a similar work-versus-genius set-to in the mid-Sixties, could not bring himself to offer Hoddle his full backing. 'He has the skill and ability to boss any match,' Greaves said in 1982, 'but he needs the audacity, even arrogance, to bridge the gap between club and international level.' Which echoed England's managerial misgivings. When Bobby Robson took over from Ron Greenwood, after England's early elimination from the 1982 World Cup, he said: 'Glenn's got to play as though he really believes he should be in the England team.'

Glenn, of course, did so believe. In his view, however, he had been repeatedly encouraged not to. Pronouncements such as Robson's, though well meant, reduced him, he has said, to near-despair. Yet protesting did no good. Neither did his occasional attempts to show that he, too, could be a hard man if he chose. It was sad to watch him try to seem excited: yelling at team-mates, lunging into hopeless tackles, racing back to cover in defence. None of it looked natural – and none of it was helpful to his cause, confirming, as it mostly did, his weaknesses in these departments of the game. In interviews, Hoddle would grumble about his treatment by the England bosses, but, again, his indignation seemed lukewarm and forced. Which, of course, worked against him, too. He lacked 'ambition' and 'appetite' was the refrain. His on-camera unease was taken as evidence that he had something to hide: well, yes, he does, we would reply – his talent, thanks to malcontents like you. Why should Hoddle have to *apologise* for being the best player in the land?

Hoddle, we now know, was much angrier in those days than he seemed. Like most footballers, he could tolerate a fair amount of terrace nastiness but disliked having his gifts questioned by the *cognoscenti*, the Greenwoods and the Robsons, guys who knew the game from the inside. As a young player, Hoddle had grown used to praise from those who mattered. His father and uncle had played for local sides in Middlesex, where he grew up, and had known enough to recognise that little Glenn was something of a miracle. They offered him unstinting adulation. So, too, did his schoolteachers. So, too, the coaches who observed him blossom from child prodigy to teenage Spurs sensation.

At eighteen, Hoddle was a regular in the Spurs first team – a regular and, frequently, the shining star. He was picked for the England Under-Twenty-ones and full recognition came when he was twenty-two. On his international debut in 1979, he scored a wondrous goal against Bulgaria – and was then dropped.

It was the first real setback of Hoddle's career, yet no one told him what he'd done wrong. Greenwood mumbled about 'disappointment' being 'part and parcel of the game'. Three years on, he was still in and out of the England team – mostly out, though he was often, and absurdly, on the bench. And then he was dumped altogether. 'I don't think I'd ever been so low in my life,' he said recently. 'Without knowing it, Ron Greenwood pretty well destroyed me when that happened.'

Understandably, Hoddle began to think about quitting England altogether. Some years earlier, he had had offers from Germany and Italy, and had turned them down, believing that his England hour was nigh. In the mid-Eighties, the offers were revived and this time he was tempted. Perhaps in Europe he'd be given the appreciation he deserved. Or was he seeking one last mammoth pay-day? Either way, no one could really blame him.

At first he looked to Italy, to Juventus, in particular, but nothing happened. Rumours flew, 'keen interest' was expressed, but for a time it looked as if Europe had developed some English-style misgivings. The Italians, perhaps, thought that they already had innumerable Hoddles. If they were to shop in England, it would be for hustling hard-men, not delicate artistes. And Juventus was still trying to remember why it had bought Ian Rush.

Having declared himself to be available, Hoddle was anxious to be off. In 1987, he surprised everyone by signing for Monaco, a French First Division side with tiny crowds and not much reputation, albeit extremely wealthy. Hoddle, *The Sun* told us, had been offered £500,000 a year, and a luxurious, tax-free, sun-drenched lifestyle. He would be housed in the same apartment block as Bjorn Borg and Boris Becker. There'd be piped music in the car park. 'People will say I've come here for the money,' Hoddle said. 'But they'd be wrong. I want to discover how good Glenn Hoddle can become.' He wanted to prove that he was up there with the very best.

Perhaps he did. Certainly, he proved it to the French. During his two years in Monaco, we English fans saw little of him. That was the way of things, pre-Sky. We did hear, though, that he had been voted France's outstanding foreign player and that Monaco team coach Arsène Wenger was on the Hoddle wavelength. When he signed Hoddle, he had said: 'I want him to make the others play . . . I want him to do all the things he's good at.' If only Greenwood had taken the same line in 1979. Glenn, we noted with despondency, would soon be thirty. It was all too late.

A knee injury cut short Hoddle's Monaco idyll, but two years of doing all the things he was good at, without Glenda jibes and Greenwood hesitations, had effected an impressive transformation. When, in 1990, Hoddle reappeared on our back pages and TV screens, he was a different man: stylishly attired, he was more intelligent, self-assured, worldly-wise. On TV, there was none of the old lip-licking and nose-scratching. He had perfected a firmly candid stare, and was now praised for his 'detachment' and 'serenity'.

The credit for this Hoddle remake did not belong exclusively to Wenger's 'deep-thinking' soccer chic, although he continues to be one of Glenn's heroes – another irritant for Spurs fans, as Wenger is now manager of Arsenal. No, the true author of Hoddle's new-found poise was He Who Shapes Us All. Hoddle, we discovered, had found God. God had found God. On a visit to Bethlehem with an England touring team, he had visited Christ's birth-place. 'I could have walked out of that cave like the rest of the lads,' he said, 'but there was this spiritual feeling inside me. It was exhilarating. I had never felt it before.'

The hacks did their research and found that Hoddle, a Catholic, always crossed himself before and after games, had consulted a faith-healer in his youth, was friendly with Cliff Richard and had links with the organisation Christians In Sport. The Bethlehem epiphany was the culmination of a lifelong tendency towards the spiritual. He'd stifled his religious feelings before, but was now 'strong enough' to let them rule his life. 'I have not been put on this earth just to play football,' he said.

But by this stage, football was no longer a clear option. His injury was serious and, even when it healed, he was reluctant to expose his knee to a full and no doubt crunching season in the English league. On his return, he trained with Chelsea, not Spurs, and when Swindon Town invited him to be their player-manager, he accepted. The playing demands would be part time and he'd get to learn about soccer management. To manage, he said, was his new vocation. God had told him so.

The media response to this career move was, to say the least, half-hearted. Hoddle, it was said, would be too 'nice' to deal with stroppy or incompetent professionals, too 'airy-fairy' in his soccer thinking. Swindon was in the Second Division of the league, where skill took second place to muscle-power. A team constructed by Hoddle would be swept aside. Two years later, such words had to be eaten. Swindon was promoted to the Premiership and was being applauded on all sides, not only for its Hoddle-like ball-play, but also for its flexible and obdurate defence.

Hoddle himself had found a new playing niche as a libero, or sweeper, a position rarely risked in this country, not least because it demands talents that English-trained defenders rarely have. Good sweepers have to be nifty on the ball and clever at anticipating their opponents' forward moves. At Swindon, Hoddle's innovation was to play himself as sweeper and to use the position not just as a last line of defence but as a springboard for attack. It was a risky strategy but, for two years at least, it worked. Hoddle, it turned out, was good at getting the best out of average players. They ran and ran, knowing that behind them the great Glenn stood guard.

On the back of his success at Swindon, Hoddle was appointed manager of Chelsea in 1993, and hailed as one of a new breed of soccer managers: ex-players of quality who had first-hand experience of the sophisticated mysteries of European soccer. Hoddle went out of his way to consolidate his image as a deep-thinking cosmopolitan. He signed the eminent Ruud Gullitt, who let it be known that he had joined Chelsea because of his admiration for Hoddle's football brain. Glenn also encouraged a buoyantly attacking style of play, similar to that employed at Swindon.

After a brisk beginning, though, Chelsea began sliding to mid-table. They were good to watch but inconsistent. The libero system, when it failed, failed on a lavish scale. In 1994, a crushing Cup Final defeat by Manchester United provoked a few uneasy mumblings at Stamford Bridge. Hoddle's transfer-dealings were called into question; apart from Gullitt, who had proved to be a wonderful success, the new manager had snapped up a series of duds or near-duds. People began talking of Chelsea as they once talked of Hoddle: gifted but fragile, insufficient steel, more style than substance, and so on. Just in time, perhaps, Glenn Hoddle was named the new manager of England in 1996.

Hoddle took the job knowing he was not by any means first choice at the FA. The position had been turned down by Kevin Keegan, Bryan Robson and, so rumour had it, Gerry Francis. But Hoddle didn't care. This was a job he'd always wanted – well, at least since his first encounter with Greenwood – and luckily, God approved. Hoddle claimed to have been guided to this task by the Almighty. He was, he said, not at all intimidated by the example of his predecessors: the haggard Bobby Robson, the near-demented Graham Taylor. Nor was he overawed by the popularity of the outgoing Terry Venables, hero of Euro 96. Whatever happened, his 'inner strength' would see him through.

But will it see *us* through? It is too soon to say, or even guess. But, on the whole, so far so good. One of Hoddle's first acts as manager was to reinstate Matthew Le Tissier, Venables's most notorious discard – and, it should be said, a boyhood Hoddle-worshipper now often accused of Glenda tendencies. At press conferences, the new manager comes across as courteous and articulate (give or take a few grammatical howlers and a general weakness for soccer-speak) and at the same time hugely distant, as if preoccupied with matters far beyond the understanding of his interlocutors. A shrewd approach, when one remembers the frantically forthcoming Graham Taylor. And in response, the press has so far treated him with caution – not to say, respect. Aside from a few God jokes – would He have allowed Southgate to miss, or even *take* that penalty in July? – and aside from the fuss about Paul Gascoigne's battering of his wife Sheryl, the mood has been agreeably provisional: let's wait and see. All in all, Hoddle is reckoned to have handled the Gascoigne issue rather skilfully.

In the face of mass demands for Gazza's expulsion, he contrived to evince an appropriate measure of reproof without damaging his own image as a steely-eyed pursuer of World Cup success. He also gained marks by undertaking to involve himself in Gascoigne's future spiritual progress; his counselling and so forth. But then, Tony Adams and Paul Merson had already been given time off for their therapy, and Glenn's approach to their delinquencies had established a general atmosphere of understanding and forgiveness. It would have been difficult for him to have dealt more ferociously with Gascoigne. And, in any case, Gascoigne himself – a longtime protégé of Venables – must now feel that he owes Hoddle at least one glorious, match-winning show. Let's hope so.

England's next game, against Italy on 12 February, is already being seen as the first test of Hoddle's management. His victories so far – against Moldova, Poland and Georgia – have not really been credited to him. The shade of Terry Venables still lingers. If England does well against Italy, at least some of the applause will go to Venables. But if England loses, Hoddle will know that his new job has finally begun. Will God be on our side, or does He secretly prefer the flashy wiles of Zola, del Piero and the like? Rather depressingly, Glenn Hoddle thinks that God may give the game a miss. 'I don't think God cares too much about who's going to win the World Cup,' he has said. Well, *He* may not care, but we do; and so, too, does *The Sun*. To be on the safe side, Glenn had better not stop praying.

Punch, 1997

Just What Are Those Teeth For?

'I do not come to Lilliputia with a measuring stick'. This was Gore Vidal, a week or two ago, when asked to say which of our two main parties was the more right-wing. The British election, in Gore's lofty view, was 'parish-pump politics', a juvenile charade compared to America's great billion-dollar circuses. Even our sleaze struck him as laughably small-scale: 'just kindergarten stuff'. In Vidal's native land there was no need of cash-for-questions. The deal there was cash-for-answers. And the answers were delivered in the form of 'special legislation'. In America sleaze makes a difference.

At first, the spectacle of Vidal pulling his New-World patrician stunt was pretty irritating. How dare this Yank, however posh, sneer at our little votes, our feeble bribes-machine? Since when has the sheer magnitude of a government's corruption been a cause for patriotic pride? At the same time, though, his presence was unsettling. Too often, he seemed to have a point. There were more than a few moments when the election did, alas, seem tailored to his scorn. Thus, when the headless chicken stuff was going on, or when the Tories wrapped the Albert Hall in a blue ribbon, it was hard not to hope that our disdainful visitor was spending the day somewhere else. But where? On every side, there seemed to be some Toytown farce in progress. What, for instance, would Gore make of Christine Hamilton? What would he make of Martin Bell? Too British to be true, the pair of them, in their quite different ways. It was a relief to learn that several of Vidal's hours here were being spent discussing Montaigne (so he said) with Michael Foot.

Sadly, when Vidal showed up on one of *Newsnight*'s election panels,

Jeremy Paxman failed to cut him down to size. In fact, he didn't even try. Vidal was allowed to preen himself at leisure. Next to him, the two British panellists – Lord Archer and Fay Weldon – seemed dwarfishly over-anxious to make points: Archer, of course, trumpeting the Tory party line, and Weldon semi-weeping for Old Labour. 'Where does an old radical like you *go*?' Paxman asked her, somwhat rudely. He would not have dared to put the same question to Vidal.

There is, after all, a touch of the Vidals in Paxman's own approach to British politicians. Disdain is famously his TV stock-in-trade. Unlike Vidal's, though, Paxman's sneers come with a furrowed brow. He and his co-anchormen enjoy the needling, come-off-it stuff but they are keen also to be thought of as concerned champions of the electorate – as closer, somehow, to the common people than vote-hungry politicians are, or want to be. Their televisual-duty, they would have us think, is to cut through all the electioneering double-talk and – on our behalf – focus on the 'real issues': health, Europe, education. No easy task, this focusing, they say, since politicians at election-time are more than usually evasive. They are also more than usually absurd. Look at those silly clips of Paddy Ashdown playing hopscotch or John Major on his knees in a day-nursery or Tony Blair in his Newcastle soccer-strip. Who do these people think they're fooling? Why don't they treat us as grown-ups? What's happened to the issues?

To this, the politicians might retort: where did those clips come from in the first place? As they see things, it's television that is to blame for the low level of election discourse. Paxman and his colleagues never let them have their say – their 'issues' say, that is to say, with all the necessary parentheses and footnotes. Television's whole cast of mind is childishly reductive: inquisitorial, gaffe-avid, scared of boredom, its and ours. If there is any silliness around, Paxman and Co will surely seize on it, and build it up. Good politics, the politicians claim, does not make good television. But good television, they also claim, is usually bad politics.

After a week's television election-watch, I'm rather surprised to find myself siding with the politicians. Yes, they are guarded, cliché-prone, mendacious – but such habits are not discouraged by the compulsively hostile scenarios they are faced with on television. Consider what tends to happen when politicians agree (as they're obliged to) to be interviewed, or to take part in a television-panel 'discussion'. Before any of them get to say a word, they are usually made to sit through one of those five-minute vox pop films: on 'Poverty in the North East' or 'Education Now' or 'Scottish Devolution'. These films are presented as The People's View: perhaps not comprehensive, perhaps a little too italicised in places, but humanly compelling. 'I'd like to know if that Peter Lilley could survive on sixty seven pounds a week?' enquires some grizzled pensioner. Cut to Lilley in the studio: he's looking, natch, complacently amused. And when the film is done, Paxman or whoever will at once turn to his guest, or guests, and growl: 'Well, there it is, Minister (or Shadow Minister or Lib Dem spokesperson for X, Y or Z). What are you/will you/might you be doing about *that*?' And then we get the 'Jeremy, if I may say so, with the greatest possible respect, that film of yours does not begin to . . .' And so on. To which Jeremy is likely to reply: 'Answer the question!' But if the answer turns out to be too lengthy, or too heavily freighted with sub-clauses, the Paxman axe will surely fall: 'Look, I don't want a shopping list,' 'Spare us the speeches, please,' 'Answer me this: yes or no' – and then, triumphantly, 'We're running out of time.'

All in all, I get the feeling that television overrates its audience's blood-lust, or squirm-lust. Take David Dimbleby's grilling of Tony Blair on *Panorama*. Most of the interview was spent raking over Blair's Old Labour past. At first this line seemed fair enough. Blair, after all, had on that very day been assuring his new City chums that almost nothing the state owns is – what's the word? – unprivatisable. But Dimbleby went on and on. 'Ten years ago, you – Tony Blair – said so-and-so, and now you're saying – and I quote – the very opposite.' Blair blustered about the need for change – 'I'm not going to roll the clock – turn the clock back – roll back the tide' – but Dimbleby would not let go. David the People's Mouthpiece had turned into Dave the Dungeon Dentist. Blair soon began to sweat, and we began to ask ourselves: how much can the guy take? And this, as with a heavily one-sided boxing-match, became the chief thrust of our viewing pleasure. And David Dimbleby seemed to be feeling the same way, with his newly close-cropped hair and his magistrate's half-moons. 'So people were *right* not to vote for Michael Foot. Is that what you are saying?' 'David, *please!*' Blair whimpered at this point. He was pleading not for mercy but for Dimbleby to quit the sadist-histrionics, to turn back into that cuddly, sane chap who supervises *Question Time* so even-handedly. And by this stage, I would guess, most of the audience was on Blair's side. Enough's enough. We don't want our next P.M. to be a nervous wreck.

Fat chance, you may think, but when Gore Vidal witnessed the launch of the New Labout manifesto, he did detect a certain 'nervousness' in Tony Blair's demeanour. 'He's like a kid who's having a wonderful dream but at the same time fears that the dream might turn into a nightmare.' In his set-to with Dimbleby, Blair once or twice seemed perilously close to cracking – which, in the politician's style-book, means 'betraying a few seconds' irritation'. Poor Blair: he's not allowed to smile; he's not allowed to snarl. Just what – as Dimbleby the Dentist might have asked but thankfully did not – just what are those teeth for?

Politicians, it is generally agreed, must never lose their tempers. In spite of what you and I might think of as gigantic provocation – 'Answer me this: yes or no!' – a pol must always keep his cool. A single lapse and he is finished, as he – and David Dimbleby – well know. How do skins get to be so thick? Is it congenital or do they learn it from each other? Either way, in politics, insensitivity is thought of as a mark of elementary professional prowess. Paxman and Dimbleby might yearn, on our behalf, to find out what Gordon Brown conceals beneath his mask of stony moderation, or how Ashdown would shape up in a pub-brawl, but I'm not certain that the public greatly craves disclosures of this kind. Someone like Max Clifford will tell us that MPs make up for their professional sang-froid by going in for seamily hot-blooded private lives. I wonder if that's really how it works. Or is it just that MP's with hot blood ought not to be MPs? David Mellor, for example, always seemed a bit too, shall we say, impulsive for high office. Watching him nowadays, yelling at people on television, it's tempting to conclude that he has found his proper niche.

The most 'human' politicians I have seen this week have tended to be Liberal-Democrats: Charles Kennedy, Conrad Russell, Menzies Campbell. But then, it will be said, politicians such as these can well afford to be themselves. From the two interested parties, Kenneth

Clarke is, of course, known to be attractively 'robust', not to say quarrelsome, but he is always in control. Supremely so, I'd say.

Clarke has the knack of seeming both competent and flammable. So too, in his donnish way, does Robin Cook. Indeed, Cook – of all the pols I've scrutinised this week – has been perhaps the most intriguing. He keeps his temper not just in order to be liked, nor simply to be seen as a safe pair of hands. Knowing that, in TV terms, he'll never come across as specially likeable or charismatic, Cook settles for an image of preoccupied aloofness. For him, self-mastery has higher ends: only a calm head can cope with the grave, complex issues he has been entrusted with. 'Don't break my concentration,' seems to be his plea, 'Our country needs it.' And usually this works.

It does help, of course, that Cook is Shadow Foreign Secretary, or Shadow Minister for Europe, an area which television has long ago despaired of as a likely source of thrills and spills. No 'issue' is more weighty, and yet no issue is more boring. Thus, when prodded by a Paxman, Cook can always reach for his well-thumbed copy of the Maastricht Treaty, or dawdle over a few paras from the Social Chapter, knowing that Paxman – and the rest of us – will soon enough be nodding off.

On the subject of early nights, I ought to mention Vincent Hanna's *Midnight Special*, an after-hours 'political supper-party' put out by Channel Four. The show bills itself as committed to 'accentuating the embarrassing, extolling the provocative, and venerating the destructive – that special kind of pleasure that comes from inflicting pain on politicians'. In fact, it's a relaxed and genial affair. The supper menu, for instance, includes lollipops shaped in the likenesses of the three main party leaders: guests are asked to 'take your pick. A Major, an Ashdown or a Blair. Lick it or bite it, according to your taste.'

Vincent Hanna neither licks nor bites. Indeed, his massively world-weary style is something of a model for TV-interrogators. 'Speak on if you have to' is his general line with eager pols. At the same time, though, he is smart enough to know when they are exploiting his goodwill. He listens well, prompts when a prompt is needed, and his interruptions are almost as well-mannered as they might be in real life. On the whole, he seems to quite like politicians: at any rate, he knows their game and doesn't hate them for it. How he does brighten, though, when it is time for him to introduce his 'special guests'. On the programme's cleverly-constructed sleaze-night, he was glad to welcome Sarah Keays, Max Clifford and Cynthia Payne, the Streatham sex-hotelier who continues to believe that what the world needs now is love, love, love. To which *Newsnight* would surely answer: 'That's all very well. Who's going to pay for it?'

London Review of Books, 1997

Chunnel Crossing

Last December I needed to get to Paris and back in a hurry and someone suggested, with a smile that might not have been a smile, that I should 'take the Tunnel'. It's more expensive than most aircraft, I was told, but just as quick. Best of all, it gets you right into the heart of town. No airport hassle; no costly taxi rides. 'Also, it's new. It might be fun. You haven't tried it, have you?'

You bet I hadn't. When I did go to France, which wasn't very often, I always went by boat. The ferry was slow but it was cheap, and it had sound literary backup. 'On the French coast the light/Gleams and is gone; the cliffs of England stand/Glimmering and vast, out in the tranquil bay.' I was writing a book on Matthew Arnold, the author of these lines and, in his day, a great connoisseur of distances and chasms. Indeed, my quick trip to France had to do with my Arnold researches. How dismally unfitting that the poet of 'Dover Beach' should be the spur to my cross-channel haste! Arnold liked to move slowly, when he moved at all. He liked to listen and to look. 'The sea is calm tonight/The tide is full, the moon lies fair/ Upon the straits – on the French coast the light/Gleams and is gone . . .'

I too had to gleam and go, in service of this stately bard. At 8 a.m. on 10th December, I presented myself at Waterloo's new International Terminal and booked what I still liked to call 'my passage'. Waterloo is the name of the ancient railway station to which the Tunnel facility has been – rather stylishly – attached. Had no one thought to give the terminal a different name, a Euro-name? Or was the decision not to meant to be a sort of bitter jest: if the French come here, let them be greeted with reminders of what we did to them two hundred years ago?

If so, the jest was firmly in line with a large and lively section of the British press. On the weekend before the launch of the Tunnel's passenger train service, one of our tabloid Sundays had provided its readers with a list of the '101 Things You Might Have Suspected About the French'. Our cross-channel neighbours, we were told, are lazy, gluttonous, unclean. They eat horses, snails and frogs. They hardly ever brush their teeth. They invented handkerchiefs but don't like using them. They wear berets and striped sailors' jerseys. They call their French letters 'English overcoats'. *The People* concluded: 'They are only a giant frog's hop away but they could be the men in the moon for all we've got in common with the French.'

This was familiar, feeble stuff but it was drawn from a deep well. For *People* people, and for quite a few who read the posher Sunday sheets, the Channel Tunnel represents just one more step towards the extinction of what's left of Britain's 'national identity'. For some, it is the step too far, since it dares to evoke images of steps, or stepping-stones: of foreign legions approaching us on foot, or – if they choose – by car, or train, or tank. It is the final cutting-off of our cut-offness. What price Dunkirk or D-Day? Who now can speak of sceptred isles, gems set in silver seas? Napoleon once tried to mole his way across to us by way of the seabed. So too, it's said, did Hitler.

Over the years I've learned to be suspicious of arguments that end with the word 'Hitler', especially when the arguments are mine, as some of these have been from time to time. Lining up for my first trip on Eurostar, I wondered: am I really against the Tunnel, or is it just that I can't stand the advertising – all this Euro-togetherness, this guff about our Continental cousins? Why don't they just *say* that the whole thing is about money? Or is it that some infantile defensiveness lurks at the core of Britain's – and my – self-esteem?

For all our imperial conquests, many of the most stirring British myths are to do with protecting our back-lawns. For us, the Channel has always been more barrier than bridge. Good fences make good neighbours: so too do thirty-four kilometres of water. The idea of making the Channel *easier* to cross is, well, foreign to our thinking. Although tourist-board statistics suggest that the French are much less interested in seeing Britain than the British are in seeing France, we hold fast to the belief that this Tunnel must surely have been drilled for their benefit, not ours.

And even those Britons who for years have been deploring British insularity seem to be less than thrilled at the prospect of having their Provence hideaways invaded by flocks of *parlez-vous* sightseers from back home. For them, the main point of Provence has been that the yobs they've left behind at Dover know nothing of *vins, pâtés* and *fromages*. Hence the advanced Francophile's deep loathing for the likes of Peter Mayle, the guy who made merry with the Provençal mystique. For them, France should have stayed a secret, hard-to-get-at source of *chic:* food, fashions and the 'ferment of ideas'. *Quel cauchemar* to think of these *délices* as just a chunnel's length from Kent.

One day, perhaps, the ferry service will be classified as *chic*. To go to France by boat will signify that you're the meditative type, that you have feeling for what travel really means. Not yet, though. The ferries are nice and slow but they are slaves to the quick sell. Their corridors are lined with fruit machines and souvenir shops. Everyone you see or bump into is weighed down with travel-goodies, most of which seem to have been purchased on the boat. It is possible to observe people playing the machines *without letting go* of their five shopping bags. Not easy, but some of them do it rather well. And on the return leg from Calais, the 'lounge areas' are packed with fiercely-barbered Brits sitting astride huge crates of the low-duty beer they've picked up from harbourfront warehouses. Their plan is to sell it on to British pubs.

But still, a boat's a boat, and even with these floating malls it's possible for travel-aesthetes to take to the decks, breathe in the spray, and watch for the first sight of foreign land. Also, in spite of a few recent mishaps, the ferries are generally reckoned to be safe. Could the same be said of our mysterious new Tunnel? At Waterloo, my co-passengers showed no signs of anxiety. There was none of that strained *bonhomie* that can usually be sensed in airport bars. But then at airports there are more things to nibble at the nerves: protracted check-ins and passport-controls, duty-free shops, airport novels. And after take-off there are life-jacket demos, sickbags, safety-belt routines, each serving to remind us what we're up to. If we look out of the windows, we see clouds.

With Eurostar, the main idea is to annihilate our awareness of both time and distance, to make travel seem deeply unmomentous. You check yourself in by running your ticket through a machine just like the ones you use on subways. Your bags are X-rayed, your passport checked, but the attendants at both rituals seem detached and over-brisk, as if in amused mimicry of some other, more authentic, style of vigilance. When you climb on to the train, a stewardess too glassily smiles through you. Is she dreaming of getting a job with British Airways?

On the day I travelled, a few Eurostar first-timers trekked along the platform's length to take a look at the train's snout, which is rather tactlessly piscine in appearance, resembling a dolphin's, or a shark's. 'Let's hope this thing can swim,' quipped one of them. Then it was all aboard, a whistle, and away. As we settled into our cramped, aircraft-style seats, a not-quite bilingual voice assured us that in three hours we'd be in Paris. There was a rustle of excitement in my carriage, as if the news came as a surprise. Somewhere behind me a champagne bottle popped, and I could hear a full English voice demanding a 'full English breakfast'. At weekends, apparently, Eurostar can only manage a few snacks. The Englishman had never heard anything so preposterous in his 'born days'. Try translating that one into French.

The train, meanwhile, was making short work of the London suburbs. In no time at all, we were gliding through what seemed to be the greenish fields of Kent. This was going to be easy. But then why shouldn't it be easy? My problem is that I have lots of literary friends. During the week before I left, I'd been bombarded with all kinds of chunnel doomspeak. Practically everyone I told about my trip had pulled a face. Didn't I know that the Tunnel was thought of as 'ill-starred'? Well, yes, I did. I too had read the papers. Right from the start, even the upmarket British press has viewed the Tunnel project with suspicion – or rather, with a sort of fidgety disdain. Each setback in the construction process has been written up near-gleefully, as if to say: 'Well, what did you expect?' And the project itself has now and then seemed to assist in the making of its own doom-laden image. Nine workers died in the early stages of the drilling. There were reports of a huge overspend and of bickering among the ten building companies involved. The opening was more than once delayed, and when at last – in January 1994 – the Queen and President Mitterand were called to cut the ribbon, the train still wasn't ready to do business.

There were rumours that the Tunnel might have sprung a leak, or a near-leak, or that it had at the eleventh hour revealed some deadly flaw. Other stories alleged that the whole tube was aswarm with rats: French rats. And the old British rabies-phobia was merrily re-stoked. Foreigners are not allowed to bring pets into Britain; if they do, their animals are seized at Customs and put into quarantine for months. The idea is that foreign animals have rabies and ours don't. Thanks to the Tunnel, we were now at the mercy of deranged poodles and foam-flecked killer dachshunds. The IRA also rated a few mentions. How easy it would be for terrorists to decorate the Tunnel walls with Semtex.

One or two of my friends even described the Tunnel as being 'against Nature'. There is a difference, they said, between river-tunnels and sea-tunnels. Rivers, by definition, have been tamed. Seas, though, can turn nasty when they're crossed – and nastier still when they're crossed by the wrong means of transportation. Neptune, after all, is not particularly keen on boats: every so often he sucks one into his great maw. What would he make of all this burrowing? Land and sea, like the British and the French, are not *meant* to overlap. To walk on water is one thing; to walk under it is, as they say, a different kettle of fish.

Suddenly it was 9.40 and we'd reached the coast. The Tunnel runs from Folkestone to Calais and I had imagined that, before 'taking the plunge', we would catch a glimpse of what we were up against, or getting into. But there was no sign of the sea: just fields and farmyards, and the odd oasthouse. That's how I knew we were in Kent. The train did stop, but only for a few seconds, as if to ready itself for the big moment. Then the 'chef de bord' announced, in what I took to be a dead or deadpan voice, that we were about to 'penetrate ze Channel Tunnel'. The champagne bibbers let out a half-hearted cheer and everything went dark – at least, everything outside the window went dark: our cabin-lights had been turned up a notch or two. So this was it: the Tunnel, black as night. And in we went.

But what did I expect? An aquarium effect, perhaps, with trailing seaweed and little fishes nosing up against the window-panes, a mermaid paddling by, a lobster, a French rat? In order to get anything at all out of the experience, you had to work hard at it. You had to sit back, close your eyes, and tell yourself: 'I've never *been* under a seabed before; this is my first time; Neptune, be gentle with me.' But this way madness lies. It was easier by far to take a short walk to the bar, where a couple of elderly Spaniards were talking economics. On the table in front of them, each had arranged various banknotes and several rows of French and English coins. 'This ten-franc,' said one. 'This fifty-pee,' came the reply. Outside the dark whizzed by.

I was halfway through my glass of beer and readying myself for another bout of what Keats used to call 'negative capability', when all at once light struck, the light of day. 'Welcome to France!' came over the loudspeaker. And then, outside the window, fields again: French fields, presumably. Trees, too; a house, a *vache*. The time was 10 a.m. – or 11 a.m. French time. The Spaniards were synchronising watches. The Tunnel crossing had taken a mere twenty minutes.

And now we were in France. But were we? As Eurostar gained speed, the landscape blurred into a slant green-and-brown, with flying blobs of black. From time to time, I thought I could identify a church – *was* that a church? – and even an avenue of slender, pointy trees, as in the painting by who-was-it? But all was indistinct, fast-forward. After five minutes, I stopped looking. Someone said: 'I wish it would slow down.'

Slow down? If he had heard this, the driver would have laughed. So far as he was concerned, being in France meant being able to let rip. The run of technical faults that had delayed the Tunnel's opening had been to do with Britain's reluctance to grant Eurostar its own railtrack, or its own electrification system. As with the Tunnel itself, the Brits wanted to have the train but they also wanted to pretend it wasn't there. When in England, the highspeed silver missile is required to to conduct itself like any other locomotive, sharing its track and its power supply with the run-of-the-mill commuter trains that shuttle between London and Kent. On the specially-built French tracks, Eurostar can reach 186 miles per hour. In Britain, it has to chug along at less than 100. The need to switch from one power system to another, with a third adjustment required when Eurostar passes through the actual tunnel, has been 'at the heart of all the [tunnel's] problems', according to Christian Wolmar, the *Independent*'s transport correspondent. Wolmar reckons that Britain's Eurostar track will 'now not be ready until 2002, at the earliest.'

Well, I can wait. I'd wanted speed, but this train was *too* speedy. All I could remember of my journey were the English bits, and I'd seen them before. But now the train *was* slowing down. We were on the outskirts of what seemed to be a city. Motorways had become visible, with cars driving on the wrong side of the road. A sign read: 'Ventilation'; another said 'La Chambre – Nuit'. And yes, we did seem to be in Paris, France. During our charge through Normandy, there had no doubt been other signs: according to my map, we must have passed through half-a-dozen towns. But Eurostar is not designed for map-readers, rubbernecks, contemplatives. Its job is to get you where you say you want to go: but fast.

At 12. 15 French time, we pulled into the Gare du Nord, a short taxi-ride from the Eiffel Tower, within walking distance of the Louvre, Notre Dame, the Place de la Republique, and just across the *rue* from a McDonald's. Disembarking, my co-travellers made swiftly for the exits. One or two of them looked as if they might have trouble slowing down. Perhaps, like me, they were day trippers. We had five hours before we had to report back for the journey home. Eurostar would leave Paris just after 5p.m. and reach Waterloo in time for a night out on the town. The other town.

At the Bureau de Change, the Spaniards were at the head of a long queue and I found myself standing next to the full-English-breakfast-man, a florid, silvery-bald type in blazer and club tie. 'What did you think of it?', I asked. 'Speaks for itself. We're here. Three hours. Not bad. Not bad at all. Spot on.' But didn't he too feel slightly cheated, cheated of the full *voyaging* experience, the heaving waves, the distant shores, the gradual sense of spiritual enlargement that sea-crossings can induce? This train was super-quick but, essentially, was it not a kind of *thief*, a thief of time, a thief of the imagination? I mean, did he for instance really *know* that, just one hour ago, he had been sitting on a train beneath the sea? At this, he gaped at me. 'Of course I bloody know. What *are* you: French?'

Vogue (USA), 1995

Anti-Star: A Profile of Julie Christie

In her latest film, *Afterglow*, just released, Julie Christie plays a character called Phyllis Mann, a one-time Hollywood film actress. Middle-aged and locked into a dire marriage to the gregariously lustful Lucky (played by a half-asleep Nick Nolte), Phyllis spends lonely evenings, drink in hand, staring at videos of her old movies: black-and-white horror flicks which she has taped from the *Late, Late Show*. 'Is there no end to your horrors?' Phyllis cries in one of these. 'None whatsoever,' says Count Falco, her merciless co-star. Phyllis's facial expression as she watches her young on-screen self is anything but friendly.

Afterglow, directed by Alan Rudolph, is a slickly-made, somewhat pretentious tragi-comedy of sexual, or marital, bad manners. Partner-swapping shenanigans occupy most of the main plot: by accident, the marriage of Phyllis and Lucky has got intertangled with the equally dire union of Marianne and Jeffrey, a (much younger) pair of yuppies. Everyone is pretty miserable before, during and after the partner-swap. Childlessness emerges as a big issue for the women; male sexuality preoccupies the males. There are some witty moments but the film is fatally undone by its uncertainty of tone: Feydeau keeps bumping into Strindberg (or *Shampoo* into *Don't Look Now*) and we don't know if we are meant to laugh or cry. And neither, we suspect, does Alan Rudolph.

The whole thing does come alive, though, whenever Phyllis is at centre-screen. And this is not just because the role has more subtlety and depth and is performed more persuasively than all the others. What really seizes the attention is the idea of a fifty-seven-year-old Julie Christie impersonating an over-the-hill movie star. Are we in on something *autobiographical* here? Is horny handyman Lucky meant to remind us of the stud-crimper in *Shampoo*? Is the Manns' runaway daughter meant to be an echo of the dead child in *Don't Look Now*? And if so: does Julie Christie sit at home nights watching tapes of her old movies?

Try putting such a question to the real-life Julie Christie and you will get stared at rather in the way that Phyllis stares at re-runs of *The Curse of Count Falco*. How can anyone, the stare will say, be dumb enough to ask a thing like that? Julie Christie's movie stardom was much starrier than Phyllis Mann's but, in interviews at any rate, she takes about as much pride in her screen-acting backlist as Phyllis does in hers. The difference is that Julie Christie has erased the tapes. Or, rather, she would erase them if she could.

I met her recently in London and again, soon afterwards, at the San Sebastian Film Festival, where *Afterglow* was premiered (and where Christie won the Festival's Best Actress prize). I made an effort to get her talking on topics like: 'How did it feel to win an Oscar (for *Darling*) at the age of twenty-four?' and 'Which of your films do you look back on with most satisfaction?' The blanks I drew seemed practised but authentic – if bored and impatient adds up to authentic. Still pleasing to behold, Christie is tinier, frownier, more fidgety than I expected from an actress whose most haunting screen appearances have been abstractedly reposeful (see *The Go-Between*, *Return of the Soldier*, *Doctor Zhivago*, and even – when the opium gets to her – *McCabe & Mrs Miller*). The famously alluring lower lip juts forward in determined style. She had agreed to be interviewed, I'd been advised, because of her new film. She was, she said, 'quite pleased' with her own contribution to *Afterglow*. She admired Alan Rudolph: 'he dances with his camera'. She was a friend of Robert Altman, Rudolph's mentor and *Afterglow*'s producer. And she was full of praise for Toyomichi Kurita, the film's cinematographer. Had I not been impressed, as she had been, by the lighting in *Afterglow*? It was, she said, a 'character in its own right'.

Christie was extra-fidgety today, she said, because she had just completed eight weeks on the stage in a Marguerite Duras play called *Susannah Andler*. The part had required her to occupy the boards for two hours every night, and she was drained: 'On stage you really do go into disturbing places you'd rather not go into and that has to have an effect on your real self. This was a character who was suicidal from beginning to end. You can't just pretend to be suicidal. You have to find those parts of you, that we all have, that are suicidal.' Stage acting was for her a nightly 'terror', rather like going into battle: 'Terror – and *overcoming* terror. You actually feel this terror which you hope not to feel in your life, and then you overcome it. That it's *possible* to overcome that terror.'

For Julie Christie, this stage-fright has a special edge. She is, she says, almost amnesiac. She can't remember lines. 'I forget them all the time. In this last play I had too much to learn. It's always too much, but this was quite clearly too much, two hours of Marguerite Duras, it's just too much to hold in your head. So it sort of slips away.' She had been helped through it all by her co-actors. 'Some lovely person says: "Did you tell him?", because your line is meant to be: "I told him". And there is nothing in my brain. Absolutely nothing. And the other person is going through that absolute terror, thinking: "Has she forgotten? Is she acting? What's going on here?". Then they get to know you and they think "Uh-oh. I see her hands going up to her face, and she's doing that thing she does whenever she forgets her lines – which is, *pretend to think*."'

When I continued to press her on the matter of her early films, Christie's hands did not go to her face. Just as she could not remember lines, so she could recall almost nothing of her youth. And she was fed up with being asked to try. Her big-star phase – from the mid-Sixties to the late Seventies – she now thinks of as little more than a pre-adult folly, something her beautiful young face did, years ago. But does she not like to be remembered by her fans, those who drooled over that walk in *Billy Liar*, that bed-scene with Donald Sutherland in *Don't Look Now*, that dinner-party indiscretion in *Shampoo*? 'Because I haven't got any memory, when people connect me with something I did in the past I can't find it particularly pleasant because I don't know who they're talking about or what they're talking about. There is no connection whatsoever. It is absolutely void. So who is this person? If I was more generous I would probably just be able to embrace their fantasy – or their need, or whatever it is . . .'

Quite clearly, she was keen to change the subject. Why didn't we talk about interviews, for instance? Had I read Janet Malcolm's book, *The Biographer and the Murderer*? Wasn't there something innately duplicitous and fake about the relationship between two strangers meeting as she, Christie, and I had: the one seeking to appropriate and publicise the other's inner narrative? On this question, she assured me, Janet Malcolm's book was a must-read: 'There's a line in it, something about how the interviewee almost inevitably becomes a child when they start to be interviewed. Even the most intelligent person in the world, even people who have been interviewed a lot. Everything slips away and they suddenly become a child to the father – or is it the mother?' She did not have Malcolm's book with her but at our next meeting – scheduled for San Sebastian in three days' time – she would bring with her a marked copy.

We were having lunch and so the next thing we talked about was food. After much intense study of the menu, she had settled for lentil soup and vegetable lasagne. She was not a 'pure' vegetarian, she explained, although she greatly respected those who were. From time to time, then, she ate meat? 'I would rather avoid it, but I might take on some free-range meat because I think it's so wonderful that farmers are actually trying to even do it – against all the odds, against sort of huge amounts of national odds, and the power of the . . . If they're actually fighting the biggest powers in the whole world, the pharmaceutical companies, which actually more or less own the world . . . so any farmer who decides to take that on is a hero, or a heroine.' She went on to describe the horrors of factory-farming, the dangers of organo-phosphates, the need for constant gastronomic vigilance. She was, she said, 'quite obsessive about food'. Even as she ate her lentil soup (so 'comforting') she was planning tonight's supper: beetroot stew. As for me – well, I was just glad I hadn't opted for the burger.

And this, I began to see, was Julie Christie's strategy for dealing with irksome interviewers. Her film-star celebrity was of no interest in itself but it did give her access to the media. Her clear duty, therefore, was to exploit that access for good ends, to use it as an outlet for issues which otherwise might not get aired. Looking back over interviews she had given over the last twenty years, it was not difficult to identify a pattern. Nuclear waste, animal rights, Nicaragua, Palestine,

East Timor, Kampuchea – now organo-phosphates. Time and again, hapless interrogators had tried to nudge her back into her glitzy past; time and again, they had been forced to lend an ear to one or another of her global indignations. And I was to be no exception. After lunch, she took me shopping in London's Spitalfields Market, renowned for its organically grown vegetables. Watching Julie Christie rummaging through a tray of mud-caked beetroots, I had to concede that there was nothing affected or contrived about her food-alarm. Most of what we eat is poisoned but somewhere in that tray, or somewhere in the world, if she searched hard and long enough, there was a beetroot she could trust. And here was I, wanting to grill her about Warren Beatty, a former boyfriend she broke up with more than twenty years ago. How cheap – indeed, how poisonous. And to this extent, her interrogo-repellent had been thoroughly effective. My next question, had I asked it, would have been: but what about *that* beetroot, the big clean one at the back?

Perhaps it would be easier in San Sebastian, where Christie would be on duty in her film-star mode. After all, she *was* still in the business and *Afterglow* did have to be promoted. But Julie Christie, even at the peak of her celebrity, never really settled into film-star mode. Even in 1965, the year of *Darling* and *Doctor Zhivago*, the year of her Oscar and the year in which *Newsweek* proclaimed her as 'an idea whose time has come' – even then, the interviews she gave seem to have been tense affairs. She hated, she said, all the 'concentrated adulation' she was getting. It was 'terribly corroding', she told the London *Sunday Express* in July, 1965. 'Every whim is indulged. Look at me, talking like this to you. Everyone likes to talk about themselves but once it's indulged you don't stop. I find myself talking about myself all the time now. It's just awful. But what can you do?' Two years later, she was still complaining, this time to Orianna Fallacci: 'I mean to say . . . to be a star . . . to me it is an empty word. It means nothing except lots of publicity, lots of people watching you, listening to you and despising you. If you like it, it's wonderful. If you don't, it's hell. I wasn't expecting it and I knew it could never make me happy. All I wanted was to learn to be an actress.'

Christie learned to act at London's Central School of Speech and Drama. She had enrolled there in 1958, after an unsettled education.

Her father was a tea-planter in India, and Julie was sent to English boarding schools, where – by all accounts – she gained a reputation for wilfulness and mischief. Her nicknames were 'SO' (or 'Show-Off') and 'Bugs' (or 'Bugs Bunny', because she was so talkative). One school expelled her for telling dirty jokes. At another, she got into trouble for tucking her skirt into her knickers one hot day, thus inflaming local swains, her teachers claimed. On leaving school, she was sent to France for a year, to learn the language, and then spent a further year studenting in Brighton (she half-attended a local college and waitressed in her spare time) before making up her mind to be an actress.

Fiona Walker, a co-student at Central, remembers Christie at this time as 'very pretty . . . BB was about then: Brigitte Bardot. Julie had spent a year in France and she sort of modelled herself on the French style.' The French family she stayed with, Christie herself later said, was 'very intellectual and sophisticated about life'. She was mightily impressed. 'After a year,' she told *Newsweek* in 1965, 'my mind started going voom, voom, voom.' While studying at Central, she tended to hang out with non-acting arty types: painters, designers, bohemian-style left-wing thinkers. This, the late 1950s, was the epoch of John Osborne, Colin Wilson, Kingsley Amis and various other angry-ish young persons. According to Fiona Walker, Christie liked her young men to be somewhat dissident. She liked them to be 'cool' and 'unimpressed'. Julie herself, says Walker, was 'not in the least cool'; nor was she in the least political: Walker 'used to go on CND marches, three-day marches from Aldermaston, and Julie used to feel that she should join in for the last hour, in case she was missing out on something. "I ought to, shouldn't I? Perhaps I should." It took quite a lot of years before she became a seriously committed person.' Even today, Walker detects an element of the 'hair shirt' in Christie's politics.

In 1959, though, Julie Christie was first of all one of the prettiest girls at drama school. As Fiona Walker recalls it, her friend had already been singled out for future stardom:

> First year students at Central would be selected to sell programmes at the public performances given by the third year. I was never asked to do that. But Julie would be. For one thing, she had

the right middle-class credentials, but also the school knew very well what they were doing. Put this little thing on show and all the agents aren't looking at the stage, they're looking at the girl in the aisle. I remember John Arden's *Live Like Pigs* was the first public performance we gave in our third year. The third year is the shop window. You're all trying to get an agent. *Live Like Pigs* is a play about gypsies who are living in a council house. Real scavengers. Real kind of squalid people. And Julie played Rosie who had a little baby and looked like . . . in fact, I think she was discovered under a pile of rags. That's how Rosie emerges: I can't quite recollect. Julie did not look like Julie and it was not a big and important part by any means. But at the end of that performance, a very long telegram arrived from one of the top agents in the country – very long, praising her performance and saying: *could* he represent her? That man had clocked Julie at least a year before, probably. He was just waiting.

The agent shortly afterwards got in touch with a television producer, Michael Hayes, who was preparing a sci-fi drama series for the BBC. 'An agent called me,' Hayes told Christie's biographer, Michael Feeney Callan. 'He was enthusiastic about what he called "the English Brigitte Bardot at Central".' Christie was cast as a blonde android in *A for Andromeda*, which turned out to be a substantial television hit. It opened the way for several screen auditions. She had caught the eye of producer Joseph Janni and director John Schlesinger and they almost chose her for the lead in Schlesinger's *A Kind of Loving*. Oddly, the part went to an actress called June Ritchie, since forgotten.

Between auditions, Christie was supporting herself with theatre repertory work and living with a group of artist-types, both male and female, in Earls Court. But the film break, when it came, was disappointingly low-grade. The 'new Brigitte Bardot' rumour had reached comedy director Ken Annakin, who was planning three 'loosely-linked feature romps'. For these he needed some new cheesecake. The comedian Leslie Phillips was lined up for one of the male leads and some years later he recalled that Christie's casting was by no means 'a foregone conclusion. There were endless, endless discussions about the *bottom lip* . . . Some of us thought, it's too big, too noticeable. She'll look awful on film; it's not the look of today.'

At the same time, though, there was 'a touch of arrogance' about Julie Christie, 'which can be very sexy in some women'. Christie got the part, or rather parts: the female lead in *Crooks Anonymous* and in its follow-up, *The Fast Lady*: two sexy roles which had Christie confiding to the press: 'if this is all my face leads to I'll break my nose and start over again.'

Although it was Christie's screen earnings that largely paid for the Earls Court ménage, she still had to cope with the stern critical appraisals of her otherworldly 'mates', as she habitually described them. For the mates – and indeed for her – the films that mattered at this time were films like *Saturday Night and Sunday Morning* and *Room at the Top*, gritty working-class dramas set in the North of England. And if you wanted to be really cool, there was also the French *Nouvelle Vague* to be considered. Truffaut's *Jules et Jim* appeared in 1961, the year in which Christie was renting her bottom lip to *Crooks Anonymous*. It so happened that sequences of Lindsay Anderson's *This Sporting Life* were being shot in the same studio as *Crooks Anonymous*. Leslie Phillips has recalled: 'We all *wanted* to be in *Sporting Life*. That's just the natural instinct . . . We all *want* to be in the best. And Julie, from the beginning, was like that.'

A year later, her ambition was splendidly fulfilled. She landed the part of Liz in *Billy Liar*, Janni and Schlesinger's follow-up to *A Kind of Loving*. Here was a film which sought to combine social comment with *Nouvelle Vague* stylishness. The part was a small one but it was of plot-altering importance. Liz is Billy Liar's fantasy-girl and when she turns out to be real – that is to say, smart, independent and a little bossy – the fantasist runs scared, preferring to stick with his drab Northern dreams rather than risk a demanding London life with this new kind of woman. Although Christie was second choice for the Liz role (the first choice, an actress called Topsy Jane, had fallen ill), she made the most of it. Her celebrated 'walk-sequence' in the film – a smiling, loose-limbed, handbag-swinging amble (set to jaunty music) through the streets of Bradford – was ecstatically seized on by viewers of the day and is still spoken of as a screen moment of much proto-feminist significance. In 1995, thirty years after the event, *The Observer* was still calling it 'one of the most dramatic and poetic entrances in cinematic history. She didn't just walk down the grim

street of a northern city – she floated. She didn't just ooze happy
self-confidence and sexuality – she flaunted it unselfconsciously. She
was sexually free, care free. When Philip Larkin observed that sexual
intercourse began in 1963, he had probably just seen Julie Christie
in the film, *Billy Liar*.'

By the time *Billy Liar* opened, Christie was already back at work in
the theatre. She had signed a six-month, £16-a-week, contract with
the Birmingham Repertory Theatre.

When this expired she joined a Royal Shakespeare Company tour
of Europe and America, playing Luciana in *A Comedy of Errors*. The
reviews she got as a stage actress were lukewarm compared to the
raves that greeted *Billy Liar*, and this may have been the moment
when she recognised that she would never be a first-rate theatrical
performer. Paul Scofield, star of the RSC tour, said of her at the time:
'She is not yet secure on the stage. But this inexperience doesn't come
across on the screen. She has a genuine talent. I admire her enormously
on screen.'

For many would-be movie stars, a year's invisibility might well have
proved conclusive, but such was Christie's appeal in *Billy Liar* that the
film offers continued to come in. Charlton Heston wanted her for
The War Lord. John Ford sent her the script of *Young Cassidy*, a film
to be based on one of Sean O'Casey's autobiographical works. Rod
Taylor would play Sean, but even so Christie was keen to work with
Ford, whom even the 'mates' probably had some respect for. She
played a prostitute called Daisy Battles. After a few weeks' filming,
though, Ford fell ill and was replaced by Jack Cardiff, who had to
guess at Ford's intentions. Christie sensed disaster: 'I thought: this is
the end of my career.' But when she saw the film, she was astonished:
'My God, Christie. You've come out of that very well. You even
look beautiful.'

And so she did, although the film was generally panned and added
little to Christie's reputation as a new-wave star. In spite of that *Billy
Liar* walk, she was still a sexy bit-part movie presence, not much of
an actress and with no apparent appetite for stardom. She now had a
regular boyfriend, a lithographer called Don Bessant, and was still at
her happiest when pottering around with her post-student buddies.
She bought a new flat in West Kensington, and worked hard to

maintain a respectable level of bohemian clutter: 'lots of piled-up, half-read books,' says her biographer, 'the works of the artist mates crammed on to every wall.' Questioned, as she often was, about her 'marriage plans', she stalled. Marriage, she said, required a 'particular talent, like writing, like acting – and I haven't got it'.

During Christie's on-stage sabbatical of 1963–4, Janni and Schlesinger had been devising a project which, they hoped, would turn Julie Christie into a big-league, multi-digit screen sensation. The film *Darling*, scripted by Frederic Raphael, nowadays comes across as a creakingly dated morality tale but in the early Sixties it could be plausibly presented as an eloquent and timely satire on the emerging glamour-realms of advertising, fashion and television. Diana Scott, a wide-eyed, would-be model, sleeps – or succumbs – her way from Dirk Bogarde (TV documentaries) to Laurence Harvey (advertising and Paris orgies) to marriage with a Fellini-style Italian prince (old money, but also quite a few old habits, like pretending to spend weekends with his mother). Illusions crushed, Diana heads back to England, and to Dirk, but he no longer needs the hassle. Diana was brought low, we are supposed to feel, by her weakness for swinging-Sixties glamour, a glamour of which *Darling* would soon enough be seen as an ingredient. It was Christie's zeitgeisty role in *Darling*, says her biographer, that caused her to be bracketed with 'fashionable gods' like David Bailey and Vidal Sassoon. She had become, he says, 'the first female all-British all-purpose sixties icon, symbol of rebellion and success, rebellion and decline'.

As it turned out, *Darling* was more warmly received in America than in Britain, where it was thought to lack profundity. 'A performance of pure gold,' said *Life*. '*Darling* will put Julie Christie up there among the celluloid goddesses,' said the New York *Herald-Tribune*. And by the time of its release, Christie had already consolidated her star status. She had been given the key part of Lara in David Lean's much-trumpeted *Doctor Zhivago*. This was, by any reckoning, the Big One, and to this day it is probably the role for which most people know her. The film is a kind of hymn to Lara's beauty. When Julie Christie's face is not on-screen, it is being thought about by most of the characters who are. Lara even gets her own theme-tune. Although *Darling* won Christie the 1965 Best Actress Oscar, it was Lean's snow-sweeping Russian epic that guaranteed her a durable screen-goddess niche. Adolescents today who don't recognise her name will probably grunt with near-approval when told she was the girl in *Doctor Zhivago* – you know, the one in the fur hat.

When Julie Christie herself is asked these days about *Zhivago*, all she can remember is that she fell in love with Spain, where it was filmed. Certainly she has nothing to say about her reported on-set spats with David Lean. Lean, it has been written, wanted her to be less 'scatter-brained' and to conduct herself 'more like a star'. Some hope. Even in 1965, her annus mirabilis, she was usually ready to deflate the hype. 'Being on top right now is a fluke,' she said. 'If I'm a passing fad, I hope it will be over fast – voom.' For a few years, though, after *Darling* and *Zhivago*, she did find herself drawn to the Hollywood big-time. 'It is easy,' she said in 1967, 'to slip into a lotus-like existence. People keep doing things for you and you keep letting them do things for you. After a time you begin to expect them to do things for you and you get peevish if they don't.' In this same year, she met Warren Beatty, dropped Don Bessant, and moved to California.

The Beatty relationship Christie absolutely refuses to discuss. She does concede, though, that Warren helped her to get rich. During her few years in the movies, she had been tied to a contract with Joseph Janni which gave her a regular income but made it hard for her to cash in on her success. Her earnings from *Doctor Zhivago* were around £40,000. Beatty, when they met, had lately scored a multi-million dollar coup with *Bonnie and Clyde* and was expert at handling the money-men. Christie, who 'hated' money, was – for a period – happy enough to let Beatty manage her career. She told friends that this was her 'acquisitive' period. Fiona Walker recalls:

> Once Julie became famous she helped herself to all the beautiful things in life that she wanted. But lots of the things that Warren liked absolutely appalled her. He lived in hotels. He just went in for the full American film-star bit, which she never espoused, to her credit.

Instead, she bought a house in London, and a farm in Wales and shopped extensively for clothes, paintings and antiques – possessions which, some years later, she would give away to her needy art-ist friends.

Being with Beatty, though, did mean that for a time she could set aside her own celebrity-anxieties. He was a bigger star than she was, and much richer. It seems to have made sense to each of them that she should function in his shadow. *McCabe & Mrs Miller*, *Shampoo* and *Heaven Can Wait* – the films she shared with Beatty – were, first of all, vehicles for Warren. Christie's roles, though prominently billed, were essentially supportive. In consequence, perhaps, she got the chance to do some acting: especially in the excellent *McCabe & Mrs Miller*. Her cockney accent in that film had a drama-school ring to it but there was a vitality and wit in her performance that came as a surprise to some who thought of her as just a pretty, passive face. Indeed, as Mrs Miller, her face was not in the least pretty.

Around Hollywood, Christie stuck to the sidelines while Beatty did the deals. Robert Altman has recalled: 'She used to sit on the edge of those parties, while Warren mingled.' She was also to be seen 'at his side' when he campaigned for McGovern in the 1972 Presidential election. Did Christie 'politicise' Beatty, or was it the other way around? Views differ, and Christie is not saying (although she did acknowledge that Warren's approach to politics was more 'historical' than hers). A good guess might be that Beatty taught her that good politics needs good publicity. He, on the other hand, may have been tutored by her vehemence. One story has it that when Christie was filming *The Go-Between* in rural England, Beatty joined her on the set. According to her biographer: 'the couple visited a nearby pig farm where the process of animal slaughter horrified Christie. Within twenty-four hours she declared herself from henceforth vegetarian . . . Beatty, to everyone's amazement, backed her up: the procedures were shocking, he would never eat meat again. This impassioned solidarity was seen as a sure sign of paving the way for a legalised bond.' The legalised bond never happened, of course. When asked about marriage in those days, Christie became snappish and Beatty retreated into wisecracks: 'The best time for a wedding is noon. Then if things don't work out, you haven't blown the whole day.'

Throughout Christie's Californian years she had kept up her links with England. She had property in London and in Wales, and two of her best films were made in Europe: *The Go-Between* in Norfolk, England and *Don't Look Now* in Venice. When, in the late Seventies, she finally tired of America, she had an English life she could return to. 'I loved America,' she said, 'but I was resentful of America. I remember all the time I kept protesting: I don't *live* here. I'm only passing through. I couldn't believe they were wasting so much. Throw away, throw away. Do they think all that plastic just disappears?'

On her return to England, Christie took up with the rock musician-producer Brian Eno. Eno was seven years younger than her and for a time the British papers enjoyed portraying her (at thirty-five or thereabouts) as a 'faded Sixties star' who was pitiably out of place in the high-energy rock world. And it did not help at all that she seemed to have undergone a serious political conversion. She was now, without apologies, a left-wing film-star activist, Britain's answer to Jane Fonda, and she was ridiculed accordingly. Her response was to make a real effort to dismantle her celebrity, to turn herself into a kind of anti-star. It was not easy. Celebrity, she said, was 'like a nasty dog following me around. But how do I get rid of it?' She still wanted to make films, but from now on she would be more vigilant. 'She would get completely pissed off,' a friend of hers told me, 'with what was on offer. She would have liked to do films like Vanessa was doing, or Jane Fonda. She wanted to do things that were making serious statements, committed statements about living, or the human condition or whatever . . . So she found herself isolated. Scripts would arrive and she'd find something she didn't like about them: she couldn't do that and she couldn't do that. Sometimes, though, she'd pick up things: "I like that and I agree with that," and so she would sometimes commit herself to things. Or she would like a thing that a director would say because it tied in with something she believed in, and so she would assume the rest. Sometimes she would put herself in the hands of people who were not that talented, or scripts that weren't that good because she thought they were saying something that she wanted to say, something that she wanted to be associated with.'

Apart from *Return of the Soldier* (1981) and *Heat and Dust* (1982) – a film which took her back to India for the first time since her childhood – Christie during the Eighties tended to opt for independent, low-budget productions directed by women. There was Sally Potter's *Gold* in 1984 and Maria Luisa Bemberg's *Miss Mary* two years later. For much of that decade, though, she lived quietly in her Welsh farmhouse, where journalists would visit her from time to time and marvel at her rustic rigour: no heating, no make-up, no personal unburdenings. The questions she now had to field were more often to do with children than with marriage. Her answer was simple: she didn't *want* to be a mother. 'I like to pick and choose what I want to do,' she said. 'The prospect of being a spinster without any family doesn't bother me at all. I think the ideal way for humans to live is with a group of people instead of in a tiny, closed-off nucleus like a family.' Her farmhouse was shared with a couple (plus children) whom she had met in California. Nowadays she shares a house in London with what she would call 'a family of friends'. Her particular male friend, a journalist, lives somewhere else – just as he did during her Welsh sojourn.

And maybe there are echoes here of her pre-stardom life. When Christie became a film star there was, there had to be, a semi-rejection of her arty mates, a separation for which, it could be said, she still tries to make amends. 'They and I were one,' she told me. 'And then suddenly I was made into something that put me in another camp. I had the dosh.' She also had the shallowness, the glitz, the unreality. Even today, she speaks of her success in films as if it were some terrible betrayal of the intellect. 'Julie has a tremendous awe and admiration for the intellect,' says Fiona Walker. 'She envies it. This is another source of feeling inadequate: that she's not as intellectual as she'd like to be.'

Most people who meet Julie Christie remark on her low self-esteem. She is not, she will insist, a proper actress – even though, during the Nineties, she has re-emerged as a stage actress. Nor is she a proper intellectual – in spite of the Open University degree course she is currently engaged in. She has no memory, no head for figures. She finds it particularly hard to call up the statistics needed to support her various campaigns against injustice. And this can be painful to observe, since – politically – she is in an almost constant state of virtuous outrage. She knows she's right – she read a book last week that *proved* she's right – now *what* was the book called?

This tends to be the pattern of her discourse, and only a hard soul would wish to pin her down.

Friends of hers had advised me that Christie is by no means as scatty as she seems, and perhaps some of her amnesia is self-defensive. In her hotel suite at San Sebastian, she was surrounded by attendants – a hairdresser, a PR person, a Festival redjacket – and each of them was there to serve and soothe. Downstairs in the lobby lurked the Enemy: photographers, journalists and television crews. Outside, behind crush barriers, waited a hundred or so fans – not fans of Julie Christie, specifically, but film fans, hoping to eyeball a big star. Michael Douglas was expected, they'd been told. So too was Willem Dafoe. The night before, on her arrival, Julie Christie had been pursued from entrance to elevator by a small gang of paparazzi.

Up on the sixth floor, Christie seemed rather more relaxed than she had been in London. She had, she said, recovered from *Susannah Andler*. When people with clipboards reminded her that she was expected somewhere else, like now, she made it clear, but with a knockout smile, that she would not be hurried. She had promised me a second interview. A promise was a promise. The Festival would have to wait. She wanted to talk to me, she said, about celebrity, about journalists, about the death of Princess Di. She had forgotten to bring the Janet Malcolm book and in any case she was now researching the Basque separatist movement: after all, we *were* in Spain. Also, she was determined to see the new Guggenheim gallery in nearby Bilbao. At the same time, she *did* want to pursue this matter of celebrity, of Princess Di.

And so it was pursued, out on the hotel terrace, under the intermittent scrutiny of passing fans, one of whom mistook Christie for a Spanish soap star, an error she handled with aplomb. Here in San Sebastian, playing the film star once again, her memory – or some unpleasant strand of it – appeared to flicker into life: those days in the spotlight had been for her 'a nightmare'. She knew how Princess Diana must have felt. 'I knew she was going to die. That's been clear for years. It was like watching a movie made for perverts, where people paid, and watched, and continued to watch even though it was quite clear she had to die.' Diana had been 'bullied to death', she thought.

Bullied by whom? The press, the press's readers, the whole 'totalitarian' machine that we call a democracy. Had I read Milan Kundera –
she had the cutting somewhere – where he said that privacy was 'the
value we must defend above all others'? The daily life of a celebrity
in the West was like the daily lives of just about everyone in what
used to be 'the East' (i.e. the Iron Curtain countries). Hence her use
of the word 'totalitarian'. As she talked, she hunted in the knapsack
she always carries with her – a knapsack full of pamphlets, books and
newspaper cuttings. She found the Kundera: 'Famous people,' he had
written, 'have become a public resource – like sewer systems.' She read
it out to me and when she'd done she sat back and half-closed her eyes:
another tiring job well done. Then, enter left, the clipboards. They
didn't want to interrupt but they did need to firm up tomorrow's Julie
Christie schedule: press interviews, radio, TV, a publicity reception,
the screening of *Afterglow*, and so on. 'Are you guys wrapping?' one of
them enquired, and Christie's knockout smile returned, albeit wearily.
'I think so, pretty much,' she said. 'I think we've wrapped.'

New Yorker, 1998

Taste, Tact and Racism

The Di Castro Travel Agency in mid-town Alexandria has lately been mounting an eerily compelling window display: a shrine to the memory of Dodi al-Fayed and Diana, Princess of Wales. The shrine has as its centrepiece the front cover of an Egyptian picture-magazine, *al-Mussawar* – a cover depicting Di and Dodi on their wedding day that never was. The couple are shown hand in hand: she in a white bridal gown, clutching a bouquet; he in a dark morning suit with a carnation in his button-hole. They both seem very happy – or, shall we say, they don't in the least seem to mind having their heads mounted on some other couple's torsos. Di, we suspect, might not have been too thrilled with the mass-market-looking dress that she's been made to wear, but Dodi looks straightforwardly elated. What neither of them knows is that, printed in bold red letters across the bottom left-hand corner of their wedding pic, a headline asks: 'Who killed Diana?'

On either side of the centrepiece are cuttings from the condolence columns of Egypt's leading daily, *al-Ahram*: messages of sympathy from Egyptian associates and friends of the al-Fayeds. And directly below the wedding photograph there is a copy of the Koran, open at a verse which reads:

> Wealth and sons are the ornaments
> Of the life of this world
> But the things that endure,
> Good Deeds, are best
> In the sight of the Lord.

The whole montage is touching and grotesque: the simple pieties of the Koran in jarring contrast with the crude photo mock-up of the dead couple in their wedding finery. Who could have dreamed up such a folly? The Di Castro Travel Agency, according to an engraved announcement on the store-front is 'A Fayed Brothers Company' – owned, in other words, by Dodi's father and his two uncles, Ali and Salah.

I visited Alexandria only four weeks after the Paris car crash in which Di and Dodi were killed. After two weeks of British Dianamania, the Di Castro window could scarcely have failed to stop me in my tracks. For most Egyptians, though, the shrine, and what it seemed to say, were unremarkable. Far from being thought of as spooky or sensational, the di Castro display merely summarised a general, and wholly settled, conviction in the Middle East: that accident was no accident.

Within days of the event, the columnist Anis Mansour was writing in *al-Ahram:* 'British intelligence assassinated [Diana] to save the throne, just as Marilyn Monroe was assassinated by American intelligence. Never before, not even during the days of Cromwell, did any one person manage singlehandedly to shake the foundations of the royal family.' Once the Windsors were convinced that Diana 'would marry a Muslim who would give her a son named Mohamed or a girl called Fatma, and the son becomes the brother of the King of England, Head of the Church, there had to be a solution'. Mansour continued. 'The solution was to dispose of the princess and her groom. In that way, the royal family's nightmare would be at an end.'

It's true there had been mentions of Arab conspiracy theories in the British press but here they were instantly dismissed as 'lunatic' or Islamic propaganda, a line greatly assisted by Colonel Qadaffi's intervention. Qadaffi told journalists in Sirte that Diana 'was clearly hunted by the royal family, which wanted to get rid of her. It is very clear that they did not want the brother of a British prince to be an Arab Muslim.' In an earlier statement, he accused Britain of 'executing an Arab citizen and a British citizen simply because the Arab wished to marry a British princess. British and French Intelligence planned this together. It is an act of racial and religious discrimination.' Qadaffi, everyone knows, is barking mad: ditto, therefore, the theories he espouses. And in any case, I had heard it asked in London, where did these Arabs get the idea that Britain's MI5 would have been *clever* enough to pull off such an elaborate and chancy execution? The whole idea was nonsense.

The fact remained that in Egypt – and probably throughout the Arab world – few people were ready to accept that the two lovers died by chance. On an Alexandrian newstand I picked up three books on the subject: *Assassination of a Princess* by Ahmad Ata, *Diana: A Princess Killed by Love* by Ilham Sharshar, and *Who Killed Diana?* by Muhammad Ragab. This last was subtitled: By Order of the Palace – the Execution of Imad al-Fayed. When I asked the newsvendor: do you believe all this? his answer was: 'All of Egypt believes it'. He seemed almost apologetic, as if he didn't want to be the one who broke the news. I got a similar response from the head waiter in a Cairo restaurant: 'The whole world knows it.' He too seemed to feel sorry for me: a dim Briton gulled by his homicidal rulers.

During the four days that I spent in Egypt, the assassination theory was on everybody's lips – except that it was not a theory. There was confident talk of Diana being pregnant. She pointed at her stomach, did she not, when that French doctor came to her assistance in the tunnel – or was it another doctor, later on, after they had got her to the hospital? There was talk, too, of Diana having converted to Islam, in preparation for her Muslim wedding. I heard and read stories of British MI5 agents staying at the Paris Ritz on the night of the crash, of Dodi having received phone-calls over dinner, phone-calls warning him that something was afoot. One call had made him 'extremely tense'. Soon after, he 'decided to leave the hotel'. This story, reported in *al-Ahram*, seems to have originated in a French magazine called *Nouveau Détective*.

On one of the two evenings I spent in Cairo, I went to a dinner at which several prominent Egyptian journalists and editors were present, including Anis Mansour, the columnist who had first floated the assassination theory. By the time I met him he had, he said, published a further seven columns on the subject. I half-expected Mansour to be viewed with condescension by his journalistic colleagues. A couple of days earlier, I had read of him (in an Egyptian English-language weekly) that he was 'well-known for his fondness for discovering design where others only see accident'. In fact he was the evening's star turn. Most of the other guests seemed to approach him with great reverence, hanging on his words, nervously glancing at him when they spoke. And when the Di/Dodi liaison came up for discussion, nobody made any serious attempt to quarrel with the Mansour line. I asked the journalists about Mohamed al-Fayed, but they said little that I had not heard before: he had come from Alexandria, from nowhere, and had been out of Egypt for some thirty years.

His son Emad – 'Dodi' was a nickname – proved to be a subject of much keener interest. For them, he had clearly been a figure of high glamour – his Ferraris, yachts and jets, his Hollywood starlets, his successful courtship of Diana. I asked about Dodi's relationship with his father but was soon made to feel that this was not a question that should properly be asked, not now, not during this period of mourning. I formed the impression while I was in Egypt that Dodi may have been a little backward – 'simple' was a word I heard quite often used – and that he conformed to some familiar image of the feckless first-born son of a rich father. Mohamed would always have bankrolled him, people said, if only in order to safeguard his own status as a loving parent.

The journalists were more forthcoming about Dodi's mother, Samira Khashoggi. After the break-up of her marriage to Mohamed in 1957 (the divorce came through in 1958), she had founded a magazine called *al-Sharqiyya*. She had written romantic novels, married again (twice), and in 1986 she had committed suicide – though it was more often said that she died of cancer, or a heart attack. During the early days of her separation from Mohamed, when Dodi (b. 1955) was two or three years old, there had been an unpleasant custody dispute. Mohamed kept little Dodi 'under guard' in Alexandria because, he said, Adnan Khashoggi, Samira's brother, planned to kidnap the child. Eventually there was a court order forbidding Khashoggi to make any approaches to his nephew.

Journalists are, of course, terrific gossips, and this was an informal evening. On the following day, I interviewed an Egyptian diplomat who had spent several years in London and had had close dealings with the al-Fayeds. Did he buy the assassination theory? Did al-Fayed himself buy it? Mohamed, said the diplomat, would accept the French judicial findings; he believes in French justice, and of course he hopes that the car crash will turn out to have been an accident. But what about the Di Castro window display: does this not indicate that the al-Fayeds inclined somewhat towards the idea of a conspiracy? 'This was possibly the work of an over-zealous manager', he said. He had not himself seen the faked wedding picture, but he did not seem particularly shocked when I described it to him.

The 'Who Killed Diana?' issue of *al-Musawwar* is dated 5 September, six days after the crash. On the same day the Queen, somewhat reluctantly, paid tribute to her former daughter-in-law as an 'exceptional and gifted human being' but made no mention of the princess's final lover and co-victim.

Before he died, most of what was written about Dodi had been prurient and disapproving. Some regarded it as racist. Edward Said, for instance, spoke of 'an orgy of racist fantasy and sexual peeping tom-ism'. 'It was as if every threadbare Orientalist cliché about "fabled" Oriental wealth and sexual prowess was marshalled to conquer (read "violate") the blonde English snow fairy,' he wrote in *al-Ahram Weekly*. And in impressive support of his opinion, he cited the 10 August issue of *The Sunday Times*:

> Does he [al-Fayed senior] hope that William's coronation, in however many decades' time, will have an Alexandrian air due to the dark-eyed presence of the new king's half-siblings Cleo and Mo, the dashing children of Dodi and Di? And will old Grandpa Mohamed, the matchmaker, be there himself, rubbing his hands in victory?

After the Paris deaths, hostility to Dodi became quite explicit, and it was presumably in order to combat this line of disparagement that Dodi's bereaved father decided to put his own spin on the tragedy – and, indeed, on the romance. Within days of the car crash, Michael Cole, al-Fayed's ultra-Brit PR man, was feeding the newspapers sugary tidbits from the couple's final hours. Diana, he said, had given Dodi a pair of cufflinks that had once belonged to her father. Dodi had responded with a 'Tell me yes' ring. There was also a silver plaque on which Dodi had inscribed 'a poem', seemingly authored by himself.

Cole also refuted press suggestions that Dodi was a fast-car freak: 'In point of fact', he said, 'Dodi did not like speed'. He also dismissed speculation that Mohamed had dreamed of becoming step-grandfather to the future King of England. All the Fayed family loved the princess and wanted nothing from her. Their only wish was that she should find personal happiness and contentment after her years of difficulty. And on 17 September, on the Geraldo Rivera TV show, he mused on the several ways in which the two lovers had been suited to each other:

> When they were together they were quite similar . . . they had such a lot in common. They both liked the films. I mean Dodi was besotted with the film business. And Diana was a film fan. Somebody was saying to them, you know, they should go and see a stage play in the West End which was just wonderful, and both of them agreed simultaneously that they'd rather see even a second-rate film than go to the theatre.

'The mouth-piece doth protest too much methinks', wrote one reader to the *Sunday Telegraph*. Al-Fayed, though, was not to be restrained. When *The Sun* (which, pre-Paris, had run the headline 'Dodi is a Dud in Bed') reproduced a letter which al-Fayed had despatched to the 'hundreds of ordinary folk' who had sent him their condolences, there were suggestions that the letter had been leaked. 'I take some comfort', the letter signed by al-Fayed read, 'from my absolute belief that God has taken their souls to live together in Paradise . . . If the planet lasts for another thousand years, people will still be talking about the terrible event we are living through. But what they will remember most is the love that existed between two wonderful people'.

Two weeks earlier, Michael Cole (accompanied by al-Fayed) had addressed a 9000-strong crowd at Fulham Football Club: 'If this planet lasts another thousand years, people will still be talking about the terrible events we are living through together. But what they will remember most is the affection that existed between two wonderful people.' On the appearance of these same words, more or less, in *The Sun*, A.N. Wilson, writing in the *Evening Standard*, warned that 'Mr al-Fayed should be wary of losing our sympathy':

> Mr al-Fayed is yet again giving a very unfortunate impression

to that public he wishes so desperately to please. The impression received is that he is exploiting the situation for all it is worth, and almost claiming that, in Paradise if not on earth, he has at last secured marital kinship with the greatest in the land.

The general view of Mohamed al-Fayed is riddled with 'unfortunate impressions'. Time and again, he has made errors of timing, taste and tact from which competent advisers should surely have been able to protect him. His English is not all that it might be – and is regularly cluttered with expletives. But better a few expletives than the mailshot-prose that gets foisted on him by his PR men.

I talked recently with a friend who once sat next to al-Fayed at an embassy lunch. For most of the lunch, he said nothing: he had to make sure that his food was not poisoned. (A germ-phobic, al-Fayed, when eating out, always calls for a cut lime, which he then rubs around the edges of his cutlery, glass, plate, etc.) He stirred himself only twice: the first time to ask the woman on his right to let him look at a fancy silver notebook-holder which, for some reason, she had with her. 'We could make that. The Harrods logo would fit *there*', he said, then gave it back; the second time was when my friend asked him about Harrods. He at once gestured towards a distinguished-looking Brit sitting opposite. 'Fucking racist', he said. 'I've got Harrods now. My face in Egyptian Hall. Never take it away from me. There for the next thousand years. Fucking racists.' He is a big man and he was not whispering but nobody reacted. His Finnish wife – 'very pretty, very blonde', according to my friend – was also sitting opposite. She smiled at him. 'Maybe he smiled back but maybe not'.

Before the Harrods – or, to be precise, House of Fraser – takeover in 1985 Mohamed Fayed (the 'al' was added later) had been seen in business circles as a wealthy middleman, a fixer who had useful contacts in the Middle East and in Brunei. He was not considered a big player. Sure enough, in 1979, he had bought the Ritz Hotel in Paris. But the Ritz was a bauble, an unprofitable self-indulgence. Certainly al-Fayed was reckoned to be small-time by global tycoons like Tiny Rowland, who, when he met al-Fayed, had been refused permission to acquire Harrods by the Monopolies and Mergers Commission.

Hoping to have this decision rescinded at some future date, he had the bright idea of parking some of his own House of Fraser shares with al-Fayed. In due course, he would buy them back.

As it turned out, al-Fayed used the former Rowland shares as a platform for his own takeover bid. Rowland was astounded and enraged – and all the more so when the bid was nodded through at high speed by the authorities. Why, he asked, didn't the Government treat al-Fayed as suspiciously as they had treated him? Was it because al-Fayed, a year earlier, had persuaded the Sultan of Brunei to keep his billions in sterling and thus 'save the pound'? Al-Fayed, Rowland claimed, could not possibly be as wealthy as he said he was. The House of Fraser cost about £600 million. Al-Fayed was rich, certainly, but was not in the nine-figure league; Rowland believed that he was fronting for another buyer – perhaps the limitlessly loaded Sultan of Brunei.

Al-Fayed (and the Sultan) denied any collaboration. Mohamed's millions were all his, and his alone. And he was supported in this claim by Kleinwort Benson who testified in November 1984 that the Fayeds were 'members of an old established Egyptian family who for more than a hundred years were shipowners, landowners and industrialists in Egypt'. Al-Fayed, Kleinwort's representative told Channel 4, had left Egypt after his businesses there were nationalised by Nasser in the early Sixties, but had already salted away some £20 million, offshore. This £20 million was the basis of his future mega-fortune. The 'real build-up of the family wealth came from the period in Dubai when they became involved in large construction contracts and the oil service supply.'

So far, so plausible. The trouble started for al-Fayed when he began talking to journalists who urged him to add a few autobiographical details. He was, it seems, all too happy to oblige. He told reporters that his grandfather, Ali al-Fayed, had founded a cotton-shipping business in 1876 and had used his own ships to supply the Lancashire mills, that he had then invested in property in Paris and Switzerland and in time had built up a 'major fleet of ships'. The riches thus amassed had eventually passed to Mohamed's father, a keen Anglophile, who had seen to it that his sons were 'educated at British schools and had British nannies'.

In November 1984 the *Daily Mail* described the al-Fayeds as follows:

> Mohamed and his brothers Ali and Salah have climbed a commercial and social Everest since their grandfather Ali al-Fayed founded the family fortunes a century ago by growing cotton on the banks of the Nile and exporting it in his own ships to the mills of Lancashire . . . One half of the explanation for his 'Englishness' can be attributed to his English nanny and to his education in one of the pre-Nasser English-style public schools, Victoria in Alexandria, where he was caned and stuffed full of crumpets by Oxbridge-educated masters.

Less than six months later, on the eve of al-Fayed's Harrods takeover, the same story – give or take a crumpet – was still solidly intact. Ivan Fallon in *The Sunday Times* wrote of the al-Fayeds' 'disdain for the nouveaux riches of the Arab world'. The al-Fayeds had 'delicately pointed out that their family lived in some luxury when even the Saudi royal family lived in tents in the desert':

> The family does not see itself in the Arab tradition at all but as part of something much older. Egypt, Mohamed pointed out, was the cradle of civilisation. He and his family, he implied, are inheritors of the tradition of the Pharaohs, not that of the desert.

This boast of a pharaonic lineage is, apparently, not uncommon with socially aspirant Egyptians. Egypt may not be oil-rich, but the country is rich in history, and from this point of view the oil barons of Saudi and the Gulf can be seen as little more than jumped-up tribesmen. Wishing to signal an innate superiority – Egyptian over Arab – the al-Fayeds permitted a fable to develop. After all, with Harrods almost in their grasp, they needed to project their superiority in terms which would be comprehensible to British readers. To the British, 'superiority' meant old money, crumpets, nannies, public schools – and pharaohs too, if you insist.

In Alexandria in the 1930s, when Mohamed al-Fayed was growing up, 'superiority' meant being on good terms with the British. The

British were the occupying force and they were in charge of all the places at which smart-set Alexandrians might wish to be seen: the Sporting Club, the Yacht Club, the Officers' Club, and so on. There is a story, probably apocryphal, that little Mohamed used to go down to the docks in Alexandria and watch the British ships at berth there. He was impressed, so it's said, by the spectacle of British sailors lined up on the decks, in their crisp white uniforms, saluting the Union Jack, and apparently experienced some kind of Anglophile epiphany, from which he has not yet recovered.

This story has often been related in the press here but when I repeated it in Egypt people laughed. Mohamed, they said, may well have visited the docks and seen the well-dressed sailors but the feelings he had were unlikely to have been straightforwardly admiring. Those Egyptians who cared about who ruled them and who were not actually profiting from the occupation, tended to despise their British masters. These colonial governors, they'd say, were not really in Egypt in order to get the country on its feet. They were there to safeguard the Suez Canal – the route to India. Far from nurturing or even encouraging native self-government, the British held it back. Whenever possible, they would stir up trouble between Muslims, Copts and Jews and then say: Look, how *can* we leave these people to themselves?

There was resentment, then, aplenty – the understandable resentment of the colonised, the condescended to. But there was also, in some quarters, a kind of envying attraction. The British got things done. The British gentleman was looked up to, I was told by one Anglicised Egyptian, for his 'probity, his administrative skills, and his well-ordered mind'. The British, she said, lack candour but possess 'a sense of fairness which can be appealed to'. Is this how al-Fayed saw the British? If so, he may by now have changed his mind. One way or another, the British were a powerful presence in his early life in Alexandria. He may not have wanted to *be* British but he may well have wanted to belong to that Alexandrian élite who were accepted by the British and who led a semi-British way of life: nannies, public schools, accounts at Harrods, and the like. He may also have wanted revenge.

Once the fable of al-Fayed's Alexandrian background had been publicised – and added to by 'journalistic hallucination', as he himself would later call it – he was not going to go out of his way to contradict it. And this proved to be an error, an error that haunts him to this day. Tiny Rowland knew the al-Fayeds' autobiography was a fake, and launched into what would turn out to be an eight-year-long vendetta, or campaign of exposure. 'I have been accused of being a bad loser', Rowland later told *Forbes* magazine, 'but I refuse to lose to a cheat'. In 1987, two years into his House of Fraser reign, al-Fayed found himself, thanks to Rowland's tireless proddings, the target of a full-scale investigation by the Department of Trade and Industry. Called to testify on their personal and business background, the al-Fayeds stuck to the fable – old family, cotton, ships, the English nanny – and even added a few new details to it. The DTI's verdict was unequivocally negative. It found that 'the Fayeds dishonestly misrepresented their origins, their wealth, their business interests and their resources to the Secretary of State, the OFT (Office of Fair Trading), the press, the HoF Board and HoF shareholders, and their own advisers.' The money to buy House of Fraser had, the DTI suspected, been raised by the al-Fayeds making use of 'their association with the Sultan of Brunei and the opportunities afforded to them by the possession of wide powers of attorney from the Sultan of Brunei'.

Several new 'early background' details had been added to the al-Fayed fable. These included '20 companies, spread between Port Said, Suez, Ismailia and Alexandria', a family yacht named *Dodi*, and – in the late Fifties – the shipping of 'both cargo and pilgrims round the Gulf'. All of the al-Fayed assets – apart from the £20 million which had already been spirited away – were seized by the Nasser government in 1961. It was at this point, the inspectors were informed, that the al-Fayeds decided that 'there was no hope for them in Egypt' and had set off, first for Europe and then to the Gulf. Mohamed, they said, had predicted the Gulf's oil boom and had got into the act very early. Hence their properties and businesses. These soon became available at knock-down prices – and Mohamed was on hand to take advantage. In 1957, he acquired a small but once thriving shipping agency, 'at a low price', says the DTI. The business had been owned by 'a wealthy Alexandrian Jew, Mr Leon Carasso, whose business had been destroyed by the events of late 1956'. This agency, the Middle East Navigation Company, was the first al-Fayed company, the first of many.

During the late Fifties and early Sixties, the al-Fayeds expanded their activities in Egypt, buying into hotels, property and shipping. By the time of Nasser's 1961 nationalisation programme, they seem to have been doing very nicely, even though – as the DTI Report labours to make clear – 'the sums involved . . . were still small in comparison to the size of the inherited wealth the al-Fayeds later claimed that they enjoyed in these years'. And this becomes the familiar DTI refrain: yes, the young al-Fayeds were successful, but not on the scale that they pretended, not on the scale that would have enabled them to buy the House of Fraser. Millions, yes, but hundreds of millions, no.

After a few dozen pages of the DTI Report, an unbiased reader might easily be inclined to feel sorry for the al-Fayeds. After all, what have they done? They have been guilty of 'big talk', but isn't this normal practice in big business? And al-Fayed gives the impression that he believes in his own legend:

> Hum, on my children's life, it's mine. All mine. Me and two brothers . . . nobody. And the British Government, they don't give permission . . . they give me permission in 10 days because they know who is Mohamed Fayed for twenty-five years. I give this country business, over six billion sterling worth of business, in the last ten years. They know who is Mohamed Fayed. This is why they give me permission and before they give that, they have to know that this is my money . . . right? . . . Not anybody money, because the man who has, who owns this Lonrho, Tiny Rowland who's always writing . . . bad man.

This snatch of authentic-sounding speech appears in the transcript of a tape-recorded conversation between al-Fayed and two representatives of the Sultan of Brunei. Tiny Rowland acquired the tape-recording (it's said to have cost him a million dollars) and later had the transcript printed in a booklet called *The Sultan and I*. Much of the dialogue on the tape is gibberish (al-Fayed's interlocutors were a couple of Indian 'holy men' who had the Sultan's ear) but every so often Mohamed does come out with an affecting line, or paragraph:

For me, I need nobody, only my God, you know, what I have
between me and him [the Sultan], just spiritual things'

I have a message in my bottle, that wealth you know I have,
half of it will go to God.

Whatever we do there is nothing can keep us safe except the
goodness we make, for others and for ourselves and not only for
ourselves only, but for others and this is a big thing. I mean 50,000
people I look after okay? Their homes, look after them and this is
a pleasure you know and as much as I can make I'm always here . . .
I like to take from people can afford to give. I like to do things for
India like Mother Theresa, like you know, which very important
I like you to see where we can do to also offer to do things for
people, which is very important.

Tiny Rowland, in an appendix to the booklet, lists all of these snippets
as 'examples of a claimed idealism which is a part of Mohamed Fayed's
technique as a confidence trickster'. But I am not so sure. Admittedly,
Fayed is talking to a pair of Indian holy men, and this might well
account for the wish to 'do things for India like Mother Theresa'.
At the same time, though, not even Tiny Rowland can question
al-Fayed's generosity. In Egypt, I heard many tributes to his charitable
deeds and his record in Britain can scarcely be dismissed (though it
often has been) as an effort to buy good publicity. At Great Ormond
Street, al-Fayed is a hero. His baby son (he has three children by his
present wife) was once treated there for meningitis and as a gesture of
gratitude al-Fayed bought the hospital a magnetic resonance scanner
that is said to have cost around £6 million. He has also paid for a
Selectron scanner at the Royal Marsden and gives £50,000 a year
to meningitis research at Queen Charlotte's Hospital and £100,000
annually to Childline. The list goes on. In Egypt, al-Fayed's acts of
charity have been on a smaller scale – and there are some Egyptians
who believe that he could have done better. The charitable deeds I
heard of there involved consignments of wheelchairs or sticks for the
blind, although it was rumoured that he had built a hospital in Upper
Egypt. None of this was of much interest to the DTI inspectors, whose
tone is steadily judicial, bordering now and then on the contemptuous.
Rarely is al-Fayed granted even an approving nod, a crumb of praise

for his, well, energy and acumen. In terms of 'Trade and Industry', al-Fayed – as he often boasts – has brought millions to British industry, especially during his sojourn in Dubai during the early Seventies, when he arranged for major construction contracts to go to British firms. According to the DTI, these contracts would anyway have gone to Britain, since the Ruler of Dubai was solidly pro-British. The British contractors, on the other hand, were full of gratitude for al-Fayed's mediating skills.

It was skills of this sort, without question, that pitched the al-Fayeds into the big money. In the early Sixties, they were well-off Egyptian expatriates, capitalists-in-exile, on the look-out for whatever deals might come their way. By the mid-Eighties (*pace* Tiny Rowland and the DTI) they had become seriously rich. 'It is easy to make money,' al-Fayed has said, and he certainly made it look easy. His commercial history during the middle years of his career revolves around a series of highly successful acts of infiltration. He got himself into Dubai by offering to assist with the construction of a dock. Dubai, at the time of his approach, had not yet become oil-rich; indeed, the country was quite poor. Did al-Fayed know what was coming? Presumably he did. In any event, by the time the oil-cash started to pour in, he was already installed as one of the Ruler's trusted friends.

He scored a similar success with the Sultan of Brunei. Within weeks of their first informal meeting, he had become the Sultan's 'trusted confidant', and was wielding the Sultan's power-of-attorney throughout Europe: a power which Tiny Rowland and the DTI believe he exploited for his own, Harrods-buying ends.

Al-Fayed's brief foray into Haiti in 1964 is closely and scathingly examined in the DTI report. But the episode is surely more comical than criminal. Al-Fayed showed up in Port-au-Prince claiming to be an oil-rich Kuwaiti sheikh at a time when Haiti, labouring under the effects of a US economic boycott, was almost on its knees. Sheikh al-Fayed found himself given a free hand, and access to the harbour's funds. He installed lights on the pier and set out one or two buoy markers, but full-scale renovation never quite got going. Al-Fayed's real interest in Haiti, it would seem, was to check out stories he had heard that the country might be rich in oil. When he discovered that the stories were unfounded, he hastily decamped – bearing with him, said Duvalier, the port authority's remaining funds: around $150,000, it was claimed. Al-Fayed, on the other hand, complained that Duvalier owed *him* a pile of cash.

Comical or not, the whole episode does argue for a certain flair, a certain courage, on the part of al-Fayed. The DTI inspectors, though, were unimpressed. What mattered to them was that yet again the defendant had been guilty of self-misrepresentation. Or, at the very least, al-Fayed had allowed a myth to burgeon and had made no effort to deflate it. (The Haiti newspapers called al-Fayed a sheikh and he chose not to set them straight: to Haitians, he said, all Arabs are called 'Sheikh'.) In Cairo, a friend of al-Fayed's chuckled when I asked him: 'Why *does* the man tell so many lies?'. 'Lies', in his view, was too strong a word. Why not call them 'fantasies'? 'But why are the fantasies always to do with rank?' 'Ah, well . . .' – and then the spreading of the hands, as if to say: 'Your guess may even be as good as mine.'

In this country it would appear to be al-Fayed's persistent uppishness that gets on people's nerves. His agenda, as the press perceives it, is quite plain. He wants to buy what cannot, in the end, be bought – authentic class. To watch him try to pull off such a deal is risible: the chairmanship of posher-than-posh Harrods, the castle in Scotland, the sponsoring of royal horse shows, the tarting up of the old Windsor house in Paris – it is all so laughably transparent. And look what happens when acceptance is refused, when the DTI exposes him as a misrepresenter, and when – on this basis – he is twice denied a British passport? What happens? The vulgarian turns vulgar. 'This guy has been shitted upon,' he tells the world, and then proceeds to seek revenge. He bribes MPs to speak up for him in Parliament and when this manoeuvre brings in no returns, he shops the MPs to the papers and thus brings down a Tory government to which, over the years, he had donated massive sums, and brings it down so heavily that he will almost certainly not live to see another one. And then – the crowning payback, so to speak – he arranges for his wastrel son to marry into the Royal family.

For some, the awfulness of al-Fayed lies first of all in what he has revealed about Britain. Even he was shocked by the eagerness with which Members of Parliament fell victim to his not-all-that-enormous bribes. 'Compared with ministers, MPs and other Tory fixers I have had the misfortune to encounter', he – or was it Michael Cole? – has said, 'the average carpet dealer in the Cairo bazaar is a man of great probity and honour.' The refusing of al-Fayed's passport can now be read as a petulant, last-ditch attempt on Britain's part to show that although individual Britons can quite easily be bought, true Britishness somehow cannot. No wonder this pro-British foreigner is angry. No wonder that, in certain moods, he has wished to tear the whole thing down.

Al-Fayed has been mocked most relentlessly on account of his supposed obsession with the royals. It is easy enough, though, when one takes a look at Harrods, to understand how the owner of all this – six floors, thirty-five acres, 4,000-plus employees and *ubique*, wherever the eye falls, luxurious profusion – might be subject to monarchical delusions: might feel himself to be a king. The store's motto is 'Omnia omnibus ubique' but that is not quite how it feels. Harrods is, self-consciously, the Citadel of Privilege, the Palace of Big Bucks, the Shop of Shoppes. The store, sure enough, can get everything from anywhere but only somebodies can easily afford to place an order. To have become boss of this cornucopian palazzo was surely worth a dozen DTI reports, a score of Tiny Rowlands.

Al-Fayed's business career has repeatedly brought him into contact with absolute rulers, kings, dictators of small countries: the Emir of Kuwait, the Ruler of Dubai, the Sultan of Brunei, rich men whose whim is law. At Harrods, once his helicopter has landed on the roof, Mohamed becomes just like them. On the sixth floor, he is welcomed by his palace guards, his grand viziers, his PR men. And down below, his proles begin to quake, five floors of them, from Ladies Underwear to Leather Goods. I have talked lately to some former Harrods employees, and each of them spoke of al-Fayed in quasi-regal terms. They told of his peremptory sackings, his impulsive edicts, his ferocious eye for detail, his vindictiveness. None of them was willing to be named, but each was ready to laden me with anti-Fayed gossip. My impression was that they were still afraid of him, and always would be. The shop was 'like a police state', one ex-employee told me.

Even al-Fayed's customers are made to feel that, when visiting the principality of Harrods, they must defer to Harrods' laws – in particular, its immigration laws. Customers can be expelled from Harrods if they happen to be wearing the wrong clothes: jeans, vests, slacks. A few years ago, there were headlines about an American customer being told to leave the store because she was wearing an unsightly pair of leggings – Chanel leggings, it so happened, and purchased from Harrods on some earlier occasion. Nonetheless, she had to go, by order of the Chairman. Al-Fayed, an ex-employee told me, hates it when customers dawdle in the gangways. Sometimes they are ordered to keep moving. He likes his customers to be 'actively shopping'. He also dislikes it when customers are carrying too many bags, even bags full of Harrods merchandise. The passageways must not be clogged. After all, he himself might at any moment decide to go on one of his daily patrols: at high speed, flanked by bodyguards, but missing nothing. 'He adores it,' I was told. 'He loves to parade around. He hates to see any boxes on the shopfloor. He wants it to seem as if it has all happened by magic.'

In Harrods the other day, clad in a suit and tie, I bought a sumptuously produced and disastrously expensive book called *Harrods: A Palace in Knightsbridge*, 'published', said the title-page, 'by Mohamed al-Fayed'. One of the main objectives of the book is to establish the idea of a Harrods lineage, a dynasty running from the shop's founders (in 1849), through some of its subsequent owners – in particular the Burbridge family who owned Harrods for some sixty years and made it most of what it is today – all the way down, or up, to the store's present owner, the 'merchandise magician', Mohamed al-Fayed:

> 'Fantasy' is a word fequently on the lips of Mohamed al-Fayed, the Chairman and owner of Harrods. Fantasy, glamour, the romance of retailing – more than ever before, these are the hallmarks of Harrods today . . . Like his Edwardian predecessor, Mr al-Fayed has vision, and the determination to realise his vision. Moreover, his love of history has meant that now more than ever Harrods is aware of its fascinating past.

'Harrods', al-Fayed goes on to testify, 'is not just a money-making venture for me; it is part of Britain's heritage. It is a place which I love.' And certainly, in spite of ex-employee talk about a 'police-state' atmosphere, the place – when you walk around in it – gives off a deeply pampered air. Al-Fayed, since his purchase, has poured millions into renovation and refurbishment. As the book says, 'boardings and fittings erected over the past half-century were torn down to reveal original features. Back into public view came those splendours of the past: Edwardian Rococo ceilings and capitals, Art Nouveau mouldings and ceramic tiles, Art Deco marble pillars, bronze grilles and wrought-iron banisters' All this is most imposing to behold and al-Fayed should be applauded for having made it happen. Once again, however, we run up against the familiar al-Fayed gaffe, the extravagance-too-far, the foot-in-it: the store's brand-new Egyptian Hall and the Egyptian Escalator are the nadir of self-glorifying kitsch.

In the Egyptian Hall, the face of Chairman al-Fayed has been set into each of the twelve sphinxes that peer down from the borders of the ceiling. Each sphinx bears on its chest the name 'al-Fayed', spelled out in hieroglyphs. In one corner of the Hall there is a motorised waxwork of Queen Nefertiti, strumming on a harp, and mounted on what seems to be a giant lotus plant. Everywhere you look there are pharaonic apparitions: a vision of Egypt as promoted by the gift shop in a Cairo Hilton, but on a hugely grander scale. And the Egyptian Hall is mild stuff compared to the Egyptian Elevator. This stupendous construction soars from the basement all the way up to the domed ceiling, now tricked out with zodiacal symbols. The whole thing is supported by vast pillars decorated with hieroglyphics (some of which spell 'Harrods') and all the rest of it. Halfway up the escalator, facing you as you arrive at the second floor and chiselled on the wall in giant letters, is the familiar line from 'Ozymandias': 'Look on my works, ye Mighty, and despair!' I wonder whether anyone told al-Fayed how the poem continues.

My first thought on encountering this soaring edifice was that destroying it would cost a fortune. But al-Fayed has already said that Harrods will stay in his family 'for a thousand years' and that he himself intends to be buried on its roof. My second thought was that this whole Egyptian folly was a joke: a whimsical, if grandiose riposte to a country which had stripped al-Fayed of his youthful assets and forced him into exile. In Cairo, a friend of his had advised me not to underestimate Mohamed's continuing bitterness on this score. My joke theory, though, did not last more than a few seconds. Even as I pondered it, I found myself forced to step aside in order to make way for three full-dress, full-blast Highland pipers who had begun marching through the store. Later in my Harrods book I read that 'the Chairman's love of Scotland has also left its mark on the store. To the surprise and delight of customers, kilted pipers are often to be found parading through the various departments.' Nefertiti's harp, sphinx Fayed, Ozymandias, and now 'Scotland the Brave' . . . Once again, I was forced back to the conclusion that what this man al-Fayed really needs is some *advice*.

But kings don't like, or take, advice. If it is true that al-Fayed sees himself as king of a small country, or as baron of a realm-within-a-realm, his courting of the royals at once seems wholly plausible – inevitable, even. Even the most junior of visiting foreign monarchs can expect the red carpet treatment when supping with the British Queen. On this reading, one can see how al-Fayed may have come to regard Dodi as his royal heir, the future king of Harrods, and thus perhaps something of a catch for Princess Di, whose shopping skills were world-renowned. Diana, after all, was no longer an authentic royal. Nor was the Duke of Windsor. Nor is Mohamed al-Fayed. After the humiliating DTI Report, and after the refusal of his applications for citizenship, al-Fayed apparently shifted the focus of his regal aspirations. Spurned by the real-life British royals, he turned to an alternative, ex-royal line: the exiled Windsors (whose relationship he described, pre-Di and Dodi, as 'the greatest love story of the century'), the cold-shouldered Princess Di. They too, he believed, had been 'shitted upon' by the British establishment.

What next for al-Fayed? Much surely depends on the attitude al-Fayed takes to the outcome of the French investigations into the Paris car crash. If, as seems possible, he shows signs of inclining towards the Middle East's assassination theories, he will find himself totally ostracised in Britain. After what he has been through, he may well decide: what's new? – and make a break. Should he return to Egypt – his family still keeps a house in Alexandria – many would greet him as a hero: a hero victimised by Western racists. In Egypt at the moment, attitudes to al-Fayed are necessarily coloured by the tragedy of Dodi's death. Mohamed is a grieving father and should not be talked about in other than respectful terms. Before the Paris crash, feelings about him seem to have been mixed. The upper classes saw him as *baladi* ('a vulgarian'). In the good old days (i.e.pre-World War Two) 'people like that would not have got through the gates of the Gezira Club, not for any amount of money'. Intellectuals faintly despised him because of his kow-towing to the British, his bad taste, his absurd pretentiousness. The man in the street had never heard of him.

Now, Mohamed al-Fayed is probably the world's best known Egyptian. Egyptians back home would like to be proud of him, I think, because of his symbolic usefulness (East v. West) but for the moment they can't quite make up their minds. 'On the one hand,' an Egyptian writer told me,

> in a line-up of possible Egyptians to represent Egypt to the world he might not be my own personal first choice. On the other hand, he is representative of a certain Egyptian-ness. He's like the hero of an Egyptian folk tale – not a heroic epic but a folk tale. He's from the people, he's got larger-than-life dreams; he sets off into the world and he's wily and resourceful and lucky enough to find the treasure and secure it, to make his dreams come true. And that was all very well until the end of August when, with his son set to marry the Princess, the story suddenly vaults over into tragedy. And this is when you have the dislocation, the change of genre. Now if Dodi and Di were to be found living happily in an enchanted castle in the Waq el-Waq mountains guarded by an MI5 genie, that would be more fitting. I wish they would. But the feeling I mostly have about Mohamed al-Fayed is that he has been badly advised. If I were his friend, if I could advise him now, I'd tell him to come home. I'd say stop letting your British agent give odd-sounding statements to the British Press, stop pouring your money into *there*. Just come home for a while, and grieve. It doesn't have to be forever.

It is a nice thought, but I doubt that al-Fayed considers Egypt sufficiently stable and therefore safe for big business. In December, Jack Straw announced that he is reconsidering al-Fayed's application for British citizenship. And in any case Britain – passport or no passport

– happens to be where he lives. It is his home; or, rather, it is where most of his homes are now located: the mansion in Surrey, the castle in Scotland, Craven Cottage, the apartments on Park Lane. And when he crosses the Channel he has the Ritz as well as the Duke of Windsor's old house, which he still owns and which may have been meant for Di and Dodi, had they married. Before the Paris deaths, al-Fayed was set to auction the contents of the Windsors' house, which included some tasty items of royal memorabilia, exported into exile by the Duke after his abdication. Al-Fayed's hugely expensive renovation elicited 'not a word of thanks' from British officialdom, he has complained. (Thanks for what?) And when he offered to return some of the Windsors' more 'historic' possessions to the British Crown, the offer was ignored. The sale (at Sotheby's, New York) is scheduled for next month.

London Review of Books, 1998

5

From Walking Possession *(1994)*

A Biographer's Misgivings

My life and times as a literary biographer began about fifteen years ago, in 1979, when I started researching a biography of the American poet Robert Lowell, who had died two years earlier, aged sixty, at the height of his considerable fame. In the summer of '79, I was taken by Lowell's widow, Caroline Blackwood, to the house in Ireland where she and Lowell had been lodging during the last weeks of his life. It was a chaotic visit, for one reason and another, and I didn't learn a great deal – but I did come away with a few relics: postcards and letters written to the poet, some fragments of unpublished verse, an old passport, a couple of photographs and several bits of conflicting 'oral testimony', as I believe it's called, from local witnesses – a shopkeeper, a publican, a caretaker and, of course, from the widow herself, who naturally enough found the visit acutely depressing.

When I got back to London I sat at my desk before examining my treasure trove, and I have to say that I felt a bit daunted by the prospect that now lay ahead of me. What did these bits and pieces mean? Where did they fit? Who were these strange – to me – people who signed themselves 'Blair' or 'Frank' or 'Peter'? They were old friends of Lowell's, I supposed. Older, anyway, than I was.

At this stage, I knew little about Lowell beyond what many others knew, from interviews and general gossip and from the evidence of his own heavily autobiographical writings. In my case, the bit extra came from having met him for lunch from time to time during the last half-dozen years of his life, and from a brief and unsuccessful professional collaboration which I will come to in a moment. Did I really want to spend the next half-dozen or however many years of *my* life attempting to inhabit this other, now-dead personality? And what level or quality of habitation was actually possible or desirable?

As I sat there, I got to imagining what it would be like if some biographer were to inspect the contents of the desk in front of me, my desk, as I had just inspected Lowell's. What would such a biographer make of – for example – this note from my mother complaining that she hadn't heard from me in weeks, this letter from my former wife tackling me about some unpaid electricity account, this perfumed postcard from someone called Priscilla, thanking me for a 'wonderful, enriching encounter' and expressing the fervent hope that she and I might 'do it again very soon'. Who *was* Priscilla? I later remembered that she was a research student writing a paper about literary magazines, a subject on which I'd written a book. I'd spent half an hour with her in a noisy London pub, and that had been the extent of our 'encounter'. But if *I* didn't know who she was, some three weeks after the event, what would my biographer make of her? He would probably spend months trying to establish her identity, and the harder it was to do this, the more interesting she would become. He would question all my friends and relatives about her, this mysterious Priscilla 'who clearly meant so much to the ageing Hamilton as he approached the end'. Before long, my friends and relatives would start believing in her too. 'If it hadn't been for that curious Priscilla business, who knows what he might not have gone on to achieve.' And so it would continue.

I ripped up the postcard from Priscilla, sent my former wife a cheque, and telephoned my mother to tell her that I'd be coming to see her next weekend. Biography, or the idea of it, had made me a better person – if only for an afternoon.

But it was not I who was under investigation; it was Robert Lowell, and I was not at all sure that I would become in any way more virtuous by attempting to track down *his* Priscillas, of whom there had been several dozen in his life, by all accounts. By whose accounts? Lowell's life had been of the sort that gives rise to anecdotal reportage. There were dozens of Lowell stories, most of them to do with his conduct during one or another of the manic episodes that afflicted him throughout his life. I knew the stories and had no doubt passed around one or two of them myself, but it was different now. Lowell dead would carry on being gossiped about, but not by me. It was my job to write the stories down, with footnotes, to authenticate.

Up to this point, I had, I supposed, held the usual ambivalent views about literary biography. I read biographies of writers with some pleasure but I was not always certain that knowing about the life was necessary to an understanding of the work. Lowell, it could be argued, was a special case. He was categorised as a 'confessional poet', a writer who had gone beyond customary bounds of reticence or personal embarrassment. There seemed to be a sense in which, more than most, he used his art to master and survive the often terrible circumstances of his life.

Much of Robert Lowell's celebrity since the publication of *Life Studies* in 1959 had had to do with people seeing in him a sort of literary heroism: a willingness to be led by Life into realms of experience that would exert the maximum pressure on his Art. John Berryman once said, 'The artist is extremely lucky who is presented with the worst possible ordeal that will not actually kill him. At that point he's in business.' Lowell himself might not have agreed with this, but a number of his admirers thought he did, and he was not always disposed to contradict them. By the early 1970s, there was nothing that Lowell would not *say* in a poem even though the saying of it might cause serious damage in his life – damage which would in turn provide the subject matter for more poems. In a sense I was embarking on a biography that had already been written, or made up. This meant, or so I thought, that there would be no problems of secrecy, no suppression of materials, no challenging of the essential biographical endeavour. On the other hand, it raised the question: since we knew so much already, did we really need to be told more?

On this, I was unsure. The best I could say was that I was curious to measure the self-created, self-nourished Lowell version of the Lowell life against other, less well-scripted versions: versions that might be provided by those who had muddled up their lives with his. One can never write a Life without also writing, or touching on, several other subsidiary or lesser lives. And in doing this, how judicious, how fair-minded could one actually hope to be? Just by calling such lives 'lesser' one was treating them rather as Lowell himself had treated them in reality. And yet how else could this biography get written? One might, for instance, wish to reprove Lowell's destructive self-absorption; at the same time, though, my narrative could hardly deny him centre-stage. It would be a weird sort of biography that made heroes of its subject's victims, if victims was indeed the right way to describe those who had, at some cost to their own tranquillity, elected to serve the poet's cause.

People would say of Lowell, as they have often said of many other artists, that he caused suffering to others and that no work of art, however marvellous, could compensate for what he did. But then, without the art, we would probably not care much what he did. And why not, in Lowell's case, see the poems as having mitigated the harmfulness rather than having in some way been the cause of it? On the other hand, if the art had not been so admired would he have felt licensed to believe that his life mattered more than those of his admirers? And did the work prosper because of that belief?

Lytton Strachey called biography 'the most delicate and humane of all the branches of the art of writing'. Someone else called the biographer 'an artist on oath'. Biographers love to quote these tags, and no wonder. Contemplating the difficulties of investigating Lowell's life, I could indeed at moments feel myself to have been nobly challenged: we all like to think of ourselves as 'delicate and humane'. But in some other part of my memory I could hear W.H. Auden's dictum about biography being 'always superfluous . . . usually in bad taste' – or, more tellingly, T.S. Eliot's even more magisterial pronouncement that 'curiosity about the private life of a public man may be of three kinds: the useful, the harmless and the impertinent'. If my Lowell project turned out not to be useful, I could hardly be sure that it would also manage to be harmless. Nor could I guarantee that it would not be 'impertinent' – an impertinence of some sort lurks at the heart of all biography, it seemed to me.

These, then, were some of my initial reservations. Perhaps more important was another question: what were my credentials for the task? Well, here I didn't feel too uncomfortable. I had seen quite a lot of Lowell since his move from New York to London in 1970. I had published his poems, I had interviewed him, I had visited him now and then at home and in hospital. We weren't friends, exactly, but we were friendly enough allies, of a sort.

A couple of years before he died, Lowell told me that he was thinking of writing a prose autobiography. He was having difficulty in getting started, he said, and we agreed that maybe if he spoke his recollections into a tape-recorder and then worked on the transcripts, this might get him going. I was editing a magazine at the time, *The New Review*, and we agreed that in exchange for my asking the questions and then getting his responses typed, and so on, he would give me first opportunity to print instalments from the work, as it proceeded. This seemed to me a good arrangement – all I had to do, really, was to give him a few prompts and then sit back and listen. Any magazine at the time would have been happy to print chapters from Robert Lowell's own version of his life.

We had two sessions of tape-recording, and the second was – if anything – more disastrous than the first. In each session, Lowell so rambled and digressed and parenthesised that when we came to type up what he had said it read like the night-mumblings of a drunk. Perhaps he *was* drunk. More likely, though, there was something wrong with our whole method of enquiry. In our two sessions, which dealt with Lowell's student years at Kenyon College, and his friendships with John Crowe Ransom, Randall Jarrell, Peter Taylor and others, we managed to cover about ten days of his life. At this rate of progress, it would have taken about fifty-seven years to cover the whole story. And Lowell was fifty-seven at the time.

Anyway, it didn't work out, and we abandoned it. A number of poems in Lowell's last book, *Day by Day*, to me show signs of having been encouraged by these sessions, so it was not a complete waste of time. And there was a lesson to be learned: biography and autobiography are not close bosom friends. For Lowell, almost every name and date that came up in our conversations was saturated with feeling and significance and mystery. For him, the whole process seemed painful and bewildering. Was he remembering, or misremembering; how much had been forgotten, how much had been embellished, altered by later experience? He would remember a door opening, a pair of shoes, the sound of a voice on a particular afternoon, in a particular sunlight. How to get *that* across, that mixture of the too-blurred and the too-precise, was the sort of challenge that might sponsor the writing of a poem. For a biographical essay, though, it was exasperating that Lowell couldn't remember whose door it was that opened, who the pair of shoes belonged to, what the voice said that afternoon. Why had these images lingered when so many others had been lost? On another day, talking to someone else, would he remember it all differently? For the biographer, seeking a narrative outline, it was important to find answers to these questions, or to propose answers to them. But the autobiographer, the authentic rememberer, would know that there was no point in seeking patterns. The only way to know more was to remember more; and some things had, yes, been forgotten. Which things, though? What sort of things?

And this was Lowell's method, or non-method, with the tape-recordings. He spoke his memories as they came back to him and, host-like, was courteous and welcoming – curious, even, to see how they were dressed, how they looked these days, and so on. And yet at the same time, for him the whole act of remembering was full of sadness, sadness for what had been lost – not just to memory, but lost. From my point of view, sitting there with my editor's tape-recorder and my editor's wish to have all this material explained, the whole thing was both touching and infuriating. I was half-priest, half-torturer, and in neither role was I much of a success. Although I still have the tapes, I have played them back just once, as his by-then biographer, and they were almost completely useless – incomprehensible without a yard or two of explanatory footnotes (not all of which I would be able to provide) and even then too disjointed to be accurately quoted.

For a year or two after Lowell died, there was talk of appointing a biographer. When the time came, it happened that my magazine had folded and I was vaguely looking for some kind of job, or occupation. Caroline Blackwood, together with some other London friends of Lowell's, might well have remembered those tape-recording sessions. If Lowell had entrusted me with the role of his recorder, or sound-man, then maybe he would not have objected to the idea of me as his biographer. I really don't know the background, but when the job was offered I said yes.

This makes it all sound splendidly straightforward, but of course it wasn't. With biographies nothing ever is. Indeed, having said yes, I was immediately pitched into the centre of the very conflict which was to dominate the final chapter of the book I would eventually write. In case you are not familiar with the story, Lowell in 1970 had left his American wife Elizabeth Hardwick and set up house in London with the Anglo-Irish writer Caroline Blackwood. It was an acrimonious transfer, hugely complicated by the poet's long history of mental illness. Was this English adventure just another manic episode from which he would emerge, chastened and apologetic, as so often in the past, or was it the 'real thing', whatever, in his case, that may mean? In America Lowell had a loyal and, it might be said, heroically sympathetic wife and a number of good friends – these people had, so to speak, served time in the Robert Lowell saga: they had rescued him from police stations, sat with him for hours in hospitals listening to him talk lovingly of Hitler and Napoleon, extricated him from absurd romantic and financial entanglements, repaired or tried to repair whatever damage had been done during his various mad periods. They had done all this out of a love and admiration for the man which even now seems awesome. And then, in 1970, he was announcing that he had left America (and them) behind: he had a new life, a new woman, a new house, a new team of helpers, English helpers. Most of his American friends had heard this kind of thing before and expected the episode to be over in six months. Indeed, some of them carried on not quite believing in his new life even after he divorced, got remarried and had a son with Caroline. Others recognised quite early on that this time Lowell meant it. There had become, in many people's minds, two Robert Lowells: the American Lowell and the post-1970 English Lowell. There had become two camps: essentially the Hardwick camp and the Blackwood camp – with overlaps, of course.

For Elizabeth Hardwick there was much to be endured – not least the suspicion that Lowell in England was a dangerous absurdity: he was going against his nature, his background, the true grounding that had kept him sane and creative for long stretches during their marriage and before. For Caroline Blackwood, on the other hand, it was America that drove him mad. In England, away from his own chaotic history, away from the 'glare' – as he himself described it – he would be healed and renewed. It was a terrible situation and Lowell often felt that it was tearing him apart. It might even have shortened his life. Certainly it is hard to forget the very last moments of that life and hard not to find in them a perfect image of the conflict which he had come to feel was both insoluble and inescapable. Lowell died of a heart attack in a taxi cab on his way from Kennedy airport to Elizabeth Hardwick's apartment on West 67th Street, their former home. He had quarrelled with Caroline, the last of several quarrels they had been having over the past few months, and he had probably determined to return to his American life – or to try to, because he was by no means out of love with Caroline. But he was dead on arrival at the house. Elizabeth Hardwick found him in the back seat of the taxi. In his arms there was a brown paper package: inside was a portrait of Caroline by Lucian Freud, *her* former husband. Lowell had brought the painting to New York, it was said, 'to be valued'. Somehow Lowell, the great self-mythologiser, had contrived to write, or stage, the last, marvellously chilling paragraph of his biography, his Act Five, Scene Five. There was a prosy, common-sense reason for him having that picture in his arms; there was also a poetic aptness. It would be up to me to register the one without diminishing the other.

For the biographer entering this complicated world of recrimination and counter-recrimination, there was straightaway what one might call an 'innocence' problem. I had spent many hours in London, in pubs and restaurants, listening to Lowell fret about his two worlds, his two lives, and the unbearable tension that was building up between them, and I had no more idea than he did about what he should or shouldn't do. What I did have was a much more vivid grasp of his English unhappiness than I did of whatever it was that had driven him from America in the first place.

It was natural enough, then, that in the eyes of Lowell's American friends I would be seen as belonging to his 'English' world, a world which they believed had finally destroyed him. And this was the most daunting of the many obstacles I found when I presented myself in New York in 1979 as the prospective chronicler of Lowell's life. Which Lowell life? was the obvious first question that sprang to people's minds.

At first, doors were opened with great caution. I was given lists of names from Lowell's past, introductions to X and Y, but at this stage I didn't really know what questions to ask. And Lowell's American friends, although they were polite and amiable, were not eager to answer anything they did not have to answer. I soon realised that information was not going to *originate* from any of these so-called 'living witnesses'. Before approaching a witness I needed to know a lot more than I did about the history of that witness's relationship with Lowell. But how would I find out?

A typical situation was that I would approach A (who had been recommended to me by B) and he would ask me 'what I wanted to know' – actually he was trying to find out what I already *knew*. He would then, unfailingly, ask me who else I had seen and who else I was planning to see. 'Well, tomorrow I intend to visit C,' I might say. 'Oh no. Not C. Don't talk to him or, if you do, don't believe anything he says. He resented Lowell. He'll pretend he didn't but he did.' Or it would be: 'I wouldn't bother with D. You won't get anything out of him. He adores Caroline and Lizzie quarrelled with him years ago.' Now and then, I was even told: 'I'd be careful when you talk to X. He's totally on Lowell's side.' What, I had to wonder, could *this* mean: on Lowell's side. And whose side did they think I was on?

Anyway, so much – at first – for the 'living witness' method of research. Later on, I read with much sympathy a comment by Mark Schorer on his researches into the life of Sinclair Lewis. Schorer said:

> Sometimes I wished that I had ten years more, for in that time most
> of these people would have gone away and I would no longer be
> confused by their conflicting tales and would in fact be free to say
> what I wanted about *them*.

I left New York for Harvard and spent the next three months or so in the Houghton Library. A few years before his death, Lowell had sold his 'archive' to the Library – an extensive collection of his manuscripts and notebooks and a vast pile of correspondence: the bulk of it, of course, being letters that had been addressed to him. From these letters I was able to build up a chronology of his life and a fairly reliable map of his relationships over the years. The Priscilla factor, as I now called it, had to be kept in mind. Not having Lowell's side of the correspondence made it difficult to know quite what was going on or – as in the case of his turbulent first marriage to the novelist Jean Stafford – to know who to sympathise with.

The Stafford letters, in fact, cast an interesting sidelight on the whole business of biography. They are superb pieces of marital polemic, detailed and lengthy and almost – though never quite – hysterically high-pitched. They are full of anger and resentment. There are no replies from Lowell – indeed, this is partly what is making Stafford so angry. But I knew, when I read these Stafford letters, that I had heard this voice somewhere before. And sure enough I had – in Lowell's long poem, *The Mills of the Kavanaughs*, written not long before the breakup of the Lowell–Stafford marriage.

It was a poem that had always rather puzzled me, not just because there were a number of local obscurities and a narrative that was extremely hard to follow but also because it gives so many of its best, or at any rate its most ferocious lines, to a vengeful, recriminating female. Women, up to this point, had not featured other than passively in Lowell's verse. Without the Stafford letters, I would now contend, the peculiar energies and intensities of *Mills of the Kavanaughs* would have remained mysterious, without any graspable source or context: although they would not have lost the slightly artificial or transplanted tone that worried me when I first read the poem.

Knowing the source of the poem also tells us something of Lowell's methods as a poet, about his habits of assimilation and mimicry. Lowell, it seems, was as much impressed by the *literary* power of Stafford's letters as he was troubled by their judgements on him as a husband who'd deserted her. After all, the desertion had already happened and he had no intention of going back on it: the poetry had yet to be written. Is this mean self-servingness or is it the icy detachment of the genuine artist? Later on, Lowell would once again make use of a wife's wounded letters in his poetry, with rather more controversial results. Finding the Stafford correspondence made it possible for me to view this process more as a literary compulsion than as an isolated personal outrage – although it was that, too. But I'll come back to this in a moment.

The experience of reading other people's private correspondence is always faintly thrilling and delinquent. Biographers, if they are honest, will admit that the pleasure they take in this branch of their research is not all to do with literary scholarship. In the Lowell case, there was a slightly embarrassing example. In the Harvard Library I came across a handful of letters written to Lowell by a woman we'll call G. It was evident from these letters that G and Lowell had had an affair, an affair that had meant a lot to her at the time – the late Forties. What it had meant to Lowell was, as usual, not entirely clear. I later tracked down G – in London, as it happened, although she was American – and I asked her if she would be interviewed about her relationship with Lowell. She agreed, and I – and my tape-recorder – went along to see her. Not knowing what I knew, she had prepared a presentation in which she and Lowell had been, as she put it, merely 'literary friends'. They had talked a lot about books, they had admired each other's writings, and that was all there was to it. She knew 'very little', she said, about his 'private life'. The interview proceeded along these genteel lines for about half an hour, until I could stand it no longer. I had to tell her: *But I've seen your letters.* There was a silence, and G's mind was evidently racing: 'Which letters?' 'How?' What did they say?' After all, they had been written thirty years ago, in haste. Maybe, since she wrote them, she really had come to believe that she and Lowell had been no more than literary soul mates. She seemed genuinely stricken, as if I had callously, or stupidly, broken an important spell. The silence went on for a bit longer and then I switched off the machine. 'You mean, he actually *sold* them to Harvard University?' she said. I tried to make it better by explaining that he had also sold several thousand other letters, and that most writers did the same, but she was half-listening. 'All right, I'll tell you what really happened,' she said. But she told it with bitterness, and one could not be sure that this bitterness did not have more to do with Lowell's treatment of her *letters* than with his treatment of *her* thirty years before. But then opening old wounds is something else that the biographer needs to be good at. I did not tell G that in the same Harvard Library I had come across some gossipy letters to Lowell by supposed friends of my own – a couple of them making not very friendly reference to me. After all, I was in no position to claim any sort of fellow feeling in the matter.

One of the arguments in favour of writing biographies of the recently dead is that, if you leave it too late, the living witnesses will not be living. But the eagerness to get hold of testimony while it is still hot does have its, shall we say, unseemly aspects. 'The quick in pursuit of the dead', as Elizabeth Hardwick once put it. People don't write letters in the way they used to, and public figures have become more sophisticated in their efforts to forestall and thwart biographers. In the nineteenth century it was possible for a public figure to think of his biographer as a friend – in fact he usually *was* a friend. Nowadays it is taken for granted that, at the very least, there will be a degree of tension between the life-writer and his subject. Thus, in future, there will be an increased reliance on the testimony of contemporaries, and no doubt these 'living witnesses' will themselves acquire a skill and sophistication in the practice of their craft. Their affidavits will become ever more polished and composed; the raggedness of what actually happened will be tidied up. And some witnesses will learn to be expert in biographical double-talk: blackening a name they are pretending to revere. A lot will depend on who, among the witnesses, dies first. If best friend A dies without having been asked to say his piece, we will be forced to rely on second-best friend B for a ranking of A's actual involvement in the studied life. For all we know, B might have resented A and might now wish to downgrade him. And to check this out, we would really need to talk to C, if he is still alive. When it comes to lovers, wives, children even, the competitiveness between the witnesses becomes of course even more hazardous. The closer you are to the action, the more delicate the choice you're obliged to make. In the case of Lowell, I actually suppressed mention of more than one involvement because there was a clear possibility of damage, and I also left out other material because it was put to me that there was a need to protect the Lowell children. But of course it is not always possible to judge the damage, or the misery, that can result from biographical writing.

With Lowell, there were moments when the biographer had to be far more circumspect than Lowell himself had ever been. I often felt that Lowell might find my reticence a bit feeble-spirited. After all, he had pulled no punches. When in the Seventies, he took passages from Elizabeth Hardwick's brilliant, angry letters and incorporated them into poems about their separation, he was widely attacked – this was surely the ultimate betrayal. But Lowell could never quite see what the fuss was all about. In quoting Hardwick's letters in his verse, he was responding to them, to her, not as an ex-husband but as a co-writer, a maker-over of pain into poetry. In some important way, he was proud of Hardwick's letters, as he had been proud of Stafford's. And he had found them painful to read, so in this sense they were to be seen as *his* experience, and thus material for art. For Elizabeth Hardwick, at the time, there was nothing in all this except bitterness. Twenty years later, she may be feeling differently. After all, without the lines from her letters, some of these Lowell poems are not very good.

My Lowell book was completed in 1982 and appeared in the winter of that year. After I'd finished it, my publishers immediately began asking me *who* I would be doing next – not what but who. The assumption was that my next book would be a biography. I was now, it seemed, a biographer-elect. Ahead of me lay a possible new career in which I would move from one 'case' to another. It was suggested to me that I might write a life of Ezra Pound, then the name of John Berryman was mentioned. A quite different publisher wrote to ask how I would feel about tackling the life of Sylvia Plath. I described this last proposal to a sardonic friend of mine who said that I should agree to it, of course, but only on condition that the very last sentence of the finished book should read: 'As to her final months, I believe that we should draw a decent veil'. The common factor in these propositions was, it seemed to me, insanity. I was in danger of being set up as an expert on mad poets. As a bit of a mad poet myself, from time to time, I was not at all sure that this would be good for me. So I declined these offers, or semi-offers, and returned to London – where I had another career of sorts waiting for me, as the reviewer of other people's books about mad poets.

It was during this period that the subject for my next adventure was presented to me, quite by accident. My sixteen-year-old son came home from school one day and announced that he had just read this 'terrific book'. His face wore the look it sometimes had when he came back from a heavy-metal concert. 'Terrific books' were not, at that time, part of his cultural curriculum. 'And what terrific book would that be?' I asked, hoping – at best – for Stephen King or Robert Ludlum. 'It's called,' he said, struggling somewhat to remember, 'It's called *The Catcher in the Rye*.' I was genuinely stunned. *The Catcher in the Rye* was a book I hadn't thought about for a long time. Once, though, about thirty years ago, it had been the key 'terrific book' of *my* adolescence. I'd read it so many times that I almost knew it off by heart. For months, I had gone around *being* the book's hero, Holden Caulfield, until I learned that thousands, perhaps tens of thousands of other adolescents were doing the same thing – and had been doing it since 1951, when *The Catcher* first appeared. I had then followed Salinger's subsequent career, through *Franny and Zooey* to *Raise High the Roof Beam, Carpenters*, trying hard to sustain the same level of enthusiasm, as a devout disciple should. Then Salinger had stopped publishing; he'd disappeared from view and, after a bit, I'd more or less forgotten about him – although every so often, whenever I heard myself come out with a phrase like 'big deal' or 'goddam phoney', I would half-remember where it came from.

And now, years later, here was my adolescent son telling me that he had fallen victim to the same infatuation. I was, of course, delighted; and impressed too that the book still had this power to charm the young. We began comparing notes: 'Remember the bit when old Stradlater leaves his razor in the washroom?' 'What really happened with Mr Antolini?' and so on. And then, a bit later, my son asked me the question that would determine, for me, the shape and substance of the next four years. He asked me, 'Who *is* J.D. Salinger?'

Well, I told him what little I knew, most of it remembered from my own junior researches thirty years before. Salinger was a New Yorker, from a prosperous half-Jewish business background; he was born in 1919; he had attended military college as a boy; he was in the US Army during World War Two, possibly working in Intelligence; he had published short stories in *The New Yorker* during the 1940s; *The Catcher* was his first novel; it had been a best-seller when it appeared and became a cult text for rebellious teenagers from the mid-Fifties to the early Sixties. Salinger had then embarked on a long fictional saga about a family of geniuses called Glass – one of these, Buddy

Glass, seemed to have been modelled on Salinger himself. Buddy was
a novelist who had written a successful book about an adolescent and
who was now greatly troubled by the attentions of his fans. With
the publication of *Franny and Zooey* in 1961, Salinger's celebrity had
reached such a pitch that, for reasons partly to do with this and partly
unknown, he had withdrawn completely from the public arena – not
just refusing to give interviews or answer fan-mail but refusing even
to publish what he wrote – if indeed he did still write.

To my son, this last bit, the bit about refusing to publish, was the
most interesting. In his culture, the pursuit of celebrity was crucial to
any so-called creative undertaking. Fame was the sharpest spur. The
idea of popular success being voluntarily rejected was perhaps more
strange to him than it was to me, but this did not mean that I was
able to give him any persuasive account of what Salinger was up to.
I muttered a bit about the corrupting effects of collaborating with the
media, I threw in a bit about Salinger's Zen Buddhism, I recalled the
passage in *The Catcher in the Rye* where Holden Caulfield yearns to
go off into the woods and live as a deaf mute. But I could tell he
wasn't impressed and, after we'd stopped talking, I found that I was
asking myself the question he'd asked me: Who *is* J.D. Salinger?

I then re-read the books and I lingered particularly over the long
story, *Seymour: an Introduction*, the story in which Buddy Glass,
Salinger's supposed alter ego, talks directly to his audience – the
audience he says he wants to reject. Buddy's manner, rather like
Salinger's own manner in the one or two odd statements he had
made in his own person over the years, was not the grouchy,
inattentive manner of the misanthrope. On the contrary, it was
energetically playful and flirtatious. Salinger the author seemed to
be using Buddy Glass as a means of both fostering and toying with
the curiosity of his worshipping young fans. It was a deeply social, or
even a theatrical manner – the manner of one who is sure enough of
the affection of his readers that he can afford to play games with it.
It was the manner, so I thought, of one who wanted, and expected,
to be loved – but loved on his own terms, even though the terms
might turn out to be more harshly absolute than those which normally
prevail between a writer and his readership.

This at any rate was how I read it at that point. Having just emerged from spending three years inside the psyche of a writer to whom reticence meant nothing, and who was intensely involved in all aspects of his fame, I was perhaps over-disposed to be sceptical about Salinger's reclusiveness. I didn't really believe that he wanted to be left alone. It didn't fit with what he'd written. In other words, in this special case, I was ready to project a literary interpretation on to the personality of the author, something I knew in the abstract to be dangerous. But I kept coming back to the idea of play, of theatre, in Salinger's later work. Was his refusal to publish in truth something of a tease? Had we, his readers, failed him in some way? Had we misread him, been insufficiently respectful, not responded ardently enough to his late work? I knew that he had rejected numerous requests for interviews from journalists. Perhaps he was waiting for the really *serious* approach – from *the biographer*. Perhaps he was waiting for *me*.

Some hope. But even so, what if Salinger *was* genuine in his wish to be ignored, forgotten, written off? Did this mean that we, his readers, had to suppress all curiosity about him? I began to get intrigued by the notion of trying to construct a version of Salinger in much the same way as I had constructed a version of Lowell – and using much the same sort of materials: my reading of the works, the testimony of people who knew or had known him, and any documentary evidence that might be there to be uncovered. The difference would be that, with this book, the author under scrutiny was still alive. And yet, so far as biography, or even literary history, was concerned, he would prefer us to think of him as dead. Or so he said.

Without the Lowell experience, with its super-abundance of bio-graphical material, and without the coincidence of my son's encounter with *The Catcher in the Rye*, I don't suppose I would have pursued the matter any further. Fatally, though, I mentioned the idea to my agent, who had also been puzzling over the question of what – or who – I might do next. He suggested, as agents do, that I set down a few thoughts on paper, and I did. I came across this synopsis not so long ago, and in the light of all that has happened since, I was – well – almost reassured by its *naïveté*, its deep *mis*reading of the Salinger conundrum. It starts off with an account of my early attachment to *The Catcher* and it even quotes that line in which Holden Caulfield defines a good writer as someone who makes you feel that you can call him up on the phone. Salinger, in his works, comes across as just that sort of writer. And this observation is not meaningless. After all, who would want to call up the author of *Finnegans Wake* or *The Love Song of J. Alfred Prufrock*? And yet, in life, Salinger had made himself uniquely unapproachable. The synopsis, dated 1983, continued as follows:

> What would happen, I wonder, if – without invading his privacy (underlined), without attempting to 'get to' him in any of the obvious ways, one simply set about building a portrait of Salinger's life and personality based on (a) the books themselves (b) records available to the public (c) interviews with people who knew/know/know about him?
>
> The idea would be not to approach Salinger himself until one had reached the end of the 'public' research. He would no doubt hear of one's endeavours, as the thing developed, and he might in the end be tempted out of hiding. The book would not at all depend on his capitulation although the final chapter might well give an account of what happens when, at last, he is approached.
>
> The book's method would have to be one of extreme delicacy and propriety – one should not be seen to push or pry. One should be seen as simply gathering together what is already in the public domain, or recording whatever is willingly, and responsibly offered in the course of the research. In this case, the biographer would be a character in his own book. His rebuffs might be as interesting as his collaborations. The idea would be to arouse in Salinger a sort of grudging curiosity – a counter-curiosity.

Salinger's counter-curiosity was indeed stimulated by my efforts, but it came not in the form of a melting, an unburdening – or whatever it was I had in mind in my painstakingly 'decent' outline for the book. It came in the form of a lawsuit. My book, when it appeared, was called *In Search of J.D. Salinger* and it gives a full account of the whole business. The upshot of my attempts to get closer to my admired subject was that I ended up as his arch-enemy. As I say in the eventually published book: 'The book I fell for has at last broken free of its magician author. But even so I can't rejoice that, whatever happens, my name and J.D. Salinger's will be linked in perpetuity as those of litigants, or foes, in the law school textbooks, on the shelves of the US Supreme Court, and in the minds of everyone who reads this, the legal version of my book.'

To sum up, then. I have written two biographies – one of a dead author whom I knew, one of a live author whom I've never met. In each case, though, I have come away from the project with a sense of having failed, with a sense of having got it wrong and of not having greatly liked myself when I was doing it. I am not complaining, nor am I looking for sympathy. I was well paid for this work, and there is clearly something about the whole business of poking around in other people's lives that I quite like. And, in the end, I would probably defend the books I wrote – as books. It is only when I hear biographers talk high-mindedly about the delicate and humane aspects of their calling, or when they refuse to acknowledge that there is in what they do some necessary element of sleaze – it's only then that I remember my own biographer's misgivings: all those letters I read, those tape-recordings I transcribed, those wounds I re-opened, those emotions I guessed at, those lives I plundered or played with so that I could tell my tale.

1990

Philip Larkin: 1. The Collected Poems

Philip Larkin, we are told, left instructions in his will that certain of his writings had to be destroyed, unread. His executors obeyed: the word is that several of the poet's notebooks, or journals, are now ashes. Did Larkin expect to be so obeyed? Or did he imagine that perhaps someone, somehow, might take a peek at the material before it reached the flames? And if such a thought did cross his mind, why didn't he destroy the stuff himself? He must have known that, by not doing so, he was bequeathing at least the possibility of a dilemma. But then some of his most moving poems contrive a subtle, unsettlable dispute between revelation and concealment. There is a wanting-to-be-known that can desolate or undermine our self-sufficiency.

And now, it seems, there are things about Philip Larkin that we'll never know. So what? Well, put it like this, the loss can be made to sound not at all what Larkin, as we know him from the poems, would have wholly wished. But then again, who knows? After all, those now-incinerated notebooks might have been full of household accounts or noughts and crosses: the instruction to destroy them a librarian's last, bleakest joke. Throw these away and you are doomed to imagine that my life was not really as boring as I always used to say it was. Having something to hide is generally reckoned to be better than having nothing to show, he might have thought.

There are no explicit instructions in Larkin's will concerning the publication or re-publication of his poems. He seems not to have minded the idea of having his most early work exhumed. Nor did he leave any advice about what ought to happen to the various unfinished pieces he would leave behind. We can assume, therefore, that he must have envisaged a *Collected Poems* rather like the one we've now been given: a volume that adds something like eighty poems to his lifetime's known tally. This is a hefty addition, since the poems we already know him by and most admire total a mere eighty-five. I'm thinking here of the poems collected in *The Less Deceived*, *The Whitsun Weddings* and *High Windows*. So his 'output' has been almost doubled. (I say 'almost' because *The North Ship*, reprinted 'with considerable hesitation' in 1966 and offered more as a curiosity than to be admired, adds another thirty titles to the list.) What it all boils down to, or up to, is that Larkin the thrifty now has a *Collected Poems* of substantial bulk.

Ought we to think, though, as he generally did not, that adding means increase? Kilograms aside, the plumpened Larkin oeuvre does not carry a great deal of extra weight. On the contrary, a poet whom we value for his sparingness, for not out-putting work that he wasn't 'pretty sure' amounted to the best that he could do, is now to be seen as somewhat cluttered with botch-ups, immaturities and fragments. It's as if this most bachelor of poets had suddenly acquired a slightly messy family life.

Apparently, it could have been messier. Anthony Thwaite has decided not to include various squibs and limericks (these will appear later on in Larkin's *Letters*), and has also ruled against certain of Larkin's unfinished pieces; he mentions an 'attempt at a long poem called "The Duration" . . . which takes up fifteen pages of drafts between April and June 1969; and what was apparently his final struggle with a substantial poem, "Letters to my Mind", drafted in October and November 1979'. I am not sure that these items don't sound to be more interesting than some of the bits and pieces Thwaite has chosen to include. But then, ought we to have any 'fragments' at all in an edition of this sort? And if we do have them, ought they not to be herded off into a section of their own? This was Eliot's method, and it might have been Larkin's if he'd had the choice and if – a big if – he had thought as highly of his own 'The Dance' fragment as Eliot did of *Sweeney Agonistes*.

Was there not a case, in Larkin's case, for two *Collected* volumes: the first a one-volume reprint of the three grown-up, finished books plus the handful of poems he completed after publishing *High Windows* (these, of course, would include the marvellous 'Aubade'); the second, a mop-up of juvenilia, fragments, occasional light verse, even limericks and squibs? Thwaite's edition does divide itself in two, with mature Larkin at the front of the book and learner Larkin at the rear, but it makes no other formal separation between the poems Larkin passed for press and those which, for one reason or another, he hadn't wished to see in print.

I find this a bit disconcerting. The beauty of Larkin's three grown-up books, or one of their beauties, is that you can open them at any page and find something that only Larkin could have written. And even his most light-weight pieces are consummately 'finished' – there is nothing slovenly or make-weight or derivative. With this *Collected Poems*, there is an almost fifty-fifty chance that 'any page' will reveal lines which you'd swear could not possibly have sprung from Larkin's pen.

> I declare
> Two lineages electrify the air
> That will like pennons from a mast
> Fly over sleep and life and death
> Till sun is powerless to decoy
> A single seed above the earth:
> Lineage of sorrow; lineage of joy . . .

The next line does not, alas, read: 'Going well so far, eh?' In fact, there are about fifty similarly exalted lines to go before the thing finally deflates:

> Joy has no cause
> Though cut to pieces with a knife,
> Cannot keep silence. What else could magnetise
> Our drudging, hypocritical, ecstatic life?

This poem, entitled 'Many famous feet have trod', was written in October 1946, and thus earns its place among the 'mature' work. 1946 is the year in which Anthony Thwaite believes Larkin's 'distinctive voice' can first be heard. So it can, in the poems 'Going' and 'Wedding Wind', which we already know. In the other 1946 poems printed here, we have to strain to pick it up, in odd lines, now and then; and in 'Many famous feet . . .' I'm afraid I can hear no trace of it at all. Larkin used to chuckle that he of all people had once written a never-published volume called *In the Grip of Light*. I'm inclined to think that the chuckle was intended to cover those 'pennons from a mast', that 'lineage of joy'.

1946 was in fact the year in which Larkin read Thomas Hardy's 'Thoughts of Phena' and experienced a literary conversion, 'complete and permanent'. Hardy rescued him from Yeats, just as Yeats – three years earlier – had captured him from Auden. Under the Hardy regime, he was indeed able to find his own distinctive voice, but the Yeats and Auden periods offer almost nothing in the way of even potential Larkinesque. To peruse the eighty or so pages of juvenilia that are reprinted here is to discover scant line-by-line poetic 'promise'. Anthony Thwaite finds Larkin's Auden poems 'astonishing and precocious' and they are, to be sure, pretty good going for a kid of seventeen. But they are also fairly stiff and dull, and, because of their enslavement to the icy Master, we have no way of guessing what their author might or might not do should he ever manage to break free: it could be everything or nothing. Larkin himself, writing of these poems at the time, said: 'As for their literary interest, I think that almost any single line by Auden would be worth more than the whole lot put together.' Now there we *do* hear the later man's distinctive voice, and that was in 1941.

The sheer bulk of Larkin's juvenilia might seem irksome when presented as part of a *Collected Poems*, but biographically the bulk does matter quite a lot. This juvenilia period, 1938–46, would be later looked back on as a lost idyll of aliveness and fertility. By the age of twenty-four Larkin had written two books of poems – *The North Ship* and *In the Grip of Light* – and two novels – *Jill* and *A Girl in Winter*. Three of these books were published, but none of them had made much of a splash. In 1947 and 1948 he seems to have written almost nothing, and when the poetry does start up again in 1949 it is a poetry of failure, loss, rejection. In 'On Being Twenty-six', the poet regrets the flagging of his 'pristine drive', the withdrawal of 'Talent, felicity', and is bitter about having now to settle for something 'dingier' and 'second best':

> Fabric of fallen minarets is trash.
> And in the ash

> Of what has pleased and passed
>   Is now no more
> Than struts of greed, a last
> Charred smile, a clawed
> Crustacean hatred, blackened pride – of
>   I once made much.

Thus burnt-out, and 'clay-thick with misery', the poet falls silent yet again. There is nothing between May 1949 and January 1950. In this month, Larkin's first really spectacular development takes place. In 'At Grass' the theme is still to do with 'what has pleased and passed', but the subject is thoroughly *out there*: retired racehorses perhaps plagued by memories of erstwhile triumphs. In the next few months, we have 'If, My Darling', 'Wants', 'No Road' and 'Absences'. Within a year, the clay-thick self-pity of 1949 has become lighter, wiser, more sardonic:

> Always too eager for the future, we
> Pick up bad habits of expectancy.
> Something is always approaching; every day
> *Till then* we say.

It's an extraordinary falling-into-place, and the month-by-month dating of the poems gives the whole business a certain narrative excitement: although we will have to wait for Andrew Motion's biography to tell us what happened, or didn't happen, in 1947–8.

Throughout the book, the precise dating of the poems (meticulously recorded in the poet's worksheets) can evoke a sort of mini-tale: we learn, for instance, that January is a strong month for Larkin poems but that July is almost always a complete write-off, that 'Home is so sad' was composed on New Year's Eve, that the anti-marriage poem 'Self's the Man' immediately follows 'The Whitsun Weddings' and was completed on Guy Fawkes Day, and that in one month (January 1954) Larkin wrote 'Reasons for Attendance', 'I remember, I remember', 'For Sidney Bechet', 'Born Yesterday' and 'Poetry of Departures'.

Although I have grumbled about Thwaite not separating the unfinished pieces from the finished, there is undeniably a drama in observing that straight after finishing the expansive 'Dockery and Son' (just in time, one guesses, for it to be included in the *Whitsun Weddings* book), Larkin spent over a year grappling with a longish narrative poem, to be called 'The Dance'. The wish, evidently, was to build on the 'Dockery' model, to combine narrative relaxation with verse-strictness, but Larkin seems to have discovered that relaxation, for him, usually means a drift towards light verse, or over-surly self-parody – not at all what he wanted for this essentially angry and distressed love poem:

> In the slug
> And snarl of music, under cover of
> A few permitted movements, you suggest
> A whole consenting language, that my chest
> Quickens and tightens at, descrying love—
> Something acutely local, me
> As I am now, and you as you are now,
> And now; something acutely transitory
> The slightest impulse could deflect to how
> We act eternally.
> Why not snatch it? Your fingers tighten, tug,
> Then slacken altogether. I am caught
> By some shoptalking shit who leads me off
> To supper and his bearded wife, to stand
> Bemused and coffee-holding while the band
> Restarts off-stage, and they in tempo scoff
> Small things I couldn't look at, rent
> By wondering who has got you now . . .

The very awkwardness reminds us how many of Larkin's best effects depend upon him sounding both superior *and* vulnerable, unloving and in need of love. It's a difficult balancing-act, breathtaking when it works; when it doesn't, he can veer uneasily between the boorish and the sentimental. 'The Dance' was, it seems, en route to failure, and Larkin was probably right not to persist with it, but there is a memorable painfulness in watching him trying to wrench this exposed and ambitious poem into shape.

Since 'Aubade' in 1977, Larkin published only four poems – two rather charming birthday poems (one for Gavin Ewart, the other for Charles Causley), a poem about a dead hedgehog, and a couple of stanzas specially written for a *Poetry Review* special number on poetry and drink. After his death in 1985, a handful of unpublished poems was found. The strongest of these are desperately miserable, indeed inconsolable, as if Larkin had grown weary of trying to fathom 'whatever it is that is doing the damage'. The last poem of any weight was written in 1979 and it isn't easy to read, if you care at all about what happened to this awesome yet companionable poet. But unhappily it does help to explain the six-year silence:

> Love again: wanking at ten past three
> (Surely he's taken her home by now?),
> The bedroom hot as a bakery,
> The drink gone dead, without showing how?
> To meet tomorrow, and afterwards,
> And the usual pain, like dysentery.
>
> Someone else feeling her breasts and cunt,
> Someone else drowned in that lash-wide stare,
> And me supposed to be ignorant,
> Or find it funny, or not to care,
> Even . . . but why put it into words?
> Isolate rather this element
>
> That spreads through other lives like a tree
> And sways them on in a sort of sense
> And say why it never worked for me.
> Something to do with violence
> A long way back, and wrong rewards,
> And arrogant eternity.

Philip Larkin: Collected Poems, edited by Anthony Thwaite (Faber and Marvell Press)

1988

Philip Larkin: 2. The Selected Letters

There is a story that when William F. Buckley Jr sent a copy of his essays to Norman Mailer, he pencilled a welcoming 'Hi, Norman!' in the Index, next to Mailer's name. A similar tactic might happily have been ventured by the publishers of Philip Larkin's *Letters*: the book's back pages are going to be well thumbed. 'Hi, Craig', see p. 752, you 'mad sod'; 'Hi, John', see p. 563, you 'arse-faced trendy'; 'Hi, David', see p. 266, you 'deaf cunt', and so on. Less succinct salutations will be discovered by the likes of Donald Davie ('droning out his tosh'), Ted Hughes ('boring old monolith, no good at all – not a single solitary bit of good'), and Anthony Powell, a.k.a. 'the horse-faced dwarf'. There is even a 'Hi, Ian': he calls me 'the Kerensky of poetry'. Not too bad, I thought at first. Alas, though, the book's editor advises me that Larkin almost certainly meant to say Dzerchinsky, or somebody – some murderer – like that. He had probably misread a communication from Robert ('the great terror') Conquest.

Anyway, it is already pretty clear that one of the chief excitements of this publication will be in finding out who has been dumped on, and how badly. Few well-known names escape the Larkin lash and although Anthony Thwaite seems in this area to have been abundantly forthcoming, we can surmise that he must have done *some* toning down. After all, this is merely a Selected Letters and there are over three hundred [. . .]'s sprinkled throughout.

Apart from Thwaite himself, the few who are spared include figures like Vernon Watkins, Gavin Ewart, Barbara Pym: allies who are genuinely liked and admired but who are nonetheless junior to Larkin in talent and repute. The really big hates tend to be reserved for sizeable poetic rivals. Ted Hughes is a recurrent, near-obsessive target, with S. Heaney advancing on the rails. Even John Betjeman is given a few slap-downs here and there. All in all, I think it is true to say that Larkin has not a kind word for any contemporary writer who might be thought of as a threat to his pre-eminence. Kingsley Amis seems to be the exception but actually isn't, quite: in this complicated case, the kind words are often double-edged. And as Larkin got older, he became increasingly disposed to downgrade the literary heroes of his youth. Auden, once worshipped, becomes a 'cosmopolitan lisping no-good'; Yeats turns into 'old gyre-and-grumble'. Only Lawrence, Larkin's earliest 'touchstone against the false', survives more or less intact.

It would be easy enough, then, to argue that – fun and games aside – the really important revelation of these letters is that Larkin, the above-it-all curmudgeon and recluse, the arch-self-deprecator, was in truth nursing a champ-sized fixation on matters of literary rank – a fixation perhaps Maileresque in its immensity and scope. The settings, we might say, are different, drabber, Hull not Brooklyn, and so on, but the ache for supremacy is much the same. Mailer, in his *Advertisements for Myself*, set out to annihilate the opposition, rather as Larkin seems to here. The American made a show of his megalomania; he overplayed it, with a grin. Larkin, being English, being Larkin, chose a public stance that was meant to disguise the ferocity of his ambition.

This sounds plausible, and could be backed up with some fairly unappealing extracts from these once-private letters. Larkin *was* surprisingly alert to questions of literary-world status and to the encroachments of his rivals. No attempt to account for his lifelong unhappiness can now possibly pretend that he was not. But his ambition, as its largely dismal narrative unwinds, seems anything but Maileresque. There is no zest in it, no Tarzan-calls, no muscle-flexing self-delusion, no . . . well, no ambition, really, as somebody like Mailer would define it. The yearned-for bays are withered; they may even turn out to be made of plastic – *withered plastic*, if this boy's luck runs true to form. Larkin knew himself to be the champ – but he knew also that he was a smalltime, local sort of champ. He was unlikely to make it in the heavyweight division, nor was he a serious contender for world titles. He was at best perhaps a bantam-weight or – ho ho ho – a cruiser. But then, God bugger me blue, what did *that* make all the other craps and shags – the Wains, Hugheses, Davies, *Holloways*, for Christ's sake? At least he, Larkin, didn't show up for readings in a *leather jacket*.

'You've become what I dreamed of becoming,' Larkin wrote to Kingsley Amis at a point quite late on in their careers, seeming to mean by this that Amis was an esteemed, successful novelist and that he himself was a mere poet. But there were other ways in which he envied Amis – or rather there were other ways in which he measured himself against what Amis seemed to represent.

In a very early letter – not to Amis – Larkin finds himself brooding, as he often does, on 'ways of life', and he ends up contrasting two types of literary artist: there is the 'ivory tower cunt . . . who denies all human relationships, either through disgust, shyness, or weakness, or inability to deal with them', and there is 'the solid man with plenty of roots in everyday living by which his spiritual and mental existence is nourished'. Although Larkin would surely have guffawed later on had Amis proposed himself as an example of the second type, he knew that he, Larkin, had grown into a pretty fair example of the first. What was it that had made him stay put, miss out, cave in, while his comrade voyaged out to grasp the goodies?

'After comparing lives with you for years/I see how I've been losing', Larkin wrote, in a poem which was not published in his lifetime but which he tinkered with for two decades. The addressee may not have been Amis but one's guess is that it was. Even after the pair of them have become grand figures, Larkin still has the Amis model on his mind. When *The Oxford Book of Twentieth-Century Verse* clocks up sales of 85,000, this is 'chickenfeed compared with *Lucky Jim*'. On the other hand, Larkin is delighted to find that his entries in *The Oxford Dictionary of Quotations* outnumber Amis's by five to one ('Poor Kingsley only has one, and that "More will mean worse". I haven't searched beyond that').

Twenty years' worth of the Amis–Larkin correspondence has gone missing, so it is not easy to track their rivalry in detail. From what there is, though, we get the sense that Amis's worldly success had some significant bearing on Larkin's precocious sourness, his posture of exclusion and defeat, the sense even that without the Amis irritation Larkin may not so readily have found *his* subject, his unlucky Jim. At the beginning of their friendship, Larkin took it for granted that he was the more serious, the more loftily destined of the two. On the face of it, in 1941, the two were neck and neck, a couple of randy bachelor types who didn't give a bugger, partners in pornography, swapping smut, comparing readings on their ever-active masturbation charts, and all the rest of it. Each of them was working on a novel, and although we don't know what Amis thought of his own work at this time (or, come to that, of Larkin's) we are in no doubt of Larkin's intensity of purpose.

'I so badly want to write novels,' he wrote (again, though, not to Amis), novels that would be 'a mix of Lawrence, Thomas Hardy and George Eliot'. In order to achieve this aim, he is already shaping up to distance himself from enfeebling human attachments: 'I find that once I "give in" to another person ... there is a slackening and dulling of the peculiar artistic fibres ...' As early as 1943, he is looking forward to a 'lonely bachelorhood interspersed with buggery and strictly monetary fornication'. At this stage, such resolutions are for art's sake and are anyway half-joking. Amis's readiness to get sexually involved is to be envied in some ways but it also suggests a failure of essential seriousness. On the very few occasions when Larkin does address Amis solemnly, as writer to writer, the tone is close to condescending: 'You know that the putting down of good words about good things is the mainspring of my endeavours.'

By the age of twenty-five, Larkin had published two novels and one book of poems, with another book of poems ready, as he thought, for publication. Amis had managed but one volume of his verse; none of his fiction had appeared. Six years later, Larkin had one further publication to his credit – the privately-printed *XX Poems* – and Amis had come out with *Lucky Jim*, a novel that had its comic roots in the ribald world which he and Larkin had once shared and which (so Larkin may have thought) they had invented. Its spectacular success, coming when it did, must have been hard for Larkin to endure. Or maybe he didn't give a toss.

It is unusual for a writer's letters – all foreground and virtually no background – to come out in advance of a biography, and the Amis connection is just one of several areas on which conjecture is rather teasingly encouraged. More familiar, perhaps, than the idea of Larkin-the-careerist is the idea of Larkin-the-depressive, but here too we have too many gaps in the life-story, too many possible crisis-points, too many relationships that are insufficiently explained. Even so, as a chronicle of ever-deepening wretchedness, this book has weight enough. From 1945, when he takes his first job as a librarian in Leicester (having already written his two novels), until his death forty years later, the pattern of complaint remains more or less the same: the job is boring, the writing is going badly or not going at all, the relationship he is in – if there is one – is dreary, futureless and guilt-inducing, the world – and England in particular – is going to pot, thanks usually to lefties, foreigners and niggers.

Pornography, cricket, jazz, gin, Mrs Thatcher and the occasional spring day provide relief but even these oases are eventually discovered to be tainted. Pornography is all very well but where – in real life – do you get to see 'schoolgirls suck each other off while you whip them'? Test matches have to be avoided because there are 'too many fucking niggers about', too many 'Caribbean germs'. Even good jazz gets boring in late middle age and the trouble with spring is that you're *supposed* to like it. Gin, he was advised, is killing him. Only Mrs Thatcher (along with D.H. Lawrence) fails in the end to disappoint, but Larkin lashes himself for having disappointed *her*: he refuses the offered Laureateship because, he says, he has become 'a turned-off tap'. 'A Laureate can fall silent but he cannot be dumb from the start.'

Larkin stopped writing altogether in 1977, the year his mother died, and in his last years the routine misery takes on a sharper, more urgently self-loathing edge, as if the one thing that had made the rest just about possible to bear had, by withdrawing, left him exposed – to the world, and to himself – as an imposter, a grotesque: 'In the old days, depression wasn't too bad because I could write about it. Now writing has left me, and only depression remains.' 'So now we face 1982, sixteen stone six, gargantuanly paunched, helplessly addicted to alcohol, tired of livin' and scared of dyin', world-famous unable-to-write poet.'

Now and then, Larkin's misery sounds clinical, there from the start, as when he writes that 'Depression hangs over me as if I were Iceland' or (in 1949) that he feels as if he has been 'doctored in some way, and my central core dripped on with acid'. At other times, of course, it comes across as Larkinesque, the act he opted for because it was so easy to perform, so 'true to life'. What might have made a difference? In 1944, he wrote:

> You see, my trouble is that I simply can't understand anybody doing anything but write, paint, compose music – I can understand their doing things as a means to these ends, but I can't see what a man is up to who is satisfied to follow a profession in the normal way. If I hadn't the continual knowledge that 'when all this bloody work is through for today I can start work again' or 'this half-hour is simply ghastly, but one day it will have been digested sufficiently to be written about' – if I didn't think that, I don't know what I should do. And all the people who don't think it, what do they do? What are they striving for?

The great novel never happened and perhaps Larkin recognised – and hated to recognise – how little of the true novelist's generosity, or curiosity, of spirit he could actually muster or sustain. But he was proud of what he did write, even though it was in the nature of his gift that its appearances would be intermittent, and it is unlikely that he was all that tormented by his failure to write fiction. He may have wanted to *be* Kingsley Amis (now and then) but it seems doubtful that he would have wanted to swap oeuvres.

The love of a good woman? Larkin's misogyny was well entrenched by his early twenties – all women are stupid, he would say, they make scenes, they cling, they are forever parading their 'emotional haberdashery', they want babies, and so on – but who knows how things might have turned out if he had been luckier in his liaisons? Or, he would no doubt have retorted, more courageous, better-looking, or more ready to fork out for endless boring dinners (with no money back when it's all over)? In the early Fifties, there was one affair (described by the editor as 'passionate') which seems to have made more than the usual impact. Patsy Strang, a married woman, actually has Larkin addressing her as 'sugarbush' and 'honeybear'.

The episode is short-lived but the recollection of it somehow hangs over all subsequent involvements. When it ended Larkin wrote to her:

You are the sort of person one can't help feeling (in a carping sort of way) *ought* to come one's way *once* in one's life – without really expecting she will – and since you did, I feel I mustn't raise a howl when circumstances withdraw you, however much I miss you – it would be ungrateful to fortune, if you see what I mean . . . do you? At least, that's what I try to feel! But oh dear, oh dear! You were so wonderful!

There is no other moment quite like this in the book. To turn the screw, Patsy Strang died – of alcoholic poisoning – in 1977, two months before old Mrs Larkin died. This was, of course, the year of Larkin's 'retirement' from writing poetry, and the year too in which he finally completed the poem 'Aubade': 'the good not done, the love not given, time/torn off unused.'

Selected Letters of Philip Larkin, 1940–1985 edited by Anthony Thwaite (Faber)

1992

Philip Larkin: 3. The Biography

A couple of weeks ago, there was a write-up in the *Independent* about a rap performer name of Ice Cube, author of 'A Bitch is a Bitch' and 'Now I Gotta Wet'cha'. Ice Cube, we were told, is notorious for his misogyny and racism and for whipping up his fans into ecstasies of loathing: he has them 'grooving to a litany of hate'. Only one of Ice Cube's lines was quoted – 'You can't trust no bitch. Who can I trust? Me' – but the reviewer did attempt to pinpoint his subject's characteristic manner of address. He called Ice Cube's language 'incessantly Larkinesque'.

Larkinesque? Did this mean that Ice Cube, for all his appearance of commercialised aggression, was secretly a somewhat poignant type of artist, wry, subtle, elegiac; that his dignified, distressful lyrics were likely to linger in the memory for decades? It seems not. In this context, 'Larkinesque' signified 'foul-mouthed'. And the *Independent*'s readers were supposed to know this. Oh, Larkinesque, they'd think as one, *that* means Cube uses the word 'fuck' a lot.

And who can blame them if they do so think? After all, in the week before the Ice Cube notice, these same readers were treated to a daily dose of Philip Larkin's more repulsive aperçus: sexual intercourse is like having someone else blow your nose, women are stupid, kids should be sent away to orphanages more or less at birth, and all the rest of it. At the bottom of one page, in a little box, we would get the *Independent*'s 'Daily Poem' – usually some workmanlike concoction without a flicker of inspiration or originality – and on another, similarly boxed, there would be the ugly mug of Philip Larkin, together with a line or two of his off-the-cuff plain-speaking. What a busy newspaper: encouraging *les jeunes* and les no-hopers even as it chips away at the repute of the best poet we have had since Auden.

A few years ago, 'Larkinesque' suggested qualities both lovable and glum. Nowadays, it means four-letter words and hateful views. As Larkin once predicted, his 'Lake Isle of Innisfree' has turned out to be not 'Church Going' or 'The Whitsun Weddings' but 'This Be The Verse': 'They fuck you up, your mum and dad'. 'I fully expect to hear it recited by a thousand Girl Guides before I die,' he said.

How did this come about? Many would say that last year's *Selected Letters* are to blame. Without meaning to, the edition showed Larkin to be a fairly unpleasant piece of work, mean-spirited and – yes – foul-mouthed, and there was not enough in the way of biographical context for his would-be defenders to get hold of. The *Letters*, amusing as they sometimes were, gave us a mouthpiece not a man. But even so, the widespread outrage seemed excessive. It was not as if the living Larkin had gone out of his way to make us want to be his chums. Unlike John Betjeman or Stevie Smith, two poets he admired, he did not set out to be 'much loved' – although he did like to be much mentioned. There was a vein of coarseness on display from the beginning. Larkin turned it to advantage in his work, setting it off against an equally strong vein of tender sentiment, but we always believed him when he said that 'self's the man'.

We knew too that this poet's personality, his off-colour ribaldry and slang, had been shaped in the 'come-off-it' postwar years and nurtured in dreary provincial towns, in seedy digs and gas-lit libraries. We had no proof, but we rather suspected that Larkin collected hardish porn, had it in for blacks and queers, was careful with his money and, when it came to relationships, too morbidly obsessed with his own failings to be much of a lover or a friend. Plenty of this we were able to pick up from the poems but these were usually so well judged, as dramas or confessions, that we could speak also of a Larkinesque 'persona' – a self-projection that might in part be a disguise.

When Larkin died in 1985, at sixty-three, the obituaries were full of warmth; there was much talk of our 'nation's loss'. He was known to have gone a bit funny in his final years, falling in love with Mrs Thatcher and giving out with some reactionary comment, but all this was reckoned to be amiably bufferish, a

bit of a self-parody, and somehow valuably English in its con-
cern for old-style ways. Only a few people knew that there was
nothing at all funny about the way Larkin had gone funny, that
his conservatism was tinged with the same vehemence that marked
his ever-deepening self-hatred and despair. There was also a drink
problem, a port-for-breakfast kind of drink problem. Since the death
of his mother in 1977, he had stopped writing poetry, or stopped
expecting to write poetry, and when he did take up his pen it was
either from duty or from rage – and it was not always easy to tell
which was which.

When Larkin's *Collected Poems* appeared in 1988, Anthony Thwaite
– the book's editor – was criticised for certain policy decisions, but
nobody complained that he had left out late, unpublished pieces like
'Prison for strikers/Bring back the cat/Kick out the niggers/What
about that'. Some readers, though, did wonder about his inclusion
of a startling poem called 'Love Again', which he had discovered
among Larkin's papers:

> Love again: wanking at ten-past three
> (Surely he's taken her home by now?),
> The bedroom hot as a bakery,
> The drink gone dead . . .
>
> Someone else feeling her breasts and cunt,
> Someone else drowned in that lash-wide stare,
> And me supposed to be ignorant,
> Or find it funny, or not to care,
> Even . . . but why put it into words?

It might seem at first that this poem should not have come as a
surprise, that it was just another bit of grumbling about girls. And
yet it did. None of Larkin's earlier unburdenings had had anything
like the same unmerciful ferocity, the same screaming-point force of
attack. There is no attempt here to mitigate the central emotion of
the poem, no 'Well, what do you expect?', not even much of a
late bid for plangency, for general wisdom – indeed, on this score,
it is the failure of his attempt to open the thing out that does the
clinching:

> Isolate rather this element
>
> That spreads through other lives like a tree
> And sways them on in a sort of sense
> And say why it never worked for me.
> Something to do with violence
> A long way back, and wrong rewards,
> And arrogant eternity.

If Larkin had lived, he probably would not have published 'Love Again'. On the other hand, one's guess is that he rather badly wanted us to see it. We knew he was 'fucked up' because he'd told us so, in poem after poem, but the Larkin we admired *was* 'supposed to find it funny or not to care' or at any rate to have the gift of transmuting daily glooms into great haunting statements about love and death – ours as well as his. In 'Love Again' the unhappiness strictly belongs to him: our share in it is that of the pitying spectator.

Andrew Motion knew Larkin during the years of 'Love Again' and although his biography begins at the beginning, and has many interesting revelations about the poet's early years, there is nearly always a sense that he is working backwards from that poem, or from what he had learned from that poem about the essential hopelessness of his subject's predicament. Motion has said that he wrote this biography 'with love'. He loves the poems, certainly, and leads us through them, one by one, with easy reverence, but his feelings about their author often seem to be equivocal. He wants to love Larkin but much of the time the best he can muster is a sort of muffled, reluctant pity-cum-contempt. Much of the time also there is simple bewilderment: why *did* Larkin get so little sense of achievement out of what he had achieved?

A sense of achievement is not the same as a need to be acknowledged as the tops. Larkin from the start believed, or said he did, in his own 'genius', but even as an adolescent he seems to have spent more time worrying about how to make it as a writer than he did enjoying the satisfactions of a job well done – or, come to that, making sure the job *was* well done. He was constantly checking his age against the ages of his rivals, both alive and dead, his progress against theirs, and when he first met Kingsley Amis he was appalled to find himself 'for the first time in the presence of a talent greater than my own'.

And this Amis rivalry was all-important later on. Larkin fancied himself as a novelist and when he finally conceded that fiction was beyond him, or beneath him, he also had to concede that, unlike Amis, he would never be able to 'live as a writer': the toad work would squat on him for keeps. And this meant that other puerile fantasies had to be relinquished: the villa in the South of France, the quilted smoking-jackets, the under-age groupies, and so on. The young Larkin had a somewhat raffish, Maughamesque notion of how writers lived, and he would dress the part: bow ties, cerise trousers, poncy kerchiefs, lashings of Brylcreem – the stuff, verily, of fiction.

When Larkin abandoned fiction for verse, out came the cycle clips. Poems may be wonderful but being a poet was for him a bit like being, well, himself – the self he hoped Art would help him to escape. As a novelist, he might have got rid of his stammer, his thick specs; he might have become better-looking and mastered his awkwardness with girls. As a poet he would be condemned to relive or to perpetuate his grotty adolescence. It would be introspection all the way. No routes would open into the thrilling, despicable, exterior 'real world'. Poetry would ensure that he stayed where he was, stayed who he was.

We have now seen enough of Larkin's early unpublished poems to be certain that, had he not stayed where he was, he might have grown up to be a cut-price Yeats or Auden. Immobility became his subject, and the Hardy influence intruded just in time. And it is the Hardy biography that often comes to mind as we scrutinise Larkin's dull, complicated life. There is the selfishness, the stinginess, the petty vanities. There is the clenched and murky wistfulness about sex, the near-sentimental veneration of animals and landscapes, the yearning for romantic absolutes. Remorse is a powerful emotion in both poets. Larkin spent most of his life complaining about his mother's trivial-minded possessiveness but when she died he knew exactly how to feel.

Larkin once predicted of himself: 'I believe when I am old I shall bitterly regret having wasted my life, which I may have done. This is because I shall never attain the absolute – in other words the *continual* ecstasy – because it doesn't exist. Therefore in addition to being afraid of death, I shall feel cheated and angry.' This is the kind of talk that gets poetry a bad name. In Larkin's case, a whole lifetime was spent avoiding not just the 'continual ecstasy' that 'doesn't exist' but also the non-continual fragments of near-ecstasy that actually did come his way, the sort of ecstasy that costs money, wastes time and is productive of much personal inconvenience. One of the last poems he wrote was about a hedgehog he had accidentally killed. 'We should be careful of each other,' he wrote, 'We should be kind/While there is still time.' To which we might feel like responding, as to some of Hardy's similar laments: perhaps there was still time.

'We should be careful of each other' assumes an ambiguous import when we explore, with Motion's guidance, Larkin's dealings with 'his' women. It turns out that far from being cut off from the world of sexual entanglements, he was up to his neck in them, to the point sometimes of near-strangulation. The strongest part of Motion's book comes with his coverage of the final years, when Larkin had at first two, then three women who felt themselves to have a claim on him. There was the long-serving Monica, his mostly absentee companion for more than thirty years. There was Maeve, a Roman Catholic with strong views about pre-marital sex, who kept Larkin at bay for seventeen years before finally submitting. And then, five years before he died and about five minutes after Maeve's capitulation, there was Betty, his 'loaf-haired' secretary at the Hull University Library. Maeve knew nothing of Betty (nor did she know, until after Larkin's death, about his porno mags; the revelation made her feel unclean). Monica and Maeve knew about each other, but Larkin assiduously kept the two apart, and mostly in the dark: he was always telling the one that he had stopped caring for the other. For a long stretch, then, of his adult life, Larkin was able to see himself as under siege, his dismal bachelorhood a citadel. Much of his anguish, in the later stages, was to do with his fear that the invaders might simply pack up and go away. The crunch came when Monica's ill-health required Larkin to allow her to move in with him.

Andrew Motion skilfully prepares the ground for all this complication. He has at least one eyebrow raised but decently tries to see things from the Larkin point of view. And in the book as a whole, he is in no doubt that sex is the narrative main-spring. Early on, Larkin's sex-life was as we had imagined it: all in the mind. He had no luck at school, and not much luck at Oxford, where the bluestockings he ineptly groped would cry: 'I'd really rather not, thank you.' There was a fleeting homosexual liaison – 'a few messy encounters', recalls the favoured swain, one Philip Brown, a co-student at St John's – and after that a period of ambivalent dream-jottings in which Larkin recorded visions of male-membered girls. This was followed by a sado-masochistic inter-lude, during which he wrote fiction about schoolgirl swishings at St Bride's.

Real women began to enter his life in 1943, when he started work as a librarian – work, as Motion shows, which he took far more seriously than he let on. By this time, though, he had already devised his Philosophy of Sex. His parents' marriage – the father a bookish, imperious Nazi-fancier, the mother a vacuous slow-drip complainer – had instilled in him a determination to stay unattached. Their union, he said, had 'left me with two convictions: that human beings should not live together and that children should be taken from their parents at an early age'. When he was twenty-one, and stepping out with his first girl (a schoolgirl, Ruth Bowman, whom he had been helping with her literary research), he was telling his male friends: 'I *don't* want to take a girl out and spend circa £5 when I can toss myself off in five minutes, free, and have the rest of the evening for myself.' When he did briefly get himself engaged to Ruth, he made it clear that 'marriage would not automatically follow'. Poor Ruth has described one of their typically lacklustre dates: the young poet had fallen strangely silent, she recalls, and when she asked him what the matter was, he'd said: 'I've just thought what it would be like to be old and have no one to look after me.'

And this rather set the tone for the relationships that followed. One affair, with Patsy Strang, does seem to have carried a romantic-erotic charge, but this was perhaps because Strang was safely married and anyway a bit of a bohemian; she was also quite well off. Even so, one of the few touching letters in the Thwaite selection from

the *Letters* was the one Larkin wrote to Strang when she ended
their affair:

> You are the sort of person one can't help feeling (in a carping sort
> of way) *ought* to come one's way *once* in one's life – without really
> expecting she will – and since you did, I feel I mustn't raise a howl
> when circumstances withdraw you, however much I miss you – it
> would be ungrateful to fortune, if you see what I mean . . . do
> you? At least, that's what I try to feel! But oh dear, oh dear! You
> were so wonderful!

Motion, in his printing, unaccountably lops off 'You were so wonderful!' so that the letter feebly ends: 'Oh dear, oh dear! . . .' This
seems unfairly dampening when one considers how rarely Larkin let
himself catch fire.

A question is raised here about the relationship between Andrew
Motion's biography and Anthony Thwaite's *Selected Letters*. Most
people found it odd that the *Letters* preceded the *Life* and after reading
Motion they may find it odder still. It seems that, whenever possible,
Motion avoids quoting from letters which are already available in
Thwaite. Thus, in a few instances, he appears to deny himself
evidence which is more powerful or telling than his own. For
example, the letters Larkin wrote to his friend Jim Sutton seem to
have been shared out between Motion and Thwaite. There are about
two hundred letters in existence, Thwaite has said. Of these, Thwaite
prints over seventy and Motion cites about one hundred and twenty.
Forty of the letters to Sutton that appear in Thwaite are not referred
to in Motion and some that Motion does quote from sound more
interesting and important than one or two of those picked out by
Thwaite. Now and again, in order to get a full picture of Larkin's
response to this or that event, we are obliged to turn from Motion to
Thwaite and back again. You may not want to know the full extent
of Larkin's worship of D.H. Lawrence or about his early interest in
the visual arts, but if you do, don't throw away your Thwaite. Are the
two books meant to dovetail in this way or is it just that a biographer
instinctively prefers new material to old – six months old, in this case?
Either way, it seems a bit rough on the reader. Larkin would have

thought so, to be sure. One remembers his response to the break-up of the marriage of two friends: 'I suppose I shall have to start seeing them both now – take double the time. Arrgh!'

Andrew Motion has taken five years to write this book and his industry can be applauded. He has dug up many gems – an autobiographical fragment, pocket diaries, not-known-of early drafts – and he has persuaded people to talk to him who had good reason to refuse. Maeve Brennan's testimony is surely something of a coup, although she may not be delighted to read here that Larkin used to get excited by her hairy arms ('PAL to author' is the source). We don't get as many letters *to* Larkin as we would have wished, so that it is not always clear what *he* is having to put up with, but presumably Motion's witnesses drew the line at this more intimate kind of exposure.

As a biographer, Motion is painstaking and intelligent and he has some valuable insights but for my taste he is too solemnly intrusive: he likes explaining things and is forever teasing out supposed internal conflicts, in case we can't see them for ourselves. The teacher in him is often at war with the narrator and, in the early sections of the book, where he is guessing, he slips easily into an inert biographese: 'It was a tentative step towards the high mountain of art', 'By the summer of 1938 the fountain of creativity was jetting up poems as well as stories'. 'Fountain? Mountain?' we can hear his subject growl, 'make up your mind.'

Philip Larkin: A Writer's Life by Andrew Motion (Faber)

1993

Seamus Heaney's Anonymity

'About the only *enmity* I have is towards pride.' Seamus Heaney said this in an interview and, since we know him to be the most over-interviewed of living poets, perhaps he shouldn't be forced to say it again here. Put in its context, though, this too-worthy sounding protestation has much to reveal about the disposition of Heaney's work so far, and can even be read as a riposte to those critics who complain that, for all its verbal richness and its moral courage, his work is strangely without 'personality'.

In the interview, Heaney was talking about his Catholicism, about how his sensibility had been 'formed by the dolorous murmurings of the rosary, and the generally Marian quality of devotion' afforded by the Roman Church – a Church which Heaney, even in his twenties, continued to go to for Confession and which 'permeated' the whole life of his Northern Ireland childhood. Thanks to this Church, its doctrines and its rituals, Heaney's sensibility was from the start centred towards what he calls a 'feminine presence'. It was this presence that induced in him his 'only enmity':

> A religion that has a feminine component and a notion of the mother in the transcendental world is better than a religion that just has a father, a man, in it. I also – just in my nature and temperament, I suppose – believed in humility and in bowing down, and in 'we' rather than 'I'. I hate a *moi* situation, an egotism, a presumption, a *hubris*, and I'm used to bowing down to the mother as a way of saying that. About the only *enmity* I have is towards pride.

When people complain about the absence of 'personality' in Heaney's work, they are at some level complaining also that the '*moi* situation' has been skirted or suppressed, and that as a result his poems lack the sort of sharply individual human *tone* that Larkin has, or Frost, or Lowell. I have heard it said that Heaney's work is 'teachable but not memorable', that lines of his don't linger in the mind, and it certainly seems to be true that admirers of his do tend to remember images or situations or stylistic brilliances rather than cries from the heart or haunting melodies. He has written few 'inter-personal' poems that are any good, and he is better at addressing the dead than he is at confiding in the living.

Of course, when Heaney started writing – in the late 1960s – there was '*moi*-poetry' aplenty to be haunted by, and we can now see that the literary-historical moment was precisely right for the eventual, if not imminent appearance of a poet for whom none of all *that* held any magnetism. A new Auden, a new Stevens might have seemed to be the answer, and shortly there were indeed new Audens, new Stevenses to choose from. But neither intellectualism nor playfulness nor mere perfection of technique would be enough to reclaim glamour for the impersonal, or anti-personal. The only real challenge to the over-intimate would have to come from a poetry that risked its opposite: the too-theatrical. A poetry to be listened in on would be most effectively displaced by a poetry that dared to resurrect some of the art's discredited rhetorical/theatrical presumptions. (These, it should be said, had by the early 1970s been 'discredited' not just by the aching whisperers of Confessionalism but also by cute performance stars and by sloganisers of the 'left'.)

In terms of the desirable 'next step' for British poetry, Seamus Heaney had some obvious natural advantages. After all, confessional poetry was unlikely to seduce a Catholic. And, for the wishing-to-be-humble, there was not much allure either in the mock-humilities of Larkinesque. Even so, Heaney did not at first seem to offer much of a challenge to anything, or anyone – he was too much like Ted Hughes, minus the Lawrentian, black-magical ingredients, and he was a shade too youthfully delighted with the plopping, slopping, thwacking sounds of spade on soil, or milk in pail, etc. (Donnish critics have always loved this onomatopoeic side of Heaney, though: maybe because it gives them the chance to exhibit their own 'sensibilities' –

'You'll notice how the "thwa –" of "thwack" is shyly answered by the "plu –" of "plump"'.)

And yet, if one looks back now at Heaney's first two books, *Death of a Naturalist* and *Door Into the Dark*, it becomes evident that he had already there begun a sort of rebellion against the '*moi*', against the autobiographical 'I', the nervously racked victim 'me'. The voice he spoke in, or rather the voice in which his poems spoke, already had a tinge of bardic anonymity, a suggestion that the self had indeed been humbled, but momentously: Seamus Heaney the man was being elected, so it seemed to him, into the role of Seamus Heaney, poet.

If this makes him sound like George Barker, it absolutely shouldn't. What is attractive about Heaney's response to his vocation is that he is never entirely happy that it is *he* who has been chosen: a childhood spent wondering how to avoid the priesthood had perhaps ill-prepared him for such singularity. And it is the marvelling near-reluctance with which he acknowledges his own election that silences, or ought to silence, any post-Movement tendency to scoff.

Like Dylan Thomas, like Graves, Heaney assumed the noble vestments, but he did so with an engaging awkwardness, a persuasive lack of flourish. One of the fascinations of Heaney's work, read from the beginning until now, is in observing how he shifts this way and that to find a genuinely comfortable *fit*, a non-fake, non-proud way of living in the sacred robes he knows he has the obligation and the right to wear. He can neither fling them off nor swap them for the more workaday gear which, in certain moods, he might feel more 'at home in'. But there is always a touch of 'Why me?' in his sometimes effortful transcending of the 'me', and this has given him a rare sturdiness of posture – rare, that is, for the 'chosen' sort of poet he's become. Indeed, it could be said that one of Heaney's principal achievements is that he has re-dignified the bardic stance.

There are those who would say that he has been helped in this by having something to be bardic *about*, by having arrived on-stage at a place and time when it was possible for him to say:

> To forge a poem is one thing, to forge the uncreated conscience of the race . . . is quite another and places daunting pressure and responsibilities on anyone who would risk the name of poet.

Certainly, it is hard to think of how an English poet could get away with saying this; but with Heaney 'getting away with it' does not arise. A Heaney without the Troubles that erupted just as he was finishing his second book would maybe have been all vocation and no job: archaeological, etymological, nostalgic, literary-grandiose and 'good on nature'. He might even have fallen victim to some Irish version of the thin-spined Californian-meditative which showed faint signs of enticing him around the time of his third volume, *Wintering Out*. From his first two books, it's hard to tell. These were much concerned with the *discovery* of his vocation, with measuring the distances between his sort of digging and that of the farm folk he'd grown up with, and with registering a sense of awe at the mysteries which seemed to lie ahead. When he has spoken of this period he has usually portrayed himself as almost-passive: the poems were already *in* him, he would say, and his task was to uncover them, to excavate, or even just to make himself available to their arrivals. He was also reading a lot of modern poetry, late in the day and in something of a hurry, it might seem, as if to seek directions, signs. The dark behind *The Door into the Dark* was, simply, dark.

The Troubles did erupt, though. Heaney wintered out the first few months, tinkering with place-names and imperilled Irish crafts, but he sensed from the start – from 1969 – that the bard's moment had almost certainly arrived, that from now on 'the problems of poetry' had changed 'from being simply a matter of achieving the satisfactory verbal icon to being a search for images and symbols adequate to our predicament'. Again, it is 'our' predicament, not his, although as a liberal, bloodshed-hating Northern Ireland Catholic with strong ties to the British, both personal and cultural, he could hardly have felt all that 'representative'. The 'we' at this point could so easily have surrendered to the '*moi*', and Heaney could respectably have withdrawn to the margins of his maddened tribe. He could even have done this without handing in his robes.

But he didn't, and his poetry since then has been a moving drama of discomfiture, of trying to reconcile the 'magic' aspects of his calling with, so to speak, the 'duties' of the tribal bard. He has never been confident that the two can be reconciled and whenever he has had to make the choice he has almost always chosen to safeguard the 'mystery' of his vocation. There have been wobbly moments, as in the second part of *North*, where he has tried to confront the 'Irish thing' in ordinary speech, as Seamus Heaney, but all in all he has held honourably fast to the objective he set himself at the beginning of the 1970s: 'to discover a field of force in which, without abandoning fidelity to the processes and experiences of poetry . . . it would be possible to encompass the perspectives of a humane reason and at the same time grant the religious intensity of the violence its deplorable authenticity and complexity'. These words must have been arrived at with some anguish, and much care. It is not easy, perhaps not even possible, to speak of 'deplorable authenticity' without seeming to favour the 'authenticity' aspect of that formulation.

Heaney has looked for his 'field of force' in some out-of-the-way places, as remote sometimes from the present tense as he could reach: not in order to seek comfort from the past – unless there is comfort in knowing that history is comfortless – but to bring back 'befitting emblems of adversity'. Befitting they have been, and delivered with a curt or stoic shrug, as if to say: 'What can I say?':

> I am Hamlet the Dane,
> skull-handler, parablist,
> smeller of rot
>
> in the state, infused
> with its poisons,
> pinioned by ghosts
> and affections,
>
> murders and pieties,
> coming to consciousness,
> by jumping in graves,
> dithering, blathering.

It was with his fifth book, *Field Work*, that Heaney found a voice that is neither bleakly antiquarian nor awkwardly portentous. By this time the Troubles really had become *his* troubles. Friends and relatives of his were being killed: the '*moi*' could no longer be prevented from intruding some of its own nervous cadences. In poems like 'The Strand at Lough Beg' and 'A Postcard from North Antrim', Heaney sounds

that 'heartbreak' note which Robert Lowell used to talk about. Maybe
Lowell talked to *him* about it. *Field Work* has an elegy in memory of
Lowell ('the master elegist'), and the two poets saw each other often
during the mid-Seventies. In this book, even the 'love-poems' (a
genre Heaney says he hates the sound of) are unaffectedly meant to
be listened to by the beloved – and thus listened in to by the rest of
us. But it's Heaney's Irish elegies that hurt the most:

> Across that strand of yours the cattle graze
> Up to their bellies in an early mist
> And now they turn their unbewildered gaze
> To where we work our way through squeaking sedge
> Drowning in dew. Like a dull blade with its edge
> Honed bright, Lough Beg half shines under the haze.
> I turn because the sweeping of your feet
> Has stopped behind me, to find you on your knees
> With blood and roadside muck in your hair and eyes,
> Then kneel in front of you in brimming grass
> And gather up cold handfuls of the dew
> To wash you, cousin. I dab you clean with moss
> Fine as the drizzle out of a low cloud.
> I lift you under the arms and lay you flat.
> With rushes that shoot green again, I plait
> Green scapulars to wear over your shroud.

Field Work, to my mind, is the book of Heaney's which we ought
to keep in mind (how can we not?) when there are grumbles about
'anonymity' or 'suppression of the self'. His '*moi*' poems are all the
stronger, all the more hard-won, it seems to me, not because they
go against his notion of a tribal role but because – at their best –
they don't: it's just that, in these poems, the 'I' lurks behind the 'we',
and vice versa. And the elegy is, of course, the perfect form for such
lurking, or entwining: an intimacy meant to be made public.

In *Station Island* (1984), Heaney returned to pondering the 'poet's
role', but with a new despondency. He enlists the assistance of other
artists, from Dante to James Joyce, and yearns guiltily for the 'clumps'
and 'clunks' and 'clogs' of his most youthful verses. Not so guiltily,
though, that he cannot welcome some jeering Joycean advice: 'Keep

at a tangent./When they make the circle wide, it's time to swim/out on your own'. After all, what had those grand elegies in *Field Work* actually *done*, except perhaps to 'saccharine' with literature the suffering of those they claimed to mourn? The Dantesque apparitions contrived by Heaney in *Station Island* are accusatory, and our instinct (also contrived by Heaney?) is to spring to the defence of the accused, to tell him to 'Let go, let fly, forget/You've listened long enough. Now strike your note'. In the 'Sweeney' versions and translations which appeared in this country at the same time as *Station Island* the central fantasy is one of flight – of elevation *and* liberation.

Heaney's new book, *The Haw Lantern*, does strike one or two new notes, but it is slight and low-powered, by his standards. It shows signs not so much of high vocation as of obedient professionalism: a Phi Beta Kappa poem for Harvard, a poem for William Golding on his seventy-fifth birthday, a poem for Amnesty International, Irish Section, on Human Rights Day, 1985. And there are signs too that Heaney has set himself to learn from the oblique, clandestine parables and allegories which poets of Eastern Europe use to fox the censors. I am not sure that he has a light enough touch for modes like these (and in any case does their 'lightness' not thrive on necessity?) but perhaps for the moment they offer a relaxing middle path between the druid and the *'moi'*. A sense of exercise prevails throughout the book, except in the group of sonnets written in memory of the poet's mother, who died in 1984. These are touchingly uneven: fondly anecdotal, with some strongly sentimental moments, but sometimes almost breathtakingly ill-made:

> She'd manage something hampered and askew
> Every time, as if she might betray
> The hampered and inadequate by too
> Well-adjusted a vocabulary.

Or is Heaney himself attempting to avoid a similar betrayal? Certainly, throughout the sequence, there is a reluctance to reach for anything that might be thought of as poetic grandeur.

'Silence' and 'emptiness' are what these sonnets register, and one senses that silence and emptiness are at the emotional centre of this book. Weariness, also. Dutifully, mechanically almost, Heaney continues to be full of words, and full of worries about what to do with them. But he has been tired of such worries for some time: those robes, it seems, will never fit. In a poem called 'From the Frontier of Writing' he describes being stopped at an army road-block where 'everything is pure interrogation'. When he is eventually let through, he feels 'a little emptier, a little spent/as always by that quiver in the self,/subjugated, yes, and obedient'. The same kind of thing happens, he says, at the 'frontier of writing': the writer is interrogated, guns are aimed at him, data about him get checked out, he could easily be shot. If all goes well, though, he's allowed to cross the frontier, 'arraigned yet freed'. Seamus Heaney has been arraigned often enough, by himself and by others' expectations of him. Why is it so hard to think of him as ever being 'freed' – he who has dared to 'risk the name of poet'?

The Haw Lantern by Seamus Heaney (Faber)

1987

Innocent Bystander – The Forgetfulness of Damon Runyon

Damon Runyon is famous for shunning the past tense, as in: 'I am going to take you back a matter of four or five years ago to an August afternoon . . . On this day I am talking about, the Lemon Drop Kid is looking for business.' Even when one of his stories has been told, is over, and he permits his protagonists a little late-night deconstruction, there is still this unrelenting attachment to the present. '"Well, Mrs B," he says. "You almost get a good break when old Doc News drops dead after you stake his wife to the poison because it looks as if you have her where she can never wriggle off no matter what she says. But," Ambrose says, "my friend Mrs News is cute enough to seek my advice and counsel."' This speech belongs in the past tense, but the author is determined not to put it there. By this stage in Runyon's career, to have done so would have brought professional dishonour.

Runyon did not always write this way, but once he had learned how to, he never – so to speak – looked back. According to one commentator, there is in Runyon's New York tales 'only one single instance of a verb in the past tense [and] I will lay six to five that it is nothing but a misprint'. Jimmy Breslin reckons that Runyon caught the habit either from Samuel Taylor Coleridge or from listening to hoodlums testifying evasively at court hearings. A more likely bet is that he caught it from Ring Lardner, from whom he picked up several other hard-boiled/soft-centred tricks of style. The fact is, though, that the ploy does fit snugly with the kind of stories Runyon liked to tell, stories whose charm insists that we are not often invited to reflect on origins and consequences. In Runyon's wide-eyed gangland, everyone talks as if he has been taken by surprise. A counsel for the defence can usually plead that his client was obliged to act before he had a chance to think.

In most of Runyon's tales of Broadway low-life in the 1920s, the narrator has no past and not much of a present – or perhaps, like his characters, he has more past than he cares to remember and a future that is, to say the least, uncertain. He is a Mr X, and he functions as a warm-up man for the main action. He can be found most nights in Mindy's Restaurant 'putting on the gefillte fish, which is a dish I am very fond of', when in come these three parties from Brooklyn'. The parties have names like Harry the Horse or Nick the Greek or Johnny Uptown and they are mostly small or medium-time bad guys: thieves, extortionists, kidnappers, racketeers or killers. The word 'killer', however, is a word that's never used. These men with funny names also have funny names for what they do. They speak of giving their foes 'a little tattooing', 'a boff over the pimple', or of whipping out 'the old equaliser' in order to aim some 'whangity-whang-whang at Louie the Lug' or at whoever has been foolish enough to make a party feel 'somewhat disturbed' or 'very much excited'. The narrator does not object to such euphemising because equalisers usually equalise each other – well, almost usually. Like the papers say, innocent bystanders can now and then get caught in other people's crossfire. But then, what's innocent about bystanding at a time like this?

This is a question that is never put to Mr X. Although he knows this world, he is not of it. For some reason, though, the Mindy's hoods practically queue up at his table for the chance to bend his ear: 'Maybe you will like to hear the story'; 'It's a very unusual story indeed, and is by no means a lie, and I will be pleased to tell it to someone I think will believe it.' This hunger to narrate is portrayed as common to all gangsters of the epoch. None of them can read or write 'more than somewhat', and none has even a rudimentary knowledge of life outside his little stretch of urban jungle. On politics and geography, for instance, they are particularly weak. In one story, Harry the Horse and friends find themselves at a political party convention and have no idea what is going on; in another, set in wartime, someone wants to know where – indeed *what* – Europe is. But then, as Mr X would have us bear in mind, these outlaws have long ago handed in their right to vote, travel is not permitted by the terms of their parole, all politicians are owned by the very gang bosses who own *them*, and all foreigners seem to be living in New York, so what's the point?

What the hoods do have, thanks to Mr X, is a natural aptitude for speaking Runyonese, a lingo invented to convey the simultaneous workings of a slow brain and a speedy tongue. The vocabulary is alive with colourful demotic but the syntax is stately, uncertain, pseudo-British. It is as if these self-confident slack-mouths suspect that what they are saying might get written down and used in evidence. Maybe this is why they talk to Mr X: they know – as we are not supposed to – that he is actually a hotshot columnist, that he is an associate of Arnold Rothstein, Al Capone and Mayor Walker, that he can get your name in the papers as easily as he can keep it out, that he has clout in places where it matters: in baseball, boxing, the racetrack, City Hall, the Mob. Certainly, this is how Runyon himself liked to be seen – as the invisible string-puller, the shrewd appraiser on the sidelines. 'I am the sedentary champion of the City,' he once said. 'In order to learn anything of importance, I must remain seated. Why I am the best is that I can last an entire day without causing the chair to squeak.'

Mr X likewise does not often squeak his chair. He also wishes to present himself as an all-knowing neutral. But he is shifty too, and timid, and nothing like as grand-mannered as Runyon, his inventor. He is, he tells us more than once, 'a law-abiding citizen at all times' and 'greatly opposed to guys who violate the law', although he also makes it his business to steer clear of the police: 'Personally, I do not care for coppers, but I believe in being courteous to them at all times.' Luckily, the cops usually steer clear of *him*: 'They know there is no more harm in me than in a two-year-old baby.' Mr X is not 'a guy who goes around much', but now and then he is asked to do small favours for the hoods – he runs errands for them, delivers messages, fixes pow-wows between warring parties, and so on. His chief duty down at Mindy's, though, is to sit still and listen while they talk.

Mr X is sometimes reluctant to do this – maybe because most of the hoods' plotlines turn on a contrived misunderstanding or on some implausible offstage machination – but at such moments he reminds himself that cute guys like Izzy Cheesecake and Rusty Charlie are likely to turn not-so-cute if they don't get to tell the tale. So he listens, and we listen with him: as eavesdroppers, we are even less likely than he is to make sniffy moral judgements or offer to help out with the grammar or even to request a bit more detail when it comes to the descriptive stuff. On dolls, especially, the guys tend not to throw away the words. 'I never see such a wide doll. She looks all hammered down.'

We know nothing about Mr X beyond the very little he lets slip. He seems not to have a regular job, and our guess is that he pays for his meals at Mindy's out of his racetrack winnings, or that he has some fringe role in the bootlegging business – he certainly knows all the joints. Unlike the guys he eats with, though, he wants nothing for himself: he is not in pursuit of money, power or women. He is what Damon Runyon, who pursued all three, would now and then have dearly wished to be: an uncommitted ear.

Runyon, though, according to his biography, dearly wished to be all sorts of things. Born in cowboyland (actually his birthplace is Manhattan, Kansas), he was the son of an ill-tempered Indian fighter turned newspaperman, a drinker and a brawler who, when Runyon's mother died, did not take kindly to the business of to-wing a small boy from bar to bar. Damon thus early on 'acquired a veneer of hardness covering a heart of loneliness'. He tried his hand at writing poetry, he became a bellhop, a jockey, a boy soldier. But it was not long before Daddy turned him into a small replica of Daddy: he taught the boy boozing, whoring, telling lies, and other necessities of frontier-town living. And little Damon learned fast: by the age of fifteen he was a hardbitten newshound on the Pueblo (Colorado) *Chieftain*, covering lynchings without spilling his whisky and discovering how to hero-worship visiting gunmen celebrities like the ludicrous Bat Masterson, on whom Runyon would later base one of his most dreamy-eyed character-confections, 'The Sky' – or Marlon Brando in the film of *Guys and Dolls*.

Sky Masterson is Runyon's fugitive ideal. As a sports writer, and as a close-up hanger-on of gangsters and tycoons, Runyon was in the business of constructing heroes, but none of the heavyweight boxers he secretly bought shares in, nor any of the bigshot racketeers he took to ball-games and played poker with, would ever shape up to the image of unfettered manliness embodied by the wondrous Sky. Maybe the fact that Runyon's shoe-size was a near-freakish five and a half or that he lived in daily terror of running out of funds meant that he was in the wrong business from the start. Not so – indeed the money he was earning told him otherwise. As long as he was making such big bucks, he could still reach for The Sky – well, couldn't he?

So far as he was able to, Runyon played the glamorous urban cowboy role: he talked tough, he dressed snappily, he mixed with the right wrong people and tried not to let on that for health reasons he had in young manhood been forced to quit the drink; he married above himself, but not too far, treated his wife badly, took a Mexican showgirl for his mistress (and in time his second wife), telling everyone that she was really a Spanish countess, neglected his children and was nice to animals, especially horses that ran fast (although he did keep a pet cockroach for a time; it slept in one of his bedroom slippers and was considered thoroughly trustworthy). Throughout all this, he drilled out several million words of high-class copy for his lord and master, Hearst.

'I never bite the hand that feeds me' was Runyon's motto as a journalist, and over the years he made sure that he never had reason to fall out with Hearst, even during the proprietor's pro-Nazi phase. By the end of the Thirties, he was America's most highly paid columnist, and the Broadway stories – of which there were numerous Hollywood adaptations – made him a millionaire. Indeed, his price was about to go through the roof when, in 1946, he died of throat cancer at the age of sixty-two (or thereabouts; he always lied about his age). For the last months of his life he could not speak. But then he never did speak much. His son Damon Junior records, in a 1954 memoir, that when the dying Runyon was angry about some business having been transacted through a third party, 'I replied: "But I understand he was very close to you." His fingers jabbed emphatically at the keys of the typewriter he was using as a voice. He rolled the paper up so I could see what he had written. "No one is close to me. Remember that."'

Damon Jr did as he was told: he remembered, and his memories, although they labour to achieve a note of fondness, are saturated with resentment. Runyon is blamed for the death by drinking of his first wife, the mental instability of his daughter, and the general fouled-upness of his son, Junior himself, who at the time of writing was emerging from a long struggle with the booze. Runyon's own early flight from the bottle seems to have made him pretty good at driving other people to it.

This certainly would be the view of Jimmy Breslin, who suggests also that Runyon's sense of his own superior detachment must have been well nourished by the atmosphere of Prohibition. In those days, when booze was at the heart of everything, the great spectator was on coffee. This is one of several acute but unfriendly assessments in a biography which, on the whole, is something of a mess. Breslin is for ever jazzing up the action with invented — or is it reconstructed? — dialogue:

> There was a poolroom in the basement of the corner building at 95th and Broadway, and the first day Runyon went in there, one of the guys said to him: 'The people in here are all right. Don't go near Tenth Avenue. They got a lot of killers there.'
> 'Where on Tenth Avenue?' he said.
> He began walking. If there are killers, he reasoned, then that means there are also a lot of crap games and, even better, loose dolls. When he got to the corner of Tenth Avenue and 47th Street, he took one look at the guys standing around and wishing mightily for trouble, and at once he felt at home. Baseball was nice, but murder was the main event.

Jimmy Breslin is himself a big-name New York columnist, and he covers the Runyon low-life beat. For him, too, murder is the main event. Like Runyon, he writes with lots of mush and muscle and he prides himself on knowing the Big Apple right down to its rotten core (hence his six-page digressions on subjects like the construction of the city's subway system). He even wrote a novel called *The gang that couldn't shoot straight*. And he shares many of Runyon's attitudes — to high-brows, Columbia University professors, the Algonquin set; and like Runyon, he always has the dope that's inside the inside dope. For instance, Breslin knows for certain that Jack Dempsey had lead in his gloves when he knocked out Jess Willard, he has the actual *name* of the guy who shot Arnold Rothstein, and he was pretty much *in the room* when Bugsy Siegel watched his screen test.

All in all, the example of Damon Runyon must have guided Breslin's career 'no little and quite some'. His biography, however, is far from homage-ful: on the contrary, it reads more like an attempt by Breslin to get Runyon off his back, once and for all. The disciple misses no opportunity to cut the master down to size: Runyon 'believed in writing only for money, even ahead of vengeance'. 'He wanted phrases that would make the reader think only of him.' 'While he pretended that bellhops were his people, he usually situated himself close to the money.' By the end of it, Runyon's pimple is well boffed, and Breslin rules. Indeed, there really is a tone of exultation in Breslin's account of Runyon's young second wife's affair with the muscleman Primo Carnera. The by-then aged Runyon, who collected dumb heavyweights and saw himself as 'the ultimate Broadway wise guy', was for years in ignorance of the affair, and there was much chortling at his expense in Mindy's, chortling Breslin now rather nastily sits in on. Breslin might retort that Runyon would have done the same for him. But would he? *Damon Runyon: A Life* tells us plenty about Runyon, but it doesn't tell us this.

Damon Runyon: A Life by Jimmy Breslin (Hodder)

1992

Kingsley Amis's Self-Love

Kingsley Amis has a reputation for not liking other people, but – these so-called *Memoirs* might seem to permit us to enquire – does anyone, *could* anyone, like him? Is Kingers himself, at the end of the day, the sort of bloke you'd want to run into at – well, at the end of the day, at the club, or the pub, or at some crappy dinner party?

On the face of it, no thank you. The faint hope might have been that, in writing directly about himself, the irascible old shag would come over as somewhat, shall we say, cuddlier than his usual public image makes him seem. To any such tender expectations, though, Amis offers here a close-to-gleeful 'In a pig's arse, friend' – i.e., you bastards will get nothing out of me, or not much, and what you do get you won't like.

For starters, he confides, there will be zero in the book about anything that is private to him. Dodgy material of that sort will be restricted to privacies other than his own. He will tell us nothing of real interest about his wives, mistresses or kids (although he chucks Martin the odd walk-on here and there), or about any living loved-ones – a species defined by him as those 'who have emotional claims on me'. He doesn't want to hurt types like these, he says, or hurt them any more than he already has (mind your own business), and he doesn't want to be boring.

He also promises not to tell us how he thought up the plots of his novels, nor to go on about reviews and sales: writer's-life data that nobody, he thinks, wants to know about – and if anybody does, too bad. As it happens, quite a bit of such data does leak through, and we are two or three times referred to page so-and-so of *Stanley and the Women*, or wherever, and he even lets fall the occasional bibliographer's nugget, if you please: for instance, did you, or *Private Eye*, know that Amis's very first piece of published writing was called 'The Sacred Rhino of Uganda'?

Thirdly, there will be a near-embargo on genealogical bullshit, Tony Powell stuff about the ancient Amises of Virginia, USA. We get a grandad with hairs sticking out of his red nose ('how much I disliked and was repelled by him'), a grandma – 'large, dreadful, hairy-faced' – whom he remembers having 'loathed and feared', and an aunt who was, no question, off her head. A few Pritchettian genteel-weirdos are to be chanced upon around the margins of young Kingsley's suburban London childhood, but the general picture of those years is as blurred for us as it evidently is, and maybe was, for him. (And no, we do not get told whose idea it was to call him Kingsley – something to do with Charles of that name, we conjecture, or perhaps it was Henry, C's blacksheep brother, a figure whose curriculum vitae reads very like some of those that Amis has in store for us: pissed all the time, terrific sponger, no good at writing novels, and so on.)

We are, however, vouchsafed a glimpse or two of Amis's mother and father, whom he seems to have quite liked. Too much on them would have meant having to tell us more about a certain adolescent culture-vulture who used to tick his dad off for not liking Brahms, but we do learn that Amis *père* was a pretty good cricketer (possessing 'a late cut I have never seen surpassed') and had a talent for mimicry 'that made him, on his day, one of the funniest men I have ever known'. And Mum? Well, like many another boot-in merchant, Amis does tend to go a bit trembly on the subject of his Mum: 'She was a jolly little woman for all her nerves, and shortness of breath, fond of a giggle, a fag, a gin and tonic (no more than a couple) and, I am sorry to record, an occasional glass of Empire wine, Keystone or Big Tree, for the "iron" in it. But she was more than that. It was that gentle creature who, when I rendered my first wife pregnant before our marriage, told my father not to be such a fool with his threats of excommunication and persuaded my future parents-in-law not to boycott the ceremony as they had been intending – the first of the appallingly long line of figures in my life who I have come to value altogether more highly, to appreciate the uniqueness of, now they are gone.'

The grumpily workmanlike prose style finds it difficult to cope with unaffected warmth. But this is Kingsley on his Mum, choked up; normally, he is careful to avoid such challenges to his composure. As to that 'appallingly long line' of valued and unique associates, it has to be reported that very few of them put in an appearance in this book. They, too, come under 'privacy', no doubt. Altogether, he vows, we will not be hearing much about 'merely good chaps, or fairly good chaps', nor about self-restrained' chaps, or 'secretive' chaps.

And fair enough, we have to say: these are *his* memoirs, after all. But what then is left to tell? Luckily, Amis possesses a good memory for anecdotes, or so he says, and he is also not too choosy when it comes to embellishing what he remembers – in this sphere, he would rate himself as 'fairly conscientious'. He has few scruples, either, about putting words into people's mouths – especially dead people's mouths – if it helps to liven up the narrative or lends support to some malign character sketch. 'Of course,' he says, 'I have invented dialogue,' and if this means giving himself some of the more trenchant ripostes, the more dignified silences, so be it. There are moments, though, when we would like to know just how much inventing has been done. Did Philip Larkin really say of John Wain: 'No advantage of birth or position or looks or talent – nothing, and look where he is now'? If I was John Wain, I would want to be sure of the exact words. According to Amis, Wain used to think of Larkin as a friend. And Larkin, although he is here said to have groaned when Wain 'invited himself' to stay with him in Hull, is also said (not here) to have refurnished his house in preparation for Wain's visit. Admittedly, this does not mean he was looking forward to the visit, but even so, he did a bit better than just groan, or so it seems.

Another sort of scruple Amis doesn't have is the sort that might have restrained him from recycling bits of writing from the past. These old bits – always acknowledged – do tend to stop us in our chortling tracks: strange, unexamined reminders of an earlier, more solemn Kingsley Amis: 'His hands looked strong and deft, like a precision mechanic's. But his face held the attention. With its clear blue eyes, thin upper lip above delicate teeth, and generally flattish planes, it was both grim and gay, seeming to hold both these qualities at once when in repose and lending itself to swift alternation between the one mood and the other.' Eh? No parody, this is Amis on Yevtushenko, c. 1962. Amis's point in reprinting such blurbese is not, alas, to show us what a prat he used to be but (I think) to persuade us that there was nothing personal about the Amis/Levin campaign in 1968 to prevent Yevtushenko's election to the Oxford Professorship of Poetry: 'If successful, it' – the election – 'would have installed a trusted ally, if not a total minion, of the Soviet regime in a highly sensitive and influential slot.' The highly sensitive slot, incidentally, went that year to Roy Fuller, who, when asked, declared himself 'absolutely sympathetic to Marxist ideas' and spoke of his 'fundamental belief in the materialist conception of history'. And five years after that, it went to the highly sensitive John Wain, thus prompting Larkin's sneers, cited above. Oxford undergraduates, take note: Sir Kingsley, CBE, Dip. Booker, is perhaps not so honour-laden that he might not, if pressed . . . etc. Just a thought.

We ought not to downplay Kingsley's sense of his own worth – that's for sure. Wounded or ruffled vanity is the trigger for several of the score-settling tales he has to tell. John Wain has not been forgiven for patronising Amis early on, and both Enoch Powell and Roald Dahl might have been rendered more benignly if, when given the chance, they had evinced a surer grasp of Kingsley's stature. When Andrew Sinclair and James Michie are sniped at for being mean, for not picking up the tab, we get the feeling that Amis's ire comes mainly from his not having been treated with sufficient deference. Surely it wasn't just the *money* – and yet maybe it was: they say it takes one tightwad to nail another. And is there not a certain meanness of – um – spirit in making public a chap's way with his wallet? The retribution seems excessive.

But then it often does. Even Amis's famous right-wing politics seem to be standing in for something else, some deeper enmity. Certainly, they have as much to do with loathing the lefty element in our domestic cultural arena as they have with plotting any new world-orders. And his literary judgements seem similarly tainted with a sort of oppositional vigilance, with protecting his own turf. The writers he likes pose little or no threat – Elizabeth Taylor, Elizabeth Bowen, Anthony Powell: either safely senior or safely underrated by the mob. Philip Larkin used to exhibit the same tendency when asked to name *his* lineup.

Larkin, of course, is the one contemporary to whom Amis is prepared to yield high marks (Robert Conquest, perhaps the most 'all right' of Kingsley's literary cronies, is shunted off into 'light verse'). Larkin is named as Amis's second-favourite poet (Housman is tops, though he might not have stayed tops, we suspect, if Amis had ever sat next to him at Trinity High Table), and as his 'best friend'. Mysteriously, though, the pair of them seem rarely to have met: in thirty years, Larkin never invited Amis up to Hull – not even to look over his new furnishings. The friendship was given its shape and its vocabulary when they were undergraduates and perhaps each of them was nervous about risking too much adult intimacy. It's odd, though, and it prompts the question of how often Amis got to see his other friends. He says that altogether in his life, he has had seven friends.

Amis's memoir of Larkin is affectionate enough. Most of it was written for a book of tributes, when Larkin was alive. There are now a few posthumous additions and they leave a taste – not a nasty taste, but almost. There are the quoted indiscretions, and there are disclosures that put Larkin in a bad or embarrassing light (it seems he was a tightwad, too). And there is also a wish, not obvious, to take the poems down a peg or two. On the subject of Larkin's much-celebrated 'Aubade', Amis is dead right to pick on that dreadful 'think with/link with' rhyme, but he is surely too heartily commonsensical in his summing-up: 'on first reading "Aubade" I should have found a way of telling you that depression among the middle-aged and elderly is common in the early morning and activity disperses it, as you tell us in your last stanza, so if you feel as bad as you say then fucking get up, or if it's too early or something then put the light on and read Dick Francis.' And then what? Sit and wait for it to go away – the feeling, and the poem? Amis believes it was 'fear of failure' that prevented Larkin from persisting in his attempts to be a novelist. 'No poem of Philip's preferred length lays your head on the block in the way any novel does.' Yes, *any* novel.

Behind so much of Amis's jesting, we discern a rigidly straight face, an obscure but powerful thwartedness. He tells us that he has had a lifelong fear of going mad, and we believe him. Maybe if he was not so afraid of sounding like an American poet, he could have told us in this book what sort of mad he has in mind. We do get a description of some hallucinating he once did when he was in hospital – he calls it 'A Peep Around the Twist' – but this chapter is as boring as most dream-writing tends to be, as boring as Amis himself would doubtless find it, were it not about him. I suppose what's really missing is any sense of Amis as a plausible character in his own narrative. Without wanting him to get stuck into a stretch of fearless self-analysis, we would quite like him to tell us what he thinks is wrong with *him*.

As it is, all the drunks drink more than he does, or can't handle what they drink as well as he can. All the narcissists and time-servers push themselves and try to get ahead, as he does not. All the talent is either wasted early or absent in the first place – not true of his own. To which he might retort: but that's what being a writer of fiction is all about – you get to be in charge, you get to lay *their* heads on the block. Instead of presence, we get authorial persona, by the yard: Amis the observer, the interlocutor, the recollector, the top judge, consistently projected as the shag who got things right that other shags kept getting wrong. And as the shag, moreover, who's been given precious little credit for his efforts, since you ask. Well, actually, we *didn't* ask, but still . . . good God, is that the time? One for the road? We'll pay.

Memoirs by Kingsley Amis (Hutchinson)

1991

The Comic Strip

Raymond's Revuebar is usually thought of as Soho's superior strip club. It stages not mere skin shows but Festivals of Erotica, it sells Dunhill or Lambert Butler cigarettes, and it gets itself listed in the daily papers under Theatres. Svens and Ottos have no need to look shifty when they sidle into Raymond's. This is no quick stop-off for provincial wankers. Raymond offers leisured pornography for the international connoisseur.

This summer, though, the joint has worn a faintly puzzled look. At the front door, visitors have been greeted with two contrasting slabs of artwork – one celebrating the genteel enticements of *les girls*, the other showing a large Blitz-vintage bomb descending on a city centre. The bomb carries a chalked slogan: 'Have a nice day.' On the night I went there, the tuxedoed bouncer was having a hard time explaining to the punters that Raymond's Revuebar was now in fact *two* theatres. 'Turn right for the Festival of Erotica,' he'd instruct the plumply cufflinked; 'Upstairs for *The Comic Strip*,' he'd tell anyone in jeans. Raymond, you see, had leased his Boulevard Theatre to an 'alternative comedy' ensemble, and for two nights a week his de-luxe foyer had become a jostle of conflicting styles. The bouncer boasted that he could tell at a glance who'd come for what: the problem was making sure everyone ended up in the right place.

The idea of satire in a strip club began a few years ago with the Comedy Store in Meard Street: here, on weekend evenings, amateur comics were invited to try out their acts on audiences made tolerant by the sleazy ambience and the prospect of a late-night drink. Most of the seven *Comic Strip* performers had built up small reputations at the Store (or at the Elgin pub in Ladbroke Grove) before moving into Raymond's. For them, this was a step-up to the big-time: four pounds a ticket and a stone's throw from Shaftesbury Avenue. Raymond's, though, was still 'alternative' enough for them to mount a show which Shaftesbury Avenue wouldn't even dream of putting on: a show more 'offensive', I would think, to those who use words like 'offensive', than anything *les girls* were offering next door.

The Comic Strip's compère and guiding star is a Meard Street veteran called Alexei Sayle, a portly, spring-heeled Liverpudlian with a convict haircut, a Desperate Dan chin and an Oliver Hardy silkette suit well buttoned at his bulging gut. A rock version of the theme from *Crossroads* starts the show, and Sayle hurtles on to the stage, spraying the audience with saliva, sweat and a deluge of fucks, cunts and bastards (flat 'a' – *bas*-tards!). A big man who can move like lightning; a pathologically aggrieved pub lout who's read some books; a 'cheeky monkey' from the Kop. Sayle's posture is manically contemptuous, his rhythm a hysterical crescendo of obscenity with spat-out satirical asides. Both the stance and the timing are near-perfect, and within seconds he has the audience agape. Most of them, it seemed, had never been called *cunts* before.

'Silly fuckers from Hampstead and Islington' who have been conned into paying 'four fucking quid' in the hope of seeing something 'alternative' (Sayle whines this in a poncey voice), or 'political' (this in a yobbo-radical-type grunt): so much for the fans. You've come to the wrong place, Sayle taunts. Just because he happened to look like a 'fucking East German playwright' they needn't expect any Berlin-in-the-Twenties *significance*. His own philosophy of life was simple: all you need is 'to have a fucking good grip on your *temper* – *cunts*!!'

If anything was to be learned from a night out at *The Comic Strip* it was that bad language still has an awesome potency. It was obvious to everyone that Sayle was getting laughs for some really rather thin material, but the laughter never stopped: the hectic speed and the vein-popping intensity of his delivery was part of the secret – but it was the 'fucking' element that really guaranteed his triumph:

I can't understand why they're always picking on the Afghans –

fucking nice dogs. Who ever heard of fucking Toxteth – Tox-*teth* [saliva spray] before the fucking riots, eh? That Willie Whitelaw, half-man, half fucking bumblebee, the wanker. The proceeds of tonight's show are going to my favourite London charity: 'Help a London Child – kill a Social Worker'. Toxteth – two hundred fucking *years* some of those cunts have lived up there. What about the fucking Soho *Vikings*, eh . . .

And so on. It may not look much on the page, and has perhaps been imperfectly transcribed (Sayle's-pace is about fifteen words a second) – but think how enfeebled it would be without the 'dirt'. As Rik Mayall (on *The Comic Strip* bill as one half of a duo called Twentieth Century Coyote) patiently explained to me: 'The rhythm – that's one of the reasons why we swear a lot on stage. The rhythm of the thing is very careful – the laugh has to come just right. It's almost poetic – if a sentence is not quite long enough before the laugh, we put in a "fucking".'

He might have added that the swearwords also inject meat and venom, an illusion of anything-goes rebelliousness: if you can say *that*, then surely nothing's sacred. It is only after the show is over that you register what *hasn't* been treated with contempt. Women's lib, gay pride, black power – indeed any cause likely to be favoured by the average 'silly fucker' from Islington or Hampstead. Such audiences don't mind being mocked for their yoghurt and stripped pine – but it might have been a different story if *The Comic Strip* had ventured an assault upon their reflex liberalism. Rik Mayall acknowledges all this:

> The next stage, yes, is to get to where you can take the piss out of anything. At the moment, though, with Brixton and all that you can't go around saying: Who are these niggers with big fat lips? It would be great if you could. Short people, tall people, people with big ears, why not people with black skin? It's when you get too specific – so it's *just* blacks – that it gets wrong. At the moment I suppose we feel that you don't take the piss out of the man at the bottom.

Mayall, who has written an MA thesis on Pub Theatre, teamed up with Ade Edmundson at Manchester University, and the pair of them spent a few years touring the college circuit before hitting London. Twentieth Century Coyote is perhaps the least 'meaningful' item on the bill: Mayall and Edmundson specialise in on-the-edge neanderthals like the Dangerous Brothers or (played by Mayall) the catatonic Kevin Turby. Kevin's *tour de force* is a long, intricately plodding monologue about His Average Day. He gets up very late and goes down to Tesco's where he buys some cornflakes which he then takes home and puts into a plate before sitting down at a table with the flakes in front of him . . . etc. 'I was just sitting there eating my cornflakes. I don't know how many I had had. Fifteen, sixteen, maybe. I wasn't counting.' All this is delivered in a bombed-out monotone: you couldn't really call Turby one of the unemployed because the simple business of getting through the day demands his total concentration, his entire stock of 'resources'. There is, to be sure, a great army of the unemployed, but, as Turby makes clear, there is also an army of the unemployable.

Much of Twentieth Century Coyote's act consists of making jokes about old jokes. The Knock-Knock routine, for example, is maybe the most easily graspable of all 'response-jokes'. For the Dangerous Brothers, however, it's a tough one: the brothers' combination of low intelligence and a short fuse turns any sort of inquisition into a threatening 'set-up'.

> 'Knock knock, open the door.'
> 'Open the door – who?'
> 'Open the door please I want to come in.'
> 'Open the door please I want to come in – *who*?'
> 'Look, just OPEN THE FUCKING DOOR, WILL YOU?'

And by this stage the pair will come to blows – Mayall extraordinary to watch with his electrocuted stare and clockwork arms, Edmundson almost coquettish as his cringing victim. And the fighting, of course, isn't custard-pie. It's kneeing, nutting, nipple-twisting stuff: a punk version of the traditional music-hall chastisement.

Coyote operates a similar trick with the famous gooseberry joke, which is: 'What's round and hairy and goes up and down?' 'A gooseberry in a lift.' Adrian Dangerous doesn't get it. 'How did a gooseberry get in a lift?' he wants to know. 'How do I know, it's a fucking joke, it's *implicit*.' 'Yuh, well, how does a fucking *gooseberry* push the button in the lift? Gooseberries don't have *arms*.' '*Bas*tard, how many fucking gooseberries do *you* know?' Nervous pause from Adrian, then (boldly): 'Three.' 'All right then, let's have the fucking *names* of these gooseberries you're so matey with.' 'What?' '*Names*, you cunt.' 'Names? Well, there's Derek, int-there? Derek Gooseberry.' 'Derek Gooseberry. All right, where is he? Go and get the bastard.' 'He's got a headache.' 'A headache! That's very fucking convenient.' Mayall is now advancing and there is a giggling masochism in Edmundson's retreat – this time he'll make the beating *really* bad. 'Anyway the point is: Derek has got fuck-all arms.' Mayall is now on the brink, eyes like ray-guns, both fists twitching: 'So fucking what if he's got fuck-all arms, he could have jumped up and NUTTED the fucking button, couldn't he?' and even as the first savage blow connects, Edmundson screams out his last request: 'BUT HE'S GOT FUCK-ALL LEGS!' And yes, the beating really is quite bad this time.

The Comic Strip's other double act, the Outer Limits, is more hooked into the media than is Coyote, and more conventionally slick. Peter Richardson and Nigel Planer have been together now for eight years – 'We do everything together. We piss into each other's mouths' – but for most of that time they played music, with the jokes as decoration. Now a lot of the jokes (many of them too esoteric for my tuned-out ear) are to do with current or quite recent pop: a big-band crooner's delivery of hits by groups like the Stranglers and the Sex Pistols was greatly enjoyed by experts in the audience, and there was a funny routine about a music agent who has huge hi-fi speakers instead of pillars at the front door of his mansion. On the whole, I found it easier to get into their film and TV spoofs: a hard-core disaster movie in which a hijacker decides not to go through with it because the in-flight pic is *Kramer versus Kramer*, and a mincing version of Starsky and Hutch – 'those soft-talking, go-getting, bum-kissing boys of the Nancy Squad'. Although Sayle at the beginning of the show had pronounced the Art of Mime to be a 'Wank', the Outer Limits are brilliant at turning four square feet of stage into worlds of their own invention: as if to prove this, they make their most dazzling routine a mock Space Invaders set-to. In persona and physique the two are well matched – Planer cherubic and elastic-limbed, Richardson sly and demonic – and Planer, it should be said, would make a more than passable rock singer.

Peter Richardson is, in fact, the producer of *The Comic Strip* and he paces the evening with real skill. In between the frenetic stuff he places two low-keyed solo acts: one by Muppet writer Chris Langham, who has a cool line in 'disabled' jokes and does a gripping owl impersonation, and Arnold Brown, an appealingly depressed Scots Jew: 'Two racial stereotypes for the price of one'. Brown is one of those 'What am I doing here?' comedians, doleful and wry, not really expecting the audience to pick up more than a third of his material. For Arnold, all is bleak – and barely worth the effort; his catch-phrase is 'Why not . . . ?' (as in: 'I'm Arnold Brown, I come from Glasgow' [lengthy pause] 'Why not?'). He ranges from a deprived childhood ('There I was sitting in my tenement, trying to work out the meaning of the word "serendipity"') to a still-deprived maturity. The recession is a kind of gift: it means that Arnold is living in a world he understands, a world of 'second-hand food shops' and 'waiting-lists for people wanting to vandalise telephone kiosks'. A good deal older than his colleagues, Brown gloomily acknowledges that the times are bad enough for his time to have finally come. I hope it has.

And yet it is hard to see how *The Comic Strip* can 'make it' without cleaning up and thinning out their best material. They are already moving into the area of 'alternative success': an uncensored LP has just been released, a film is being made by the producers of *The Great Rock and Roll Swindle*, and the group is currently on tour around the revue-bars of provincial England. The lucrative working men's clubs are, they say, out of their range ('they don't like non-racist jokes – it's still all niggers and mothers-in-law'), and it need hardly be said that television would try to turn Alexei Sayle into Les Dawson. Still, for the moment, they must surely be the funniest live act in Britain: they have spleen to spare and they are obviously having a good time. It would take a *really* silly fucker to predict what they'll do next.

1981

The Knocking-Shop

The recent appearance of John Halperin's Gissing biography brings to mind a project which I have long thought someone ought to tackle: a fearless update of *New Grub Street*. The job wouldn't be too taxing – indeed, in many cases, it would be all too easy to attach contemporary names to Gissing's sunken literary types: his principled dullards as well as his sleek chancers. And then there are the grim trappings of Gissing's version of the Literary Career – the foundering periodical, the doomed synopsis, the already spent advance. All in all, the book's whole world of seedy, profitless endeavour *is* worryingly up-to-date.

Even so, a Gissing of the Eighties would have to make some alterations. The curse of the three-volume novel, for example, sits heavily on Gissing's greying hacks. In the 1890s the circulating libraries favoured three-volume editions of novels because readers who wanted to read on to the end would thus have to fork out three subscriptions. The publishers in turn put pressure on their authors to stretch out their plots. 'Real money' would be offered for a three-decker (enough maybe to keep your average scribbler for six months) whereas a one-volume offering would yield almost punitively dreadful rates of pay. In those days, a novel consisted of '920 pages with twenty-one and a half lines on each page and nine and a half words on each line', and that was that. If you wanted to get all experimental, you could starve. Today, of course, with Public Lending Right, it might be that novelists will start getting their own back on the libraries – a resurrection of the three-decker could triple the author's rake-off under this compassionate new scheme.

Two of the most touching moments in *New Grub Street* are when Reardon is forced to sell his books in an attempt to make ends meet

– well, not meet, exactly, but at least set up some distant, mocking contact. In Gissing's day, it seems, a dealer would visit the impoverished author at his by then semi-furnished lodgings and, for a handful of guineas, bear off the best of his prize leather-bounds – the only things the poor devil really cared about: real books, not like the rubbish he and his colleagues were obliged to churn out day by day.

Here again, I think, things may well have changed for the better. For most modern Reardons, these rending scenes will instantly evoke images of Chancery Lane – or, more precisely, that small alley off the Lane where generations of book reviewers and literary men have known the confused pleasure of securing the price of their next drink(s) in exchange for a mint copy of *Giles Goatboy*, or of swopping some multi-volume reissue of John Cowper Powys for a night out on the town.

The Chancery Lane idea is (or used to be) that you can sell off review copies for half their published price. The books had to be in really good condition (hence the loving care with which one would sometimes see a reviewer handling a text which that same day he had damned as 'worthless' in the public prints) and they had to be less than four months old. In the mid-Sixties, I remember, it was even possible to take *poetry* down the Lane, but I understand this is no longer so. In fact, rumour has it that things are altogether stickier now and that it is not unknown for a dealer to turn down some quite nicely priced volumes on the grounds that they are 'boring'.

In the days when I used to go down there, though, he would take almost anything. And on Fridays the Lane would be alive with reviewers struggling in from Blackheath with their holdalls, or nipping round the corner from the *Telegraph* with a fistful of Robert Hales or Arthur Barkers. One esteemed figure at *The Times* used to order a taxi for noon on Friday and when it arrived he would have a flunkey load it up with art books and American encyclopedias. He would then squeeze in beside his booty and, with twinkling eye, instruct the driver to stop off in the Lane en route for Garrick Street, or Paddington. To the novice bookman with only a Catherine Cookson and a Roland Barthes between him and the workhouse this was indeed a stirring image of literary success. Gissing would have loved it.

Now and then, of course, one pondered the doubtful morality of these Friday expeditions. After all, these books were – presumably

– sold off to public libraries for less than their published price. This meant that the author would not collect his 10 per cent (again, this was all pre-PLR). Thus, in the case of a book you had already savaged in the prints, here was an additional chastisement. Could this be just? But then, more creatively, it could be argued that the Lane simply provided an opportunity for one limb of the industry to help another, that pennies lost to the novelist brought pounds to the reviewer and that a healthy criticism could only mean a healthy . . . and so on.

Of course, many novelists are themselves fiction reviewers, and several of the Lane's best anecdotes are to do with novelist A catching novelist B attempting to sell A's latest book. Along these same lines, I know of at least one reviewer who could not bear to take his swag along in person because this would mean him once again having to view a shelf-long stock of his own most recent publication: 'It had such *good* reviews,' he'd wail, 'but now I know they didn't mean it.' A greenhorn, he had clearly not heard the one about the hapless scribe who was once seen shuffling down the Lane with a carrier-bag containing six 'author's copies' of his brand-new 'breakthrough' novel. When quizzed, he said he wanted to celebrate publication day 'in style'. Each of these yarns, it seems to me, could be gruesomely fleshed out by the author of my new *New Grub Street*. And if he cares to get in touch, I can tell him a few more.

On the topic of 'the knocking-shop' – as the Lane vendor was once widely known – I still can't quite suppress a flicker of excitement when I come across a book like *The Oxford Illustrated Literary Guide to the United States*. It has all the qualifications for a quick and unashamed dispatch to EC4: it is expensive, lavishly but boringly illustrated, virtually unreviewable except by someone as madly knowledgeable as its two editors, and almost entirely without point. Without point, that is, unless you really want to know that Thomas Wolfe rented a cottage in Boothbay Harbor in July 1929 or that Rex Stout wrote four short stories in a boarding-house in Burlington, Vermont or that in Bridgwater, Connecticut on 1 July, 1949 'Van Wyck Brooks and his wife moved to a house on Main Street in which they were to entertain many literary visitors. A Sunday supper they gave in 1957, for example, was attended by Norman Mailer, Katherine Anne Porter and William Styron.' The authors call people who want to know this kind of thing 'literary travellers' and they plead that such travellers have in the past been handicapped by the lack of a guidebook that covered the whole of the United States. Well, I'm not sure how literary travellers travel, but they should perhaps be warned that for a guidebook of this size they should also pack a portable lectern. It's about a foot square and almost five hundred pages long.

I wonder how the editors imagine their book will be used. Will the literary traveller work by place or by author? That is to say, will he happen to find himself in Blowing Rock, set up his lectern in the market square, then discover from his literary guide that yesindeedy in this vurry town John Hersey wrote his *Hiroshima?* Or should we envisage a more dogged, gumshoe type – one who picks an author and then tracks him all the way from New Sybaris to Purgatory Pond? In either case, it is hard to fathom the rewards. I mean, what does one say or think on finding oneself outside the front gate of 61 Maeaug Avenue, New London, Connecticut: is it enough simply to know for certain that John Hollander lived there from 1957 to 1959? And what of the Auden sleuth who drags himself from campus to campus ('W.H. Auden also taught here' is the *Guide*'s usual formulation) and finally ends up at Swarthmore, only to be told: 'He lived at various addresses, including 16 Oberlin Avenue, and often took his lunch at the Dew Drop Inn, now the Village Restaurant, at 407 Dartmouth Avenue'? No problem about where to eat, but even so . . .

Leafing through the *Literary Guide* is rather like gawping impotently at the For Sale pages of *Country Life*, and it would be easy to get the impression from this book that American writers live only in mansions which are situated in spacious, leafy grounds, or pillared brownstones which look as if they've been borrowed from the mayor. Page after page of enviably huge residences are on show throughout. There are no garrets, no mental institutions. There are no obvious fleabags – although, since most of the pictures seem to have been taken with an estate agent's camera, it is not always possible to slap a fair price on individual properties. The thinking here seems to be that, in addition to his thirst for history, the literary traveller will usually prefer staring at real estate that is worth staring at. A reminder, though, that even to this day, an American *New Grub Street* is not all that easy to imagine.

1983